Women and Politics in France 1958–2000

Gill Allwood and Khursheed Wadia

London and New York

First published 2000
by Routledge
11 New Fetter Lane, London EC4P 4EE

Simultaneously published in the USA and Canada
by Routledge
29 West 35th Street, New York, NY 10001

Routledge is an imprint of the Taylor & Francis Group

Typeset in Baskerville by
Florence Production Ltd, Stoodleigh, Devon

Printed and bound in Great Britain by
Biddles Ltd, Guildford and King's Lynn

British Library Cataloguing in Publication Data
A catalogue record for this book is available from the
British Library

Library of Congress Cataloging in Publication Data
Allwood, Gill.
    Women and politics in France 1958–2000 / Gill Allwood and
Khursheed Wadia.
        p.   cm.
    Includes bibliographical references and index.
    1. Women in politics—France.   2. France—Politics and
government—1958–   I. Wadia, Khursheed.   II. Title.
HQ1236.5.F8 A45   2000
306.2′082′0944–dc21   00–036632

ISBN 0–415–18492–4 (hbk)
ISBN 0–415–18493–2 (pbk)

In memory of Claire Duchen whose
contribution to the study of women in
France has inspired so many of us

Contents

Tables

Acknowledgements

Many people have contributed to the completion of this book, and our gratitude goes to all of them. The following deserve a special mention: the late Claire Duchen for her constant willingness to provide help, information and comments; Heather McCallum and Victoria Peters, at Routledge, for their enthusiasm and help in publishing this book; CPEDERF for carrying out essential research in Paris and for their unfailing ability to find information of all kinds and to answer any questions; to the archivists and librarians at the Bibliothèque Marguerite Durand and the press cuttings service of the Fondation Nationale des Sciences Politiques, both in Paris; to Henri Sinno of the CGT's Institut d'Histoire Sociale, in Paris, for documentation sent.

Gill Allwood would like to thank colleagues in the Department of Modern Languages at Nottingham Trent University for providing the time, the money and the support necessary for the research and writing of this book. Marianne Howarth and Martin O'Shaughnessy deserve a particular mention for being supportive, flexible and accommodating throughout, as does Trevor Pull for solving any problem thrown at him. Finally, the biggest thanks of all must go to Dave, Kristina, Caitlin and Ben.

Khursheed Wadia owes thanks to the University of Wolverhampton Research Committee for granting sabbatical leave, to colleagues in the School of Humanities, Languages and Social Sciences at the University of Wolverhampton for their support and to Penny Welch for ideas and useful discussion. A particular debt is owed to Jean Gilkison for her thoughtful and encouraging advice throughout the writing of this book. More personally, special thanks go to Rustom and Zubin for their patience and love.

Acronyms and abbreviations

AFPA	*Association féministe pour une politique alternative*
CADAC	*Coordination des associations pour le droit à l'avortement et à la contraception*
CAMS	*Commission pour l'abolition des mutilations sexuelles*
CDS	*Centre des démocrates sociaux*
CDU	Christian Democratic Union
CEVIPOF	*Centre d'´tude de la vie politique française*
CFC	*Commission féminine confédérale*
CFDT	*Confédération française démocratique du travail*
CFTC	*Confédération française des travailleurs chrétiens*
CGC	*Confédération générale des cadres*
CGT	*Confédération générale du travail*
CINEL	*Centre d'initiatives pour de nouveaux espaces de liberté*
CNFE	*Cercle national femmes d'Europe*
CNIR	*Conseil national interrégional*
CPNT	*Chasse, pêche, nature et traditions*
DL	*Démocratie libérale*
DOM-TOM	*Départements et territoires d'outre-mer*
EDF–GDF	*Electricité de France–Gaz de France*
ENA	*Ecole nationale d'administration*
ETUC	European Trade Union Confederation
EU	European Union
FLN	*Front de libération nationale*
FMA	*Féminin, masculin, avenir*
FMH	*Des femmes en mouvements – hebdo*
FN	*Front national*
FNS	*Fédération nationale des syndicats*
FNSPN	*Fédération nationale des sociétés de protection de la nature*
FO	*Force ouvrière*
GAMS	*Groupe de femmes pour l'abolition des mutilations sexuelles*
GE	*Génération écologie*
IFOP	*Institut français d'opinion publique*
IPU	Interparliamentary Union

LCR	*Ligue communiste révolutionnaire*
LFDF	*Ligue française pour le droit des femmes*
LO	*Lutte ouvrière*
MDC	*Mouvement des citoyens*
MDF	*Mouvement démocratique féminin*
ME	*Mouvement d'ecologie*
MEP	Member of the European Parliament
MFPF	*Mouvement français pour le planning familial*
MLF	*Mouvement de libération des femmes*
MP	Member of Parliament
MPF	*Mouvement pour la France*
MRG	*Mouvement des radicaux de gauche*
MRP	*Mouvement républicain populaire*
MWR	Ministry for Women's Rights
NGO	Non-governmental Organisation
OECD	Organisation for Economic Cooperation and Development
OSCE	Organisation for Security and Cooperation in Europe
PCF	*Parti communiste français*
PR	Proportional Representation
PR	*Parti républicain*
PRG	*Parti radical de gauche*
PRS	*Parti radicale-socialiste*
PS	*Parti socialiste*
PSU	*Parti socialiste unifié*
RPF	*Rassemblement pour la France*
RPR	*Rassemblement pour la République*
SGEN	*Syndicat général de l'education nationale*
SME	*Small- and Medium-sized Enterprises*
SOFRES	*Societé française d'etudes par sondage*
SUD	*Solidaires, unitaires et démocratiques*
UDF	*Union pour la démocratie française*
UFF	*Union des femmes françaises*
UNESCO	United Nations Educational, Scientific and Cultural Organisation
UR	*Union régionale*
USSR	Union of Soviet Socialist Republics

Introduction

Since the mid-1990s, the relation between women and politics in France has been almost constantly in the public eye. The campaign for parity, established in 1992, brought together feminists and women politicians from across the political spectrum in a demand for numerical equality between men and women in elected bodies. Its main success was to raise awareness of the under-representation of women in politics. With a growing majority of the population in favour of the idea of increasing women's public presence, politicians began to find it politically advantageous to support the idea, and by 1997, only the *Front national*, one or two deputies (for example Christine Boutin (UDF) and Didier Julia (RPR)) and a significant number of senators publicly declared their opposition. The left-wing Prime Minister, Lionel Jospin, and the right-wing President, Jacques Chirac, already engaged in the competition for legitimacy and support which cohabitation engenders, adopted the cause of women's representation as part of their respective campaigns to modernise politics. The Constitutional Reform Bill which they both supported was passed by a special Congress of both houses of parliament at Versailles in June 1999.[1] During the Bill's passage through parliament, an intense public debate took place around the question of whether or not republican universalism would be irreversibly damaged by the recognition of sexual difference.

Women's place in politics was thus secured on the public agenda and seemed set to expand. Since June 1997, women have constituted a record 10 per cent of the National Assembly and 30 per cent of government ministers, occupying the prestigious posts of Minister for Justice and Minister for Social Affairs. In the June 1999 European election, 50.8 per cent of French candidates were women, the highest proportion for any member state,[2] and 40.2 per cent of French MEPs returned at this election were women.

The overall picture is more complex than this would suggest, however. First, although the proportion of women in the National Assembly has increased from 6 to 10 per cent since 1993, France remains in fifty-fourth place internationally and next-to-last in the European Union as far as women's representation is concerned. Moreover, not only has the constitutional reform of June 1999 taken the wind out of the sails of the campaign for parity, but as it stands, it is very tame. It therefore remains to be seen what concrete change will occur. Second, the supposed consensus around the idea of bringing more women into politics has not removed some of the worst aspects of the masculine culture which confronts them when they get there. Just before the Constitutional Reform Act was passed, government minister, Dominique Voynet, attending the agriculture show, was greeted with cries of 'get your knickers off, you slut' (*L'événement du jeudi*, 23–9 September 1999: 49). The ever-increasing number of personal accounts by women politicians suggest that this was not an isolated incident.

A survey of the media in the late 1990s could easily lead to the conclusion that the whole issue of women and politics is contained in the idea of parity. This is misleading for two major reasons. First, the term 'parity' has assumed a number of meanings. For the campaigners who popularised its use in France, as for the Council of Europe which first applied it in the context of women's political representation in 1989, parity meant the numerical equality of men and women in elected institutions. For politicians of all persuasions since then it has been used to refer to any measure favouring the increased presence of women in politics. And for the media, it has come to replace the terms 'feminism', 'women's rights' and even 'women' as a means of attracting attention. The advantage of the popularity of the idea of parity is that it has kept the issue of women's representation and related rights on the agenda. The disadvantage, however, is that it has reduced the question of the relation between women and politics to this one aspect, and this is the second reason why the exclusive focus on parity is misleading.

The NGOs (non-governmental organisations) at the United Nations conference on women in Beijing in 1995, the student and social movements of 1995 and 1998, the demonstrations by '*sans papiers*' (people without official papers legalising their presence in France), the activities of the Coordination of Associations for the Right to Abortion and Contraception (*Coordination des associations pour le droit à l'avortement et à la contraception* – CADAC) and the 1997 National Conference on Women's Rights are all concrete examples of fervent political activity by women and feminists at a time when feminism is portrayed as either a thing of the past or as an example of American excess, and when politics is still considered to be what happens within the formal structures of public life.

International and European initiatives

France does not operate in isolation from the rest of Europe and the world. Although it has a specific culture and history which continue to influence the quantitative and qualitative representation of women in politics, pressure has grown in recent years from European and international bodies, conferences and treaties to address the inequality of men and women in politics. For example, the UN platform for action on Women in Power and Decision-Making, adopted at the 1995 Beijing conference and agreed by France, contains two strategic objectives: to take measures to ensure women's equal access to and full participation in power structures and decision-making and to increase women's capacity to participate in decision-making and leadership (http://www.un.org/womenwatch/daw/index.html, accessed 3 November 1999).

In 1988, the Council of Europe passed a formal declaration on equality between women and men, stating that this is a principle based on human rights, an essential condition of democracy and a requirement of social justice. The participation of women in politics had already been included in the Council's Second Plan (1981–6) and a committee of experts had been established, whose report, submitted in 1985, proposed a programme of action for the Council of Europe. The programme included specifically political issues (for example, selection of candidates, positive action and so on) and more general issues, such as civic education and women's position in the labour force and the media. The Council of Europe continued to call on member states to move towards equality between men and women in politics and decision-making. At the end of 1989, the term 'parity' was introduced, and the question of the relation between parity and democracy was raised for the first time. It was the subject of much debate during the following years and was broadened to include all sites of decision-making, although, in reality, politics remained the focus of discussions.

The European Commission's interest in sexual equality gradually broadened from its initial concerns with equal pay and protection for women workers during pregnancy and following childbirth to include equal opportunities in employment and education, the representation of women in the media and sexual harassment in the workplace. The presence of women in decision-making appeared on the agenda in the early 1990s. The Third Programme of Action (1991–5) established a network of experts on 'women and decision-making', set up research projects and encouraged cooperation with NGOs. It also made several recommendations to member states concerning the appointment of women to posts of responsibility in government and the civil service and encouraging parties and administrative bodies to introduce measures favouring women's access. More precise measures were included in the Fourth Programme of Action (1996–2000) which advocates 'mainstreaming'[3] as the way to introduce equality in every policy area. The fourth of six main objectives in this Programme is the promotion of the equal participation of women and men in decision-making. Further legitimacy was added to this objective when EU heads of state and government met at the European Councils of Essen, Cannes and Madrid and declared that reducing unemployment and establishing equal opportunities for men and women were priorities for the EU and its member states. Article 2 of the 1997 Treaty of Amsterdam states that equality between men and women is a major aim of the EU, and Article 3 states that it is a compulsory component of all policy areas.

The impact of these initiatives is the gradual emergence of a culture in which women's participation in decision-making is expected. In accordance with this expectation, the French Prime Minister, Lionel Jospin (1999b), has declared that increasing the number of women in politics is part of the fundamental modernisation of democracy which he has promised to undertake. Further, he has declared that the government will examine the implications of all public policies for equal opportunities between men and women. He has committed the government to delivering a national plan of action on equal opportunities in all areas (politics, economics, work and society) in 2000. This plan is intended to unite all the measures taken and envisaged in these areas in a global strategy for equality (Jospin 1999a).

The study of women and politics

The literature on women and politics is now vast, and it would be impossible here to provide a just review of its contents. Monica Githens, Joni Lovenduski and Pippa Norris (1994: ix–xvi) provide an excellent summary of its main contours. This brief overview is intended simply to situate the approach which has been taken in this study and which is presented later in this introduction.

Women were for a long time excluded from political science, and were later to become the objects of studies of political behaviour, most of which demonstrated that women were inadequate. Early feminist analyses began by filling in the gaps left by masculine political science, providing information on women's voting behaviour and participation in élites. Initially, there was a tendency to regard men as the norm to which women were compared, but later, explanations began to be offered for women's apparently lower rates of participation. These focused on the exclusion of women by male-dominated institutions and élites as well as on the material constraints which prevented women from participating at the same levels as men.

Women's movements of the 1970s challenged traditional definitions of the political which, they claimed, exclude women by confining them to the private (non-political) sphere. Their claim that 'the personal is political' not only brought new issues such as abortion and violence onto the political agenda, but also expanded the definition of the political to include activities in which women were involved. Thus, the study of women's political activism came to include their involvement in new social movements and campaigns to change public policy. This approach revealed a rich history of women's political participation, obscured by the traditional focus on institutional politics. Rather than applying the methods of the study of mass and élite political behaviour, this approach combined searches of historical archives and primary materials, interviews with activists and studies of the law and the policy-making process (Githens, Norris and Lovenduski 1994: xi).

A third approach to the subject of women and politics focuses on the exclusion of women from political thought and develops a critique of concepts such as democracy, citizenship and equality. Increasingly, this area of research has raised questions of multiplicity and difference (for example, Dean 1997, Phillips 1993, Yuval-Davies 1997) and examined the relation between gender, politics and the state (for example, Waylen and Randall (eds) 1998).

This study attempts to combine these three approaches in order to provide information on women's participation in mainstream politics, their 'alternative' political activity, including feminist politics and attempts to influence policy outcomes, and the critique of theories of citizenship and equality.

Why France?

France, along with Britain and the United States, has been a favoured subject of American-dominated comparative political science. When political science emerged as an academic discipline in the 1950s, the history and politics of France were perceived as exceptional. The main aspects of this exceptionalism were: the presence of a large and influential communist party; the history of quasi-revolutionary upheavals; the instability of institutions; the large number of political parties, which meant that parliamentary majorities depended on coalitions; the highly ideological nature of political debate; and the strict separation of religion and politics in a secular state (Rémond 1993: 204–5, Bell 1995: xiv).

The establishment of the Fifth Republic in 1958 was expected to end exceptionalism and stabilise the political system. Indeed, the turnover in prime ministers has been considerably lower since 1958 than it had been under the previous constitution. The power of the executive increased in relation to the power of the legislature, the complexity of majority coalitions was reduced, and the highly centralised nature of the state has somewhat diminished. The debate around Catholicism and secularism has declined, as religiosity has decreased and as secularism has apparently become more tolerant of different beliefs (Rémond 1993: 205–7). However, as David Bell (1995: xv) writes, 'the development of an adventurous foreign policy, the "events" of May '68, and the collapse of Gaullism created as many problems as they resolved, thus confirming France as the exception to many generalisations about Western Europe'. He states (1995: xxviii–xxix):

> Leaving aside the obvious and urgent need for an extended comparative field, there are still reasons why France should continue to be

one of the 'big four' analysed by political science students everywhere. One is the drama of French politics, along with its intense and endlessly self-reflective capacity. French politics is distinctive in nature, in content and in style, a distinctiveness which has not lessened with the decline of the PCF or the departure of de Gaulle. The rise of the National Front and the ecologists is one aspect of this 'exceptionalism'; the nature of leadership is another. France has retained its capacity for political surprises as well as for highly-charged issue politics which remains fascinating to the student of politics.

Howard Machin (1994: 2), however, underplays the distinctiveness of French politics:

> Domestic politics are increasingly normal, in the sense of resembling those of France's similar-sized European neighbours, West Germany [*sic*], Britain and Italy. For many years, and sometimes by deliberately nationalist policies, this was not the case . . . In the 1970s there was still a vast literature which argued that France was a special case, irrelevant for comparisons with any other state. If some of these writings reflected misperceptions by their writers about the rest of the world, they were not all completely wrong. In the 1980s, however, it is appropriate to focus on French politics as an interesting variant of a European pattern.

Machin (1994: 3) identifies some of the significant changes of the 1980s which brought France into line with comparable Western democracies as: a trend towards less conflictual politics, with a growing consensus among the main political forces about the basic parameters of politics; a retreat of the state, as a result of Europeanisation, decentralisation, and deregulation of the economy; and a disappearance of the resistance to pluralism.

Debate continues about whether or not France is exceptional, but beyond the reasoned debate, there seems to be a need to believe that it is. René Rémond (1993: 209), for example, concludes his essay on changes in French politics with the following:

> It is still justifiable to claim that the gradual disappearance of the French political uniqueness is far from certain. There is every possibility that our native genius will invent yet more original ways to act out our relation to politics.

This insistence on perpetuating French exceptionalism is no doubt related to the threat to national identity posed by the globalisation of the economy, the Europeanisation of decision-making in many policy domains and the Americanisation of culture. French exceptionalism continues to be evoked in many areas of public debate and certainly in debates around gender. Two issues are frequently focused upon: the apparently special understanding between the sexes which, at times, is even elevated to a peculiarly French variant of feminism, and the relation between Catholicism, or at least Catholic family culture, and women's involvement in politics.

First, it is argued that gender relations are organised differently in France, where there is a special understanding between the sexes. This argument was heard across the political spectrum during the debates around sexual harassment in the early 1990s, when France was compared, favourably, with the United States, where gender relations, it was claimed, are antagonistic and violent. More recently, campaigners against parity have similarly stressed French exceptionalism. For instance, Elisabeth Badinter (1997: 40) argues, 'This feminist tradition, which is not at all warlike, has allowed us to preserve a tacit agreement with men and to impose ourselves in the name of the law, but without ever departing from the principle of universalism.' This study implicitly questions the extent to which this claim can be justified.

Second, since commentaries on French politics frequently state that 'France is a Catholic country', attributing a greater or lesser number of its political characteristics to this factor, it is interesting to situate it in relation to other European countries in order to assess the extent to which this is a relevant observation. This is especially important in the context of a study of women and politics, since religiosity has frequently been found to interact with gender as a significant factor in studies of political behaviour. In Catholicism or Catholic family culture, women have long been placed at the centre of the family, which represents the stable ideological and structural basis of society, in opposition to politics which is considered divisive, hence disruptive and dangerous.

The influence of Catholicism has not always been clear, however, as French political scientist, Maurice Duverger, found in the 1950s. He writes (1955a: 151), 'The Protestant countries, both Anglo-Saxon and Nordic, have a lower percentage of women deputies than France, which is both Catholic and Latin, and where women's rights were more recently introduced.' By 1997, this was no longer true for the Nordic countries: Sweden, Norway, Finland and Denmark, all Protestant, had an average of 37.2 per cent women in their parliaments compared with France's 10 per cent. Moreover, Spain, at least as Catholic and Latin as France, had 24.6 per cent (Hochedez and Maurice 1997: 78).

Not only do these figures cast doubt about the influence of Catholicism on women's political behaviour, but other findings actually question the extent to which it is appropriate to refer to France specifically as a Catholic country. Eurobarometer (1985: 49) finds that, on the question 'How important is God in your life?', European countries can be divided into three groups: those in which at least four interviewees in ten felt that God was 'very important' (10 on the scale) – Ireland and Portugal (46 per cent),

Italy (43 per cent), Greece (41 per cent) and Spain (40 per cent); those in which between one-fifth and one-quarter of interviewees considered that God was 'not at all important' (1 on the scale) – Denmark (21 per cent), France (23 per cent), the Netherlands (26 per cent), and Belgium (18 per cent); and the three other countries – Germany, Luxembourg and the United Kingdom, which fall somewhere in between. The report states that 'the five most religious countries, according to this yardstick, are clearly those where Catholicism or the Orthodox Church plays a major role, although Belgium and France, traditionally Catholic countries, are not among them'. In terms of atheism or indifference, then, France occupies third position after Denmark and the Netherlands (Eurobarometer 1985: 50).

Interestingly, the 1995 Eurobarometer presents different findings to the same question and creates slightly different categories, France's position proving even more intriguing. There are three groups: those countries in which the distribution of answers tends towards 'important': Greece, Spain, Ireland, Italy and Portugal; those countries in which the distribution of answers tends towards 'not important': Denmark and East Germany; and the remaining countries which show a certain equilibrium between the extreme ends of the scale. The report states, however, that France should be considered as a separate case, 'since the score "not important" is double that of "important")' (Eurobarometer 1995: 75). Compared with the 1985 survey, a 13 per cent drop in positive answers to the question was found in France, and only in Greece was there an increase in the number of people who say God is important in their life (+19 per cent). Some 63 per cent of French respondents who consider themselves as belonging to a particular religion consider themselves Roman Catholic, but although this is a large majority, it is smaller than the other European Catholic countries (Belgium 67 per cent, Spain 79 per cent, Ireland 91 per cent, Italy 88 per cent, Luxemburg 89 per cent and Portugal 91 per cent) (Euro-barometer 1995: 76). The 1994 survey also found that there is a high concentration in France of those considering themselves atheist (EU average 8 per cent, East Germany 39 per cent and France 19 per cent) (Eurobarometer 1995: 76). One in five European citizens claim to attend religious services 'once a year or less' (39 per cent of Danes, 36 per cent of East Germans and 32 per cent of French). Thirteen per cent of the EU population claim they never go to religious services, the highest being 21 per cent in France (Eurobarometer 1995: 77).

The study of women and politics in France

The choice of France as a focus of study means that there is a vast literature in English on French politics. However, in mainstream studies of French politics, women are consistently ignored, or confined to a few cursory paragraphs or, at best, pages.[4]

Between 1955 and the late 1980s, the study of women and politics in France was limited. Maurice Duverger (1955) synthesised the results of four national surveys on women and politics, which had been sponsored by UNESCO. The surveys were conducted in France, Yugoslavia, West Germany and Norway. The findings of the French study, by Dogan and Narbonne (1955), were published in the same year. Almost a decade later, Andrée Michel and Geneviève Texier's (1964) wide-ranging two-volume study of the status of French women included sections on the law, work, the family, institutional politics, religion, trade unions, interest groups and reproductive politics. Again, there was a ten-year gap before the subject was re-examined. Two political scientists, Janine Mossuz-Lavau and Mariette Sineau began prolific research careers in this area. Together they published (1983) the results of a survey on women and politics. Mossuz-Lavau has published widely on voting behaviour and political attitudes (for example, 1994, 1997a, 1997b, 1997e) and on the gendered impact of the law (1991). Mariette Sineau has conducted a number of studies on women in the political élite (1988, 1997a, 1998a) and has written, with Jane Jenson (1995), a full-length study of the impact on women of policies pursued during François Mitterrand's two presidential terms. Janine Mossuz-Lavau and Mariette Sineau are the only two researchers who have worked consistently on women and politics within a political science framework, although some of Françoise Gaspard's more recent projects also fit within this framework, notably an investigation into women and the parties (1995) and the 1993 election study of women's candidacies (*Parité-infos*, no. 0, 1992).

The bicentenary of the Revolution in 1989 prompted numerous conferences and publications around the themes of the Republic, democracy and citizenship. Feminist historians such as Eliane Viennot, Françoise Thébaud and Michèle Riot-Sarcey undertook their own explorations of the place of women in each of these constructs and began to develop ideas about what women's citizenship could be.[5] Philosophers such as Françoise Collin and Geneviève Fraisse developed further theories of women's place in democracy and citizenship. This is one of best developed areas of French feminist research on women and politics.

Parity and associated debates have spawned numerous publications. The first was *Au pouvoir citoyennes* (Gaspard, Servan-Schreiber and Le Gall 1992), and it has been followed by the proceedings of various conferences, for example at UNESCO in 1993 (Halimi (ed.) 1994a) and at Toulouse in 1998 (Martin (ed.) 1998); special issues of journals (for example, *Nouvelles questions féministes* 15, 4, 1994 and 16, 2, 1995, and *Projets féministes*, 4–5 1996); and books in favour of the campaign (Mossuz-Lavau 1998c, Bataille and Gaspard 1999) and against it (Amar 1999).

Some edited volumes have combined the interests detailed above. *Les femmes et la politique* (Le Bras-Chopard and Mossuz-Lavau 1997) and a special issue of *Pouvoirs* (no. 82, 1997) include articles on democracy and the Republic, voting behaviour, women in the political élite, European law and parity.

Research on women's participation in politics outside the formal parliamentary system includes studies of feminist politics (Picq 1993), of women in the trade unions (Colin 1975, Maruani 1979, Laot 1981, Simon 1981 and Zylberberg-Hocquard 1978, 1981) and of women in the social movements of the 1980s and 1990s (Heinen and Trat 1997 and Kergoat 1992).

To summarise, the seminal works by Duverger (1955), Dogan and Narbonne (1955) and Michel and Texier (1964) did not launch a field of study within French political science, as they might have done. Instead, it was many years before Mossuz-Lavau and Sineau began to research in this area, and, until the late 1980s, they were more or less alone. The most developed areas of research on women and politics in France are the study of voting behaviour and women in the political élite and reflections by historians and philosophers on the exclusion of women from the Republic. Since 1992, the parity debate has stimulated interest in the relation between women and politics and has led to an increase in publications in this area. A large section of the literature is made up of personal accounts by individual women politicians, for example Yvette Roudy (1985, 1995), Frédérique Brédin (1997) and Elisabeth Guigou (1997) and records of interviews with women from the political élite (Mangin and Martichoux 1991, Adler 1993, Sineau 1988, Freedman 1997). Although individually these accounts would bear little weight, the sheer number of them, all concurring in particular on the masculinism of French political culture, has to be taken as additional evidence.

The available literature in English on women and politics in France is limited. Comparative studies of women's participation have relied heavily on translations of findings by Mossuz-Lavau and Sineau (for example, Lovenduski 1986 and Randall 1987). Amongst the more important contributions to the study of women and politics in France are the following: Andrew Appleton and Amy Mazur (1993) have conducted research into women and two major French parties, the *Parti socialiste (PS)* and the *Rassemblement pour la République* (RPR). Dorothy Stetson (1987) has published a full-length study on the impact of public policy on women's lives and has co-edited a comparative study of state feminism (1995), in which Amy Mazur analyses the French Ministry for Women's Rights. The French women's movement is the subject of Claire Duchen's now classic study *Feminism in France* (1986) and an article by Jane Jenson which originally appeared in *New Left Review* (Jenson 1990) and has now been updated and republished in an edited volume by Monica Threlfall (1996). Maggie Allison (1994) has analysed the politics of abortion in France and Joan Wallach Scott (1996b) has written a full-length study of sexual difference and citizenship.

Aims, objectives and global structure

This book is the first full-length study of women and politics in Fifth Republic France 1958–2000. It has several interconnected aims. On one level, it is concerned with political activity. This is examined in three parts. The first part aims to provide essential information about the participation of French women in traditional political structures and organisations, including governments, representative assemblies, state bureaucracies, political parties and electoral politics. The second part examines the role of women in relatively new alternative forms of political activity, including new social movements. The third part examines the activity of women in the campaign calling for their greater representation in political institutions.

Participation refers to the activities by which a citizen engages with political institutions and representatives. These include registering to vote, voting, discussing politics, taking part in an election campaign, and attending meetings. Some commentators include less conventional activities, including protest activities, such as demonstrating, signing a petition or occupying a building, but most studies of participation have focused on narrowly defined party politics.

Studies of participation investigate both the level of participation, usually measured in terms of the effort required to perform certain activities, and political orientation or electoral choice. They investigate the factors which influence both these aspects, in an attempt to find which ones are determinant. The first part of this book will apply these methods to a study of French women's participation in order to bring women into studies from which they have to a large extent been excluded.

This is not simply an account of women's political participation, however. Although the first part of the book uses the methods employed by traditional political science in order to provide information essential to an understanding of French women's participation, it situates this approach within a feminist critique of the limitations of a narrow definition of politics. It is argued that, by focusing on the processes of government and the state, this approach, first, ignores forms of political activity in which women are more likely to be involved, and, second, reinforces the representation of the public arena as almost exclusively masculine. The analysis of women's participation is therefore located within a broader questioning of the definition of political participation and the theoretical and strategic consequences of attempts to redefine it.

The second part of the book thus moves away from the narrowly defined area of political participation, expanding the meaning of the term 'political activity' to include, for example, participation in the new social movements. The feminist redefinition of the political has placed issues which were previously relegated to the private sphere firmly on the political agenda. The aim of this part of the book is, then, to demonstrate the feminist claim that the personal is political, and to reassess women's political activity in this light.

Since the victory of the Socialists in 1981 and the five-year experience of the Ministry for Women's Rights, French feminism has turned its attention towards public politics, arguing that there is a complex inter-dependence between the 'private' and 'public' spheres of political activity and that women need to be present in both. Since 1992, there has been growing support from feminists, women politicians, intellectuals and public opinion for a campaign for the equal representation of men and women in political institutions. This campaign has brought an urgency to the need to establish whether integrating women into a masculine political system will advance the feminist project. It raises many questions, such as whether parity alone can improve women's citizenship rights or whether feminist objectives will only be achieved through a fundamental reworking of the principles which underlie the current political system. The third part of the book considers the contribution of French feminism to these debates. It also questions whether notions of national citizenship are still relevant at a time of increasing European political integration and argues that the current French feminist solutions based on a reworking of the traditional republican model of citizenship do not venture beyond national boundaries.

In France, as in many other Western liberal democracies, economic crisis has contributed to the destabilisation of established politics. The decline in the political parties, the relationship between the National Assembly and the government, scandals surrounding the financing of political parties, concerns that the EU undermines national government, and popular disaffection with political institutions are all seen as signs that representative democracy is in crisis. The debates surrounding these questions take place in the context of a broader debate on the meaning of democracy and citizenship. Disillusionment on the part of the electorate and the disenfranchisement of groups of the population, including the homeless and immigrants, illustrate the need to redefine citizenship.

The third part tries to locate French women within political theory and examines their contribution to it. An analysis of the French feminist critique of the exclusion of women from the republican tradition of universalism is accompanied by an assessment of the feminist contributions to the current debate on democracy, citizenship and equality.

Methodology

Drawing on the methods developed by prominent feminist political scientists and notably Joni Lovenduski, Pippa Norris and Vicky Randall, this study aims first to 'bring the women back in' to accounts of French politics, identifying the ways in which mainstream studies have excluded them and integrating all the information which can be found into these standard frameworks. Second, however, it highlights the limitations of this approach and examines movements which have sought to expand the definition of the political and political activity. Finally, it discusses French feminist contributions to current understandings of political concepts, especially universalism and citizenship.

A wide variety of sources has been used. These include the existing secondary literature, presented briefly above and in more detail in the relevant chapters of the book. Primary sources include the data bases of the Interparliamentary Union, the European Women's Lobby, the Council of European Municipalities and Regions, Eurobarometer, and the European Database – Women in Decision-Making; information from the women's sections and press offices of the political parties and trade unions; newspaper and periodical articles, including those held in the press cuttings service of the Fondation Nationale des Sciences Politiques in Paris;[6] and the websites of the French government, parliament, parties and organisations. In many parts of the book, information from these sources has been brought together for the first time and is not always comprehensive. Until pressure from international and European organisations became difficult to resist, French official state bodies did not collect statistics on the political participation of categories of citizens, on the principle of the indivisibility of the French people. This means that it is very difficult to carry out the most basic counts of the numbers of women in various bodies. Similarly, until very recently, parties and trade unions were unable to provide details of the proportion of women in the membership and internal organisation, and some still cannot whilst others provide incomplete data.

The problems associated with the limited nature of the information available are exacerbated by the distortion of the results of some early studies, especially in the area of voting behaviour. Here, the results of small-scale local studies were extrapolated, without comment, to the national level and regarded as general findings. The interpretation of opinion polls has similarly produced exaggerated claims about the political behaviour of women. This study attempts where possible to demonstrate how these misrepresentations have occurred and constructs a more faithful picture of the relation between women and politics. Although beyond the scope of this project, further research based on large-scale empirical work will enrich our understanding of women's political activities. In particular, studies which move beyond the falsely homogeneous category of 'women' and investigate the variety of women's situations in relation to politics are essential.[7]

Difference – or which women and politics?

It is important to explain here why we have decided not to make specific reference (either in one special chapter or throughout this book) to ethnic minority women (whether migrants or of migrant origin).[8] There are two main reasons why this decision was taken. The first relates to the difficulty of obtaining both qualitative and quantitive data on ethnic minority women and the second, which is more important, relates to the contention (Carby 1992) that it is problematic, if not impossible, to incorporate the experiences and problems faced by ethnic minority women into an analysis of those faced by white women without conflating and over-simplifying the processes of racism and sexism which in turn reinforce the sense of exclusion that ethnic minority women experience in white society.

First, although interest in international migratory flows and migrant populations has increased since the early 1980s, academic, governmental and party political literature and discourses on ethnic minority women are insignificant if not non-existent. Immigrants constitute a neutral category in which women are made invisible in both comparative and single country studies. In 1986, at the OECD's first Conference on Immigration, it was reported that 'so far migrant women have been the subject of systematic research only in a restricted way' and that 'owing to the economic recession, other issues such as the labour market position of the second generation migrants, unemployment and illegal immigration have been given priority' (Abadan-Unat 1987: 24). At the end of the 1990s, information is no more available than it was previously. Michèle Aulagnon, writing in *Le Monde* (20 March 1998: 10), notes:

> We do not hear them. Official statistics published monthly give very little information about their presence. Politicians mention their existence only rarely. Although they represent 45 per cent of the migrant population and form almost a third of all foreign workers . . . in France, migrant women are absent from all the important sociological and historical literature on migrations.

In order to make specific reference to ethnic minority women in France, it is important to know who they are and yet the very first step of establishing their numeric presence is fraught with difficulty. The term 'migrant (women)' (*[Femmes] immigrées*)[9] can and has been used interchangeably with 'foreigners' (*étrangers*)[10] and '(women) of foreign origin' (*[femmes] d'origine étrangère*)[11] to describe ethnic minority women, whether migrants or of migrant origin. Yet, if ethnic minority women are mentioned in official statistics, then it is as part of the categories 'migrants' (*immigrés*) or 'foreigners' (*étrangers*). Those of migrant origin, born in France, are left out. Consequently, any information relating to their presence and collective experience is subsumed under those of white French nationals. However, the lack of statistics and other information is in itself revelatory of the various discriminations to which ethnic minority women are subjected from the time of entry into France and this brings us to the second more contentious question of whether to include a chapter or series of sections on ethnic minority women in a book which speaks of 'white women' generally (although even this term does not a cover a homogeneous reality).

It is no secret that to date, the bulk and mainstream of theory and politics in feminist writing have reflected the experiences and hopes of white women and is neither applicable nor responsive to those of ethnic minority women. The lack of feminist writing exploring the political experiences (in the widest sense) of ethnic minority women is even more acute in France. The sex-based norms of French and other western societies which give rise to certain expectations and demands amongst white women are denied to ethnic minority women through the operation of racism. This has been most recently demonstrated in the context of the debate and campaign in favour of parity. What meaning can gender parity in elected bodies have for women who, along with ethnic minority men, are either denied the right to vote or whose lack of resources (based primarily on racist prejudice, practice or laws) prevents them from gaining presence within the polity?

Originally, the majority of ethnic minority women arrived in France as wives and daughters, in the framework of family reunion policies introduced in the mid-1970s. Historically, therefore, they have no autonomous legal status and hence little stake in the society of their destination country. The lack of autonomous legal status denies them access to political and other resources and structures, while their lack of stake acts as a demotivator to involvement in political activity. Although the circumstances of ethnic minority women have changed in that they are now significant participants within the labour market, and many participate in associations and non-governmental organisations and informal networks, their image as women closeted in a culturally foreign, isolated domestic sphere is perpetuated; for example, if and when ethnic minority women are mentioned or studied, it has been mostly in terms of sexuality (for example, genital mutilation, the wearing of the veil) so that eventually those (including feminists) who speak about them and/or for them end up reinforcing the ways in which western culture exoticises and sexualises ethnic minority women and, consequently, ignores other parts of their existence.

Hence, in this book, when we speak of women's needs, interests, experiences and rights we do not speak for ethnic minority women. We are aware that for the aspirations, interests and demands of ethnic minority women to be expressed, feminism, in this case French feminism, needs to include an analysis of race which is informed by the collective reality of the totality of ethnic minority women's lives. Just as feminist studies of 'women' challenged the way in which politics was understood and structured in traditional political science, so the experience of ethnic minority women (in France and elsewhere) constitutes an area of study that is crucial in expanding that challenge, and ensuring that once 'women' are included, the latter does not become a universal concept which ignores the specific discrimination experienced by ethnic minority women.

Other issues fall under the heading 'difference'. The difference debate has split French feminism throughout its history and is of particular pertinence to a discussion of the relation between women and politics. Is the goal of feminism in this context for women to accede to sites of power until now occupied almost exclusively by men, or is it to change these sites of power and, indeed, all conceptions of power, from the outside? Or should feminism be trying to do both at once? If they do enter male-dominated institutions, will women act like men or transform them from within? Do women do politics differently from men, do they have different political interests and does the answer to either of these questions justify the claim for women's greater presence in political institutions?

This book focuses on gender as a basis for exclusion from political decision-making and as a basis for organisation in order to challenge this exclusion and influence policy decisions. In doing so, it may contribute to the understanding of the exclusion of other subordinated groups. However, women's relation to politics (their ability to participate in policy-making, to influence policy outcomes and the impact that policies have on their lives) is influenced by factors other than gender or which interact with gender.

The question of the complex and multiple interactions between the various power axes on which women are positioned has occupied British and American feminists since the early 1980s, following criticisms of the white, middle-class, largely heterosexual bias of the movement which claimed, explicitly or implicitly, to speak for women as though this category were unproblematic. Largely unexplored in the French women's movement, this issue is at last on the agenda (ANEF 1998). Speaking at the 1998 ANEF conference on feminism and racism, Claudie Lesselier (1998: 50) underlines one of the main threads of the conference, which is that further work needs to be done on the interrelation between social relations and different forms of oppression. Two examples of specific contexts in which this needs to be done are Vichy and colonisation. She states that research could also usefully be carried out on the gendered nature of social movements (for example, the movement of 'sans papiers' and anti-racist movements); and on feminist and women's practice and theory on racism and anti-Semitism.

The interaction between women as political actors, the institutions and processes of policy-making, policy outcomes and women as direct or indirect consumers or objects of public policy is highly complex. At each point, power relations are at play. The women who attempt to influence policy outcomes may be very different from the women who are most affected by them.[12] Class interests can be in conflict with gender interests. This explains, for example, why the labour movement of the nineteenth century, in defence of the interests of male workers, vigorously opposed women's entry into the labour market, why the PCF in the 1950s failed to support campaigns for the legalisation of contraception and abortion, which it saw as a means of controlling the reproduction of the working class, and why the first meeting of the *Coordination des femmes noires* (Co-ordination of Black Women) in November 1977 was disrupted by men and women of the extreme left, who, calling the speakers '*petites bourgeoises*', insisted that bringing an end to imperialism and capitalism was more important than 'cultural' issues (*Le Monde*, 2 November 1977).

Numerous questions arise: Does a focus on participation in mainstream institutional politics mean a focus on white middle-class women? Does the demand for women's greater presence in mainstream political élites concern only those women with access to the resources necessary to partici- pate at this level? What impact could this form of participation have on the lives of all women and does it contribute to the feminist project?

The recognition of multiplicity and differences is especially difficult to integrate into the analysis of women's participation in the first part of the book. Although some information is available on differences according to age and class, there is no information on participation according to ethnic origin, as explained above.

Gender and public policy

A second set of issues relate to gender and public policy. Gender as a social cleavage does not fit neatly into the ideological categories created by a political system constructed primarily around social relations of class. Gender cuts through political affiliations and does not align with left and right. Although policies constructed with class issues in mind (whatever the terminology used by those who claim that class is no longer a valid way of viewing social divisions) frequently have a markedly different impact on men and women, this is rarely intentional, or even noticed, by policy-makers.

What is the most effective way to produce policy outcomes which are favourable to women? Is it for women to agitate outside or inside formal politics? Is it for gender considerations to permeate the entire policy- making process or to be dealt with by a specialised body such as the Ministry for Women's Rights? Would the problem be solved if there were an equal number of women and men in sites of decision-making? These questions recur throughout the book in the analysis of the effectiveness of state feminism (the institutions which are established with the express aim of improving women's status and the women who are active within them); the influence of women within the political parties and trade unions; women's political activity outside the formal arena; and the debate around the difference that it would make if women and men were equally present in politics.

Dorothy Stetson's *Women's Rights in France* (1987) focuses on the policy- making process and what happens when feminists try to influence it. She

argues that the central issue in all political conflict is the battle over meanings, and her book explores 'the changes in women's rights in France by
focusing on the conflict about the definition of issues' (21). She finds that
issues which are least threatening and most incremental have the greatest
chance of success. Demands for legal equality of the sexes without changing
sex roles are more acceptable and attract the support of many more groups
than those which propose a basic reorientation of the roles of men and
women (4). Some researchers have found that new proposals can attract
support from mass publics, however. This seems to be the case with parity,
which is represented as a new idea, even though it is not. It has been
consciously packaged as revolutionary and subversive and explicitly
opposed to worn-out demands for quotas. The struggle continues around
the meaning of the term 'parity', but at its best, it still means only equality
with men, thus fitting in with Stetson's 'least threatening' category of policy
issues and therefore the most likely to be widely accepted.

Stetson (1987: 5) reports that in the US, feminists have not succeeded
in mobilising mass publics and convincing the government to define
women's rights issues in terms which come anywhere near role change,
and this is the case in France, too, where the law passed on sexual harassment ended up having nothing in common with the feminist definition of
this issue (Delphy 1996: 152–3) and where abortion had to be repackaged
in order to gain acceptance (Allison 1994). The problem is that narrow
definitions bring limited effects: equality is not radical. Its impact occurs
at the level of the individual, and has little effect on the status and participation of women as a group (Stetson 1987: 6). The major issue, then,
is the redefinition of issues in feminist terms, whether this is 'the political',
sexual harassment or parity. The parity debate is a struggle over definitions. What could be radical or subversive has been turned into a simple
demand for equality or, worse, equal opportunities.

The gendered impact of public policy is not examined in detail in this
book. Issues which could be addressed include the gendered effects of obviously gendered policies, for example sexual harassment, rape and abortion,
but also the gendered impact of less obviously gendered policies, such as
the shortening of the working week, the ratification of the Maastricht
Treaty and changes to the nationality laws. A gendered analysis of the
impact of a wide range of policy decisions is the subject of a separate
study, the results of which are forthcoming.

Research problems

Some of the problems which arose during this research have been solved
or circumvented. Others, despite numerous searches and much discussion,
have not.

A problem that arose unexpectedly and at a late stage in the research
process is how to present political activities carried out by women but

clearly anti-feminist. The most obvious examples are activism in the anti-abortion movement and in extreme right-wing movements and parties. Lilane Kandel (ANEF 1998: 36) raises the underexplored issue of women's autonomous active participation in Nazi politics, arguing that it is too easy to claim simply that the men or the system which oppressed them are solely responsible for their actions:

> Oppressed, no doubt, but not necessarily 'elsewhere' or 'innocent' for all that. We cannot, however, decide that they are social and historical actors only when they become feminists. It is therefore necessary to undertake both analyses at the same time. If not, we run the risk of finding ourselves in the fairy-tale world of 'feminist realism', with its pious images of women who are all victims or all martyrs – or even all resistance fighters or, even worse, all heroines.

One partial solution is to direct readers to studies of women in these movements (Venner 1995, Lesselier and Venner 1997). Another is to clarify the stance of the authors and the selection process which has had to take place in order to keep this research within reasonable limits. Not all studies of women and politics are inherently feminist: feminist research is defined not by its subject, but by the perspective taken on this subject. This is a consciously feminist book in that it starts from the premise that women are subordinated to men and explores possible ways to change this power relation. Since it is impossible to include everything which is relevant to the subject women and politics in France, selection of topics has had to take place, and those which have been chosen for inclusion are those which further the main argument. Thus, in part one, women's activities in mainstream politics are examined. In part two, the sites of alternative political activity which are selected are those which seek to redefine the political. The numerous associations in which women participate, but which do not challenge definitions of what is political or how political activity should be organised, are not included. Part three focuses on the movement which aims to bring about the better representation of women in politics.

Chapter summaries

Chapter 1 provides a picture of French women's presence, not only within elected assemblies at local and national level, but also within the state executive. It also analyses and comments upon the role and influence of women within these structures with regard to public policy-making and in particular that relating to women's rights. In doing so, the problems which exist in trying to provide such information and analysis are borne in mind: bias of traditional political science literature, the lack of information and secrecy regarding the means of distributing power within the institutions of the state, and the lack of data on women in élite politics due to the traditional assumption that women are neither suited to, nor interested in, élite politics.

Chapter 2 examines women's presence in the membership and internal organisation of the main political parties. It discusses party policy towards the promotion of women in politics, including candidate selection; party policy towards women's rights; and the parties' attempts to attract women voters. It finds that, with a few exceptions, the number of women decreases as one ascends the party hierarchy, and the selection of women candidates, until very recently, was in inverse proportion to the chances of the party winning a particular seat. It finds that the parties are heavily implicated in the exclusion of women from politics and are only now responding to growing pressure to increase women's presence.

While trade unions do not, strictly speaking, operate within the political sphere, it is true that women's participation and influence within politics reflect their position within socio-economic institutions. Besides, in France, perhaps more than in any other European country, trade unions consider themselves to be political actors, motivated as much by ideological concerns as purely economistic ones. In this respect, they constitute an important channel of influence on political parties and political agenda setting and women's position within them needs examination and comment. In the 1970s, feminist activity within the unions forced them to consider the category 'working women' and its specific needs. It also forced union involvement in issues previously defined as 'private'. However, a period of union commitment to improving women's rights as workers has been followed by a return to more conventional concerns. Chapter 3 examines existing material on this subject, but also adds to it to provide a useful and comprehensive synthesis of women within trade unions.

Chapter 4 shows that, despite the fact that as early as 1955 commentators found the gap between men and women's electoral participation barely significant, much time and energy has been devoted to identifying such a gap and trying to explain it. This chapter examines studies of voter turnout, political interest and knowledge about politics, finding that, in many cases, the research methods and expectations of the researcher have exaggerated the gap. It then examines studies of political orientation, finding that there are differences in the ways men and women use their vote. It analyses factors which may be more pertinent to this difference than gender itself, in particular religiosity, age and position in the labour market.

It is argued that the evidence may be used to support the view that women's political participation is very similar to men's, and that differences can be attributed to their relative lateness in acquiring political rights, to factors other than gender or to problems with research methods. On the other hand, the evidence may be used to support the view that the study of women's political participation has been constrained and distorted by the narrow definition of the political, which has excluded many areas in which women are particularly active.

Chapter 5 examines a question which has aroused media and academic interest since the 1950s: why do women participate less than men? It discusses the various explanations which have been offered: the historical exclusion of women from public politics and the creation of a male-dominated political culture; women's alleged lack of interest, confidence and ambition; women's lack of the resources necessary to enter public politics; the type of electoral system; the role of the parties; and the impact of the 1970s' women's movement.

It finds that the evidence supports the argument that women are excluded by the political system, rather than that they exclude themselves, although it is clear that numerous factors contribute to their under-representation. It is argued that the dominant construction of 'political participation' contributes to the apparent absence of women, since areas in which they are active, including social movements and campaigns to change public policy, are excluded from the analysis. The following two chapters therefore focus on 'alternative' sites of political participation.

Chapter 6 examines women's participation in mixed movements out-side the formal political arena, taking as examples the ecology movement and the social movements of 1988 and 1995. It finds that, despite repeated references in the literature on the ecology movement to the participation of women, the information available on their involvement is patchy, and no firm conclusions can be drawn. However, it shows that women led a number of important protests, were active at all levels of the ecology movement both before its entry into mainstream politics and afterwards, and that a debate took place within the movement around the links between ecology, femininity and feminism.

Chapter 7 examines the various forms taken by feminist politics during the Fifth Republic. It discusses the extent to which the MLF of the 1970s represented continuity or discontinuity in women's political practice; the relation between feminism and institutional politics; and the extent to which feminism successfully challenged the definition of the political. It does this by analysing core debates around, for example, the public/private divide and the relation between revolution and reform. It is found that feminism expanded the definition of the political and produced a critique of masculine institutional politics, but it did not find a sustainable alter-native to traditional political activity.

Chapter 8 provides an overview of the numerous attempts which have been made since the 1970s to increase the number of women in politics. It shows that there is a wide consensus around the principle of increasing women's representation, but that there are two contentious issues associ-ated with it. The first is what difference it would make if there were more women in politics and the second is the practical question of how this increase should be brought about. It is argued that, although the equal

presence of men and women in elected bodies would have symbolic significance, it would not on its own address the problem of the access of different
social categories to the resources necessary for political activity, nor would
it guarantee women's access to sites of real power. It is also argued that
the Constitutional Reform Act passed in 1999 fails to satisfy the demands
of the campaign for parity and that continued pressure will be necessary
if the goal of the campaign is to be achieved.

While campaigners for parity have claimed that the equal representation of men and women in political institutions would solve the democratic
deficit, feminist critics of the campaign have argued that a fundamental
reworking of democracy and citizenship is necessary if parity is to improve
women's lives. Chapter 9 examines the debates which have taken place
around these issues in order to assess the extent to which parity could
improve the status of women as citizens and their ability to participate
fully in politics and civil society.

It is argued that, on its own, parity would not address some of the main
problems of contemporary democracy, nor would it solve the problems
caused by the exclusion of women. Instead, it is necessary to focus on
locally-based active citizen participation, which would enable democracy
to work from below, rather than imposing it from above. It is also necessary to redefine citizenship in a way which encompasses the private and
domestic spheres, as well as the public political. It is argued that parity
has placed the question of women's relation to politics firmly on the political agenda, but that it cannot on its own give the majority of French
women access to full citizenship. It is up to feminists to maintain pressure
in a wide variety of areas if this is to be achieved.

The conclusion summarises the main themes of the book. The first is
that women's participation has taken place in both mainstream and non-
traditional sites of political activity, although at different rates and with
the relation between them varying over time. They have been caught in
two conflicts. The first is that, by entering mainstream politics, they risk
sacrificing the force of their critique of it, while by remaining outside mainstream politics, they risk merely agitating on the sidelines, while men
continue to make the important decisions. The second is that, if women
stress their difference from men, they risk having this difference turned
back on them and used as a basis for continued discrimination. However,
if they stress their sameness to men, they can no longer seek to rectify the
damage done by falsely gender-neutral policies and practices. If they deny
that women are excluded from politics as a group, they cannot fight to
increase the presence of this group. The main conclusion which can be
drawn from this study is that it is essential that women participate both
in mainstream and non-traditional political activities; that they both use
the system and try to change it; and that they do this in the name of their
sameness and, at the same time, their difference from men.

1 Women and the state

In traditional political science, the state has long been regarded as a privileged site of political participation and representative democracy. Hence, apart from focusing on voting, parties and pressure groups, studies of political participation have emphasised the importance of involvement in state structures and processes in order to assess the contribution of various social groups or classes to the preservation or transformation of political life and of society in general. In examining political participation in the state, traditional political science has paid very little, if any, attention to women's political involvement. On the basis of crude sex-stereotyping, it has argued that women are uninterested in, uninformed about or psychologically unsuited to politics and therefore, that their levels of participation are low and by implication unworthy of study. The French political scientist, Maurice Duverger, who synthesised the findings of a UNESCO-funded survey in the 1950s of women's political participation in France, the German Federal Republic, Norway and Yugoslavia, noted, 'the survey seems to have encountered ... a certain degree of indifference. The political scientists and most of the organisations invited to supply information often tended to regard its purpose as a secondary one, of no intrinsic importance' (1955b: 8). Such indifference and dismissiveness were also clearly demonstrated by Mattei Dogan (1955: 292) who studied the social background of deputies elected in June 1951, but who refused to include women, arguing that not only did they form a mere 3.5 per cent of deputies but that most of them were housewives rather than profession-holders. Where traditional political science has shown an interest in women, it has only done so in order to demonstrate women's similarity to or difference from men's political behaviour (taken to be the norm) within a strictly defined 'political' sphere. For example, Duverger's study, mentioned above, does just that.

The contention that traditional political science has defined 'politics' and political activity to include a set of roles which are male stereotypes did not gain currency until the beginning of the 1970s when burgeoning women's movements across the industrialised world began challenging sex-roles generally, and the differentiation that these roles reproduced in the political sphere. Feminist academics and activists in France and elsewhere[1] challenged the type of data chosen by traditional political science in its analysis of women's participation and the interpretations which flowed from such analysis. In 1965, Andrée Michel wrote in criticism of political scientists:

> The majority of works within this new [political] science emphasise the study of political behaviour more or less exclusively in the context of political parties. It is from such an angle that Dogan and Narbonne, [and] Maurice Duverger study the political behaviour of women (electoral behaviour, the presence of women in parties, female candidatures, the activity of elected women representatives, etc.).
>
> (61)

In contrast to traditional political scientists, feminists sought different reasons to explain the disparities in political participation of men and women, reasons which did not place the blame for women's under-participation on their supposed lack of knowledge or interest. They questioned not only the interconnection between roles, status and power distribution in politics but also the definition of politics itself, and in doing so they rejected politics as an activity only carried out within the restricted sphere of state institutions, parties and elections (sites of representative democracy). Since its beginnings, the women's movement set out to enlarge the definition of politics to include feminist activism in favour of women's rights. Feminists, engaged in the study of activity and activism beyond traditionally defined politics, deliberately chose to act (without men) outside that restricted patriarchal domain:

> In opting for separatism, in affirming the principle according to which the struggle against oppression belongs to the oppressed themselves . . . the feminist movement of the early 1970s had brought about a fundamental break in the traditional conception of politics. But there is another central idea within feminism which is that, in order to understand as well as to fight women's oppression, one cannot build on any form of existing 'top-down' social analysis: one has to 'build collectively from below'.
>
> (Viennot 1984: 167)

This approach held sway throughout much of the 1970s. However, in the 1980s a new interest in women's participation in formal political structures, in particular the state, emerged amongst feminist academics and activists. Again, this is as true for France as for other countries. A number of reasons explain this emergence of interest in the state.

First, the post-1968 feminist movement had started to disintegrate by the late 1970s as a result of internal dissension over ideology and strategy.

This left a sizeable proportion of women activists who were prepared to reconsider more traditional or formal ways of acting politically. Although the women's movement had been 'anti-state' it had nevertheless made demands on the state to further women's rights, and in making demands a large number of feminists had found themselves dealing with parliamentary parties or state agencies which could be influenced and which had, in return, influenced them.

Second, the conjunction of women's growing presence within education and the labour market and the influence of feminist ideas had pushed thousands of ordinary women out of the private sphere of the home into the public arena and the further this process continued, the more women saw themselves as holding a stake in society. Consequently women outside the feminist movement gained a greater interest in traditional policy agendas onto which so-called 'private' issues (such as abortion and contraception, violence against women, divorce, etc.) had been placed in the 1970s. In the 1980s, then, there emerged a desire to further influence such agendas by reshaping the existing organisation of public roles. Also, at the same time, male politicians were having to re-examine the needs of their women constituents who were not the passive and private beings that they had always perceived.

Third, in France, the establishment of a Ministry of Women's Rights in 1981 focused public attention, whether critical or supportive, on the relationship between women and the state as never before. The choice of title, 'ministry', indicated that the state was approaching the aspirations, experiences, interests, and rights of women in a more dynamic way than it had done in its previous history. The new Minister for Women's Rights, Yvette Roudy, stated that the ministry would represent a permanent dialogue between French women and the state: 'The moment a group exists, an association is registered, in short can be identified, as soon as there are people who have faces, a constitution, they must be recognised and a dialogue must begin' (Ducrocq 1985: 64). The construction of this dialogue was to be based on feminist demands to empower women's associations through the allocation of real resources,[2] to fund specific projects (e.g. the Maison des femmes and the Simone de Beauvoir Audio-Visual Centre in Paris), to establish vocational training programmes, especially in new technologies, to introduce feminist studies and research in higher education and to extend women's rights through legislation.

Fourth, initiatives throughout the 1980s and 1990s, at European[3] and international level,[4] to encourage the presence of women in the state have helped to create a climate within which the question of women's political participation in the highest decision-making bodies cannot be avoided by established parties and politicians.

The increased interest among feminist academics and activists in women's engagement with the state has led, in the 1990s, to a gradual development in feminist theory of a different conceptualisation of the (liberal democratic) state as either a privileged public political space or at least one which cannot be ignored, in which women (among other 'different' and under-represented interests) can contribute to the revitalisation of democracy and citizenship and where the realisation of feminist ideals can be pursued.[5] However, on the whole very few feminist academics,[6] whether French or otherwise, have made the state a central part of their concerns and consequently a distinct and coherent set of feminist theories of the state has still to emerge.

In France, the 1980s and 1990s have produced numerous works on women, democracy and citizenship in the context of the debate on parity (see Chapters 8 and 9), a number of works on what one might conveniently term 'state feminism' (Batiot 1986, Jenson 1987, Mazur 1995a, 1995b, and 1996, Mossuz-Lavau 1986, Stetson 1987) and an abundant literature (comprising empirical analysis, essays, biographies and autobiographical accounts by women who have held decision-making responsibilities within state structures) on women and decision-making (Adler 1993, Gaspard 1996, Jensen and Sineau 1995, Mossuz-Lavau and Sineau 1983, Sineau 1988).[7] While none of these works focuses exclusively on the state, together they provide a bank of information, albeit far from complete, and analyses from which a picture of women's participation in the state can be constructed and developed. The importance of the state in traditional political science studies of politics and political participation, and the recently developed interest within feminism in the state's structures and processes, as outlined above, constitute the rationale for considering the question of women's involvement with state structures and processes in Fifth Republic France.

The aim of this chapter is threefold. Its main aim is to assess the extent of women's participation in decision-making state structures at national and sub-national level. But it also considers, albeit briefly, the type of roles that women have played within these structures, and the issue of their performance. The study of women's involvement with the state in a country like France is subjected to a number of limitations. For instance, an examination of the small numbers of women present at national decision-making level will not offer generally applicable conclusions about the way in which women act and affect outcomes. Furthermore, the study of women's participation at regional and municipal levels can lead to conflicting findings as there are often considerable disparities between regions and local municipalities and in any case, as far as France is concerned, studies of women and local politics are few and far between (Junter-Loiseau 1998, Rieu 1998, Gaspard 1998c). Nevertheless, it is hoped that this chapter will make a useful contribution to a growing body of comparative literature (including individual and cross-country studies) on women's participation in political decision-making within the state.

Women and political decision-making in the Fifth Republic

Women's participation in élite offices of the state, just as their participation in voting and other forms of formal political activity, is linked to their socio-economic and domestic status. Hence, the better placed they are within the education system, the labour market and cultural networks on the one hand and the more equal the division of domestic labour in the home on the other hand, the higher the level of their participation in politics in general and more specifically at decision-making levels where a significant time commitment (*disponibilité*) and level of experiential skill (*compétence*) is required.

In Fifth Republic France, women's participation within the state has been unremarkable when compared with that in other European Union countries and yet, over the last forty years, France has fared well as far as other gender equality indicators are concerned. For instance, French women make up almost half of the working population, representing one of the highest labour force participation rates in the world. Furthermore, France is placed seventh in the world according to the UN Development Programme's sex-specific indicator for human development (*Le Monde* (supplement) 31 August 1995: 4).

It is argued (Adler 1993, Sineau 1997a) that the establishment of the Fifth Republic, in 1958, furthered and consolidated the masculinisation of power within the French state. The introduction of a number of particular institutional features gave rise to 'a sort of republic of males which assured the latter of the monopoly of legitimate power' (Sineau 1997a: 45). These features include: the investiture of extensive powers in a state technocracy whose members, trained at the élite *grandes écoles*,[8] have been nominated by the President of the Republic to the highest state administration and government positions; the election, by universal suffrage, of the head of state who has served as a potent figure of masculine power;[9] a majoritarian electoral system which has produced and intensified certain outcomes and practices (highly personalised, gladiatorial electoral contests, the holding of multiple mandates, the marginalisation of smaller parties) with extremely unfavourable consequences for women's participation (see Chapter 5). It is not surprising therefore that the establishment of the Fifth Republic coincided with the 'political exit' of women from both the executive and legislative branches of the state which have subsequently remained stubbornly opposed to measures and processes of feminisation until relatively recent times.

This section aims to present as full a picture as possible of French women's participation within mainstream institutions of the state at both national and sub-national levels. It will, therefore, focus on women's presence in the national legislature (the *Assemblée nationale* and the *Sénat*), government and the civil service and within sub-national assemblies and executives with particular emphasis on the regions and municipalities. As women have not been considered as political partners until recently, there exists a profound lack of statistical data on their participation within the state. Where data does exist (for example, within inter-ministerial surveys and reports), it has not been made widely available. Instead, it has been left to academics and political activists, interested in women's political participation, to seek out, analyse and publicise relevant information.

Women in national electoral office

While women have had the right to vote since 1944, it was not until the 1970s that they began, in a very small way, to contribute to the making and voting of laws. During the first twenty years of the Fifth Republic, the proportion of women present in both houses of parliament was negligible. The proportion of women representatives remained at 2 per cent for most of this period, rising to 2.1 per cent, in the National Assembly, only once in 1967 (see Table 1.1). This stands in contrast to figures for the Fourth Republic (1945–1958) when women formed over 5 per cent of deputies in the first seven years and over 5 per cent of senators in the first three years.

It was only with the arrival of Valéry Giscard d'Estaing to the presidency in 1974 that these unremarkable figures began to rise, albeit insignificantly. Giscard d'Estaing's message to electors contained the twinned themes of liberal reform and modernisation in politics, economy and society. His publicly stated ambition of constructing an open, democratic society in which all social groups would participate, included improving the status of women and the feminisation of politics. This ambition was fashioned not only by the experience of May 1968 (a massive strike movement begun by

Table 1.1 Percentage of women representatives in parliament

Level of office	1958	1962	1965	1967	1968	1971	1973	1974	1977	1978
Legislative (Assemblée nationale)	1.5	1.7	–	2.1	1.6	–	1.6	–	–	3.7
Legislative (Sénat)	1.9	1.8	1.8	–	1.8	1.4	–	2.5	1.7	–

Level of office	1980	1981	1983	1986	1988	1989	1992	1993	1995	1997	1998
Legislative (Assemblée nationale)	–	5.3	–	5.9	5.7	–	–	6.1	–	10.9	–
Legislative (Sénat)	2.3	–	2.8	2.8	–	3.1	4.3	–	5.6	–	5.9

Sources: Parité-infos (1997); Jenson and Sineau (1995); European Database: Women in Decision-Making, http://www.db-decision.de/english/Wahl.htm, accessed 24 July 1998.

students in response to the Vietnam War; see Reader and Wadia 1993) and the developing feminist movement but also by the desire to keep up with the reform-oriented democracies of Northern Europe where women's presence in politics has always been more marked. Consequently, the renewal of senatorial seats in 1974 led to a rise in the proportion of women senators to above 2 per cent for the first time in the Fifth Republic (although by 1977 this figure had again fallen to 1.7 per cent). The 1978 legislative elections returned twelve women (representing 3.7 per cent of deputies) to the National Assembly (mainly due to an increased feminisation of Communist candidates).

The increase in the number of women parliamentarians continued in the 1980s and 1990s under the presidency of Mitterrand. The latter's election promises to advance the cause of women in politics, as in other spheres of French life, led to a 39 per cent increase in the proportion of women deputies (from 3.7 to 6.1 per cent), during his two presidential terms. Although the upward trend of the above mentioned figures appears positive, a closer examination of the legislative elections which took place in the 1980s and 1990s reveals a gloomier picture. Following Mitterrand's victory, the left swept to power with a sizeable parliamentary majority in 1981. After the presidential election and during the legislative election campaigns, feminist activists had vigorously canvassed the main left-wing parties to select more female candidates especially in view of the fact that Mitterrand's victory was due in large part to the swing registered among female voters towards the left's candidate.[10] Nevertheless, the PS, which increased its percentage vote from 25.7 per cent in 1978 to 38.3 per cent in 1981 (Chagnollaud 1993: 449) and gained the largest number of seats, fielded only 40 women candidates (representing 8.5 per cent of all Socialist candidates) of which 19 were elected (Sineau 1997a: 52). Communist women were unable to make an impact given that the PCF vote had declined from 20.6 per cent to 16.1 per cent (52).

In 1988 and 1993, the result for women was not much better, as their representation within the National Assembly increased by a mere 0.4 per cent and 0.8 per cent respectively in comparison with the 1981 figure.[11] And if the presence and impact of women have been marginal in the National Assembly then it is even more so in the upper house where the proportion of women remained stagnant, between 2 and 3 per cent for the duration of the 1980s.

In the late 1990s, it is the legislative elections of 1997 which have marked a turning point in that the proportion of women candidates (at 23 per cent) rose above 20 per cent for the first time since the majoritarian system of elections was introduced in 1958. This result was due mainly to the fact that the two main parties of the Left, the PS and the PCF, had made pre-electoral commitments to adopt a 30 per cent quota in favour of women which in fact resulted in quotas of 27.2 per cent in the case of the PCF and 27.8 per cent for the PS (Gaspard and Servan-Schreiber 1997: 2). The legislative elections of 1997 raised the percentage of women deputies up to 10.9. However, the fact remains that just over 90 per cent of parliamentarians (both houses included) are men and this figure continues to keep France second from bottom in the league table for EU countries.

Women in national government

To date there have been a total of twenty-nine governments, composed of between thirty and forty ministers, under five presidents of the Fifth Republic. Women have been present in twenty-four of these as indicated in Table 1.2.[12] Although the numbers of women in government have increased since the early years of the Fifth Republic, their presence in what Edith Cresson has called 'real decision-making executive positions' (1998: 11) remains insignificant.

Only three women participated in government, although not all at the same time, during the unbroken period of Gaullist rule, from January 1959 to May 1974. The first woman, Nafissa Sid-Cara, was appointed by De

Table 1.2 Women in governments of the Fifth Republic

President/ Prime-Minister	Duration of government	Number of women
De Gaulle/Debré	8 January 1959–14 April 1962	1
De Gaulle/Pompidou	6 April 1967–10 July 1968	1
De Gaulle/Couve de Murville	10 July 1968–20 June 1969	1
Pompidou/Chaban-Delmas	20 June 1969–5 July 1972	1
Pompidou/Messmer	5 July 1972–28 March 1973	1
Pompidou/Messmer	2 April 1973–27 February 1974	2
Pompidou/Messmer	27 February 1974–27 May 1974	1
Giscard D'Estaing/Chirac	27 May 1974–25 August 1976	6
Giscard D'Estaing/Barre	25 August 1976–29 March 1977	4
Giscard D'Estaing/Barre	29 March 1977–31 March 1978	7
Giscard D'Estaing/Barre	3 April 1978–21 May 1981	5
Mitterrand/Mauroy	21 May 1981–23 June 1981	6
Mitterrand/Mauroy	23 June 1981–22 March 1983	6
Mitterrand/Mauroy	22 March 1983–19 July 1984	6
Mitterrand/Fabius	19 July 1984–20 March 1986	6
Mitterrand/Chirac	20 March 1986–10 May 1988	4
Mitterrand/Rocard	10 May 1988–23 June 1988	6
Mitterrand/Rocard	23 June 1988–16 May 1991	6
Mitterrand/Cresson	16 May 1991–2 April 1992	7*
Mitterrand/Bérégovoy	2 April 1992–29 March 1993	7
Mitterrand/Balladur	29 March 1993–18 May 1995	3
Chirac/Juppé	18 May 1995–7 November 1995	12
Chirac/Juppé	7 November 1995–June 1997	4
Chirac/Jospin	4 June 1997–present	10

Sources: Helft-Malz and Lévy (1996), Gouvernement français, www.premier.ministre.gouv.fr/GOUV/PMGVT.HTM, accessed 17 November 1999; Jenson and Sineau (1995).

Note: *Including Cresson.

Gaulle in January 1959 to the post of junior minister (*secrétaire d'état*) responsible for social affairs in Algeria. Sid-Cara's governmental post lasted a brief three years. Marie-Madeleine Dienesch also participated in government under both De Gaulle and Pompidou, occupying various posts at the level of junior minister. Unlike Sid-Cara, Dienesch's governmental career was successful in terms of duration[13] and included a three-month period, in 1968, as junior minister responsible for education which meant that she was invited to cabinet meetings. Dienesch was joined in government by a second woman, Suzanne Ploux,[14] between April 1973 and February 1974.

That women were appointed at all during the Gaullist years was surprising, given that neither De Gaulle nor Pompidou, despite their debt to women voters, had spoken of or encouraged women as political movers.[15] Of the three women mentioned above, only Dienesch survived the test of time. Sid-Cara was dispensed with in 1962 because her narrowly defined brief relating to Algerian social affairs had become redundant once Algeria gained independence. Susanne Ploux was arguably too socially and politically liberal to make a place for herself in Gaullist government for she was a co-signatory to the Neuwirth law on contraception, the Petit Bill to revoke capital punishment and the Perretti Bill to reduce the presidential mandate to five years. Dienesch, on the other hand, survived (by her own admission) because she was considered a woman who 'doesn't create scenes'.[16]

Under Giscard D'Estaing, the number of women increased significantly from one to six, in the first 'modernising' government led by Jacques Chirac and over the seven-year period of Giscard's presidency (1974–81), a total of twenty-two ministerial posts were given to nine women. While this increase allowed Giscard D'Estaing to claim that women were, at last, becoming visible in important structures of the the state, it is noteworthy that the majority of the posts given to women were at the level of junior minister which meant that in seven years, only three women (Simone Veil as Senior Minister for Health, Alice Saunier-Seïté as Minister, and later Senior Minister, for Higher Education and Monique Pelletier as Minister for Women's Status) could attend cabinet meetings and therefore contribute to decision-making at the highest level.

It was during the Mitterrand years (1981–95) that the promotion of women in government was accelerated as a result of presidential manifesto commitments to feminise political power. Thus, during Mitterrand's first presidency and under the Socialist government of Pierre Mauroy, four of the six female government appointments (Nicole Questiaux as Senior Minister for National Solidarity, Edith Cresson as Senior Minister for Agriculture, Yvette Roudy as Minister for Women's Rights[17] and Edwige Avice as Minister for Youth and Sports) were members of the cabinet. The government reshuffle of 1984, under the premiership of Laurent Fabius, took the number of women cabinet members up to five with the addition of Huguette Bouchardeau as Minister for the Environment and Georgina Dufoix as Minister for Social Affairs.[18] However, the first period of cohabitation between a president of the left and a government of the right (1986–8) saw the number of women in government drop to four with only one woman (Michèle Barzach for Health and the Family) occupying a ministry and hence a cabinet position.[19]

Mitterrand's second presidency (1988–95), in which executive power was shared with the Socialist parliamentary majority for all but two years, pushed women to even higher offices of the state. In May 1991, Edith Cresson was appointed Prime Minister. Her government included six other women of which all except one (Véronique Neiertz as junior minister in charge of Women's Rights) held cabinet ministerial positions (three senior ministers and two ministers).[20] And although Cresson was replaced by Pierre Bérégovoy in April 1992, the Socialists appointed a seventh woman, Ségolène Royal, as Senior Minister for the Environment, to avoid charges of disavowing women.[21]

During the 1990s, the debate over women's representation (see Chapters 8 and 9) had begun to push public opinion in favour of the feminisation of political institutions to such an extent that the visibility of women in parliament and the executive part of the state, coupled with the discourse of modernisation and democracy, often came to be used as a trump card by political leaders seeking the support of voters. Thus, during the presidency of Chirac (1995–), under the premierships of both Alain Juppé (1995–7) and Lionel Jospin (1997–), the appointment of women to cabinet and other senior positions in the state has become a matter of political competition. When Alain Juppé formed his government in 1995, he appointed twelve women in a spectacular gesture in favour of political parity for women. Similarly, in 1997, Jospin included ten women in his government (of which a record number of six attend cabinet meetings as senior ministers or ministers).

While more women have entered higher positions of political power during both Mitterrand and Chirac's presidential terms of office, their presence in such positions has been entirely dependent on the patronage of men. Thus, ministerial decision-making has included more, fewer, or no women as and when it has suited presidents and prime ministers and this is as true these days as it was in the past. Mariette Sineau (1997a) argues that women in the executive part of the state lack 'electoral cover' (*surface électorale*) given the small numbers of women present in the legislature. She asserts that, unlike the normal political curriculum vitae, whereby an individual accedes to positions of executive power via local and national electoral office, in France (because of a powerful president-led executive) women, to an even greater extent than their male counterparts, have had to rely on the 'inverse curriculum' in order to gain executive positions. In the situation of the inverse curriculum, women such as Elisabeth Guigou, Martine Aubry and other big female players (all educated at *grandes écoles*) have first been 'spotted' by a president (in their case Mitterrand), have proved themselves at the Elysée and only then have they gone on to seek electoral office and to achieve electoral legitimacy. Women's accession to power in government, in numbers equal to men, depends upon the acquisition of equal electoral legitimacy without which they run the risk of being excluded simply because a man has decided it must be so.[22]

Women in the civil service

The majority of surveys of women in positions of political power do not include an examination of the state civil service as the latter is, strictly speaking, a non-political bureaucracy. However, the decision to include a brief mention here lies in the fact that in France, possibly more so than in many other comparable liberal democracies, the most senior civil service appointments are not only political but they often provide the first step of the 'inverse curriculum' upon which women in high political office have been dependent.

The public perception has been that women have been treated fairly (in terms of recruitment, training and various social benefits) in the state civil service, since the first post-war constitution allowed them free access to it.[23] However, that perception does not match the reality as far as senior civil service posts are concerned. The most recent report on women in the civil service (Colmou 1999) confirms that it remains as much a men's club today as in the past. Women may make up 56.9 per cent of all civil service employment but no more than 10 per cent of the most senior posts are occupied by them (http://www.fonctionpublique.gouv.fr/lac. . .ands-dossiers/rapportcolmou/letatdeslieux.html, accessed 30 June 1999).

The state civil service[24] has undergone a very gradual process of feminisation since the mid-1960s. The increase in the number of women entering it over the last twenty-five years has been almost entirely due to feminisation of the category *cadres moyens* or 'middle management' (in which jobs require a high level of education and a managerial or supervisory role at intermediary levels) especially in those ministries towards which they are seen to have a 'natural' leaning: education, health, social affairs. The ministries of transport, foreign affairs, the interior and others are largely male-dominated.

The rule that the higher the level, the fewer the women present is very clearly at work within the state civil service, and the most senior jobs which remain in the gift of the government of the day have been virtually inaccessible to women until relatively recently, for example: the posts of prefect, deputy prefect, university vice-chancellor, rector of an *académie*.[25] Similarly those posts in the major organs of the state, such as inspectors of finance (*inspecteurs des finances*) including the thirty-two general inspectors,[26] state councillors (*conseillers d'état*),[27] national audit councillors (*conseillers à la Cour des comptes*),[28] are open only to those who succeed in the

Table 1.3 Women in the high civil service

	Number of women	Total
Prefects	5	109
Deputy prefects	41	448
Rector of Academy	4	30
University vice-chancellors	4	88
General Inspectors of finance	9	74
State councillors	40	201
National auditors	29	217

Source: Courtois (1999).

intensely competitive exams of the ENA and are then promoted from other high-ranking state agency posts. Such highly selective processes coupled with certain 'masculine particularities' (such as emphasis on one's professional life to the detriment of one's personal life, the working of extremely long hours as an external sign of power) (Colmou 1999) work against women's entry into these professions as the figures in Table 1.3 suggest.

A conference of EU member states on the promotion of women in the civil service, held in Vienna in October 1998, highlighted the importance of feminisation at higher levels of the civil service as one part of a general strategy to increase women's presence in decision-making sites within the state. A number of measures were suggested in order to achieve parity in civil service posts. Of these measures (transparency of statistics, the institutionalisation of recruitment pools from which female candidates can be selected, preferential measures for the recruitment and promotion of women and the close management of women's careers), none have yet been applied in France.

Women in local assemblies and government

The study of women in local politics remains a neglected area when compared with studies of their participation at national level. Yet local politics constitutes an important laboratory in which politicians in the making are trained and where new ideas for social change can be tried out before they are tested at national level if appropriate. The idea that women's presence in politics is as strategically important at local as it is at national level (in terms of the implications for the progress of democracy), was recognised in the early 1980s and led to the formation of a women's committee of the Council of European Municipalities and Regions (CEMR). This committee initiated a debate on 'women, politics and democracy' at its first conference, held in Pisa in 1983. Following this, a series of conferences discussed issues of equality in relation to local women elected representatives and culminated in the acceptance, by the CEMR's General Meeting of 1996, of the principle of parity. Valéry

Giscard d'Estaing, the current president of the CEMR, stressing the importance of women in local politics, affirmed, 'To judge the degree of modernisation of a society, one needs to look at the position of women in public life. In this regard, local authorities are a useful and pertinent place for observation' (1998).

In France, directly elected local assemblies and government currently operate at three levels: municipal (*conseils municipaux* – municipal councils), departmental (*conseils généraux* – departmental councils) and regional (*conseils régionaux* – regional councils). The municipal council, of which there are 33,804 (in metropolitan France), is elected by the inhabitants of a *commune* (the basic administrative unit of local government) for a period of six years.[29] The full council which meets at least four times a year is responsible for the budget and management of local services.[30] The municipal council executive is headed by a mayor who is elected by councillors. The 95 (metropolitan) departmental councils administer the business of the department[31] and are also elected every six years. Departmental councillors elect a leader (*président*) and an executive of between four and ten deputies (*vice-présidents*) and meet at least three times a year. The twenty-two (metropolitan) regional councils were established by the Socialists in 1985 and are elected for six years by the inhabitants of the departments within each region. The regional council elects a leader (*président du conseil*) and an executive team which is supposed to reflect the political and geographical balance of power within the region. The executive team enjoys considerable delegated power in the planning and management of the region's resources as the full council meets about three times a year. This section considers the place of women in municipal and regional councils and government.[32]

Municipal assemblies and government

If the figures for women's participation in national assemblies and government are difficult to collate and obtain, then those relating to their presence in the state's local elected bodies are even more incomplete and, it is suggested,[33] possibly inaccurate. As far as municipal councillors are concerned, Table 1.4 shows that under the presidencies of both De Gaulle and Pompidou, the increase in their numbers was insignificant and can be compared to the progress (or lack of) that they made at national level during the same period. The first notable leap forward was in 1977 (during the Giscard presidency) when the proportion of municipal councillors increased from 4.4 to 8.3 per cent. Thereafter, the number of women in municipal assemblies rose to reach just over 20 per cent in 1995, placing France in seventh position in the league table of EU countries.[34] When compared to the position of women elected to parliament, the statistics on women in municipalities appear encouraging. However, a further breakdown of such statistics reveals a less satisfactory picture.

Table 1.4 Percentage of women in local government and assemblies

Level of office	1959	1965	1971	1977	1983	1986	1988	1989	1990	1992	1995	1998
Regional council	–	–	–	–	–	8.5	–	–	–	10.6	–	25.8
Mayoral	1.0	1.1	1.8	2.8	3.9	–	–	5.4	–	–	7.5	–
Municipal council	2.4	2.3	4.4	8.3	14.0	–	–	17.1	–	–	20.3	–

Sources: Gaspard (1998c); European Database: Women in decision-making, http://www.db-decision.de/english/Wahl.htm, accessed 1 March 1999; Latour, Houssin and Tovar (1995); Vidal (1998).

In 1995, 22,000 new women municipal councillors were elected but 19,000 (representing a 21 per cent increase on 1989 figures) of these were in municipalities of less than 3,500 inhabitants (Gaspard 1998c: 39). Hence, while smaller, rural areas may have been undergoing a relatively rapid modernisation process, women continued to encounter difficulties in obtaining seats in the larger urban municipalities where the rate of increase in 1995 reached a maximum 20 per cent (Gaspard 1998c: 39). The only area with a large urban population in which the number of women councillors increased by an impressive 60 per cent in municipalities of over 30,000 inhabitants was the Rhône department where women activists from both parties of the left and right campaigned vigorously to obtain seats in greater Lyon (Gaspard 1998c: 39). However, the municipal elections of 2001 ought to see a significant rise in the proportion of women councillors, particularly in the larger towns and cities where a mixed PR list system is operated, as the inclusion of the principle of parity in the constitution will oblige parties to reserve 50 per cent of list places for women.

Furthermore, the study of the presence of women in municipal government reveals that while the proportion of women councillors increased in the 1980s and 1990s, that of mayorships gained has been much smaller (see Table 1.4). Between 1959 and 1971, the proportion of women mayors remained below 2 per cent, increasing to just under 4 per cent in the early 1980s, to 5.4 per cent in the late 1980s and to 7.5 per cent by the middle of the 1990s.

During the 1990s, mayoral office, particularly in large towns and cities, became more sought after than ever before due to: decentralisation measures in the 1980s which extended mayoral powers; and progressive European integration which has produced competition among large and medium-size cities for European development funds. Many mayors have acquired a high profile, and successful civic building and urban regeneration programmes made mayors the most popular elected representatives in 1990s' France with 42 per cent of voters wanting an increase in their powers (*Le Monde Diplomatique*, March 1998: 4). Not surprisingly, it is at this level that the picture of women's representation is most disappointing. At the municipal elections of 1995, 128 towns of over 20,000 inhabitants returned new mayors. Of these only seven were women (Cresson 1998: 11). Where the largest towns (of over 30,000 inhabitants) are concerned, women make up an insignificant 2.9 per cent of mayors and it is only the statistics relating to the smallest municipalities (of under 3,500 inhabitants) which push the national average of women mayors to above 5 per cent (Gaspard 1998c: 42). While the number of women mayors will increase in 2001, it is likely that the increase, as in 1995, will result from the success of female mayoral candidates in the smaller towns which are of less interest to experienced male candidates who want control over the bigger budgets and projects of the larger towns.

Regional assemblies and government

In spite of the fact that regional councils constitute a recent layer of sub-national decision-making and that regional elections are fought under a PR system in France, the proportion of women elected representatives at this level has been less than impressive (Table 1.4). In 1986, when the first regional elections were held, women only formed 8.5 per cent of regional councillors. This figure rose by just over 2 per cent in 1992 and it was only in 1998 when the major political parties committed themselves to quotas of between 30 and 50 per cent[35] that the proportion of women regional representatives exceeded a quarter. However, like general statistics pertaining to women in municipalities, the figure of 25.8 per cent hides the unevenness between regions in terms of women's presence in regional councils: in Corsica for instance, women did not make any in-roads into decision-making as the main party lists were completely male-dominated. In addition, the presence of two women-only lists failed to make an impact within this region.

As far as regional executives are concerned, women are even less present. A survey of 1998 statistics relating to regional government structures[36] shows that: only one out of twenty-two metropolitan regional councils is led by a woman (Anne-Marie Comparini in the Rhône-Alpes region); only one woman (Isabelle le Maréchal in the Pays-de-la-Loire region) holds the post of regional executive director (*directeur de cabinet*); the proportion of women in regional executives (*vice-présidents*) ranges from none (in Corsica and Franche-Comté) to 38.5 per cent (Nord-pas-de-Calais) and the proportion of women heads of regional council commissions[37] runs between zero (Corsica, Basse Normandie, Haute Normandie, and Picardie) to 50 per cent (Champagne-Ardenne, Provence-Alpes-Côte-d'Azur). It should be noted that the figures at the upper end of the scale relating to women in regional executives and commissions are exceptional and that the overall trend is towards the bottom end of the scale. While one expects the number of women elected representatives to increase even more significantly after the next regional elections, the present arrangement and occupation of regional executive posts suggest that women will not be selected for such posts in significantly greater numbers in 2004.

Women's role in state structures

The view that the more important the role, the more visible the office, the more powerful the position, the less likely a woman can be found in it, gains justification as one examines the place occupied by women in the state's structures. As the above sections have shown, in France no woman has ever held presidential office; there has only been one woman prime minister (Edith Cresson) to date who only occupied this office for 323 days – the shortest time for any PM in the Fifth Republic; the first woman (Simone Veil) to gain the rank of senior minister (*ministre*) only did so in 1974; the majority of women in government have held junior ministerial positions (see Table 1.5); and far fewer women have served in national parliament than in sub-national assemblies.

Alongside this vertical division exists a horizontal division of roles whereby women find themselves dealing mainly with issues that can be defined broadly as 'social' while men deal with those falling into the realm of the 'political'. The majority of elected assemblies whether in France or elsewhere suffer a lack of proper professional expertise. Consequently, deputies, senators and other elected representatives are cast in the role of experts in a wide range of policy-making fields and become members of parliamentary commissions, government ministries and local government and assembly commissions, according to their area of interest or to their profession. Other factors such as their constituency location or electoral success may also play a part in deciding the composition of the above-mentioned bodies.

However, when women enter elected assemblies the predominant factor which determines the role they play is gender, regardless of the professional or other competence and experience that they bring with them. Women, at best perceived by the men as a curiosity to be noted because they constitute such small numbers in the majority of elected assemblies and bodies in France, are subject to 'enforced specialisation' (*spécialisation forcée*) (Sineau 1988: 42) because of the so-called 'natural' sexual division of roles in the private sphere. They come to be seen as specialists in matters which fall stereotypically into the women's side of the sexual division of roles and where traditional feminine qualities can be used and developed: devotion, care, nurture in relation to their children and families. Moreover, the extension of welfare state regimes within French society, in the post-war period, has further contributed to the entrenchment of the division within the state between the 'feminine social' and the 'masculine political'. Hence, women are seen as 'experts' in education, cultural affairs, health, social welfare, consumer affairs, environmental matters and any other field in which feminine qualities and authority are useful. In addition, they are regarded as specialists in 'women's issues': abortion and contraception, equal opportunities issues, and so on. On the other hand, they are discouraged from entering the realm of the (masculine) political: economy and finance, diplomacy, strategy.

Personal accounts by women elected representatives of their enforced specialisation abound. Of her period in the National Assembly (1974–8), Hélèn Missoffe complained:

> Not a single [parliamentary] commission (other than that on cultural, family and social affairs) opened its doors to me because I am a woman. Many men don't like this commission given that it's a question of presence ... the Commission on finance tops the list you know, followed by the Commission on laws.
>
> (Sineau 1988: 42)

Missoffe's situation was not unique. Until recently, the majority of women deputies found themselves being guided toward the Commission on cultural, family and social affairs while being systematically prevented from entering the most prestigious Commission on finance which remains the preserve of male deputies – the statistical chances of being appointed a government minister increase considerably if one is a member of this commission (Mangin and Martichoux 1991: 83–4). Table 1.5 also shows that very few women – Edith Cresson (Agriculture, European Affairs, premiership), Elisabeth Guigou (European Affairs, Justice) and Martine Aubry (Employment) – have been given what are traditionally seen as men's ministerial portfolios. Moreover, the appointment of women to such posts has been a recent development with Edith Cresson taking overall charge of the Agriculture and European Affairs portfolios in 1986 and 1988 respectively and gaining the premiership in 1991. The appointments of Martine Aubry and Elisabeth Guigou to the important ministries of Employment and Justice respectively took place under Lionel Jospin's premiership in June 1997.

Women in local politics are subjected to enforced specialisation to an even greater degree where they are often put in charge of day-to-day management of school meals, crèches, general social work problems and so on while their male counterparts take care of municipal budgets, economic and industrial development, security and transport.

It is arguable that many women have used their enforced roles to influence important political decisions thereby acquiring power in the legislative process. It can be said that this was especially true in the 1980s and 1990s when certain social issues came to dominate political agendas at both national and sub-national levels, for example: the financing of the social security and pensions systems; funding and expansion of education;

Table 1.5 Ministerial positions held by women from 1958

Ministerial post-holder	Position & policy-making field	Period of appointment(s)
De Gaulle presidency (1958–1969)		
Nafissa Sid-Cara (Pour l'Algérie française)	Junior Minister Social Affairs in Algeria	January 1959–April 1962
Marie-Madeleine Dienesch (Mouvement républicain populaire – MRP/ Rassemblement pour la République – RPR)	Junior Minister Education; Social Affairs	May 1968–July 1972
Pompidou presidency (1969–1974)		
Marie-Madeleine Dienesch	Junior Minister Education; Public Health; Social Security	July 1972–May 1974
Suzanne Ploux (Union des démocrates pour la République – UDR)	Junior Minister Education	April 1973–February 1974
Giscard d'Estaing presidency (1974–1981)		
Hélène Dorlhac (Républicains Indépendants – RI)	Junior Minister Justice	June 1974–August 1976
Françoise Giroud (Divers Gauche)	Junior Minister Women's Status; Culture	July 1974–March 1977
Annie Lesur (Centrist)	Junior Minister Pre-school Education	June 1974–January 1976
Hélène Missoffe (UDR)	Junior Minister Health & Social Security	March 1977–April 1978
Nicole Pasquier (Parti Républicain – PR)	Junior Minister Women's Employment	January 1978–May 1981
Monique Pelletier (RI)	Junior Minister Justice; Minister Women's Status	January 1978–May 1981
Alice Saunier-Seïté (PR)	Junior Minister & Senior Minister Universities	May 1974–May 1981
Christiane Scrivener (PR)	Junior Minister Consumer Affairs	January 1976–March 1978
Simone Veil (Union pour la démocratie française – UDF)	Senior Minister Health; Health & Social Security; Health & Family	May 1974–May 1981
Mitterrand presidency (1981–88)		
Michèle Alliot-Marie (RPR)*	Junior Minister Education	March 1986–May 1988
Edwige Avice (Parti socialiste – PS)	Minister Youth & Sport; Junior Minister Civil service; Senior & Junior Minister Consumer Affairs	May 1981–July 1984
Michèle Barzach (RPR) *	Minister Health & Family	March 1986–May 1988
Huguette Bouchardeau (Parti Socialiste Unifié – PSU)	Senior Minister Environment	March 1983–March 1986
Nicole Catala (RPR)*	Junior Minister Education (training)	March 1986–May 1988

Table 1.5 (Continued)

Ministerial post-holder	Position & policy-making field	Period of appointment(s)
Lucette Michaux-Chévry (RPR)*	Junior Minister Francophony	March 1986–May 1988
Edith Cresson (PS)	Senior Minister Agriculture; Overseas Trade & Tourism	May 1981–March 1986
Georgina Dufoix (PS)	Junior Minister Family; Senior Minister Social Affairs & National Solidarity	May 1981–March 1986
Catherine Lalumière (PS)	Junior Minister Civil Service; Senior & Junior Minister Consumer Affairs	May 1981–March 1986
Nicole Questiaux (PS)	Senior Minister National Solidarity	May 1981–June 1982
Yvette Roudy (PS)	Minister & Senior Minister Women's Rights	May 1981–March 1986
Mitterrand presidency (1988–1995)		
Michèle Alliot-Marie*	Senior Minister Youth & Sport	March 1993–May 1995
Michèle André (PS)	Junior Minister Women's Rights	June 1988–May 1991
Martine Aubry (PS)	Senior Minister Employment & Training	May 1991– March 1993
Edwige Avice	Minister Foreign Affairs; Cooperation & Development	May 1988–April 1992
Frédérique Brédin (PS)	Senior Minister for Youth & Sport	May 1991–March 1993
Edith Cresson	Senior Minister European Affairs; Prime Minister	May 1988–April 1992
Hélène Dorlhac	Junior Minister Family	June 1988–May 1991
Georgina Dufoix	Minister Family, Women's Rights & Solidarity	May–June 1988
Elisabeth Guigou (PS)	Minister European Affairs	May 1991–March 1993
Marie-Noëlle Lienemann (PS)	Minister Housing	April 1992–March 1993
Lucette Michaux-Chévry*	Minister Human Rights & Humanitarian Action	March 1993–May 1995
Véronique Neiertz (PS)	Junior Minister Consumer Affairs; Women's Rights	May 1988–April 1992
Ségolène Royal (PS)	Senior Minister Environment	April 1992–March 1993
Catherine Tasca (PS)	Minister Communication; Francophony	May 1988–April 1992
Catherine Trautmann (PS)	Junior Minister Aged & Disabled	May–June 1988
Simone Veil*	Senior Minister Health & Social Affairs	March 1993–May 1995
Chirac presidency (1995–)		
Martine Aubry*	Senior Minister Employment & Solidarity	June 1997–
Nicole Ameline (UDF)	Junior Minister Decentralisation	May–November 1995
Marie-Georges Buffet (PC)*	Senior Minister Youth & Sport	June 1997–
Christine Chauvet (PR)	Junior Minister Overseas Trade	May–November 1995
Colette Codaccioni (RPR)	Senior Minister Solidarity	May–November 1995

Table 1.5 (Continued)

Ministerial post-holder	Position & policy-making field	Period of appointment(s)
Anne-Marie Couderc (RPR)	Junior Minister Employment	May 1995–June 1997
Michelle Demessine (Parti communiste français – PCF)*	Junior Minister Tourism	June 1997–
Elisabeth Dufourcq (RPR)	Junior Minister Education (Research)	May–November 1995
Dominique Gillot (PS)*	Junior Minister Health & Social Action	June 1997–
Elisabeth Guigou*	Senior Minister Justice	June 1997–
Françoise Hostalier (UDF)	Junior Minister Education (Schools)	May–November 1995
Elisabeth Hubert (RPR)	Senior Minister Public Health	May–November 1995
Anne-Marie Idrac (Centrist)	Junior Minister Transport	May 1995–June 1997
Marylise Lebranchu (PS)*	Junior Minister SMEs, Trade & Crafts	June 1997–
Corinne Lepage (Independent)	Senior Minister Environment	May 1995–June 1997
Françoise Panafieu (RPR)	Senior Minister Tourism	May–November 1995
Nicole Péry (PS)*	Junior Minister Women's Rights & Professional Training	June 1997–
Ségolène Royal*	Minister Education (Schools)	June 1997–
Margie Sudre (Centrist)	Junior Minister Francophony	May 1995–June 1997
Catherine Trautmann (PS)*	Senior Minister Culture & Communication	June 1997–
Françoise de Veyrinas (Centrist)	Junior Minister Deprived Zones (quartiers difficiles)	May–November 1995
Dominique Voynet (Les Verts)*	Senior Minister Environment	June 1997–

Source: Helft-Malz and Lévy (1996); http://www.premier.ministre.gouv.fr/GOUV/PMGVT.htm, accessed 17 December 1999.

*Note: Ministers in cohabitation governments.

unemployment coupled with scarcity of housing leading to enormous problems of homelessness. However, this still cannot hide the fact that women are absent from the most influential roles within state structures.

The issue of women's performance within the state

Measuring and judging the performance of women (inevitably in comparison with that of men) is a complex exercise especially in an area where structures, procedures and rules were defined in the absence of women and where women are present in such small numbers. Yet the issue of women's performance requires consideration for two reasons at least.

First, traditional political science has always measured and judged performance in terms of the ability to produce a desired outcome through the exercise of power or influence. Apart from the problem of disagreement over the definition of power and influence which makes performance evaluation of any group a difficult task, where women are concerned this problem is aggravated because there is an underlying assumption that all groups have equal potential to wield power or influence to gain desired outcomes. Clearly, women do not possess equal potential to men in this respect because, as demonstrated in previous sections, they form small numbers in elected bodies and therefore are not seen as having enough clout to enforce desired outcomes (moreover, these small numbers are further divided as women, like men, are not an ideologically homogeneous group); and women's roles within the state are limited and fall outside the traditional areas of 'male' politics and power. Hence, the application of any power-based model to evaluate women's performance would necessarily show women to be poor performers. For instance, one of the standard performance indicators in traditional political science, although increasingly used by feminist academics in the USA and Britain also, is that of legislative output, so that the overall effectiveness of female legislators can be assessed by the number of bills introduced or supported by women that get passed compared with the general range of legislation that is introduced and passed. However, there are many questions to be asked about this method, of which the following are just a few. One, over what period of time is it fair to assess women's performance? For example, given that the best chance of introducing national legislation is through ministerial office and that prime-ministerial cabinets often have a short life, women are in a particularly weak position. Under Alain Juppé as prime minister, only four out of twelve women appointed to government survived the first reshuffle to serve out their ministerial mandates up to the legislative elections of 1997 (see Table 1.5). The eight who lost their jobs six months after their appointment were given little or no chance to prove themselves. While the latter is an extreme example, generally women remain in executive and legislative office for much shorter periods of time than men and this works against a positive assessment of their performance. Two, can one arrive at accurate conclusions about women's power, hence performance, simply by calculating legislative output at either national or subnational levels, often at the level of the individual, given the small numbers of women present? For instance, parliamentary bills can be introduced under single or joint names. If a woman introduces one bill under her name only, does she wield more influence than a male colleague who introduces two bills jointly? Furthermore, does a woman who introduces a bill relating to cultural development have the same amount of power as a male colleague who introduces a finance bill, given that cultural policy, unlike fiscal policy, does not fall into the realm of the masculine political? In any case how do such individual assessments relate to an assessment of women's performance generally? Because the application of power-based indicators to women's performance is inappropriate, feminist political scientists have sought to measure women's effectiveness in other ways. The performance indicators that feminist political scientists have applied have led some to argue that women, in significant numbers, can make a (positive) difference (see Chapter 8).

Second, over the last fifteen years as the question of women's political representation has increasingly captured the attention of feminist academics, the media, politicians and the public, it would appear that much has come to be expected of women who make it into political élite structures. At the lower end of the scale of expectations, they are counted upon to brighten up a stern, boring world of grey-suited men 'with their gaily-coloured outfits' (Perkins 1999: 6) while at the upper end of this scale they are seen either as the repository of all the aspirations of women everywhere or as the vehicle for democratic renewal in a field where progress is often thwarted by the old guards of political legislatures and executives. Frequently, when the higher expectations are unfulfilled they are disproportionately criticised as they become 'a lightning rod for a wider disappointment in . . . government' (6). Arguably then, women's performance is unlikely ever to match up to public expectation.

Alternative measures for evaluating women's performance

Feminist political science research has suggested a number of alternative indicators for evaluating women's performance in the state, for example: the extent to which women in state structures espouse feminism; the way in which women in state structures react to women's issues; the extent to which women can create appropriate enough leadership styles in order to be effective.

Women élites and feminism

As a general rule women who have run for state executive or legislative office have been keen to distance themselves from feminism. When Mariette Sineau conducted a study of 40 women élites in national and local politics (between June 1984 and July 1985), she found that 75 per cent of interviewees, regardless of their party attachment, were, if not vehement detractors of the post-1968 feminist movement, then reluctant to admit to feminist ideas (Sineau 1988: 160–6). Sineau writes:

> It is possible . . . that there is a problem of 'critical mass'. Because of their small numbers in decision-making sites, the room for manoeuvre allowed to women to admit to being and saying they are 'feminist' . . . is not vast . . . Seen as 'outsiders', the balance of power is not such that they can impose their ideas. Such a situation inevitably pushes [one] towards conformity of thought and alignment with the masculine norm.

(163)

More recent studies have shown mixed results. On the basis of a survey of thirty Socialist women candidates in the 1997 legislative elections (of which twelve were elected and two appointed to the new government), Philippe Bataille and Françoise Gaspard (1999: 161–3) construct a typology (of Socialist women) consisting of three groups. First, a very small group of women who were activists in the post-1968 women's movement and whose feminism was kept alive through personal experiences of discrimination in professional life. These women have always openly admitted their commitment to feminist ideas and action. Second, a group of 'neo-feminist' women (including two ministers, Marylise Lebranchu and Dominique Gillot) whose commitment to socialism precedes their acknowledgement of the fact that their success is due, in some part, to the struggles waged by feminists of the 1970s. These women are aware that placing feminism before socialism could damage their credibility as far as their male colleagues are concerned. A third group, composed of younger women for whom 'feminism' means equality, feels there is no need to justify, qualify or mask a set of beliefs that should be considered normal at the beginning of the twenty-first century. While this typology is useful, it is based on interviews with a relatively small group of Socialist women and its application is therefore limited to those whose political home is on the moderate left of the political spectrum.

Two studies (Rieu 1998, Junter-Loiseau 1998) carried out at local level merit some comment. Annie Rieu's study of women mayors in rural areas revealed that they displayed little or no feminist awareness although they were fully appreciative of the obstacles that women faced in running for public office. In this respect, it was noteworthy that in 36 per cent of the town halls run by women, compared with 29 per cent of those run by men, the proportion of women councillors was greater than 25 per cent (Rieu 1998: 91). Rieu comments that their lack of feminist awareness was perfectly in keeping with a general mistrust of ideas of 'women's emancipation' within a rural milieu. Junter-Loiseau's study of women councillors in the municipality of Rennes presents a contrasting picture in which the majority of women concerned draw upon their gender identity to inform their work and to 'do politics differently', even though not all of them would describe themselves as feminist. However, Junter-Loiseau points out that Rennes may be an exceptional case in that it is run by a large left-wing majority (of 47 against 12 opposition members) made up of Socialists, Communists and Greens and where, more importantly, women form 31 per cent of all councillors (Junter-Loiseau 1998: 99). Because women are seen to constitute a 'critical mass' (of over 30 per cent) in this case, it is easier for them to espouse feminism either directly or indirectly.

While all these studies taken together present inconclusive evidence about women's performance in terms of the extent of their feminist commitment, they suggest that as more women enter state structures, more of them, particularly on the left, are willing to acknowledge feminism with certain exceptions: for example, the more powerful the political post occupied, the less openly feminist women are, and the more rural their background, the less the feminist awareness displayed. Finally, the antipathy between right-wing ideology and feminism has meant that women attached to right-wing politics are most likely to distance themselves from feminist ideas. On this basis, right-wing women cannot be good performers. The condemnation of a whole group of women in a performance assessment exercise based on an indicator such as self-proclaimed or perceived 'feministness', is clearly unsatisfactory.

Women élites and women's issues

Generally when women have been questioned about their interest in what are defined as women's issues, they have been keen to stress that they represent the interests and welfare of all their constituents. Nevertheless, the departments (health, social security welfare, women's status and so on) that the majority of women occupy in both national and sub-national state structures, force them, at some point of their political careers, to deal with issues that are either directly or indirectly related to women.

There are few studies undertaken to analyse the relationship between women élites and women's issues in France. As far as women at the national level are concerned, one can rely upon information about achievements or failures relating to individual women: for instance, there is an enormous body of literature on the campaign in favour of abortion and its acceptance in law which includes analyses and commentary on the role played by Simone Veil after whom the abortion law is named. Similarly, Yvette Roudy's interest in women's issues as Minister of Women's Rights and as the proposer of various bills including those on equal employment (passed) or anti-sexism (rejected), is also recorded. However, it is impossible to draw general conclusions about the relationship between women élites and women's issues on the basis of individual achievements and failures.

Two studies that one can consider are the above-mentioned ones carried out by Rieu and Junter-Loiseau, although they relate to women in municipal structures and produce different results. Rieu's study of women mayors in rural municipalities shows that women mayors did not favour women's issues above others. When asked about the various factors of local development, like their male colleagues they gave priority to the maintenance of agricultural activity, development of local craft industries, commerce and tourism and so on. None of them highlighted equality for women in any of these priority areas (Rieu 1998: 91). In Rennes, according to Junter-Loiseau, women councillors, displaying a strong feminist consciousness, forced the council to accept the implementation of a project named 'Step forward towards equal employment' ('*Démarche d'égalité professionnelle*') and the establishment of a consultative committee on 'Women and the city'. Women's issues were given a high profile within this context. However, Junter-Loiseau also points out that the arrival of large numbers of women councillors, after the municipal elections of 1995, not only coincided with the introduction of women's issues on the agenda but also with the creation of new council commissions on unemployment, citizenship, and the environment to name but a few, indicating that women were concerned with a broader range of issues.

Once again, the findings of two local studies are uneven and insufficient in terms of making generalisations about women's performance. Junter-Loiseau's study gives one an insight into how women élites could respond to the highlighting of women's issues on the political agendas of certain types of municipal, or even departmental and regional councils, if critical mass is achieved.

The creation of appropriate leadership styles

Women's ability to create appropriate leadership styles that emerge undamaged by the traditional gendered stereotypes imposed upon them, in order to work effectively, is another performance indicator that can be considered. Women are subjected to the imposition of a number of stereotypes. On the one hand, they may be perceived as too emotional, people-orientated and unassertive while on the other hand, they can be portrayed as stubborn, ambitious, domineering, 'bitchy' and anti-men. Either way, the qualities or defects attributed to them make them, according to traditional views, less competent, less independent and less logical than men. The negative effect of such stereotypes often forces women 'into playing limited and caricatured roles' (Kanter 1977: 230).

In the Fifth Republic, few women have managed to avoid being subjected to the traditional stereotypes mentioned above. If Simone Veil is described today warmly but nevertheless in stereotypical terms as Delacroix's 'Liberty leading the people', she was also dubbed a sorceress at the time when she introduced the Abortion Bill in 1974 (Helft-Malz and Lévy 1996: 341–3). In more recent years, certain women have been subject to particularly extreme stereotyping: Yvette Roudy was branded an ambitious, domineering, man-hating, 'ball-breaker' because of her role as Minister for Women's Rights but especially for introducing the Anti-sexist Bill (designed to outlaw all sexist images in the public domain but eventually withdrawn) in 1983; Edith Cresson, the only woman prime minister to date, was categorised as an ambitious and emotional seductress who had gained the top government post in return for sexual favours to the president, François Mitterrand. The campaign to remove her from the post of prime minister was orchestrated from the first day of her arrival in the job; in 1995, the twelve women appointed to Alain Juppé's government were collectively named '*les juppettes*', an epithet which at once conjured up an image of frivolity and stripped the women of their professional dignity, rendering them politically ineffective from the start. It can be argued that the gendered stereotyping of women like Cresson and Roudy and their inability to create appropriate leadership styles prevented them from performing effectively: Roudy's ministry made little impact in the long term while Cresson gained the honour of being the shortest serving prime minister in the Fifth Republic.

It is only in the more recent period that women have managed to carve out more effective leadership styles for themselves. At national level, bolstered by the increasing presence of women in parliament and the executive, the 'new breed' of women leaders since the 1997 legislative elections, such as Elisabeth Guigou and Martine Aubry have partly succeeded in escaping the damage inflicted by gendered stereotyping. To a large extent, this has been achieved by the creation of a somewhat neutral, technocratic leadership style. A large proportion of the new breed of women élites have proved themselves prior to taking up their élite posts, by virtue of having attended the most prestigious *grandes écoles* – Guigou and Aubry attended the Ecole national d'administration.

At sub-national level, Junter-Loiseau's study of Rennes municipal council also provides some evidence that having achieved critical mass, women have challenged the traditional model of the local *notable* in order to establish new leadership styles incorporating notions of service to the community and a redefinition of the skills (*compétences*) required by elected representatives to include: ability to forge closer ties with constituents, good communication skills, and avoidance of grandiose language and false promises. The establishment of these new leadership styles could then be integrated into assessments of political effectiveness. The Rennes women are certainly keen to be credited with what they see as the 'rehabilitation' of their city's political life (Junter-Loiseau 1998: 107–9). The creation of new leadership styles appears to be one of the more promising ways of achieving political effectiveness but, as the Rennes example shows, the problem women face is to get such styles accepted as alternative measures of performance.

This section has outlined the numerous pitfalls associated with assessing women's performance. The issue of performance will remain a controversial one until women can be assessed on equal terms with men – that is, until women are as present in public office as men and until their equal presence enables them to enforce changes in current political rules, role stereotypes and the way in which power is distributed within state structures.

Conclusion

This chapter has shown that women's participation in state structures has increased since 1958. However, France still lags behind countries such as Sweden where women make up 42.7 per cent of the legislature and

50 per cent of government ministers (Schneider 2000: 53). While the Constitutional Reform Act on parity within state-elected bodies will accelerate the rate of feminisation, the question of whether women will be able to challenge effectively the vertical and horizontal division of roles, and the ways in which their performance is viewed, and reviewed, remains unclear.

2 Women and the political parties

The political parties act as the gatekeepers to political office. Women's presence in the parties is important because it determines their access to local and national assemblies: if women are to be present in sites of decision-making, they need to be present in the parties. However, membership alone does not suffice. The party also needs to select women as candidates and to promote them within its internal structures. This chapter will look at women's membership and their presence at each level of the party hierarchy. It will consider party policy towards the promotion of women in politics, within and outside the party hierarchy, including candidate selection; party policy towards women's rights; and each party's attempts to win women's votes.

The literature on the French political parties, and in particular the French literature, focuses closely on the varying electoral fortunes of the parties and the structure of the party system.[1] It analyses in detail the developments from fragmentation under the Fourth Republic to bipolarisation under the Fifth Republic and a more recent return to a less severe fragmentation in the 1990s. The numerous studies of the parties provide little information on internal structures, membership, activism and candidate selection, and the information which is available is patchy.[2] Instead, they provide a historical narrative of the main organisations and their relations with each other and with the institutions, and an analysis of the roles and varying fortunes of leaders and personalities, especially presidential candidates. There has been a particular focus on the relation between the parties and presidential power struggles.

Women have only exceptionally featured amongst these prime political movers. Ministers such as Simone Veil have been appointed to government, rather than elected from within a particular party. When Veil did receive a popular mandate in 1979, this was as Member of the European Parliament, arguably a less prestigious position than that of deputy. Arlette Laguiller (LO) and Huguette Bouchardeau (PSU) have acted within tiny marginal parties, and only recently have women in the *Verts* entered the mainstream political arena. Women have not led factions, have not been involved in leadership struggles[3] and have not stood as presidential candidates with any possibility of success. It is therefore not a narrative in which women feature, and few commentators have asked what role women play in party politics.

The participation of women in the political parties is under-researched in France, and information is difficult to obtain, particularly at the level of membership and activism, rather than leadership and elected representation. When Maurice Duverger (1955a: 104) attempted to synthesise the information regarding women and the parties in the four national surveys which constituted the UNESCO study, he described it as limited and superficial. Not only was there a shortage of basic documentation, but even where this existed, the parties were reluctant to release it. These observations could have been made at any point throughout the forty years which followed his report. It is only since the debate around women's political participation began to gather momentum in 1993 that more information has become available and a greater interest has developed. However, the information is still fragmentary and varies from party to party. Most are still unable or unwilling to provide such basic information as the number of women members. This is easier to establish for parties which have formal membership procedures (especially the PCF and PS) than for those which have never sought mass membership, but have instead acted as less structured bases for election candidates (for example, the RPR and UDF). However, even in the case of the mass membership parties, the figures have not always derived from membership lists, which do not always distinguish between male and female members, but rather from more or less informed estimates.

Although there is no comprehensive study of women and the parties in post-war France, there are some notable contributions to research in this area, the first being Maurice Duverger's UNESCO report (1955a). He states that, despite the fragmentary and superficial nature of the information available, three main observations can be made (and these apply to all four countries in the study): women's membership of parties is low; the role of women in the parties' hierarchy is even more limited; and there is a tendency within the parties to oppose the constitution of women's sections with any semblance of autonomy. He observes (1955a: 105) that the highest membership is in the Christian parties. At the time of the report, for example, women constituted 30 per cent of the German CDU and 28 per cent of the French MRP. In second place, in terms of membership, were the socialist and communist parties, in which women accounted for just under 20 per cent. Women occupied a far lower proportion of positions of responsibility within these parties, however. Duverger (1955a: 108) reports that in the MRP, there were no women on the national bureau (*bureau national*) and only six (in 1951) on the executive committee (*commission exécutive*). In the Socialist party, there was one woman on the executive committee (*comité directeur*). In 1951, there were 106 women amongst the 1,843 members of the federal executive committees (*commissions exécutives fédérales*) (5.75 per cent). In the Communist Party, there was one woman on the Politbureau (*bureau politique*) and eight on the central committee (*comité central*). He adds that this statistical information does not tell the full story of women's actual influence within the power structures of the parties. He states that their role is usually minor, and that it is very rare for women to exercise any significant influence.

Duverger reports that in almost all the parties in the four countries, women's committees or sections have been formed, but that they rarely have any real autonomy and exert little influence within the party. He argues (1955a: 111), however, that this is probably not based on sexual discrimination. Instead, it is just one instance of a general tendency to oppose the development within parties of groups which could threaten cohesion, whether these are groups of women, young members, or professional or regional groupings. However, the advantage of these groups for the parties is that they are good for public relations. By demonstrating that the party cares about each social category, it can attract new members from these categories. Duverger argues that the desire, on the one hand, to maintain party unity and, on the other hand, to attract a broad membership explains the intermediate position of women's organisations. In the case of the French and Yugoslav Communist Parties, the commitment to absolute equality between the sexes has, he states, led to a refusal to allow their separate organisation within the party. Instead, they have both created associations outside the party (the UFF and the Yugoslav Women's Anti-Fascist Front), which are effective propaganda machines disguised as non-political associations.

The most detailed analysis to appear in English of the relation between women and two of the French parties (RPR and PS) is a chapter by Andrew Appleton and Amy Mazur (1993). They explore four areas: the penetration by women of party structures, including policy-making bodies and party strategies for increasing their presence in internal positions of responsibility; the existence of gender-specific organisations within and parallel to the parties; the parties' methods of selection; and party programmes on gendered political issues. The information which they gathered and the conclusions which they drew will be presented in the relevant sections of this chapter.

Françoise Gaspard (1995) has attempted to explore the question more thoroughly, but was confronted by difficulties obtaining basic information from the parties themselves. The problems she encountered included the lack of official statistics or systematic studies of the gender balance in the political parties. The parties do not have to publish details of their membership, and when they do, the statistics are not always reliable. Gaspard reports that, when asked to complete an international questionnaire on women in politics, France failed to fill in the section on women in the parties. Her own attempt in 1994 to discover from the parties how many of their members are women revealed that only the *Verts* can answer this question with any certainty (31 per cent). The PCF also gave a figure (38 per cent), but it appeared to contradict previous information and turned out to be an estimate. Gaspard concludes that it is only possible to estimate the proportion of women in the membership of the main political parties, and she places this estimate at 'a third or even more' (1995: 225).

Finally, Mariette Sineau (for example, 1994a) has produced analyses of certain aspects of the behaviour of parties and their élites around the issue of women's participation, focusing on elected representatives and the party leadership.

This chapter sets out to examine women's activities within the parties. The investigation of the proportion of women in the membership and organisation of the individual parties confirms the findings of previous studies in France and elsewhere: the number of women decreases as one climbs the party hierarchy. A similar observation can be made about the selection of women candidates, which, until 1997 and with some excep-tions, was in inverse proportion to the chances of the party winning a particular seat. The essentially descriptive presentation of women's pres-ence in the parties enables a number of conclusions to be drawn. First, the practices of the parties are heavily implicated in the exclusion of women from politics, which is examined in detail in Chapter 5. It is shown that there has been substantial resistance to women within the parties which are dominated by a self-reproducing élite. Second, only reluctantly have some of the parties agreed to select more women candidates, and rhetoric in support of increasing the representation of women in elected bodies does not necessarily translate into the promotion of women in internal party structures. Third, the action of women within the parties has been crucial in stimulating change, but has not sufficed on its own. A combi-nation of factors has been necessary to produce change in women's favour at certain moments.

In addition to presenting women's activities within the parties, then, this chapter examines the factors relevant to the parties which influence the promotion of women within their internal organisation and in elected bodies. They include: party attitudes towards the promotion of women, for example, their willingness to use positive discrimination; pressure exerted by women in the parties; the existence of pressure outside the parties, for example, a women's movement or the campaign for parity; the parties' desire to win women's votes; and the desire to project a 'modern' image, for example, Giscard's women's rights reforms in the 1970s and the battle between Chirac and Jospin in 1998 to appear the most pro-parity (see Chapter 8). Factors which may prevent or stall the promotion of women at particular times include: the culture of the party; resistance to change in the élites; the struggles between factions; the fierce competition between presidential hopefuls; and the resistance in some parties to dictates from the centre, seen to infringe on the right of the local party sections to select their own candidates. The decision to include women's rights issues in the party programme is influenced by the same considerations.

The parties which are examined here are, first, those which dominated the political scene throughout the first twenty years of the Fifth Republic: on the right, the Gaullist and centre right parties, known now as the RPR and UDF and on the left, the socialist and communist parties (PS and PCF). In contrast to the Fourth Republic, in which numerous small parties formed a series of unstable coalitions, the Fifth Republic produced an institutional framework and electoral practices which favoured the constitution of two groups of parties, one on the left and one on the right. Although the right held the parliamentary majority between 1958 and 1981, the opposition, dominated until the late 1970s by the PCF, held a sizeable minority of the vote and eventually began to provide a credible alternative. This was largely due to the deliberate formation during the 1970s of the PS as a party of government, forming an alliance and a common programme with the PCF at the same time as it tried to establish itself as the dominant force on the left. The 1978 legislative elections were the apogée of the 'bipolarisation' model, the four main parties arranged around the two poles and sharing the vote almost equally. Since then, the balance has been upset by the decline of the Communist Party[4] and the emergence of the *Front national*[5] and the *Verts*,[6] both of which are also examined here.

In the 1993 legislative elections, the three main parties (PS, UDF, RPR) won only 60 per cent of the total votes cast, while the extreme and minor parties (PC, ecologist, FN, *divers*)[7] won 40 per cent (Perrineau 1995: 474). In 1995, eight parties were capable of attracting a sizeable minority of the electorate: the PCF, PS, *Radical*, *Verts* and GE, UDF, RPR, Philippe de Villiers' Mouvement pour la France (MPF) and FN. The 1997 legislative elections resulted in a majority coalition referred to as '*la gauche plurielle*' (the plural left), the result of a series of alliances amongst parties of the left. By the summer of 1997, the *Front national* had become the third party in France in terms of electoral support, and the only party which had gained voters during the last decade (9.7 per cent in the 1986 legislative election, 15 per cent in 1997) (Schain 1999: 1). However, because its support was spread throughout the country, it gained only one seat in 1997. It has been much more successful at the local level. In contrast, the RPR and UDF had, by 1998, not only lost their parliamentary majority, but their popularity had sunk below that of the Communist Party, and the UDF had disintegrated (Knapp 1999: 109–10).

In the 1999 European elections, the PS–MDC–MRG won 21.95 per cent of the vote. Four other lists won more than 9 per cent (Pasqua–Villiers 13.08 per cent, RPR–DL 12.7 per cent, *Verts* 9.7 per cent and UDF 9.29 per cent) and four more won more than 5 per cent each (CPNT (the hunting lobby), PCF, FN, LO–LCR).

Numerous minor parties have been present in the Fifth Republic, some for the whole period, others lasting no longer than one election. Those which will be mentioned briefly are *Lutte ouvrière* (LO),[8] the *Ligue communiste révolutionnaire* (LCR)[9] and the *Parti socialiste unifié* (PSU).[10] They have been included because women have been particularly active within them and they, in response, have pursued various strategies to improve women's representation and to take gender issues into account in the party programme.

This chapter first looks at the presence of women in the membership and organisation of the parties, and their selection of women candidates. It then examines party attitudes towards the internal promotion of women, towards the selection of women candidates and towards women's rights. Finally it discusses the role of women's sections and parallel associations.

In each of these discussions, for the reasons given earlier in the chapter, there is a marked variation in the type and quality of information available for the different parties. The figures which are presented here have been obtained in a piecemeal fashion from a variety of sources and compiled into tables. Many were buried in secondary sources. Their accuracy cannot be guaranteed but, in the absence of more scientifically obtained data, they provide a useful starting point. An additional problem has been the differences in internal organisation in the parties studied and the names of the various bodies within them. It has therefore been necessary to give a brief explanatory introduction to the organisation of each party and the terms which they use. In order to facilitate comparisons between the parties, the tables have all been constructed with the legislative organ first, followed by the executive organ, then the secretariat.

Women in party membership and internal structures

In almost all the parties, women's presence in the membership is far greater than in the internal structures, and it declines as the level of responsibility grows. The exceptions are the *Verts*, LO and, during its existence, the PSU. The PSU, under the influence of feminists active within the party, had women present in the party legislature in the same proportion as in the membership. This had risen from 20 per cent in 1960 to 25 per cent in 1968 and to 38 per cent in 1980. However, the party's general secretary from 1979–84, Huguette Bouchardeau (1980: 22) states that when it came to the real site of decision-making, the policy bureau (*bureau politique*), there were very few women.

Lutte ouvrière claims that women's presence in the party is around 45 per cent in total. There is no internal hierarchy, as such, but in the national executive there are slightly more women than men. Arlette Laguiller has been the party spokesperson for many years (Rouleau 1999).

Verts

The organisation of the *Verts* is based on the regions, which can organise themselves as they wish, provided that their statutes do not contradict those of the national organisation. Membership is at a regional level and the regions elect three-quarters of the parliamentary organ of the *Verts*, the National Interregional Council (*Conseil national interrégional* (CNIR)). In line with party distrust of delegation and representation, party policy is made by a general assembly in which all members can participate. This ensures, in theory, the participation of everyone in collective decision-making, but in practice, material considerations, such as geographical position, interfere. The general assembly takes place annually and determines the orientation of the movement. It elects the fourth quarter of the CNIR which in turn elects the members of the executive college (*collège exécutif*), including the secretary, the treasurer and the four spokespersons who represent the party externally (Boy 1993: 321–2). The idea of a single leader has been rejected by the *Verts*, although certain individuals have promoted themselves in this role (Hainsworth 1990: 99).

The proportion of women members of the *Verts* has been consistently estimated at around 30 per cent, making it comparable with the other parties (Bennahmias and Roche 1992: 113). Where the *Verts* differs is in the composition of its leadership. As can be seen in Table 2.1, in 1996, 35 per cent of the CNIR and 45 per cent of the executive college were women. Along with *Lutte ouvrière*, this puts the *Verts* at the top of the table for the number of women in positions of responsibility. This has not come about by chance, but is the result of a conscious effort.

There are some very prominent women in the *Verts*, although Alain Lipietz suggests that the highly feminised élite hides underlying structures which do not respect the principle of parity at all (1996: 28). Nevertheless, the three currents which joined together at the November 1995 Federal Assembly (*Assemblée fédérale*) were each led by a woman: Dominique Voynet (Green candidate in the presidential elections), Marie-Anne Isler-Béguin (who headed the list in the European elections and had been vice-president of the European Parliament) and Marie-Christine Blandin (regional president for Nord-Pas-de-Calais) (Lipietz 1996: 26). In 1999, two of the

Table 2.1 Women in *Les Verts*

	Assemblée générale (General Assembly)	*Conseil national interrégional (National Interregional Council)*	*Collège exécutif (Executive College)*
1989	(27%)	–	–
1992	–	41/120 (34%)	3/11 (27%)
1996	–	41/118 (35%)	5/11 (45%)
1999	–	–	7/15 (47%)

Sources: Bennahmias and Roche (1992: 113); *L'Express* (6 June 1996: 38); *Le Trombinoscope* 1999: 460; Prendiville (1993: 154).

four spokespersons were women (Marie-Anne Isler-Béguin and Martine Billard) and seven of the fifteen members of the executive college (*Le Trombinoscope* 1999: 460).

PCF

In 1990, the PCF began a gradual move away from democratic centralism, which had until then determined the organisation of the party. It now recognises diversity within the party, although it still refuses to sanction the existence of official tendencies (PCF Manifesto, adopted at the twenty-eighth Congress, 27 January 1994). It stresses the importance of the individual in bringing about social change. The Women's Section (Commission Femmes du PCF 1999) writes:

> Our party has included parity between men and women in its objectives. Parity meaning perfect equality between individuals who are all unique, all different and all have their own history . . . This is a move towards the democracy that we wish to see. It is a reminder that the individual is the goal and the means of changing society.

Local or workplace-based cells are grouped into sections, which are joined at the departmental level into federations. The federations coordinate the activities of cells and sections and liaise with the national party structures. The national party Congress is the sovereign decision-making body. It elects the National Committee and determines party policy. The Congress takes place every three years or when the National Committee or one-third of the federations decide. The National Committee elects the

Table 2.2 Percentage of women in the PCF internal organisation

	Members	*Central (since 1994 National) Committee*	*Policy (since 1994 National) Bureau*	*Secretariat*
1951	18	(8)	(1)	–
1966	25	–	(1)	–
1977	30	18.3	9.5 (2/21)	0 (0/7)
1978	33	–	–	–
1979	–	26.7	23.5	16.7
1983	36	–	–	–
1996	–	25	23 (5/22)	14
1997	35–8	–	–	–
1999	–	28.1	30 (9/30)	20 (2/10)

Sources: Appleton and Mazur (1993: 101); Belden Fields (1986: 560); Charzat (1972: 58); Commission Femmes du PCF (1999); *L'Express*, (6 June 1996: 38); Gaspard (1995: 275 and 229); Jenson and Sineau (1994: 259n); *L'Humanité* (9 February 1977, 9 March 1987); *Le Matin* (5 December 1977).

Note: Figures in brackets are numbers, not percentages.

party executive, (the national bureau), the secretariat and the national secretary.

In 1951, the PCF claimed that 18 per cent of its members were women (see Table 2.2). In 1966, this had increased to 25 per cent (Charzat 1972: 58). Since 1977, the party has been estimating the proportion of women members at between 30 and 38 per cent of the total membership (*L'Humanité*, 9 February 1977, 9 March 1987; Gaspard 1995: 225; Commission Femmes du PCF 1999). Women's presence in the party's internal structure has been significantly smaller. From 1950–68, Jeanette Thorez-Vermeersch, wife of the general secretary, Maurice Thorez, was the only woman in the Politbureau, and it was 1979 before the first woman joined the secretariat (Jenson and Sineau 1994: 259 n.). Since 1979, women have made up around 25 per cent of the central committee and Politbureau, but only 15 per cent of the secretariat. In 1999, the proportion was slightly higher: 28.08 per cent of the national committee, 30 per cent of the national bureau, and 20 per cent of the secretariat. At the departmental level, 13 of the 96 federal secretaries are women (13.54 per cent); 22.5 per cent of federal committees (*comités fédéraux*) and 18.1 per cent of departmental executives (Commission Femmes du PCF 1999).

PS

The PS is organised into local sections federated at the departmental level. Membership of the PS has always been low, with the result that one in three party members are locally elected representatives, who exert considerable influence over the central party structure. The weak party structure, due, until the introduction of public funding in 1988, to a lack of resources, still holds and is exacerbated by the importance of the '*courants*' (tendencies). The seats on the party legislature (*comité directeur*) and executive (*bureau exécutif*) are allocated to each group within the party whose motion, circulated before the party conference, receives the vote of more than 5 per cent of the delegates (Stevens 1992: 240). The tendencies control the federations and the party's elected representatives and exercise strict control over internal discipline (Portelli 1993: 273).

The proportion of women members in the Parti socialiste is difficult to establish with any degree of accuracy. Philippe and Hubscher (1991: 225) give the figures as 16 per cent in 1973, 20 per cent in 1981 and 28 per cent in 1990. Subileau, Ysmal and Rey (1999) claim that women constituted only 20 per cent of the membership in 1985 and 26 per cent in 1998. Their detailed study of the membership provides further information. For example, they find that 32 per cent of the newest members of the PS are women, whereas this was the case for only 14 per cent of those who joined in 1970, 22 per cent of those who joined between 1971 and 1980, and 29 per cent of those who joined between 1981 and 1992.

Table 2.3 Percentage of women in the PS internal organisation

	Members	Legislature (Comité directeur)	Executive (Bureau exécutif)	Secretariat
1973	16	0	0	0
1977	20	13.7 (18/131)	14.8 (4/27)	17.6 (3/17)
1978	22	17.6 (23/131)	18.5 (5/27)	17.6 (3/17)
1985	21	19.8 (26/131)	22.2 (6/27)	12.5 (2/16)
1990	28	21.4 (28/131)	18.5 (5/27)	7.1 (1/14)
1994	–	–	26	9
1998	26	–	–	–
1999	–	–	30 (16/54)	29 (7/24)

Sources: Appleton and Mazur (1993: 102); Belden Fields (1986: 566); Cacheux (1996: 191); Gaspard (1995: 229); *Le Matin* (5 December 1977); *Le Trombinoscope* 1999: 456; Philippe and Hubscher (1991: 225); Storti (1978a); Subileau, Ysmal and Rey (1999).

Note: Figures in brackets are numbers not percentages.

Between 1995 and 1998, the proportion of women amongst new members rose from 31 per cent to 34 per cent, suggesting that, at the level of membership, the party is gradually feminising.

Women's presence in the party hierarchy has been much lower, however. There were no women in the leadership which emerged from the founding Congress in 1971; nor were there any women in the party structure after the Congress of 1973 (Cacheux 1996: 191). However, at this Congress, the PS established a quota for women in all internal governing bodies and in candidacies for elections fought under proportional representation (Jenson and Sineau 1994: 249). The quota was intended to match the proportion of women in the party membership, but could only be approximate, since this figure was not known. It was fixed initially at 10 per cent and raised to 15 per cent at the party Congress at Nantes in 1977, and to 20 per cent at Metz in 1979. In 1991, it was raised to 30 per cent. However, the quota was not respected and the actual representation of women during this period was much lower, as can be seen in Table 2.3.

Women entered the party leadership for the first time in 1977, when they formed 13.7 per cent of the legislature, 14.8 per cent of the executive and 18 per cent of the secretariat. In 1985, these figures had risen slightly to 20 per cent of the legislature, 22 per cent of the executive but only 13 per cent of the secretariat. In 1994, when the proportion of women in the secretariat had fallen to 9 per cent, women in the party threatened court action if the party's own quotas were not respected. As a result, the proportion of women in each body was raised to 30 per cent. In 1995, Gaspard (1995: 229) reported that, since then, the quota had been respected, but not exceeded. However, Subileau, Ysmal and Rey's (1999) survey in 1998 revealed that, of the 118 national office holders who responded, only 21 per cent were women; of the 973 departmental office holders, only 23 per cent were women and of the 1,800 section officers, 20 per cent were women.

UDF

Until November 1998, the UDF was not a party, but an alliance of parties originally brought together in February 1978 around Giscard's candidacy for the presidency, and aiming to challenge the dominance of the Gaullists within the ruling coalition. Its main components were Giscard's *Républicains indépendants*, renamed the *Parti républicain* (PR) in 1977; the Christian Democratic *Centre des Démocrates Sociaux* (CDS); the remnants of the *Parti radical*; and social democrats who rejected the Socialists' alliance with the PCF (Knapp 1999: 110). Having won 21 per cent of the votes in March 1978, it formed a separate group of 123 deputies in the National Assembly. Simone Veil headed the UDF list in the June 1979 European elections, beating Socialist, Communist and Gaullist lists. By 1981, the UDF claimed a membership of 300,000 and controlled forty-one towns with more than 30,000 inhabitants (Wright 1989: 201). It has since played an influential role, but has always been in tension, due to the wide variety of constituent parties. It presented a common programme of government with the RPR in 1986 and 1993 and single candidates in many constituencies. In May 1998, one of its constituent parties, *Démocratie libérale*, left the UDF, choosing to adhere to the electoral alliance with the RPR in its own right. The remaining members of the UDF formed a separate parliamentary group and, in November 1998, a single party.

Before this change, all the member parties were represented on the party council, which comprised a president, a policy bureau (*bureau politique*) (14 members), 20 representatives of the different components of the Union, 6 representatives of the National Assembly group and 6 representatives of the Senate group, and 3 representatives from the European Parliament and from the membership. The constitution of the UDF, combined with its lack of interest in gender issues, account for the dearth of information available on the role of women within it. It is known, however, that in 1996, 2 of the 40 members of the council were women (5 per cent). In 1999, the New UDF (*Nouvelle UDF*) had 9 women in its national leadership of 63 (14 per cent) (*Le Trombinoscope* 1999: 459).

RPR

The RPR is a highly structured organisation with a strong leadership. Its internal structure intentionally mirrors that of the Republic. The party conference (*Assises nationales*) elects the president and the two-hundred members of the legislative central committee (*comité central*). The president leads the party along with an executive committee comprised of national

Table 2.4 Percentage of women in the RPR internal organisation

	Members	Party legislature	Party executive	National secretaries
1977	40	13.3 (32/241)	12.5 (4/32)	18.8 (3/16)
1978	41	8.2 (14/170)	14.3 (4/28)	
1985	43	11.2 (19/170)	7.1 (2/28)	5 (1/20)
1990				24.1 (7/29)
1994				0
1999				12.9 (4/31)

Sources: Appleton and Mazur (1993: 102, 108); Gaspard (1995: 229); *Le Matin* (5 December 1977).

Note: Figures in brackets are numbers, not percentages.

secretaries, which he/she appoints and which is chaired by the secretary general, and a policy council (*conseil politique*) made up of fifteen members elected by the central committee (*comité central*), and of an unlimited number of members appointed by the president (Debbasch and Daudet 1992: 362–3). The president leads the party according to the line ratified by the conference. The general secretary and the executive committee (*Commission exécutive*) are accountable to the central committee (Chagnollaud 1993: 249).

Despite the high proportion of women members (40–43 per cent since 1973), women's presence in the leadership of the RPR is low. In 1977, women constituted 13.3 per cent of the party legislature, 12.5 per cent of the executive and 18.7 per cent of the secretariat. In 1985, this had fallen to 11 per cent, 7.1 per cent and 5 per cent (see Table 2.4).

In 1990, there were two women out of a total of eight assistant general secretaries (*secrétaires généraux adjoints*) or 25 per cent, and seven women out of twenty-nine national secretaries (*secrétaires nationaux*), or 24.1 per cent. Most were responsible for the family, the elderly, women and daily life. Appleton and Mazur (1993: 107) report that the increase was held by some to be a response to the eviction from the party leadership of Michèle Barzach.[11] If so, then the effect was only temporary, as by 1994, there were no women at all in the national secretariat (Gaspard 1995: 229).

In December 1999, Michèle Alliot-Marie won the first election within the party of its president. At the time of her election, there were four women in the national secretariat (13 per cent) (*Le Trombinoscope* 1999: 458).

Front national

Research on women in the *Front national* is very recent and, consequently, limited data are available. In 1998, before the party split into two around Jean-Marie Le Pen, on the one hand, and his rival, Bruno Mégret on the other, there were three women out of forty-four on the executive (*bureau politique*) (6.8 per cent), and 21 out of 120 (17 per cent) on the legislature

Table 2.5 Percentage of women in the *Front national* internal organisation

	Legislature (comité central)	Executive (bureau politique)	Secretariat
1996	15 (15/100)	5 (2/40)	–
1998	17 (21/120)	6.8 (3/44)	1 (6/100)

Sources: Barroux (1999); Lesselier (1997: 64).

Note: Figures in brackets are numbers, not percentages.

(*comité central*) (see Table 2.5). Of the one hundred departmental secretaries, appointed directly by the president, only six were women (Barroux 1999).

An important piece of research on activists in extreme right parties was carried out by Claudie Lesselier and Fiammetta Venner (Lesselier and Venner 1997). It reveals that, despite the masculine image of FN activists and despite the fact that more men than women vote for the FN, there are women active in the party, even at the highest levels of responsibility. Some of them are recruited from groups organised around the defence of the family; opposition to abortion, contraception, pornography and homosexuality; support for Christians abroad; and the defence of French traders, small farmers, workers and students. Women activists are either young (15–25) or over 45. This enables them to fulfil their primary responsibilities within the family, only becoming politically active either before motherhood or when their children are older. They are increasingly active in the party bureaucracy, in the production of the party's publications, in relations with the press, as conference organisers and as secretaries.

Selection of women candidates

Selection procedures vary from party to party. In the PS, candidates for local and national election are chosen, in theory, by party activists in a secret ballot. However, the leader of each candidate list for municipal elections, candidates for the general council (*conseil général*) and for the National Assembly and the Senate must have their nomination by the grass roots ratified by a federal and a national convention. Gaspard (1997d: 101–2) argues that the illusion of democratic decision-making in the PS, at least until very recently, hid the reality of centrally imposed nominations, which activists were asked to sanction. Since 1995, efforts have been made to democratise procedure, and Jospin was the first Socialist presidential candidate to have been selected by a secret ballot of all party members. Selection procedures in the RPR and PCF are more centralised and far less transparent. Gaspard (1997d: 102) writes:

> These methods have served to maintain the status quo as far as the representation of women and men is concerned, in that the latter, for

Table 2.6 Women candidates in the first round of the 1993 legislative elections in mainland France

Party	Ministry of the Interior code	Women candidates	Men candidates	Total	% of women
Extreme left	EXG	127	380	507	25.0
Communists	COM	91	464	555	16.4
Socialists	SOC	47	492	539	8.7
Left Radicals	RDG	2	31	33	6.1
Others from presidential majority	MAJ	16	167	183	8.7
Génération écologie	GEC	50	211	261	19.2
Verts–écologistes	VEC	38	250	288	13.2
Regionalists	REG	4	42	46	8.7
Divers	DIV	424	488	912	46.5
RPR	RPR	20	298	318	6.3
UDF	UDF	21	290	311	6.8
Right-wing *divers*	DVD	52	427	479	10.9
Front national	FRN	66	488	554	11.9
Extreme left *divers*	EXD	45	108	153	29.4

Source: Mossuz-Lavau (1997a: 456).

reasons linked to the history of the past two hundred years, tend to stick together in the public sphere and, unless they are forced to do otherwise by a social movement, co-opt each other.

The 1993 election study (Parité-infos no. 1, March 1993: 2) found that the greater a party's chance of electoral success, the fewer women candidates it selected. In the '*divers*' (independent and not otherwise classified) category, where the candidates stand practically no chance of election, 46.5 per cent of the candidates were women. The three main parties with the greatest chance of winning seats presented only 6.8 per cent (UDF), 6.3 per cent (RPR) and 8.7 per cent (PS) women (see Table 2.6).

In other words, large numbers of women were standing for parties with virtually no chance of election (424 as '*divers*' candidates). In 1997, the highest proportions were still standing as '*divers*' (33.2 per cent) and extreme left (32.3 per cent) candidates, but this time the Ecologists, Socialists and Communists were close behind with 27.7 per cent, 27.8 per cent and 26.8 per cent respectively (see Table 2.7).

However, the number of candidates selected does not on its own give a true picture of the parties' real commitment to the election of women, as they can still be selected for hopeless seats. It is important, then, to consider the proportion of women amongst the successful candidates for each of these parties (see Table 2.8). In 1997, this was Ecologists 37.5 per cent, PCF 13.5 per cent, PS 17.08 per cent, UDF 6.42 per cent and RPR

Table 2.7 Women candidates in the first round of the 1997 legislative elections in mainland France

Party	Ministry of the Interior code	Women candidates	Men candidates	Total	% of women
Extreme left	EXG	224	470	694	32.3
Communists	PCF	144	393	537	26.8
Socialists	PS	133	346	479	27.8
PRS	RDG	6	37	43	14.0
Left *divers*	DVG	86	364	450	19.1
Ecology		335	874	1,209	27.7
Divers		214	431	645	33.2
RPR	RPR	22	263	285	7.7
UDF	UDF	24	247	271	8.9
Right *divers*	DVD	167	787	954	17.5
Front national	FN	67	488	555	12.1
Extreme right	EXD	26	95	121	21.5

Source: Mossuz-Lavau (1997a: 458).

Table 2.8 Percentage of women candidates selected and elected by party, 1978–98

Election		Verts	PCF	PS	UDF	RPR	FN
1978	S	–	13.5	5.7	–	2.9	–
(legislative)	E	–	(13)	(1)	–	–	–
1986	S	–	–	18.9	–	10.3	–
(PR)	E	–	–	9.8	–	(4)	–
1992	S	–	11.5	10.8	3.2	3.3	9.2
(regional)	E	–	–	–	–	–	13.0
1993	S	13.2	16.4	8.7	6.8	6.3	11.9
(legislative)	E	–	(1)	(17)	(5)	(10)	–
1997	S	27.7*	26.8	27.8	8.9	7.7	12.1
(legislative)	E	37.5*	13.5	17.1	6.4	3.6	0
1998	S	35.0	43	39	32	34.4	–
(regional)	E	34	26	35	23	27	17

*Ecologists – all tendencies combined (*Verts*, MEI, GE, *Nouveaux écologistes*, *Solidaires régions écologie*)

Sources: Appleton and Mazur (1993: 108); Belden Fields (1986: 560); *Le Matin* (5 December 1977); Ministère de l'Intérieur, Service des Elections; Mossuz-Lavau (1997a: 460); Nolet (1980: 18); *Parité-infos* no. 1, mars 1993: 2–3; Servan-Schreiber (1996: 200); Service de Documentation et d'Archives du Centre national du RPR; Sineau (1998b: 13).

Note: Figures in brackets are numbers of candidates, not percentages.

Table 2.9 Percentage of French women elected to European Parliament, June 1999

List	Total number elected	Number of women elected	% of women
LO–LCR	5	4	80
PCF	7	3	42.9
Verts	10	5	50
PS–PRG–MDC	21	10	47.6
UDF	9	4	44.4
RPR–DL	12	4	33.3
CPNT*	5	1	20
Pasqua–Villiers	12	5	41.7
Front national	6	1	16.7

Source: *Le Figaro* (14 June 1999).

Note: **Chasse, Pêche, Nature et Traditions* (Hunting, Fishing, Nature and Traditions).

6.3 per cent. The FN had just one deputy, who was a man (Mossuz-Lavau 1997a: 460).

The tendency for women candidates to be found standing for unelectable parties or fighting impossible seats could provide a partial explanation for the impressive record of small parties such as the PSU, which presented the highest proportion of women candidates in the 1978 legislative elections (almost 40 per cent) (Bouchardeau, Goueffic and Thouvenot 1981: 102). However, the influence of feminists within the party and the commitment to increase the number of women elected must also be contributory factors, since certain parties have selected more successful candidates than others. For example, in the 1999 European elections, the LCR–LO list returned five Members of the European Parliament, four of whom were women (see Table 2.9).[12]

The parties of the left

The PCF has a variable, but at times impressive, record. It presented women candidates at elections as early as 1925 (Gaspard 1995: 224), but the proportion of women amongst the successful Communist candidates has often been much lower than the proportion of the total number of candidates. In 1978, 20 per cent of the legislative candidates of the PCF were women, but 7 per cent were *suppléantes*, substitute candidates who only come into office if the elected representative dies or is appointed to a position incompatible with that already held (for example, government minister). Nevertheless, after the elections, thirteen of the twenty women in the National Assembly, and four of the seven women in the Senate, were Communists. In cities with over 30,000 inhabitants, more than 30 per cent of the Communist municipal councillors were women and four out of the five women mayors of large cities were Communists

(Belden Fields 1986: 560). However, in the 1988 legislature, only one of the Communists' twenty-five deputies was a woman (Jenson and Sineau 1994: 249).

In the 1993 legislative election, the PCF presented 16.4 per cent women candidates and in 1997, 26.8 per cent (Table 2.8). However, in 1999, only three of the 36 Communist deputies were women (8.33 per cent). In European elections, the figures have been higher. In 1994, the PCF presented one of the six *listes paritaires* (lists on which male and female candidates appear alternately), with the result that four of the seven Communists elected were women (57.1 per cent), and in 1999 another *liste paritaire* resulted in the election of three women out of six (50 per cent) (Commission Femmes du PCF 1999).

The *Verts*, who have been present in elections only since the late 1980s, also have a relatively good record, although it does not match their theoretical commitment to parity. In the 1989 European elections, they presented a list on which male and female candidates alternated, but in 1993, only 13.2 per cent of their candidates were women. The *Verts* claim that the electoral alliance with *Génération écologie* made it more difficult for them. However, with GE presenting 19.2 per cent women candidates, this explanation seems to lose a certain amount of credibility (Lucie 1993: 4). Nevertheless, Dominique Voynet was one of the two green candidates, both women, to reach the second round of the 1993 legislative elections and was their candidate in the 1995 presidential elections, obtaining 3.32 per cent of the vote (Proud 1995: 138). In the 1994 European elections, the *Verts* list was headed by a woman, and there were nine women in the first fifteen places. In 1994, the only woman regional president was a *verte* and the only ecologist vice-president of the European Parliament was a woman (Lipietz 1994: 53).

The PS has performed better than the parties of the right, although until the watershed elections of 1997, it rarely met and never exceeded its quotas. For example, in the 1978 legislative elections, a relatively impressive 20 per cent of the total number of PS candidates were women, but this figure combined first candidates and *suppléants*. When only the first candidates are counted, the proportion fell to 5.7 per cent (25 out of 440), and only one of these was elected (Servan-Schreiber 1996: 200) (see Table 2.8). In the 1986 elections that were fought under proportional rules, the PS allocated 18.9 per cent of the places on its lists to women candidates, and 19.3 per cent of those on the lists for the regional elections held simultaneously. However, only 9.8 per cent of PS candidates elected to the National Assembly and 11.4 per cent of those elected to regional councils were women, as they tended to be placed in lower, non-electable, positions (Appleton and Mazur 1993: 105). Another reason for the failure of the quotas within the party was that they were applied to each faction, not to the overall representation of women in the party. So a slight shortfall in each faction added up to a major under-representation (Philippe and Hubscher 1991: 228).

In 1995, 75 per cent of PS members voted in favour of including a commitment to parity in the party statutes (Mossuz-Lavau 1997a: 457). The party conference in September 1996 resolved to reserve 165 constituencies for women in the legislative elections due to fall in 1997. Women accounted for 27.8 per cent of the candidates finally selected by the party, and in their constituencies the PS score rose in almost the same proportion as in constituencies where men stood, despite the fact that the women candidates were often fighting more difficult seats (Mossuz-Lavau 1997a: 457).

The parties of the right

In the case of the RPR and UDF, the small number of women candidates selected has been due to a fierce opposition to any measures intended to promote women in politics. Until recently, the RPR had no strategy for advancing women candidates. In the 1986 legislative elections, only 40 of the 388 RPR candidates were women (10.3 per cent). Of these, only two were at the top of a list, and only two more were in electable positions (Appleton and Mazur 1993: 108). In the 1993 legislative elections, 6.3 per cent of the RPR candidates were women, and in 1997, 7.7 per cent. Figures for the UDF are very similar: 6.8 per cent in 1993 and 8.9 per cent in 1997 (see Table 2.8).

In the 1998 regional election, the RPR presented 252 women candidates out of a total of 733 (34.4 per cent). Nine RPR women headed joint lists with the UDF, two headed separate RPR lists, and eleven headed joint lists with other groups (AFP 171316, February 1998). In the 1999 European election, the RPR publicised its desire to 'feminise' and 'renew' its joint list with *Démocratie libérale*. The list contained the names of 48 women and 39 men, although amongst the twelve candidates who were elected, only four were women.

The FN has selected more women candidates than the RPR and UDF: 11.9 per cent in 1993 and 12.1 per cent in 1997. In the 1998 regional elections, 46 of the 275 FN councillors elected were women (17 per cent). Claudie Lesselier (1997: 60) argues that the selection of women candidates is a conscious tactic employed by the FN in order to improve its image and public relations.

More research is evidently needed on the selection and electoral success or failure of women candidates. Until 1993, it was practically ignored as a research topic in France, but since then, interest has grown and the compilation of the data necessary to future studies has been undertaken at national elections. Studies so far have shown that the parties of the left have selected more women candidates than the centre-right, but that they have been placed in the more difficult seats contested by the party. Studies such as that of the 1993 elections have attempted to discover why there are few women amongst candidates for election in safe seats or in electable positions on candidate lists. The results of these studies and suggested explanations for this are discussed in Chapter 5.

The parties and women

This section is divided into four parts, but the division is somewhat artificial, since the factors examined in each part interact. The factors are: the parties' attitudes to the promotion of women within their internal organisation; their attitudes towards the selection of women candidates; their attitudes towards women's rights; and the existence, status and activities of women's sections or parallel associations. It is found that women's demands have met resistance in all the parties. They have had to compete with demands from the tendencies and with other priorities, for example, class struggle in the parties of the left during the 1970s, economic policy in the 1980s.

Attitudes towards the promotion of women within the party

Policy on the promotion of women varies from party to party and is reflected to a certain extent in variations in the resulting presence of women, although this rarely matches the party rhetoric. At one extreme is the commitment to the principle of the equal representation of women and men in the party organisation which the *Verts* included in its statutes in 1988 and which has resulted in a high representation of women in decision-making positions. The LCR (12 October 1999) also declares its commitment to the promotion of women in the party organisation and states that, in order to achieve this, it intends to appoint women whenever it is faced with equally qualified male and female candidates.

The PS has a complicated history of raising, yet ignoring, quotas for women in its internal structures. During the Socialist governments of 1981–6 and 1988–93, despite pressure from women in the party, the PS failed to ensure that the quotas were respected (Jenson and Sineau 1995: 344). The appointment of 30 per cent women in the national leadership of the PS in 1994, in accordance with the party's own statutes, was only realised when a number of activists threatened to take the party's first secretary, Henri Emmanuelli, to court (Lucie 1996: 2).

The UDF has ignored the question of women's position in its internal organisation. Although Giscard d'Estaing appointed individual women to positions of power, he did nothing to promote women in the parties or in elected assemblies, stating on French radio in 1975, 'Women don't like what men call Politics, which is a mixture of theoretical discussions and personal dealings' (quoted in Adler 1993: 173).

The RPR has been resolutely non-interventionist, adhering to a liberal notion of equal rights. Women have the right to join parties, to be active within them and to stand as candidates for election. Those who want to, and have the necessary skills and qualities, will succeed. Special measures to 'help' women enter politics are insulting and will result in women in political office simply because they are women. Asked by the *Nouvel Observateur* in 1978 (Evin 1978: 28) why women were so under-represented in politics, Noëlle Dewarin, RPR national delegate for women's action, responded: 'It is true that women prefer women's associations with their little routines to political parties ruled by discipline and hierarchy.' Dewarin described her role as helping women to adapt, by convincing them that women do not have specific needs. She states:

> Sometimes a woman, having gained responsibility in the movement, suddenly begins to judge the men in posts at the same level or above her, believing that she can do better than them. When that happens, it's all over. She has to be thrown out because, if you don't accept men as they are, you destroy the whole organisation.
>
> (Evin 1978: 28)

There has been some change since the 1970s. Each federation of the RPR now has a departmental delegation for women's action, which aims to encourage women to participate in politics, providing information and training, and Roselyne Bachelot, fervent advocate of measures aimed specifically at increasing women's participation, headed the *Observatoire de la parité* set up by Juppé in 1995. However, the liberal equal rights discourse has not disappeared from the party. Although Alain Juppé and Jacques Chirac declared their unconditional support for the government bill tabled in December 1999 requiring parties to select more women, Michèle Alliot-Marie, elected RPR president on 7 December 1999, is ardently opposed. Quotas, she claims, are an insult to women (*Le Monde*, 9 December 1999). National secretary for women's rights, Marie-Jo Zimmermann, argues that Alliot-Marie's success proves that 'a woman who fights succeeds' (*Le Monde*, 9 December 1999).

At the other extreme to the *Verts* is the *Front national*, which remains resolutely opposed to parity, quotas and any form of positive discrimination. Marie-France Stirbois, MEP and party spokesperson on women, states, 'It is humiliating for women to be reduced to a quota' (*Le Point*, 27 February 1999: 48). Although there are a number of high-profile women in the party (Marie-France Stirbois, Martine Lehideux and Myriam Baeckeroot are on the party executive; Marie-France Stirbois and Martine Lehideux are MEPs), their promotion is often linked to the career of their husbands (*Le Point*, 27 February 1999: 48). Women are able to become politically active, but only as an extension of their role in the private sphere, for example, in the areas of social policy, education and family policy. They may assist their husband, or replace him if he dies or is barred from office, but will always be subordinate to him and to the male leaders of the party.

Attitudes towards the selection of women candidates

With the possible exception of the PCF, which selected women candidates as early as 1925, even though they did not yet have the right to be elected, none of the parties has sought to increase the number of women elected under the party banner until pressure to do so has been irresistible. This pressure has normally come from women within the party, but it also results from competition for a share of the votes, from the effects of unilateral moves by other parties, and from movements such as the campaign for parity and, less directly, the women's movement of the 1970s. Most parties now pay lip service to parity (see Chapter 8), but only the *Verts* and the PS have been prepared to introduce unilateral measures to achieve it. *Lutte ouvrière*, in a gesture intended to expose the hypocrisy of the PS's recent focus on quotas for women, presented only women candidates in its places on the joint list with the LCR in the 1999 European elections (Rouleau 1999).

The *Verts* included a commitment to the principle of parity in the party's statutes in 1988, although they have not succeeded in attaining this goal at all subsequent elections. Francine Comte and Bernadette Léonard (1993), both members of the women's section of the *Verts*, attribute the gap between principle and reality to conflict between the commitment to parity and the commitment to other types of representation, such as that of currents within the party, to power struggles between different would-be party leaders, and to the persistence of myths about women's inferior competence. Finally, they state that there is a scarcity of women candidates.

In the case of the PS, the unilateral adoption of measures intended to increase women's election began with Michel Rocard's list in the 1994 European elections, on which the names of male and female candidates appeared alternately. Significantly this initiative followed the disastrous defeat of the PS in the 1993 legislative elections and was situated in the context of growing support for the better representation of women in politics amongst the general public. It triggered a number of other *listes paritaires*, including the one headed by Jean-Pierre Chevènement, whose *Mouvement des citoyens* (MDC) currently claims to have 30 per cent women at all levels, local, departmental and national, and to be aiming to increase this figure to 50 per cent (Morichaud 1999). In the 1999 European elections, the MDC presented nine candidates on the PS/MDC/PRG list, five of whom were women. One man and one woman were elected.

In 1995, the Communist Party's programme included a commitment to 'encourage' women's participation and to 'move towards equality of representation and responsibility between women and men in all sites of decision-making' (*Cahiers du communisme*, 1995a: 41).

The paucity of information on women and the UDF is due mainly to its lack of interest in the question. Although Giscard d'Estaing and Simone

Veil instigated certain state feminist structures and, through their policies in the 1970s, actively courted women's votes, women's role within the UDF did not excite much interest until involvement in the parity debate became unavoidable. Nicole Ameline and Gilles de Robien submitted a bill proposing the introduction of a quota of 30 per cent for candidates of either sex in elections with candidate lists (municipal, regional, sena-torial in large departments, and European), but opposition within the UDF was stronger than support (Lucie 1996: 2). *Parité-infos* (Lucie 1996: 2) reports that women in the party (Simone Veil, Nicole Ameline and Claude du Granrut in particular) have tried to put women's participation on the party's agenda, but have failed.

On the right, measures which could lead to the increased representa-tion of women in elected bodies have concerned opportunities for training, rather than positive action. By 1978, women in the *Centre féminin d'études et d'information* (CFEI), which had been created by de Gaulle in 1965 in order to attract and educate more women voters, were threatening to present their own candidates at elections if the parties of the right did not select more women. In response, Chirac claimed that the electorate was not ready to vote for women, and such were the stakes in the 1978 elec-tions that such a risk could not be taken (Storti 1978b). When the left came to power in 1981, the group, now called *Femmes Avenir* became more active and politicised. It supports women candidates who have received party nomination and it has participated in the national Congress of the RPR since October 1991 (Appleton and Mazur 1993: 107).

In 1996, eight right-wing women's organisations united under the label '*Femmes en marche*' with the aim of convincing the RPR and UDF to reserve winnable places for women on electoral lists.[13] The parties' response has not been enthusiastic although, in common with all the parties with any chance of electoral success, they have been forced to adapt their rhetoric as a result of the wave of public opinion in favour of an improvement in women's representation. Thus, in 1994, Chirac (*Le Monde*, 22 April 1994) began to talk of the need to improve women's representation in sites of decision-making, although the solutions he proposed were limited to women making an effort to improve their self-esteem and the introduc-tion of measures which would help them cope with the conflicting demands of home and work. He stated explicitly his opposition to a law on parity and to the introduction of quotas.

By 1997, however, the RPR (*La lettre de la Nation Magazine*, no. 377, 7 March 1997: 9) was declaring its commitment to improving the presence of women in politics and suggesting ways to achieve this:

> On the regional election lists in 1998, a third of the electable posi-tions will be reserved for women. Further, since it would be neither fair nor egalitarian not to reselect present incumbents who have done nothing to prove themselves unworthy, in order to replace them with

women, the RPR has opted for a first stage in the 1998 legislative elections: encouraging mixed candidate teams (deputy–substitute).

In publicity sent out in January 1998, the RPR claims to have 50,000 women members and to be resolutely committed to parity. Chirac, competing with Jospin in a mission to modernise political life, became an ardent advocate of the improved access of women to politics in 1998, although he had problems rallying the senatorial right around the cause (see Chapter 8). When the reform bill was finally passed, Marie-Jo Zimmerman, national secretary for women, stated that, although women must not be appointed to posts simply because they are women, she is confident that they will prove themselves capable: 'In many areas, their presence will even be a plus in comparison with men's' (RPR Press Office, 8 March 1999).

Party attitudes towards women's rights

It is not the intention here to undertake a detailed analysis of each party's policies on women's rights.[14] Instead, the aim of this section is to demonstrate how the factors which influence the other aspects of the relation between women and the parties interact with the parties' views on women and women's rights. These views vary enormously from the feminist analyses of the PSU in the 1970s and of the *Verts* today, to the violently anti-feminist position of the FN. They are not mapped conveniently onto the left–right spectrum, although there has always been a (hopeful) belief amongst many feminists that the left must surely be more feminist than the right. This has produced moments of disappointment, for example, the PCF's refusal to support the demand for contraception and abortion in the 1950s, the violent opposition of extreme left organisations to feminist actions in the 1970s, which it perceived as a bourgeois distraction from the struggle against class oppression, and, for some, the limited ability of the Socialist government to deliver on women's rights, especially after 1982. Nevertheless, the policies of the centre–left are undeniably more favourable to women's rights than those of the centre–right and, at the extremes today, the PCF far outstrips the FN.

Party policy on women's rights has in many cases evolved in response to pressure from women within the parties. Women have brought new issues onto the parties' agendas and into the party programmes. These have included abortion, male violence and social relations within the family.

Pressure from the wider social environment has also affected party programmes on women's rights. In the late 1970s, pressure from the women's movement led to the PCF declaring itself 'the party of women's liberation' and encouraged the PS to develop its women's rights policies. The presence of feminists in the PSU and their links with feminists from the autonomous women's movement account for the markedly feminist nature of the party's policy on women, published in the form of a booklet in 1981 (Bouchardeau, Goueffic and Thouvenot 1981). It identified two main principles which should determine party policy: the recognition of domestic labour as part of economic activity and the acceptance that women are not solely or principally responsible for domestic chores and childcare (119). As the authors point out, this implies the questioning of the institution of the family, and the association of rights with familial status. They propose an egalitarian contractual association for those who wish to live as a couple. They state that this goal is inseparable from that of a socialist *autogestionnaire* (self-managed) society in which each autonomous individual participates freely in the collective project (119).

PCF

In contrast to the recognition by the PSU of the role of the women's movement and of the participation of some of its members and activists in it, the PCF denounced it as bourgeois and as a distraction from the primary struggle against class oppression.[15] Inevitably, this provoked criticisms from feminists within the party, especially when in the late 1970s, the PCF began to refer to itself as the 'party of women's liberation' with more women members, more women officials, and more candidates at elections than any other party (Marchais 1977: 27). However, women's liberation was still situated within the context of the struggle against capitalism. Answering his own question 'is the party feminist?' Marchais (28) responded:

> No, we are not 'feminist' if that means, as is sometimes the case, opposing women to men and women workers to men workers, if that means obscuring the real solution to the discrimination, inequalities and oppression of women.
> But yes, we are feminist, if that means totally defending women's rights, taking action to create an equal and just society, a society in which men and women will finally be free and happy.

In June 1978, for the first time, the PCF recognised that women are subject to a specific oppression, which cannot be reduced to an overexploitation of class and which preceded class division. At the level of party rhetoric, this was certainly a radical change, but placed in the context of the intense pre-electoral competition on the left at the time, combined with the growing evidence that women were prepared to vote for the left, it can be seen as a transparent attempt to attract voters.

Despite, or maybe rather because of the party's claims in the late 1970s to be the party of women's liberation, women within the PCF were critical of its treatment of Communist women and its policies affecting women. In 1978, *Le Monde* (11–12 June) published a text signed by five Communist women (Michèle Guenoun, Annie Méjean, Juliette Nicolas, Peggy-Inès

Sultan, Nicole-Edith Thévenin) responding to the 1978 report of the central committee on the party's achievements in this area. The women argue that, although the party parliamentary group had presented a bill on women and the family to the National Assembly, it was little known and never discussed within the party. They argue that, although the party refers more often to women than it used to, women are almost always linked to the family. As far as the party is concerned, women's 'specific inequalities' are secondary to the struggle against capitalism, and the site of women's exploitation is the workplace. This ignores oppression and exploitation which takes place within the couple and the family and is accompanied by a refusal to consider the relation between capitalism and patriarchy.

The text also claims that, although the PCF declares itself the party of women's liberation, its women members do not feel able to speak in party meetings. They argue that the party must accept the reality of the oppression of women by men, and that the struggle against this oppression will not divide the revolutionary movement, as the party fears, but advance it. It is sexist ideology which divides the movement and turns women away. The party, they argue, needs to fight alongside women's movements, not dismiss or criticise them (*Le Monde*, 11–12 June 1978).

A year after the publication of this critique, the first issue of *Elles voient rouge* appeared, with the aim of reflecting on the role of Communist women in the women's movement and on the feminist struggle which needed to be undertaken within the party. It analysed the systemic nature of patriarchy and the relation between patriarchy and capitalism. It analysed the relation between men and women in the workplace and in the family. The response from the PCF was harsh. Madeleine Vincent denied that the PCF was late in addressing women's issues, denounced the women's movement as class collaborationist, and opposed the constitution of women's groups within the party (Bouchardeau 1978).

During the 1990s, the PCF, along with the *Verts*, joined feminist actions, such as the 1995 demonstration in favour of women's rights and the national conference on women's rights (*Assises nationales des droits des femmes*) in 1997, and it organised a 'feminist meeting for change in 1998' on 8 March 1997 at la Villette in Paris, with contributions from Marie-George Buffet (PCF), Michèle Sabban (PS), Francine Conte (*Verts*), and Michèle Emis (LCR) (*L'Humanité*, 7 March 1997).

PS

Since its creation, the PS has been subject to pressure from women within the party to increase the number of women appointed to positions of responsibility and selected for candidacies, and to recognise the specific demands of women within the context of the party's programme (*L'Unité*, 14 April 1975). It has created various mechanisms to deal with this pressure.

In 1977, the national delegation for women's action (*délégation nationale à l'action féminine*), which had been created in 1975, was replaced by a more influential secretariat for women's action (*secrétariat national à l'action féminine – SNAF*) under Yvette Roudy (Storti 1978a). The SNAF had its own budget, an office in the party headquarters, and two members of staff, and it led to the appointment of a secretary for women's action in each federation. In her capacity as national secretary for women's action, Yvette Roudy organised a National Convention on Women's Rights which took place in January 1978 (Cacheux 1996: 197–8). François Mitterrand, speaking at the conference, stated that its aim was to determine the party's policy on subjects not addressed at the party congress (Savigneau 1978). The preparatory text for the conference states that 'this conference is not the conference of the women in the PS, it is a conference of the whole party in order to take account of the feminist struggle and include it in the struggle for socialism' (Storti 1978a). Delegates at the conference were the members of the party legislature, parlementarians, and the first secretaries of the federations (only one woman occupied this position). The secretaries for women's action were also invited, but did not have a vote (Storti 1978a).

The conference approved a text (with almost 90 per cent support) organised around four themes: work, family, liberty, and activism (Savigneau 1978). However, some of the women who were present claim that it bore little resemblance either to the work of the federations or to the debates which actually took place (see *Projets féministes* 1996: 198–9). The introduction stresses that the feminist struggle is part of the socialist struggle. If feminists act outside socialism, they risk the further marginalisation of women. Feminism, it states (PS 1979: 8–9), is culturally important, but has no political or institutional base, nor does it have a social project. Feminists have two options: either they can accept capitalist structures – but the promotion of a few bourgeois women will do nothing for the liberation of all women or their access to politics; or they can attack the roots of women's subordination, denouncing, simultaneously, the economic exploitation of women and their dependence on men: 'This struggle against the overexploitation of women takes place within class struggle, but cannot be reduced to it. It must at the same time expose and destroy hierarchical relations of domination.' The text stresses that only in a socialist *autogestionnaire* society will women be truly fulfilled.

Women were an important constituency, showing signs of a growing willingness to vote for the left (see Chapter 4). The PS, recognising this, actively sought to attract women's votes and, in 1981, when the group *Choisir* invited all of the candidates for the presidential election to a forum on women's issues, Which President for Women? (*Quel président pour les femmes?*), Mitterrand was the only mainstream candidate to attend. However, the party's interest in women's rights declined after its first year in office, when the Ministry for Women's Rights saw its budget reduced and party enthusiasm for its activities waned (see Jenson and Sineau 1995, Mazur 1995a, Reynolds 1988).

The PS held its second national conference on women's rights in 1988, voting to raise the quota for women on candidate lists from 20 per cent to 25 per cent, and approving a text which underlined the attachment of Socialist women to equal rights in social justice, to autonomy and solidarity. It denounced the regression in women's rights since the right returned to power in 1986, especially in employment and the family. It called for an ambitious, modern family policy, which would include women's employment rights. Criticising the family policy of the right, and in particular, the *salaire maternel*,[16] the conference proposed a family policy based on the recognition of the sharing of domestic labour and responsibilities, and on benefits which would compensate for inequalities (e.g. parental leave for everyone, measures enabling shared parenting). The conference report in *Le Monde* (Chombeau 1988) stresses the centrality of the theme of the representation of women in politics and in the party. There were repeated calls for the quota to be raised from 20 per cent to 25 per cent in the party and on candidate lists. This was referred to as a necessary evil, and the party leadership was called upon to set an example by acting unilaterally.

The comparison between the official party text and the accounts of some of the women present at a seminar on the PS and parity eight years later is striking. Denise Cacheux (1996: 198), for example, remembers:

> Of course there had been a call for motions from the federations, but they almost all came from local women's committees. This resolution was voted almost entirely by women, because most men couldn't be bothered, just like at the national Convention . . . What was unbelievable, however, was to hear men later at party meetings or in election campaigns taking positions which were in total contradiction to our text, for example on the *salaire maternel*. They knew nothing about the text, they didn't know they had voted – by proxy – against these positions. That happens with other conference resolutions, but with women it was typical.

All the PS women interviewed by Laure Adler (1993) describe the sexism of the men in the party. They claim that it is less overt than that of the right, but no less ingrained and obstructive. Mitterrand is described in more ambivalent terms. According to some, he genuinely perceived women as equal to men and unfairly excluded. According to others, he was simply acutely aware of changes in public opinion and the shift towards the PS of women voters. Véronique Neiertz, for example said, 'Mitterrand was absolutely not a feminist, but he understood the political advantage of being one' (Adler 1993: 210).

Parity was a popular issue in the run-up to the 1997 election, and the PS was quick to profit from this, using women-only constituencies to increase the number of women candidates standing for the party. The election manifesto paid very little attention to women's rights, however, prompting feminist theorist and activist Marie-Victoire Louis (1997: 4) to write: 'And this, at a time when their Green and Communist allies, at least at the level of the party élite, are not only calling themselves feminist, but are actually present in women's protests.'

In November 1997, Socialist Prime Minister Lionel Jospin appointed the feminist historian and philosopher, Geneviève Fraisse, inter-ministerial delegate for Women's Rights. However, she had no budget and no direct authority over the Service for women's rights, which remained attached to the Ministry for Employment. Moreover, her post was removed in November 1998, and Nicole Péry, already state secretary for professional training, was given the additional remit of women's rights. The 1999 budget of the Service for Women's Rights (80.47 million francs) was a 10 per cent increase on the previous year, but only matched the 1982 budget. This suggests that, despite the high-profile rhetoric of parity, the Jospin government's commitment to women's rights is in fact limited (Aubry 1998).

The right and extreme right

On the moderate right, women's rights have received little attention. This does not mean that their policy programmes have been gender neutral, far from it, but there is no room here to expose the gendered impact of apparently gender-neutral policies. With the exception of Giscard d'Estaing's creation of a state secretariat for the feminine condition, his appointment of Simone Veil as Minister of Health and, later, Social Security, and his support for the Loi Veil, decriminalising abortion, the UDF has shown little interest in women's rights and the promotion of women in public life.

The RPR's programme has also paid little attention to women's rights. In 1979, 116 of the 154 RPR deputies voted against the continuation of the Loi Veil. The party had no position on abortion, seeing it as a question of conscience (Nolet 1980: 21). Pressure from the revitalised women's section since 1988 has had little impact on party policy (Appleton and Mazur 1993: 109).

In contrast to the lack of interest on the part of the moderate right, the FN's family policy is explicitly pro-natalist, advocating measures such as generous family allowances, available only to French families, and working patterns designed to suit mothers. The role of (French) women is to reproduce the nation physically and culturally. Opposition to abortion, a maternal income and a family vote were included in the FN's first manifesto in 1973 and have been present ever since (Lesselier 1997: 43). Although the FN does not participate overtly in anti-abortion actions, it created the *Ligue pour la vie* (League for life) in 1995 in order to do this, and numerous *associations amies* (sympathetic organisations) are active in this area, which is a meeting ground for FN, parliamentary right and Catholic activists (Lesselier 1999). The appeal to women has had limited effect, however, and women constitute a minority of FN voters (see Chapter 4).

Women's sections and parallel associations

In the 1970s, the influence of the MLF put extra pressure on the parties to demonstrate an interest in women's issues, and many either created or revived women's sections (Gaspard 1995: 235–6), although their autonomy was still severely limited. Nevertheless, women have brought their role within the parties onto the party agenda and made various demands for change. These include changes in the sexual division of labour, the timing of meetings, and the relation between the 'private' and 'public' lives of activists and candidates. For instance, the PSU women's section wrote:

> The parties fail to understand, in their language, their practice and the restricted nature of their concerns, the political nature of social relations outside production and in the family, the couple and daily life. They maintain a strict division between political and private life. They portray themselves as instruments for winning political power, tools for influencing the distribution of wealth, but they are silent on all other aspects of life. We women say that it is these other aspects of life which interest us.
>
> (Bouchardeau 1980: 78)

Women within the PS have been particularly vociferous, although they have disagreed amongst themselves over the best way to press their demands, and they were torn throughout the 1970s over the question of whether or not to establish a separate women's current. Organising separately, with the risk of ineffectiveness or isolation, or within male-dominated organisations, with the risk of subordination and being assigned to specific functions, has always been a strategic problem for women in politics. Yvette Roudy, for example, believed that 'The third tendency project and its ghetto strategy risked stalling or even blocking the new stage. Not to mention that autonomous feminism, divorced from socialist roots, risks drifting into unknown territories, or rather, too well-known territories' (Roudy 1978). The alternatives, however, were not much more attractive: promoting women within the party according to derisory quotas (15–20 per cent) or confining women's activism to social movements. Those who were attempting to form a women's tendency argued that women had a distinct political view on subjects as diverse as health, education, industry, nuclear power, economy, defence and foreign policy,

> because we have a different relationship to life, the earth and time. We have a contribution to make on left unity, class struggle, *autogestion*,

the party . . . Claiming our right to difference and organising autonomously within the party is initial proof of this.

(cited in Eyquem 1978)

It was precisely this assertion of women's specificity which was feared by others. Marie-Thérèse Eyquem (1978) argues that PS women should be seeking access to the universal, to politics on the same terms as men, not separating themselves from them.

At the 1979 party conference at Metz the women's current, referred to as the *Courant G*, represented one of the three positions on women. The other positions were represented by Roudy and by a splinter-group which included Françoise Gaspard. The *Courant G* was critical of the lack of analysis of patriarchy within the party and of the assumption that better access to employment was all that was required. Their main criticism, however, was the gap between the party's professed principles and its internal structure (Belden Fields 1986: 571–2). The *Courant G* published *Mignonnes allons voir sous la rose* until 1983 and supported Huguette Bouchardeau's candidacy for the presidency in 1981, provoking criticisms that they were undermining party unity (Appleton and Mazur 1993: 104). It brought new questions onto the party agenda including the abolition of the *cumul des mandats* (holding more than one electoral mandate at the same time), ecology, and the balance of power between men and women. It launched a petition demanding that the party select an equal number of male and female candidates in the 1979 European election, and although this was not passed by the National Convention, the quota was raised to 30 per cent. However, this small victory used up a lot of energy and, as the MLF lost its momentum, many women activists in both the PS and the PCF left politics (Gaspard 1995: 237). The *Courant G* disappeared in 1983 and became an association, *Association féministe pour une politique alternative* (AFPA), which was non-mixed, feminist and socialist and aimed to exert pressure on the PS from the outside. It lasted three years (Krakovitch 1996a: 203).

Recruitment of women to the PCF and the dissemination of the party's ideology were aided by the *Union des femmes françaises–Femmes solidaires* (UFF). Formed in 1945, it became associated with the PCF during the Cold War, acting as an apparently non-political public relations machine. Its activities during the 1950s and 1960s included education campaigns on painless childbirth, a national conference on lone mothers, campaigns for the right to professional training and the right to work, and campaigns against the stereotypical representation of women in school books. It later distanced itself from the party. In 1992, its leadership changed, and it became significantly more feminist, as can be seen in its publication *Clara Magazine* (Doumit el Khoury 1997: 55). The PCF now has a women's section at a national and a departmental level, as well as in workplace groups where there is a high proportion of women (Commission Femmes du PCF 1999).

The FN has numerous networks and satellite organisations which are particularly active on culture, morality, the family, and education. The women's organisation of the FN is called the *Cercle national femmes d'Europe* (CNFE) (Lesselier 1997: 42) which aims to inform women about social and family issues, education, politics, culture, and the moral breakdown of society (Laroche 1997: 153). It was founded in 1985 and held its first Congress in 1988. Martine Lehideux, FN MEP, has been its president since its creation. It has the full support of Le Pen and the FN. It publishes a twice-monthly bulletin and has groups and delegates in each region or department, including the DOM-TOM. It participates in FN demonstrations, rallies, and the demonstrations of Catholic fundamentalist groups, especially against abortion (Lesselier 1997: 58). Catholic organisations linked more or less closely with the FN inspire its attitude towards women. They accord French women the role of passing on their biological and cultural heritage, within a traditional family structure (Lesselier 1997: 43). In recent years the CNFE has made some concessions to the reality of women's lives in France, accepting the desire of some to work outside the home and encouraging political activity. In towns where the FN has municipal councillors, CNFE activists take responsibility where possible for pre-school children, education, and social care (Laroche 1997: 162).

Conclusion

Lovenduski and Norris (1993: 8) identify three party strategies for increasing the proportion of women in decision-making: rhetorical strategies, where women's demands are accepted and frequent references are made to the importance of having more women in office; positive or affirmative action, where special training is offered to women, targets are set and women are encouraged to put themselves forward for selection; and positive discrimination, where places are reserved for women. This, they find, is the least common, especially when it comes to elected office. They claim that the rhetorical approach often sets out with no commitment to real change (and they offer France as an example), but that it can be the beginning of a process (as was the case in the British Conservative Party).

Lovenduski and Norris (1993: 15) identify a common dynamic to claims for increased representation by women within the parties and the parties' responses to these claims. They state that once a party accepts a demand for sexual equality, it is vulnerable to arguments that the political representation of women is unjust. Women pushing for change need to secure agreement that more women should be nominated, then devise strategies to overcome the obstacles which stand before such an increase. Questions are often raised about the method of selection, and the élite's stategies for protecting its own power are often criticised. Initiatives on women's representation, then, lead to more radical initiatives on both sides. When the parties fail to respond, or respond inadequately, women increase their demands. As a result, rhetoric can be changed into positive action.

In France, demands from women within the parties, pressure from a campaign outside the party system, and strong approval from the public of the idea of an increase in women's political participation have combined in the 1990s to force parties to adopt the appropriate rhetoric. Andrew Appleton and Amy Mazur's (1993) main conclusion, drawn from their study of the RPR and PS in the early 1990s, was that:

> gender has had a significant impact upon the transformation of French political parties at the programmatic level, but less so at the organi-sational level. In other words, French parties have wholeheartedly embraced women's demands as campaign rhetoric, yet have been much more reluctant to incorporate these issues into the daily reality of party life ... Whereas parties have actively competed for 'the women's vote' by broadening their platforms to cover certain salient gender issues, they have been less forthcoming regarding strategies to promote the participation of women in party affairs. The absence of positive action strategies calls into question the extent to which trans-formed French political parties can be seen as modernised.
>
> (87)

Developments since the publication of this article mean that this is no longer entirely accurate, especially in the case of the PS. Since 1993, one of the most vocal demands from women within and outside the PS has been the equal representation of women in politics. This has meant that the parties have competed to embrace the rhetoric of parity and, in an effort to appear more committed than their rivals to such an obviously popular idea, have occasionally had to act on some of their pronounce-ments. The PS, since the 1994 European elections, has shown more commitment to feminising its own élite and elected bodies than it has to other gender issues. Appleton and Mazur's observation that this 'commit-ment' is superficial vote-seeking still holds, but it is nevertheless forcing change in one of the most male-dominated spheres of public life.

The somewhat unexpected move by the PS in the 1997 legislative elec-tions demonstrated the force of the pressure for change. At the same time as it has taken measures to increase women's representation in elected bodies and in its own internal structures, the PS has, however, failed to impress feminists with its policies, suggesting that its commitment to women is limited to moves which attract voters.

3 Women and the trade unions

French women's involvement with trade unions has a long history through which it is possible to trace a number of constant features. First, trade unions have not been able to mobilise women workers en masse in spite of the fact that the rate of their labour force participation has, since the end of the nineteenth century, been one of the highest in the world.[1] The result of this, and this is the second constant feature, is that the density of women's trade union membership (i.e. the proportion of those working who join a union) has been far smaller than that of men, and historically women have not been present in sufficient numbers to challenge the masculine model of the worker as constructed and maintained by the trade unions. At the beginning of the 1990s, figures provided by the CREDOC (Centre de recherche pour l'étude et l'observation des conditions de vie) showed that the density of women's trade union membership was 3.46 per cent compared with 10.6 per cent for men (Le Quentrec 1998: 143). Furthermore, the low density of unionisation amongst women workers has also meant that the pool of experienced women trade union activists and organisers from which decision-makers can be drawn has, in the past, been very small. According to figures relating to the late 1980s, women accounted for only 20 per cent of trade union officials, all levels included (Le Quentrec 1998: 142).

Various arguments have been put forward to explain the small numbers of women in trade unions. Women's absence from the labour movement is caused by their position within the relations of domination in the home and family which has traditionally prevented their equal participation in the labour market. Furthermore, when women become workers, it is in the economic interests of employers to reproduce those relations of domination in the workplace, and inequality in the workplace is, in turn, exploited by the unions in order to stop the progress of women in trade union work. The failure of women to get ahead at branch or company level is amplified at sub-national and national levels of trade union organisation. These arguments have been expanded and rehearsed elsewhere (Cook *et al.* 1992, Cunnison and Stageman 1993).

The lack of large numbers of activists and decision-makers has allowed trade unions, until relatively recently, to ignore women's specific or categorial issues and demands on the basis that these are not (class) mobilising. However, the growing importance of women in the labour force and their increasing activism outside the labour movement, coupled with the fact that trade union membership has continued to decline in the Fifth Republic, have forced unions to review their thinking in a bid to attract new members. It has also obliged unions to ask themselves whether the absence or silence of women within trade union structures has contributed to the low density of women members. Nevertheless, at the same time as unions have begun to ask questions about the representation of women and issues related to them, a process of integration of unions within a corporate system of interest representation at national and European level has emerged and has worked to disadvantage women greatly. Joni Lovenduski states, 'By creating gateways to governing élites through which men are vastly more likely to be qualified to pass than women, the growth of concertation impedes women's acquisition of political influence' (Lovenduski 1986: 204). It is therefore debatable as to what extent really significant qualitative and quantitative change has taken place in unions where women's participation and issues are concerned.

This chapter examines the attitudes of the two major trade union confederations (the *Confédération Générale du Travail* (CGT), and the *Confédération Française des Travailleurs Chrétiens* (CFTC/*Confédération Française Démocratique du Travail* CFDT)[2] to women workers and trade union members, the factors that have shaped these attitudes, and the impact that such attitudes have had on women's participation at the level of rank-and-file activism and that of decision-making. The original intention of this chapter was to focus mainly on the participation of women activists and decision-makers within trade unions, but this would have proved difficult as information on women who join trade unions in France is insufficient. There exist very few accounts of the experiences of women activists and decision-makers and scant statistical data relating to women's representation within trade unions from which one can build an adequate picture of women's trade union participation. Consequently this chapter's major focus is on trade unions' attitudes and policies towards women wage-earners. This is justifiable in the sense that the mechanisms of exclusion, control and resistance that are exercised within trade unions in relation to women determine the level and type of participation that women engage in. At the same time and wherever it has been possible, data relating to women's participation is included.

Two reasons explain the inclusion of a chapter on trade unions in a book about women and politics. First, it is often difficult to separate purely political activity from that carried out within the social and economic sphere. Where trade union activity is concerned, this separation becomes even more difficult as trade unions forge close links with political parties, they inform political agendas contributing to social and economic policy-making and are in return strongly influenced by party ideology, political agendas and strategies. Historically, although not from their origins, sections within French trade unionism have been as motivated by ideological and political concerns as by purely economic ones, in the belief that the working-class movement would achieve very little if it did not aim to conquer political power.[3] Certainly the two major unions today, CGT and CFDT, and the CFTC in the past, have established organic links with the PCF, PS and MRP respectively and have often operated as relay belts for the ideology of these parties.

Second, this book does not include a separate chapter on women and pressure groups in general, as research and analysis in this area are scant and are only beginning to be undertaken. Trade unions do, however, constitute important pressure groups which have advocated measures to promote the rights of women workers and which have fought against sexual discrimination in the workplace. An examination of women and trade unions may therefore allow one to draw some general conclusions about the participation of women in formal 'mixed' pressure group politics.

The continuation of a conflictual relationship: 1945–68[4]

The Fourth Republic's constitution accorded women full citizenship rights following their extensive participation in the Resistance and Liberation movements. The early post-war period saw a considerable increase in the number of trade union women (Colin 1975: 219)[5] as women participated massively in the strikes of 1947, reacting positively to the acquisition of new citizenship rights. In addition, certain measures taken by the trade unions appeared to indicate that the historically conflict-ridden relationship (arising from the long-prevalent trade union view of women as unequal partners) between women activists and their unions was set to improve and that the overwhelmingly masculine model of the wage-earner would change. For instance, as far as the CGT was concerned, among steps taken to recruit and integrate them into union structures, more women were being nominated as conference delegates and as candidates for election to union committees. Moreover, 1946 marked a first in trade union history when a woman was elected to the thirteen-strong national bureau (*bureau confédéral*) of the CGT, and in 1948 a resolution of the CGT's national conference led to the setting up of a national council of women (*conseil national des femmes*) to encourage women to become more involved in trade union activity and to resurrect and reorganise the *commissions féminines* (also referred to as *commissions femmes* or sometimes as *collectifs féminins*) which had been established at both national and federation levels during the inter-war years (Colin 1975: 219–25). In addition to these measures, the CGT launched a women's magazine, *Antoinette*, in 1955 as a means of communicating with women workers.

On the other hand, at the CFTC, a national commission for women (*Commission féminine confédérale* – CFC), made up of women only, was set up and met for the first time in April 1945, under the direction of Marie-Louise Danguy.[6] Danguy's main aims had been to push the CFTC to accept the twin principles of 'women's right to work' and 'equal pay for equal work' and to encourage women to undertake training in order to accede to decision-making posts in the union. Her successor, Simone Troisgros, was responsible for organising a series of national women's days (*journées nationales féminines*) in the 1950s and for launching a pamphlet entitled *Informations féminines*, for women activists, in 1954. In addition to furthering Danguy's goals, Troisgros' initiatives were aimed at creating autonomy for women within the CFTC (Ducrocq-Poirier and Thibault 1988: 13–19).

However, the optimism of women trade unionists and wage-earners was misplaced as, for a number of reasons, such initiatives led neither to an independent consideration of women's issues nor to the greater involvement of women in decision-making. First, the main trade unions, divided along ideological lines, were unable and unwilling to speak with one voice over women's (as over a number of other) issues. The Catholic CFTC continued to stress that the place of women was primarily in the home especially within the context of post-war depopulation and the requirement of a renewed labour force for the reconstruction of France. Thus, the CFC was never allowed to become an effective organ within the trade union; eventually 'right to work' and 'equal pay' campaigns died out while *Informations féminines* ceased to appear after fifteen issues. The CGT, also infected by party political consensus on pro-natalism, expressed support for a number of women's rights but did so mainly in terms of allowing women to work while continuing to fulfil their principal role as mothers. Hence, it favoured campaigns revolving around maternity and social security rights and the provision of childcare.

Second, trade unions, as class-based organisations, seemed incapable of adding a gender dimension to class-based strategies. Consequently, women's issues and autonomous action were always overridden by those of class. For instance, issues of reproductive rights (abortion and contraception) or of the domestic division of labour, it was argued, were 'private', and action in favour of such rights was not legitimate within the public sphere occupied by class issues. The idea that there could be a space at the intersection of the private and public spheres in which trade unionists could act in the interests of working (-class) women, was unthinkable. Madeleine Colin, a loyal communist and responsible for CGT women's issues in the post-war years, observed in retrospect, albeit in fairly muted terms: 'Insufficient consideration of women's issues by union leaders ... remained a weakness' (Colin 1975: 225).

Third, the masculine wage-earner model, which had historically constituted the focus of the trade unions' attention, persisted and, it can be argued, was even reinforced in the 1950s. The reason for this lies partly in state policies to push women back into the home but also in the evolution of the

French economy and the trade unions' response to this evolution. The sustained economic growth of the economy during this period had led to a sharp bifurcation of the French labour market which, in turn, had created a capital-intensive sector (consisting of established industries such as iron and steel, mining and oil refining, automobile, transport and machine tools, and of 'newer' ones such as nuclear, electronics and communications) where complex tasks requiring specialist training and experience were relatively well paid, and where workers gaining sector-specific (or even firm-specific) expertise had stable employment conditions, often becoming a fixed factor of production in the same way as the capital equipment with which they worked. This sector was clearly separable from a labour-intensive sector (light manufacturing and services) within which jobs attached to low pay and status increased in line with demand for goods and services but which could be easily and severely reduced during periods of economic decline. The response of trade unions to this situation was to concentrate their attention and action even more upon the key industries in the capital-intensive sector occupied by a skilled and stable male workforce, and hence a more powerful and permanent trade union membership. By contrast, trade union organisation within the labour-intensive sectors of the economy, where a high proportion of the semi-skilled and unskilled workforce was made up by women and migrants, was either weak or non-existent. Consequently, campaigns and action in favour of the right to work or against the devaluation of skills ignored women workers while identifying fundamental trade union rights and job skills with those of male workers.

It is fair to say, then, that by the time the Fifth Republic was established women were far from becoming equal partners with men within the labour force and within trade unions. Instead they were actively encouraged and educated, by the state and political parties, to become and remain mothers and homemakers.[7] During the 1960s there was little movement from these positions which can be said to have impacted positively on the lives of women wage-earners and trade unionists. The unions may have kept up a certain amount of rhetoric regarding the importance of women's aspirations and rights; for example, when the new CFDT was brought into existence in 1964, its founding principles acknowledged women's desire to be integrated into society, work and trade unionism and stated the union's commitment to involve more women in trade union organisation and activity. The CGT, on the other hand, faced with yet another competitor for increased membership, decided to use its women's magazine, *Antoinette*[8] as more of a campaigning organ in order to reach a larger number of women in and outside the workplace, with the magazine engaging a 'real team of specialists' (Simon 1981: 23) whose job was to head new features discussing 'hard' trade union, social and political issues.

However, what the trade unions did rather than what they said about women's involvement was more revealing of the fact that while they did not wish to be encumbered by the question of women's rights, they never-theless required and encouraged women's solidarity action in favour of male workers. In 1967, a massive strike of metalworkers in Saint-Nazaire, seeking equal wages with their Parisian counterparts, was joined by women office workers putting forward specific demands. The latter, supported by activists from women's associations such as the Union des femmes françaises (UFF), organised numerous women's demonstrations. These demonstrations were not welcomed by local trade union officials, even though they raised the public profile of the strike, on the basis that the core of the strike was composed of male workers whose demands would be diluted by the presence of women in protest over their own wages and working conditions. It is interesting to note, however, that previous dockers' and foundry workers' strikes in 1963 and 1964, in the same area, had encouraged and enjoyed the support of women workers and associations such as the UFF, but only because women had acted purely as auxiliaries to the men on those occasions. As such, their action as wives rather than as co-workers had been applauded, and trade union leaders were quick to thank the women involved for their solidarity action. Dominique Loiseau comments, 'In real life, if not in theory, the labour movement recognises with difficulty the organisation of "its" women, even if it raises their action as a model of solidarity' (1996: 158).

If trade unions showed interest in organising women and in defending their interests, it was because they were driven by an internal logic (that is, the desire to increase membership). The wider and external social fact that the gender profile of the most dynamic part of the working popula-tion – the intermediate age (25–45-year-olds) and occupational groups (middle management and supervisory categories and employees), had been changing, in favour of women, since the 1950s left them unmoved about addressing new generations of women workers, their aspirations and rights in a different way. That these women were unlikely to tolerate the trade union attitudes and behaviour endured by their mothers and that their different aspirations might lead them away from the traditional forms of trade union struggle, over mainly economistic issues, appeared to be unan-ticipated. This explains why the events of May 1968, and particularly the militancy of women, took the trade unions by surprise, forcing them to pay more attention to a large constituency of workers which was not willing to be ignored.

The impact of May 1968 on the relationship between women and trade unions

As far as the trade unions' relationship with women wage-earners was concerned, the events of May 1968 demonstrated two important things. First, it is clear that women constituted a sizeable proportion of strikers and demonstrators despite the fact that, unlike the case of the student movement, the images of thousands of striking workers retained by the collective memory are those at the gates of male bastions such as the Renault-Billancourt and Sud-Aviation factories. Although it is impossible to quantify the participation of women in the trade union action of this period, one can gain some idea as to its extent through individual accounts. For example, of 550,000 striking workers in the clothing industry of the (department of) Nord, almost one-third were women (Pineau 1969: 6). In certain industrial sectors female participation rates equalled or even exceeded those of their male counterparts: in textiles and electrical goods, women accounted for 53 per cent of strikers and 51 per cent in the food industry (Charzat 1972: 175). At the other end of the scale, in a sector such as the Post Office's National Girobank service, dominated by female staff (up to 95 per cent in some branches), almost all those who went on strike or occupied workplaces were women (Granger and Jersey 1988: 24). It is also fair to assume that large numbers of women were prevented from participating due to the fact that they had childcare and other domestic responsibilities.

Second, the presence of women in such large numbers had fostered a heightened awareness of the gap which existed between their aspirations and demands and those articulated by the trade unions on behalf of their members. While women workers were not the first to strike or to occupy workplaces, neither were they the first to vote a return to work. The strike movement in which they had been active participants had led many activists to think that the moment had arrived to make a break with the traditional roles they had played both in the home and at work, and while they acknowledged that important economic gains had been made in terms of wage rises, reduction of the working week and so on, the sentiment that one could go well beyond the bread and butter demands was widespread (Granger and Jersey 1988: 24). Furthermore, once back at work, the confidence that the strike movement had given them inspired many to work-to-rule, to slow down work rates or to carry out other industrial action if they felt that their employers were not respecting workers' and trade unionists' rights. A National Girobank employee and CFDT branch representative recalled that in undertaking such action, very often they received little support from their trade unions (Granger and Jersey 1988: 25). Nor did their unions always support new ways of formulating demands or organising trade union duties at work (an important right gained as a result of the May strikes). She observed, 'You could say that at National Girobank we tried to practise a different type of trade unionism which was never really recognised by the union at industry level . . . In their eyes, our work-to-rules were not real strikes' (Granger and Jersey 1988: 25). In the period following the May events, few women activists made immediate connections between this different type of trade unionism and feminism:

At the time, I made no connection between this type of action [described above] and feminism. But later, we discussed it again and analysed it differently. We realised that we had done something which did not fit the masculine model ... It wasn't feminism but we had tried to take into account the reality of our situation.

(Granger and Jersey 1988: 25)

As far as women's engagement in industrial action is concerned, Maruani (1979: 83–197) presents monographs of four major strikes which were different, she argues, from pre-1968 women's strikes not only because they gave rise to 'a collective, public consideration of problems specific to women' but also because they led to 'the emergence of a female awareness and identity which implanted itself onto class solidarities without displacing them' (78).

In addition to industrial action, women trade unionists also became involved in debates and campaigns outside work, in particular those in favour of abortion and free contraception, and the clearest expression of the awareness gained by women trade unionists through strike action and through their involvement in feminist activism outside work was to be found in the workplace women's groups (*groupes femmes d'entreprises*) which mushroomed from the early 1970s and which were brought together under the umbrella of the French women's movement, the *Mouvement de libération des femmes*. Maruani's (1979: 218–33) study of these groups indicates that they were established mainly in the Paris region and to a lesser extent in large cities such as Lyon and Marseilles. Although informal in their organisation and structures, these groups acted as a bridge not only between the trade unions and the women's movement but also between the unions and non-unionised women. In Paris, a *coordination*[9] of *groupes femmes d'entreprise* was set up and active from the mid-1970s. At the beginning it brought together representatives of workplace groups (both CFDT and CGT members) only, but by 1977 it also included representatives of CFDT and CGT women's commissions.[10] The Paris coordination of these groups was most active around issues of abortion/contraception, sexuality and violence against women.

Initially these groups were regarded with great suspicion not only by employers but also by local male trade union officials and were therefore often set up quietly, only revealing themselves at times of debate and/or action over specific issues. This was particularly so in workplaces dominated by the CGT from whose official discourse these *groupes femmes* were absent until 1977. Their presence was more easily accepted within the CFDT although even there they were often dismissed as an ultra-feminist, ultra-left destabilising influence. The presence and development of these women's groups meant that women trade unionists began to apply feminist analyses of women's place and role in society to their experiences at work, and this gave rise to a feminist critique of the trade unions.

There is little space here to do more than to summarise the feminist critique of trade unions. Besides, some of what was being said in the late 1960s and early 1970s had been debated before and a more detailed examination of it can be found elsewhere.[11] Essentially, what feminists were saying about trade unions may be condensed under four main points. First, trade unions only recognised two strictly separate categories of women: that of wage-earner, and therefore one which fitted into their economistic model of trade union organisation and action, and that of housewife, which did not. This purely economistic model was challenged by feminists on the basis that, not only did millions of women wage-earners bear the major burden of childcare and domestic responsibilities, but also that if trade unions were really interested in mobilising more women trade union members, then they had to discuss the rights of all women, regardless of whether they were wage-earners or not. Second, trade unions were male-dominated organisations which identified the rights of workers with those of male workers. Women's particular problems were therefore not given sufficient consideration. Third, not only were trade unions composed of men who displayed sexist attitudes and behaviour, but such sexism was necessarily reinforced as men were at the heart of action and decision-making. Fourth and consequently, women wage-earners had always felt dissatisfied and alienated from the trade unions despite their committing vast amounts of time and energy to labour movement activities. In the 1960s and 1970s this sense of alienation was felt more intensely as women generally became more gender conscious in the context of their growing numbers in the workforce and of the developing women's movement.

In the light of this critique, the trade unions were unable to remain unresponsive. If they were to continue to make credible claims about representing workers' interests, they had to be seen to consider seriously the problems and demands of almost 40 per cent of the workforce. Besides, it would be difficult to ignore within their own ranks the gender issues that wider society and political parties were beginning to notice and debate. The trade unions, it would appear, had to consider two main questions: increasing the presence and involvement of women at all organisational and structural levels; and proposing and fighting for solutions to problems faced by women workers.

1968–81: trade unions and feminism

Although the events of May 1968 created a culture in which trade unions, in the 1970s and beyond, considered it important to consider the place and role of women more seriously, the socio-economic context of the following years also explains why they were compelled to pursue this question more actively. By the late 1960s, France was experiencing a slow-down in economic growth. Traditional heavy industries such as steel, shipbuilding and energy were losing their world-class edge as exports fell; for example,

French energy exports were almost halved between 1958 and 1965 (Trotignan 1985: 421). These were the industries in which trade unions were well implanted and from whose workers they drew strength. On the other hand, service industries and office employment were in expansion. This sector of the economy was increasingly employing women as a cheaper and more readily disposable source of labour; for instance, between 1962 and 1968, the number of women in the aggregate group *employés* had increased by 30.6 per cent and composed almost 75 per cent of the whole group (INSEE 1973: 19). The process in which traditional male-dominated industries diminished, threatening to reduce trade union strength, was exacerbated in the 1970s and 1980s as a result of the oil crisis of 1974 and the state's market deregulation policies respectively. Consequently, trade unions in France, as in all industrialised countries, were forced to look at ways of combating the drop in membership that was concomitant with the changes described above. One of the ways to do this was to attract new generations of women workers which had entered the labour market.[12] The unions had to make themselves more gender-conscious and women-friendly.

The 1970s witnessed a radicalisation of discourse (in terms of adopting feminist ideas) as well as increased measures and action aimed at involving women at various levels of trade union organisation and taking on board women's problems and issues. However, radical discourse and women-centred action did not necessarily occur in tandem within each union. It would be true to say that while the CFDT engaged in new thinking and radical discourse, connecting class struggle and women's liberation, the CGT emphasised the development of a women-specific sector and the participation of women within it.

The CFDT: the feminist union?

As far as the CFDT was concerned, 1970 marked an important starting point of a three-stage theoretical analysis of women workers under capitalism. Maruani (1979: 39) refers to this change in terms of a pronounced, linear evolution prompted at the thirty-fifth CFDT Congress where delegates heard the union's first-stage analysis of class struggle and women's liberation. Jeannette Laot (1981: 80) points out that although this analysis was presented for the first time in 1970, research and the work of raising awareness within the leadership of the trade union, undertaken by the women-only *Commission féminine confédérale* (CFC),[13] had commenced in the early 1960s. In this first stage of analysis, it was accepted not only that women formed an 'overexploited' (*sur-exploité*) part of the working class but that they were overexploited because of so-called natural sex roles which assigned to them the additional burden of domestic labour. The Congress broke with past thinking by challenging the notion of predetermined sex roles and by denouncing the 'mentalities' contributing to such thinking.

By the time of its 1973 Congress, the CFDT's analysis had developed to put forward the notion of 'the domination of women by men', recognising that an effective struggle against women's overexploitation could not be contained within the workplace but had to be waged in wider society. Finally, the thirty-seventh Congress of 1976 confirmed the CFDT's intention to fight against the 'specific nature of women's oppression' (Laot 1981: 216). In this respect, the trade union called on both union officials and rank-and-file members to struggle against the relations of domination within the family on a political as well as personal level as part of the general struggle for democratic socialism or *socialisme autogestionnaire*.[14] The struggle against the specific oppression of women would include not only the establishment of women's rights in the workplace but also the demand for women's control over their own fertility and sexuality, the challenging of the sexual division of labour in the home, and of violence against women whether physical, verbal or graphic. In other words the CFDT had recognised a dual fight: against both capitalism and patriarchy. The Congress report encouraged the setting up of (mixed) commissions (*commissions de réflexion et d'action*) at all levels of the union in order to carry the struggle forward (Laot 1981: 216).

The CFDT's eagerness to present a feminist analysis of the situation of women workers and to defend and further the rights of women workers both inside and beyond the workplace has been variously applauded especially when compared with the CGT's early antagonism towards the feminist and other post-1968 social movements.[15] However, the CFDT's adoption of a radical feminist analysis and attendant discourse concealed a deep-rooted unwillingness to make a place for women in its decision-making structures which in turn limited its capacity to take on board women's issues and problems in practice.

In practice, the union's record was not good. In 1970, the union had already dissolved the women-only CFC which had, until then, provided a focus at national level for women's issues and problems and which had been so instrumental in hammering out the CFDT's feminist analysis of the position of women workers under a patriarchal capitalist system. The replacement of the women-only CFC by a 'mixed' national commission for women's affairs had a number of consequences. First, any form of autonomous organisation of women within the CFDT began to disappear as of 1970 and, for instance, women-only commissions (*commissions syndicales*) which had existed at federation and local levels were also replaced by mixed commissions. The emergence of the mixed commissions meant that women's quantitative presence was not only diminished within the CFCs but also in other sections of the CFDT. The CFCs had always constituted an important training ground for women who wished to work as trade union officials at various levels and in sections other than those dealing specifically with women's issues.

Second, the mixed commission decided to abandon claims for any statutory arrangements ensuring a minimum presence of women in posts of responsibility at national level and below. Instead it was argued that women would automatically gain responsibility, at all levels, in a democratically functioning trade union. However, when it became clear that this was not happening, a debate on quotas developed at the union's thirty-eighth Congress in 1979 and intensified in 1981 when Jeannette Laot, the only woman on the CFDT's thirty-one-member national bureau, left to join Mitterrand's Elysée office as head of the women's employment mission. Pro-quota activists were not to win the day.[16] Nevertheless, in 1982, the union's thirty-ninth Congress accepted the principle of a quota (of 25 per cent) for posts of responsibility amid much resistance and recrimination, but then failed to apply it in re-electing the national executive commission, instead reaching a compromise as far as elections to the national bureau were concerned: so, in order to avoid a direct replacement of men by women, the national bureau's membership was increased from 31 to 39 so that the quota of 25 per cent would be respected.[17]

Third, the mixed commission established in 1970 and which barely functioned due to inquorate meetings and general apathy, was incapable of drawing up a coherent programme of claims in favour of women workers.

Consequently, initiatives taken in the 1970s to promote women's issues and to involve women in the trade union were of an *ad hoc* nature. In the face of the obvious sclerosis of the mixed commission in charge of women's affairs and faced with the quota debate started at the thirty-eighth Congress, a women workers' commission (*commission travailleuses*), presided over by a five-member national secretariat of women workers (*secrétariat national travailleuses*), was re-established in 1979. Apart from the organisation of several conferences and study days, resulting in a couple of publications,[18] the new commission and secretariat's existence remained a gesture which failed to move the CFDT from radical discourse to a coherent and concrete programme of claims and action. This deficiency was criticised not only at grassroots level – one activist of the CFDT–SGEN (*Syndicat national d'enseignement général*) teachers' federation was to remark: 'we fought [more] in terms of a conception of trade unionism than in terms of the actual problems faced by women' (Simon 1981: 10) – it was also recognised at the highest level. In her introductory report to the CFDT's February 1978 conference on women's employment and trade union action, Jeannette Laot admitted: 'If we are clear, in terms of our analysis, our long-term project and our demands, about how to change the situation of women workers . . . we cannot say the same about how to progress to action' (1978: 17).

The lack of progress in concrete demands and action can be explained by two factors. First, the CFDT, deeply marked by a masculine culture, was doubtful about the development of women-only commissions within its organisation and structures and was resistant to the penetration of women into decision-making posts. The CFTC/CFDT's history had been marked by a tradition of women's trade unions (*syndicats féminins*) operating alongside the main union which meant that for a long period (1919–45) women did not occupy the same structures as men. The process to accept women within the trade union has therefore been long and difficult.

Second, during the late 1970s, the union became intensely engaged in a debate about general strategy, or *recentrage*[19] as it became known, which in fact allowed little or no consideration of women's place and role within the union. So, while women represented about 35 to 40 per cent of the union's total membership in the 1970s (Maruani 1979: 16), their representation in sites of decision-making was much lower. For example, in 1976 women accounted for under 19 per cent of Congress delegates (Lalu and Clément 1977) and by 1979 this figure had fallen to just over 10 per cent (Simon 1981: 58). Similarly, women represented, on average, 6 per cent of the membership of regional bureaux, 12 per cent of members of regional councils and secretariats (Simon 1981: 58) and probably under 10 per cent of regional executive commissions, based on returns from the Haut Normandie region (UR–CFDT Haut Normandie 1978: 10). Federations appeared to involve more women in their structures, with a 12 to 15 per cent participation rate.[20]

If the CFDT's awareness of women's issues can be measured by its openness to feminist ideas and the progression of its gendered analysis of capitalism and trade union action, then the CGT's approach can be described as slow on theory but more focused on developing a women-specific sector within its structures and organisation and on putting forward programmes of claims as a means of mobilising women wage-earners and recruiting new members.

The CGT: a late awakening

The development of a women-specific sector within the CGT was not new to the post-1968 period but can be traced back to the Popular Front years. Since the 1960s, however, this sector has included women's commissions at national, federation, departmental and branch level, the organisation of departmental, federation and national inter-professional women's conferences every four years, and the magazine *Antoinette*. After 1968 it was the work of the women's commissions which was particularly emphasised as crucial to the recruitment of women to the CGT and to their promotion to posts of responsibility within the union (Colin 1975: 227).

While the CGT has stressed the importance of its women's commissions at all levels, the latter have worked towards recruitment and promotion of women with little central support. It is impossible to say whether or not the proportion of women in the CGT increased during the 1970s as figures (estimates) have ranged from 25 to 35 per cent (Colin 1975: 197,

Rogerat 1978: 87,[21] Simon 1981: 13). However, evidence gathered from branch activists often suggests that women's participation in strike movements in May 1968 and subsequently resulted in increased membership for the union (Chardin 1973).[22] Similarly, as far as the representation of women in decision-making posts is concerned, the problem of availability and reliability of figures persists. In 1977, the CGT claimed to be at the top of the league as far as women's participation in trade union decision-making was concerned: for example, women made up 27 per cent of its national executive commission, almost 20 per cent of its national bureau, and on average 15.8 per cent and 19.4 per cent of its federation and departmental executive commissions respectively (Rogerat 1978: 97–8). However, the union has often encouraged and used the presence of women in its structures in order to counter criticism of its lack of theoretical reflection on women wage-earners and women's liberation.

As far as theoretical analysis was concerned, the CGT refused, in the early 1970s, to move beyond the idea of capitalist 'overexploitation' of women towards what it called a position of 'essential egalitarianism' (*égalitarisme intégral*) as advocated by the CFDT. In May 1973, at the CGT's fifth conference on women wage-earners, Christiane Gilles (confederal secretary, responsible for the women's sector) explained:

> Our critics maintain that equality between the sexes is achieved through the equal division of domestic responsibilities between men and women. We also believe that it is not up to women to carry out all or even most of the housework. But the reality lived by the great majority of women workers is still different . . .
> It is really presumptuous to state that a mother and father play a strictly equal role at all stages of a child's development when even different schools of thought in the human sciences disagree . . .
> (Quoted in Maruani 1979: 37)

The CGT position was that, in order to change women's inferior position in society, solutions had to be sought and implemented in the workplace and the struggle against capitalism had to include an attack on inequalities between men and women at work. In this respect, the CGT's fifth conference on women wage-earners presented, in 1973, a set of concrete demands which were outlined in *Le programme revendicatif des femmes salariées de mai 1973* (CGT 1973: 235–47).[23] In addition, the CGT view was that the development of a women's sector would help the union to formulate and fight for demands more legitimately and hence more effectively. The union, therefore, encouraged the establishment of women's trade union commissions from national down to branch level.

In spite of the CGT's distrust of radical feminist thinking, there were indications that the union could not remain immune to its influences indefinitely. To begin with, these indications were evident in the standpoint of the CGT's women's magazine *Antoinette*. During the 1960s, the magazine, under editor Annick Fabre, followed a safe path posing no threat to the union's position on women. However, in 1969, its editorship was taken over by Chantal Rogerat who began to make immediate changes. Under her, the 'feminine' content (romantic picture stories, good housekeeping articles) was either removed or reduced. Instead, the magazine introduced trade union news, social issue reports and, from 1975, began to introduce discussion of women's liberation issues. By 1977, the magazine's tone had become distinctly feminist.

Another indication of change in the CGT's attitude towards feminist thinking came in 1974 when, in the context of a unity in action pact signed between the CGT and the CFDT, the two unions also made an agreement on the demands of women wage-earners. The *rapprochement* between the two trade unions, concretised by the unity in action pact, took place in the context of the Union of the Left established in 1972 between the PCF and PS. One of the principles laid down in the agreement referred to the 'inferiorised position of women at work, within the family and in society' (Rogerat 1996: 118). While the interrelation between work, family and society may have long been accepted by the CFDT, for the CGT the statement of such a principle was out of step with its normal thinking. The agreement of 1974 helped prepare the ground for a turning point in the CGT's analysis of women, work and trade union activity three years later.

The period between 1974 and 1977 saw a steady build-up of pressure for the CGT to recognise feminist arguments in its analysis: in 1975, the union contracted IFOP (*Institut français d'opinion publique*) to carry out a survey ('*Femmes à l'usine et au bureau*') amongst 1,931 women workers. It found that 81 per cent of respondents felt that trade unions ought to consider and fight for solutions to women's specific problems (Simon 1981: 7). Furthermore, a Louis Harris poll two years later, showed that only 12 per cent of women thought that trade unions were willing and able to defend their interests (Lalu and Clément 1977).

The trade union's sixth national conference on women wage-earners, held in 1977, admitted for the first time that a struggle against male domination and the exploitation of women in the private sphere was as important as the fight against discrimination against women at work. Consequently, a programme of demands, updating *Le programme revendicatif des femmes salariées de mai 1973* and contained in *La charte revendicative de 1977* (Rogerat 1978: 123–43), was drawn up, presented to delegates and subsequently approved by the union's national executive commission. As Maruani emphasises, the 1977 text was fuller; it included all the demands of 1973 but was significantly different in three respects (Maruani 1979: 49). First, the right to work was recognised as a fundamental demand together with a rejection of the ideas that women, unlike men, exercised choice in going to work or that a woman's wage was supplementary to the main family income. Hence, this demand came at the top of the list whereas in 1973, it had been buried in a section on employment. Second, the CGT, in recognising male domination over women within the home and the family, demanded measures enabling men to share family responsibilities and domestic tasks equally with women. Third, there appeared a new theme related to the right of women to access cultural and leisure activities on an equal basis with men. These changes indicated a clear move away from the 1973 refusal of *égalitarisme intégral*. While it is true that in 1977 the CGT was only confirming feminist ideas which had already been embraced by a good proportion of its women activists, one cannot underestimate the effect of the contributions made at the conference by CGT secretaries Christiane Gilles and Jean-Louis Moynot. In particular, Moynot's speech came as a 'liberating bombshell' (Simon 1981: 8), provoking the majority of delegates to speak out angrily, for the first time in a large public forum, against the sexist attitudes of CGT men and 'sex segregation' within the union without fear of being marginalised or expelled.[24]

However, the openness exhibited by the leadership of the 1977 conference was not shared by the entirety of the union leadership. Conservative elements within the union's national bureau, alarmed by the fervent feminist views of women activists, were unwilling to approve the *La charte revendicative* as presented at the conference and backed by the executive commission. An amended version finally adopted by the CGT in November 1977 was guarded in its references to feminist ideas and to the use of feminist terms (CGT 1978). Besides, the union circulated a mere 6,000 copies of the conference report and programme of demands thus ensuring that only a small part of its 2 million-strong membership remained informed of the debates and expression of anger that had taken place (Simon 1981: 9). Only a year later, in 1978, it appeared that a phase of regression was setting in as far as the question of women was concerned. At the union's fortieth Congress, in the same year, not only were there fewer women delegates than in previous years, but the question of women wage-earners was hardly raised and, most significantly, Chantal Rogerat, *Antoinette*'s editor since 1969, was edged out of the executive commission. One activist's view was that, 'For the majority of [the union's] leaders and men . . . the fact that we had the sixth conference and that the executive committee had signed the programme, meant that the "women" question was resolved' (Simon 1981: 9).

The CGT's retreat can partly be explained in terms of the fact that, like the CFDT, it remained fundamentally a male-dominated union in which men were just not interested in the problems of women wage-earners. In addition, however, the union's strong ties with the PCF meant that, with the breakdown of left unity between the PCF and the PS, in the run-up to the 1978 legislative elections, the CGT was forced to review its relationship with the CFDT and to retreat to 'workerist' (*ouvriériste*)[25] positions which set it apart from those of its rival. In this, the CGT was simply following the PCF, which returned to crude workerism on a range of questions including that of feminism and feminist activism. It was in 1978 that the Communist feminist collective *Elles voient rouge* was accused by the PCF of misunderstanding the nature of oppression, and was forced outside the party as a result of a critical article published by members of the collective in *Le Monde* on 12 June (see Chapter 2).

The retreat to such positions meant that only working-class interests could be defended without risk of being diluted by specific 'categorial' demands. Nevertheless, at the beginning of the 1980s, the CGT leadership's retrograde attitudes sat uneasily next to the rebellious expression that the sixth women's conference had unleashed amongst women activists and members generally and especially in those sectors where workplace women's groups were active (banking, broadcast media, post and telecommunications, civil service). In seeking to minimise conflict with its women activists, the CGT sheltered (as always, at times of such conflict) under rhetoric about its women's sector and the quantitative presence (greater than in other unions) of women in union structures.

While the trade unions had made some efforts during the 1970s to make women more visible within their organisation and structures and to consider women workers' specific problems at work, these efforts did not produce a critical difference to the collective role and place of women trade unionists and wage-earners. However, within both unions there developed a greater sensitivity to individual problems. The 1970s saw an increased awareness and willingness, at local levels, to deal with problems relating to the working conditions of individual women members.[26]

1982–98: the (re)marginalisation of working women's rights and demands

The early 1980s marked the beginning of a difficult period for French trade unionism in which the movement experienced a considerable drop in its membership which led to a shrinking of the unions' field of action and manoeuvre. It was also in this period that the specific problems and demands of women wage-earners began to be ignored as feminist thinking ceased to challenge and inform trade unions and women's impact in decision-making lessened. The interplay of a number of factors explains why this divergence between feminism and trade unionism occurred in the early 1980s and why it has intensified from that time to the present.

First, 1981 saw the election of a government of the left for the first time since the Liberation period of 1945–7. The election of a government whose societal goals coincided with those of the trade unions meant that the latter no longer found themselves in the familiar opposition role occupied for over three decades. The importance, as they saw it, of supporting a trade union friendly government in the face of the traditional enemy, the right, robbed them of their capacity to contest government policy or to propose alternatives in the early to mid-1980s. If criticism was levelled at the left's policy, it was directed more at the way in which it was carried out rather than at its rationale or content, thus making the unions unpopular with wage-earners and weakening their position *vis-à-vis* employers. It could be argued, then, that the left in government actually contributed to a certain weakening of the unions in the early 1980s.

This difficulty was compounded throughout the 1980s and 1990s not only by the return of governments of the right from 1986–8 and from 1993–7, but also by external, global pressures. The triumph of neo-liberal policies in major world economies (USA, Japan, Germany), leading to market deregulation, a greater orientation towards competitiveness and therefore to massive cost-cutting operations by companies (under the guise of 'modernisation') meant that French trade unions, like their counterparts in other industrialised countries, saw their power considerably reduced. At the same time, the development of corporatist arrangements at the national and especially the European level (the EU's Social Dialogue since the mid-1980s) meant that the trade unions were drawn into a tripartite relationship with employers and the state whereby agreement to participate, as a 'social partner',[27] in the settlement of certain urgent and high-priority policy questions is rewarded by apparently advantageous settlements for their members. In these circumstances, the self-preservation reflexes of the trade unions and their greater institutionalisation or corporatisation in industrial relations have meant that they have been unable and unwilling to challenge the socio-economic structures and social relations in which their role has become compromised and in which the employers wield the real power. Furthermore, within this context, women wage-earners and trade union activists, in common with other groups that are more diffuse in their organisation, or that are not considered as strictly economic interest groups, are prevented from gaining representation and influence in socio-economic policy-making (Lovenduski 1986: 204).

A second factor accounting for the divergence between feminist thinking and trade union strategy is the disintegration of the post-1968 women's movement in the 1980s, in part a consequence of the destructive conflicts between the movement's different constituent currents and in part due to the institutionalisation of feminism whereby the new Socialist Ministry of Women's rights not only, arguably, appropriated MLF issues but, in addition, invited leading feminists (including leading figures from the trade unions such as Jeannette Laot and Christiane Gilles) to play a role within the Ministry or related agencies, and subsidised certain feminist groups and conferences in an attempt to control, if not remove, the focus of feminist opposition outside its bounds (see Chapter 7). The loss of focus and subsequent immobilisation of the women's movement in the 1980s meant that the unions were no longer subjected to the level of pressure which had been exerted on them by feminists (union members and otherwise) during the 1970s to integrate a gender dimension in their thinking and strategy.

Third, the institutionalisation of feminism and the co-option of women's rights issues by the Ministry of Women's Rights between 1981 and 1986 gave the unions a further excuse to withdraw from previous commitments to advancing women's specific demands. Since then, initiatives and proposals for legislation relating to women's rights have been left to government and have either been backed or contested depending on the trade union concerned and on the political climate.

Nevertheless, during the 1990s both unions have had to remain open to the question of women's representation within their own organisations and structures as a result of the campaigning work of the Women's Committee of the European Trade Union Confederation (ETUC) to increase women's representation in trade unions,[28] and the idea of parity which has enjoyed growing public acceptance, since it was raised in the early 1990s (see Chapter 8). Both the CFDT and the CGT have launched a debate around the theme and strategy of 'mixity' (*mixité*) which comprises voluntarist measures to ensure the more or less equal presence of men and women in all trade union structures.

While the above summary of the factors influencing trade union strategy towards women in the 1980s and 1990s refers to both the CGT and CFDT without distinction, there are differences in the positions taken and strategies pursued by the two unions, and these are noted below.

The CFDT: the growing divide between leaders and women activists

Between 1977 and 1979, the debate over *recentrage* or the 'return to reality' had produced, according to Marie-Noëlle Thibault (Zancarini-Fournel 1996: 219), two conflicting interpretations within the CFDT: a 'movementist' one in which workers' real problems and demands as well as engagement in mass struggle constituted reality, and an alternative 'institutional' interpretation which preferred to construct a reality in which the presence of trade unions within institutions was crucial to the interests of their members and hence to their survival. By the beginning of the 1980s, in the context of the political and socio-economic situation described at the beginning of this section, it was the second interpretation which triumphed and which was to inform the CFDT's thinking and strategy in the 1980s and 1990s. The 'realism' of institutions stifled the realism of trade union (and within it feminist) activism and struggle which has always been a key factor in the advancement of workers' rights generally and those of women wage-earners specifically.

In the early to mid-1980s, the CFDT supported socialist government initiatives in favour of advancing women's rights (for example, policies relating to employment and state funding of abortion) through its women's commission and through the office of Jeannette Laot who, in 1982, was appointed to the union's executive commission, a year after she had left the CFDT national bureau to join Mitterrand's Elysée team. At the same time, however, eager to become an influential social partner in a changing industrial relations environment, the CFDT leadership began to think and talk in terms of adaptation and modernisation. The basic argument put forward was that capitalism had changed in the 1970s, emerging in the 1980s as a system which was less rigid in its work organisation (for instance, it had moved away from Taylorist production) and that the aggressive nature of ownership had given way to a more accommodating and compromising management culture. Unions, CFDT leaders argued, could no longer respond to this change in a 'crudely anti-capitalist' fashion, which fuels conflict, as this was neither in their interests (since it alienated potential and existing members) nor in the interests of the French economy. Instead, they would have to work to promote and further the changes that had already taken place within capitalism. Following this argument then, the CFDT advocated not only the recognition of employers and management as legitimate decision-makers and the need for unions to enter into negotiation with them at company and industry level, but also suggested that certain proposals mooted by employers and government could be turned to the advantage of workers. For example, in presenting proposals to achieve full employment, the CFDT was prepared to consider so-called flexible working patterns: the expansion of short-term and part-time posts, acceptance of lower pay rises, shorter working hours and so on. As women were already the most likely group of wage-earners to be engaged in 'flexible' posts, the progression of such forms of employment would necessarily have the most impact on them.

The result of the CFDT's growing acceptance of flexibility was that, while agreeing to implement Socialist reforms, it did very little or nothing to advocate change in the situation in which reforms had to be applied. This is illustrated well by the union's attitude towards the 'equal employment' legislation of 1983. While the union accepted the principles of equal employment, it argued that the best way of implementing professional equality was through direct negotiations with employers at company level. This could involve negotiation over cases in which individual women or groups of women may have suffered unequal treatment on the basis of lesser qualifications or because of their part-time status. For instance, employers often argued that women were passed over for promotion because their qualifications did not match those of their male counterparts. Some cases were winnable, others were not, but what the CFDT refused to do was mobilise its membership and wage-earners generally over the issue of professional equality by consistently and actively demanding better training opportunities and structures for women throughout the economy. For example, at its 1987 women's conference, the union was content to point to greater opportunities for women to access new sectors of work, such as information technology. While encouraging women to seize these opportunities, which in any case were vastly overestimated, delegates were given little indication of how this might be achieved and, while continuing to adopt a feminist discourse, the ideological debate of previous years linking women's lack of opportunities and training with their role in the family was largely absent on the conference platform. CFDT women activists, dissatisfied with their union's position, found it almost impossible to gain access to the increasingly formalised gateways to decision-making at the union national level in order to influence leadership thinking.

However, certain women's commissions at sub-national levels continued to maintain feminist-inspired activity into the late 1980s in favour of women's rights issues and to lobby federation and regional leaders. This was especially true of CFDT women in the Paris region who contributed to the organisation of the 1982 national congress on women and work (*états généraux sur le travail des femmes*), the 1985 national meeting of women's organisations (*rencontre national des lieux de femmes*) and most importantly the militant nurses' coordination of strikes and demonstrations which emerged in 1988.

The CFDT's lack of commitment to gender equality demands was most clearly demonstrated in its response to the nurses' strike movement of 1988 which mobilised 90 per cent of the overwhelmingly female profession (Granger 1988: 13). The strike movement represented an enormous opportunity for the CFDT, as well as the other trade unions, to gain members in a profession with a low density of unionisation (only 5–8 per cent of nurses belonged to a trade union) and in which both the CFDT and the CGT had lost almost half of their members since 1980 (Rosehill 1988: 29). But the CFDT leadership (out of step with rank-and-file members) rejected the chance of taking up classic labour movement demands related to recognition of skills and qualifications and to in-service training, preferring instead to discredit the movement, asking 'what legitimacy does the structure [coordination] have? . . . If this [the fact that it is unelected] does not prevent the coordination from constituting a reference point for many wage-earners, it is [nevertheless] a deceitful move' (cited from an internal document, Rosehill 1988: 28). It also signed the Evin agreement, the government proposals in response to the nurses' demands, against the wishes of women rank-and-file activists and the nurses' movement. In spite of the union leadership's stance, many CFDT women were active in the organisation of the nurses' coordination. For example, in the union's Paris region health section, CFDT women provided premises for meetings, for printing and photocopying facilities and general support in mobilising nurses across the region. Furthermore, a large proportion of CFDT activists joined the 100,000 strong nurses' national demonstration on 13 October 1988 (in Paris) in defiance of their union's line and in preference to the rival demonstration organised jointly, on the same day, by the CFDT, CGC (*Confédération Générale des Cadres*),[29] CFTC and FO (*Force ouvrière*).[30]

Such demonstrations of the union leadership's disdain towards women's demands alienated large numbers of CFDT women many of whom eventually became co-founders or members of new breakaway trade unions such as SUD (*Solidaires, Unitaires et Démocratiques*) in the early 1990s. One ex-CFDT activist who joined SUD explained:

> One of the problems that we faced in the CFDT was the widening gap between our practice, our discourse at rank-and-file level, and the discourse of the union at national level relating to women's demands. There was a disconnection between the formal recognition of women's oppression and the positions of the union's national leadership which worked against women's interests, for example on part-time work . . . Women's place within trade unionism was no longer debated either in the CFDT.
>
> (Walner 1995: 18)

Furthermore, Jeannette Laot, seen as the remaining voice at leadership level in favour of feminist activism and women's demands, also left the CFDT for the same reason in 1988. Mazur (1996a: 191) argues that Laot's departure killed the activity of the union's women's commission due to the lack of an authoritative and respected voice, at the top, to speak in favour of women.

The 1990s has seen little change in the CFDT's adaptation and modernisation discourse and strategy. In fact, under the leadership of Nicole Notat, since October 1992, the union's 'realism' has hardened. If Notat's presence at the top of the union's executive allows the CFDT to claim that women play an important and active part in the union, her words and actions have strongly indicated that, unlike Laot, she is neither inspired by feminist thinking nor is she a champion of women's issues and demands. Not only has Notat separated herself from the feminism of the 1970s ('. . . as such, feminism has never formed part of my outlook. The movement for contraception and abortion and all that passed me by') but she has also denied that her rise to her current position was helped by measures (for example, quotas) designed to feminise union structures, organisation and activity (Perrot 1996: 215).

Notat's main aim has been to distance the CFDT from the parties (and currently government) of the left and to build a 'responsible' German-style trade unionism where unions and employers usually work towards compromise in situations of conflict. Moreover, under Notat, the whole thrust in membership recruitment has been towards wage-earners who would not normally fit easily in labour movement organisations. For instance, the CFDT has boasted a 5 per cent rise in its membership since 1992 but a major part of this increase comes from the targeted recruitment of wage-earners in the middle management and supervisory categories within the health and private sectors (Gilson 1997a: 28). While supporters of 'the CFDT's Iron Lady' have congratulated her for keeping the union in step with the evolution of the workforce, which has included the expansion of intermediate strata of professional, managerial and technical wage-earners and which has seen a growing proportion of women within these strata, others regret an approach which increasingly separates the union from its militant base and from the mass of wage-earners at the bottom of the employment pyramid, of which women form a more significant part.[31]

In the 1990s, then, the CFDT has been seen to back employers and government against the interests of its traditional constituency and against the interests of women. Three examples are particularly revealing of this position. First, in 1992, when employers were offered a 30 per cent reduction on their national insurance contributions for part-time posts created, the CFDT argued that the creation of part-time work signified an adaptation on the part of capitalism to individual aspirations. The union refused to support the argument that part-time work (of which 84 per cent is done by women (Gaëlle 1996: 5)), in the context of deflationary economics and deregulation, ran counter to the fundamental claims of the right to work and of equal pay which women had fought long and hard to include in trade union demands.

Second, in 1993, the CFDT (along with the FO and CFTC) approved the quinquennial employment law which opened the way for the annualisation of working hours, among other so-called flexible measures, to be agreed at company level. The measure to annualise working hours, which removed reference to the working week, allowed employers to subject work patterns to company needs and demands. This has been particularly evident in companies with a highly feminised workforce. France Telecom, EDF–GDF (*Electricité de France–Gaz de France*), companies in the banking and insurance sector which have either undergone or have been earmarked for privatisation in the 1990s and super/hypermarket chains which have vastly extended their opening hours are just some examples where women workers have been forced to accept part-time work, uneven shiftwork and short- to medium-term contracts, more often than not coupled with reductions in salary (Angeli 1995, Gaëlle, L. 1996, Gaëlle, M. 1995).

Third, in 1995, when the then Prime Minister, Alain Juppé's social security reform plan provoked anger and widespread strikes among 5 million public sector workers and students, the CFDT leadership decided to give 'critical support' to the reform plan. The protest movement included the women's '*manif du 25*' ('demonstration of the 25th' [of November]) coordinated by CADAC (*Coordination des associations pour le droit à l'avortement et à la contraception*) which brought together about 30,000 protesters defending, amongst other rights, women's right to work. While the CGT and the new breakaway unions such as SUD supported the event without hesitation or reservation, the CFDT avoided official association with it. In making this judgement, the CFDT was distancing itself very clearly from feminist activism and the further advance of women's rights as expressed by wage-earners in the late 1990s. The union's refusal to give unconditional support to the mobilisation of 1995 against the Juppé plan and in favour of women's rights provoked the departure of a number of women activists from the union who had, despite their union's position, participated in this demonstration along with other protests during this period. Activists criticised the union not just for its refusal to show clear support for women's rights but also for its compliance with employers over so-called flexible working patterns which would have the effect of reducing women trade union members' opportunities to participate in union activity. Furthermore, the CFDT's lack of support generally for issues which preoccupied the minds of women wage-earners at the bottom of the employment hierarchy has distanced it from potential members within this section of the workforce.

The fact that the union, at federation and regional levels, participated officially in the French representation at the 1995 Beijing international conference on women or at the 1997 *Assises nationales pour les droits des femmes*[32] (organised by CADAC as a continuation of the dynamic created by the demonstration of 25 November) has been of little reassurance to many CFDT activists and women wage-earners outside the union.

In the meantime there is little evidence available to suggest that the CFDT's most recent (1998) schedule of work (*plan de travail*) relating to women has brought about increased participation of rank-and-file women members who form 46 per cent of the union's membership but who remain sceptical about the union's long-term project. The *plan de travail* focuses on the issues of *mixité* (or equal involvement of women and men in all of the union's structures), equal employment and the development of trade union training for women. It also includes the establishment of a women's national networking forum ('*Actuelles*') to meet on a three-yearly basis and the implementation of the strategy '*femmes sans frontières*' (or the globalising of women's trade unionism). A vague mention is made of 'social problems' (abortion/contraception and violence) affecting women which the union will not ignore, but there is no indication of the precise nature of these problems nor of the action required to solve them (see CFDT women's web pages at http://www.cfdt.fr/etudes.htm, accessed 5 July 1999).

The CGT: from workerism to 'combative trade unionism'[33]

The CGT's return to workerist positions at the end of the 1970s, as a result of the collapse of left unity, had led the union to abandon its analysis of women's discrimination based on gender. In the early 1980s, this workerism and the impact that it had on the union's position on women's issues and demands became further entrenched as a number of key figures who had been responsible for promoting feminist analysis of women's discrimination in the 1970s left the CGT. Both Christiane Gilles and Jean-Louis Moynot, marginalised at the union's forty-first Congress in 1982 over their refusal to condone Soviet military intervention in Afghanistan, resigned from the national bureau and left the union. Chantal Rogerat resigned shortly afterwards from the editorship of *Antoinette*. Rogerat's resignation was linked to her support for the breakaway Polish trade union, Solidarity. The departure of Gilles and Moynot meant the removal of whatever little pressure there was on the national bureau to continue addressing the advance of women's rights in a wider social context, while at *Antoinette*, there was a return to the class theme of women's 'overexploitation' by capitalism.

The CGT's class-based analysis of women's exploitation sat uncomfortably with some of the thinking on working women's issues that was prevalent within the Socialist Ministry of Women's Rights. However, between 1981 and 1984, while the PCF remained a government partner,[34] the union was obliged to follow a line of reluctant cooperation with policies emanating from the Ministry of Women's Rights. The union expressed particular doubts about the 1983 law on equal employment (*égalité professionnelle*). Its main criticism was that it best served women in the more highly regarded and paid professional occupations, while neglecting the needs of working-class women in precarious, poorly paid employment and those of working mothers who had little choice but to work.

After July 1984, following the end of Communist participation in government, the union stepped up its attacks on Socialist policy and at the same time withdrew support from further implementation of the law on equal employment. At the 1985 CGT women's conference, the Ministry of Women's Rights was subjected to accusations of using the Higher Council for Equal Employment (*Conseil Supérieur de l'égalité professionnelle*) to do away with 'safeguards' (such as prohibition of night and Sunday work and the limitation of the working day to ten hours) for women at the bottom of the employment pyramid and of removing focus from maternity rights and childcare issues. Generally, the Socialists were charged with patronising the majority of working women through piecemeal legislation that was uninformed by the real concerns of women wage-earners (CGT, 1985: 15). Campaigning against Socialist policies on women allowed the CGT to mask the fact that within the union there was no discussion of alternative strategies in relation to women's rights. Even its membership recruitment strategy placed no special emphasis on women and, although the importance of women's workplace, and local and departmental collectives (previously commissions) was mentioned in union rhetoric, concrete support for these structures was lacking. In fact, due to a complete lack of data on these collectives, it is difficult if not impossible to determine what their main business was and how women were involved in them.

In the 1990s, however, the CGT has had to call into question work-erist strategy in the face of growing disaffection within its ever-dwindling membership and the increasing participation and militancy of women, young people and migrants in movements challenging established political and economic forces. Furthermore, as its main rival, the CFDT, has continued to adjust to the views and aspirations of employers and governments, the CGT has been keen to place itself in opposition to the former by demonstrating its willingness to adapt to and participate in the struggles of under- and unrepresented groups in society in order to promote change.

The trigger for the review of strategy came at the end of 1986 when thousands of students took to the streets in protest against the Devaquet reform of higher education. Student demonstrations, which had begun in November 1986, led to a call for solidarity action to workers generally. As in May 1968, student protests were followed by widespread workers' strikes, which continued throughout December and into January 1987. Unlike May 1968, however, the workers' strikes, independently organised, took place in the public sector where the CGT was strongly implanted and where it could extend its influence if it was seen to play a positive role for change. After 1986–7, then, the CGT sought to establish a dialogue with groups traditionally under-represented in the union, in particular women, migrants, young wage-earners and white-collar workers, in a bid to widen its appeal and attract new members.

Consequently, during the 1990s, the CGT launched a real charm offensive where women are concerned. Unlike the CFDT it supported the 1988 nurses' strikes without reservation and refused to sign the Evin agreement with the CFDT, CFTC and FO, on the grounds that it fell well short of nurses' demands. Similarly, the CGT has refused cooperation with government and employers on the annualisation of working hours, rejecting the terms relating to it in the employment law of 1993, which affect women workers disproportionately.

While it would be easy to conclude that the CGT has returned to a position of defending and promoting women's rights on a gender rather than class basis alone, this is not stated explicitly as was the case in 1977. The union has been careful to place its actions simply within the context of combative trade-unionism (*le syndicalisme de combat*) and 'solid, mixed struggles' ('*luttes fortes et mixtes*') in favour of women (Duchesne 1997: 45–7). In this respect, the union has clearly decided to engage in united action with feminist-inspired movements and to adopt a vastly different discourse to that of the early to mid-1980s which makes little or no reference to class. Women are presented as an undifferentiated group in which managers are subjected to the same kinds of discrimination as wage-earners at the bottom of the pyramid (Duchesne 1997: 46). However, at the same time, the CGT has also continued to support working-class women in disputes (over part-time work, 'flexible' working hours and so on) with managements at Moulinex, Thomson electronics, France Télécom,

EDF–GDF and a number of other companies in the commercial sector, and this approach has contrasted sharply with that of the CFDT which has tended to seek compromise solutions with employers.

Women activists have, however, tended to be sceptical of the CGT's willingness to support women's independent action such as the nurses' coordination of 1988, protests during 1995 and the *Assises nationales pour les droits des femmes* of 1997. Many of them outside the union have criticised CGT strategy as one where the union has entered a social movement or women's coordination mainly as a means of taking control:

> [T]he CGT enters existing coordinations and creates new ones within them, controlled by the CGT. In this way, the CGT can appear to be more left-wing than other unions who form an anti-coordination front and who sign agreements [with government] against the advice of the movement. But . . . this new and belated CGT tactic, added to the union's political weakness and lack of 'personnel' to pull it off, makes the success of this new operation highly improbable.
>
> (Rosehill 1988: 30)

Nevertheless, many have argued that the CGT no longer represents a 'monolithic block' (Rotjman 1996: 41) hostile to feminist cultures and movements. However, whether or not the CGT's charm campaign has encouraged women wage-earners to become union members is unclear due to lack of information. It appears unlikely that women are joining the union in significant numbers given the overall drop in the union's membership at a time when women form the fastest growing section of the workforce.

The unions and 'mixité'

Since 1996, both the CFDT and the CGT have begun to stress the importance of *mixité* within their respective organisations and structures. The impetus to do so has emerged not only as a result of the feminist and party political debates around the idea of political parity, which have been taking place in France since 1992, but also due to the pressure applied by ETUC on its member organisations to address the issue of women's equal representation (especially in decision-making bodies) within union structures (see Braithwaite and Byrne 1993). For the CFDT there has been an added pressure to address this question due to its emphasis on equal employment policies since the early 1980s and the reaffirmation of *égalité professionnelle* as a priority issue in its 1998 schedule of work.

As far as the CFDT is concerned, a number of measures have been taken to promote 'mixity'. These include: the introduction of voluntary gender monitoring at regional and federation levels since 1994 and the intention to extend it to other levels within the union; the development of a 'positions of responsibility policy' ('*politique des responsables*');[35] the development of trade union training and the establishment of forums in which women are able to express themselves (including questionnaires, debates, workshops). It is difficult to assess the extent to which such measures have taken or will take effect. The main reason for this diffi-culty is that voluntary monitoring procedures produce an incomplete and uneven quantitative profile of women's participation in union structures and decision-making. It is likely that such monitoring produces a more positive picture of the reality of the situation as those parts of the trade union organisation which are most enthusiastic about the promotion of 'mixity' are most likely to return gender-related statistics.

However, it would appear that in the 1990s, women's participation in the majority of union structures has remained below 30 per cent. At national level, women make up only 22 per cent of the national execu-tive commission, just under 30 per cent of the national bureau,[36] and a mere 10 per cent of national conference delegates (Loiseau 1999: 364). Further down, a similar picture is reproduced as demonstrated by Tables 3.1 and 3.2 (based on incomplete information).[37]

Furthermore, federation statistics tend to give a more positive inter-pretation of reality. For example, federation figures for women involved in development and training are much higher than the figures for those areas related to regional level because federations, unlike trade union regions, are based according to sector of economic activity. Therefore, those federations which are highly or almost entirely feminised will neces-sarily involve greater numbers of women in their decision-making structures. Finally, it is also impossible to trace the evolution of women's participation from the early 1960s to the present, due to the lack of rele-vant, comparable data. While it is clear that participation rates in union membership and decision-making structures are significantly higher in the 1990s than at the end of the 1970s, there still remains a considerable gap between the percentage of women union members and that of women at decision-making level.

The problem of data becomes even more pronounced when trying to assess the participation of women in the CGT's structures. Not only is it

Table 3.1 Women's participation in the structures of the CFDT, in per cent

	Regions		Federations	
	1997	1994	1997	1994
Conferences	24	22	29	24
Councils, bureaux, secretariats	23	21	28	24

Source: Compiled from data obtained from: http://www.cfdt.fr/etudes.htm, accessed 5 July 1999.

Table 3.2 The proportion of women in the CFDT secretariat, in per cent

	Regions		Federations	
	1997	*1994*	*1997*	*1994*
General secretaries	18	14	28	23
In charge of finance	18	18	28	14
In charge of organisation	18	18	28	18
In charge of development	14	5	33	14
In charge of training	0	0	24	27

Source: Compiled from data obtained from: http://www.cfdt.fr/etudes.htm accessed 5 July 1999.

impossible to carry out a comparable analysis over a period of time, it is also difficult to find current figures. In general the CGT appears to have done better than the CFDT at including women within decision-making structures so that (on the basis of available figures) the percentage of women in decision-making instances exceeds the percentage of women members (31 per cent).[38] This can be attributed to the existence of the CGT women's sector which has, over a long period of time, provided the union with women, experienced and trained in trade union matters, who have been able and willing to take up posts as opportunities have arisen. The small amount of data one can refer to indicates a greater involvement of women in decision-making posts. For example, the CGT's national bureau is currently almost equally mixed with a 47 per cent proportion of women (http://www.cgt.fr/01confed/07direc/dire1.htm). Similarly, the national executive commission includes 46 per cent of women members in its composition (http://www.cgt.fr/01confed/07direc/dire2.htm) although, in contrast, the union's finance commission (the only other union structure for which information can be gained) includes only 14 per cent of women members (http://www.cgt.fr/01confed/07direc/dire3.htm). As these figures cannot be compared with those before 1996 when the union's forty-fifth Congress undertook to achieve 'real mixity throughout trade union life' (Duchesne 1997: 47), it is not possible to comment on the way in which women's participation has changed and/or increased. Furthermore, it is also unclear as to what specific measures the CGT has undertaken in relation to achieving mixity.

Conclusion

Women's participation in trade unions has increased during the Fifth Republic. First, at the lowest level of participation, women constitute 39 per cent of trade union members (percentage average of women's total membership of both the CGT and CFDT combined). However, the density of women's trade union membership has remained consistently low. At a time when women's participation in the labour market has grown, when they have become more gender conscious and more prepared than ever to take part in socio-economic struggles to advance their rights, they have chosen to do so outside the arena of trade unionism. Part of the reason for this lies in the fact that women continue to shoulder the burden of domestic responsibilities which already compete with paid work for hours available in the day. In such a situation, the addition of regular trade union commitment appears impossible to the majority of working women who may nevertheless feel able to participate in more occasional social protests. Another reason is that employers structure women's work in such a way (part-time, low-grade, casualised jobs) as to make trade union membership not seem worthwhile. However, the trade unions must bear a large part of the blame for women's non-participation through their unwillingness to implant themselves within the feminised sectors of the economy, especially where unskilled jobs in precarious working conditions are concerned.

Second, women have become more involved in trade union activity and organisation at all levels. However, the higher the level of the organisation and that of decision-making, the lower the participation rate of women becomes. This is due entirely to the negligence of trade unions whose thinking and practice are designed for the participation of men: from the ideology and culture of masculinity on which unions were founded to the resultant issues which take predominance and to the organisation and timetabling of union activity.

While the unions have been pressurised to recognise the need for change in their attitude towards women, this chapter has shown that they have failed to process that recognition in order to create a public face of French trade unionism, formed as much by women as it is by men.

4   Electoral behaviour and attitudes

The study of participation has tended to concentrate on elections, not least because of the accessible and comparable nature of the available data. It is one of the most developed areas of French political science, and has been dominated by two models which have competed with each other in the search for an explanation of patterns of voting behaviour. These are 'social determinism' and 'rational choice'. Social determinism stresses the importance of the 'demand side' of electoral decision-making, focusing on the social categories which make electoral choices. The rational choice model focuses on the various components of the 'supply side' and how these influence individual voter–consumers. The social determinist model posits that voting preferences are determined by certain sociological factors, the most important being class, wealth and religiosity. It was the dominant model during the 1970s and appeared able to account for changes in electoral behaviour since the Second World War, relating these changes to socio-economic and cultural change. Economic growth, urbanisation, the growth of the tertiary sector, the decline in religious practice and the mass entry of women into the labour market were all seen as factors contributing to an increase in the number of potential left-wing voters, and the Socialist victory of 1981 seemed to confirm the hypothesis. However, after 1981, the declining support for the left amongst the very categories which had brought it to power, the rise of parties outside the parliamentary system, such as the *Front national* and the *Verts*, and the changing allegiances of voters from one election to the next, favoured the competing explanatory model: that of the informed voter–consumer, who based his/her rational decision on the salient issues of the moment (Mayer and Perrineau 1992: 84). According to this model, voters are influenced by factors such as the issues on which campaigns are run, the discourse of the candidates, and the electoral promises of the parties. The symbolic representation, or image, of a particular candidate can also influence voting choices, particularly between presidential candidates who may try to rise above left/right divisions and present themselves as, for example, 'the father of the nation', as was the case with both De Gaulle and Mitterrand.

While the rational voter model dominated during the 1980s, especially around the time of the first 'cohabitation' between a right-wing parliamentary majority and a Socialist president (1986–8), it did not go unchallenged. A study conducted by Daniel Boy and Elisabeth Dupoirier for CEVIPOF in 1988, for example, demonstrated that the political orientation of 70 per cent of the electorate had remained stable in the four rounds of voting in the legislative election of 1986 and the presidential election of 1988 (Mayer and Perrineau 1992: 86). They found that the floating voters were largely those who were least well inserted economically, politically and socially: the young and poorly educated, those who were least interested in politics. They found that, despite significant social change since the 1960s, the effects of class, religion and property ownership were still relevant to electoral choice (Mayer and Perrineau 1992: 87–9). In a more recent study, Boy and Mayer (1997) reject the hypothesis that better access to education, the growing influence of the media, the spread of post-materialist values and the declining importance of class and religion have favoured political emancipation and the emergence of a new category of individualist, rational voters, who are better informed, more politicised and less dependent on the parties. They found that in the 1995 presidential elections, Catholicism still correlates strongly with voting behaviour and that the degree of religiosity translates into a sliding scale of voter preference for the right (Boy and Mayer 1997: 106). They argue that, although class cleavages have shifted, the main difference now being between the self-employed and the employed, they have not disappeared. The third significant variable, they claim, is the variety of assets (rather than the amount). In 1995, a wide variety of assets was most likely to predict a vote for the moderate right, whereas an absence of assets predicted a vote for the left or the *Front national*. These main cleavages are cut through by others, such as employment in the public or private sector, and education, which seems to be a particularly salient factor in predicting the FN vote (Boy and Mayer 1997: 122–3, 137).

Less ardent advocates of either the social determinist model or the rational voter model favour an amalgamation of the two, arguing that sociological characteristics and short-term political factors necessarily interact in electoral decisions (for example, Mayer and Perrineau 1992: 92–111, Lagroye 1989: 326).

It is interesting to note that none of these studies have found that sex is a particularly influential factor in determining voting behaviour. Along with age, it seems to have a relatively secondary influence after religion, class and capital (Mayer and Perrineau 1992: 83, Boy and Mayer 1997). It is important to bear this in mind, while examining the differences which do exist between men and women.

The study of women's political behaviour necessarily compares it with that of men, and may risk exaggerating the difference between them and simultaneously hiding the differences between groups of women, which may be far more important. It is nevertheless useful to map out the contours of women's political behaviour, if only to expose some of the widespread misrepresentations of it.

The study of women's political behaviour

In 1955, two important studies of women's political participation appeared: Matteï Dogan and Jacques Narbonne's *Les Françaises face à la politique* and Maurice Duverger's *La participation des femmes à la vie politique*. Dogan and Narbonne (1955) took as a starting point the late arrival of women in a political system created by men, and asked how successfully they had integrated themselves into it. Did their political behaviour differ from that of men and to what extent? And did these differences vary according to the social and economic status of the women concerned, or were they based purely on sex? One of their central research questions was '*if women vote differently from men, is it because they are women, or because they are human beings who are in different social conditions?*' (15).

The study was divided into two sections. The first examined the factors which might influence women's political participation, including their social and economic status, the influence of feminism, their family responsibilities, religion and political interest. The second part of the study investigated women's political behaviour: voting, membership of organisations and associations, membership of and activism within political parties, and membership of the political élite.

They found that women voted less than men and attributed this to their lower levels of political interest and access to information, stating, for example, that women were only half as likely as men to read a daily newspaper (63). They also found that nine out of ten women voted like their husbands, claiming that this was because they were subordinate to them and bowed to their superior knowledge (63). Finally, they found that women's vote was to the right of men's, although they attributed this to factors other than gender itself, notably age and occupational status (90). The female population in 1955 was significantly older than the male, and older voters were more likely to support the parties of the right. There were also fewer *ouvrières* (female manual workers) than *ouvriers* (male manual workers), the category most likely to vote for the parties of the left.

The finding that there was no evidence of a link between biological sex and political behaviour, but rather between gender and political behaviour was one of their major conclusions, and a significant contribution to the debates of the time. They write (1955: 191): 'Men and women are, above all, human beings who exist socially as men and women. This social existence is indisputable, but nothing proves that it is the result of the biological characteristics implied by the notion of sex.'

In their conclusion, Dogan and Narbonne (1955: 191) stress that, although women are less interested and knowledgeable, the gender differences in political behaviour are small. They predict that, even if women become 'socially integrated' on the same terms as men, this will have no effect on the balance of political forces. This is because they already vote like men, to whom they are subordinate in the couple. If they become more autonomous, better integrated professionally, less subject to religious influences and better informed, they will still vote like men, because their social situation will be similar. So rather than predicting that women and men will become increasingly similar in political behaviour, they argue that simply the reasons for their similarity will change. However, one striking inconsistency in this argument is that if women's vote is to the right of men, partly because they are employed in different sectors, then if women were to become 'socially integrated' (= more like men?) then their vote will move to the left and *will* affect the balance of political forces.

The second important contribution to the study of women's political participation which appeared in 1955 was Maurice Duverger's report synthesising the results of four national surveys, sponsored by UNESCO and conducted in West Germany, France, Norway and Yugoslavia between 1952 and 1953. The surveys were divided into two parts: voting behaviour and women in the political élite. As far as participation in the political élite is concerned, all of the surveys found that women were few and far between, with their numbers decreasing as one approaches the real sites of power (1955a: 126).

In terms of voting turnout and electoral choice, however, Duverger (125) observes that women's participation does not differ substantially from that of men. He concedes that they abstain a little more than men and vote a little to the right and a little more often for Christian parties, but states that these differences are very slight. Moreover, they can often be explained by factors other than sex, for example, age. In common with Dogan and Narbonne, he writes (125), 'Nothing here suggests the existence of a fixed and feminine "nature" or of a fundamental difference in behaviour between men and women.' On the question of the similarity between the political choices of husband and wife, Duverger is more wary than Dogan and Narbonne of jumping to hasty conclusions. While noting that this similarity exists, Duverger does not assume that women simply adopt their husbands' already established views. He suggests that there may at least be a sort of dynamic at play. He writes (125), 'it seems proven that women bring their vote into line with the wishes of their husband, but is the husband's decision not unconsciously influenced by the couple's whole lifestyle and the presence of his wife?'.

These early studies compared women's voting behaviour with that of men, finding that, although the differences were small, women participated less, were less interested in politics, and were more conservative than men. Later studies of electoral behaviour, which often devoted only a small section to women, exaggerated the difference and portrayed women as inadequate citizens. Alain Duhamel, for example, in an article in *Le Monde*

(10 March 1971) writes, 'French women are bad citizens. They hardly vote, rarely engage in political activism, only exceptionally stand as candidates and do not make the effort to find out what is going on.'

The first attempt to refute such assertions formed part of the ground-breaking two-volume study by Andrée Michel and Geneviève Texier (1964) who combined evidence drawn from the 1955 studies with a strongly argued feminist analysis which reads today as far ahead of its time. However, it did not mark the birth of feminist political science in France, as it might have done. It was the late 1970s before Janine Mossuz-Lavau and Mariette Sineau began to produce methodical analyses of women's political behaviour, which are situated within mainstream political science and still today form almost the entire corpus of work on this subject. Using the framework for investigation which has dominated the area since the seminal studies of women's participation conducted by Dogan and Narbonne and Duverger in the 1950s, they examined women's voting behaviour (turnout and orientation) and their political attitudes (interest, knowledge and affinity for the left or the right). Until the early 1990s, their work showed that women's relative under-participation was a '*retard*' ('time lag') and that, mainly due to social change, their political behaviour was evolving and would soon 'catch up' with that of men. Later, Mossuz-Lavau began to argue that women's vote was no longer 'catching up' with that of men, but was developing an autonomy of its own.

Voting turnout

It is interesting to note how much energy has been devoted to the search for a difference in voting turnout between men and women, given that Duverger had already stated in 1955 that the differences were so slight as to be insignificant. Even in the earliest years of universal suffrage, women's abstention rate was at most seven to ten percentage points higher than that of men, and the evidence on which this was based is not indisputable. When Alain Lancelot stated in 1968 that 'In France, women abstain on average more than men', he immediately qualified this by adding that 'this has rarely been proven on a national scale, due to the imperfect nature of opinion polls on the question of abstention' (Subileau and Toinet 1993: 105). Subileau and Toinet (1993: 105) concede that surveys and other studies have often demonstrated women's higher rates of abstention,

Table 4.1 Abstention rates for men and women, in per cent

	1981 Presidential	1988 Presidential	1993 Legislative	1995 Presidential
Men	10	15	23	16
Women	12	17	24	18

Sources: Ysmal (1995a: 22); Mossuz-Lavau (1997b: 36).

but they also cite numerous exceptions, 'so many, in fact, that when it is claimed that women now vote as much as men, one wonders whether that has not always been the case'. It is certainly true that, since 1981, abstention rates for men and women have not differed. And at the 1977 municipal elections, women under the age of 25 actually abstained less than men (Subileau and Toinet 1993: 105–6). Since 1981, the difference has been no more than one or two points (see Table 4.1).

Those who accept that there has been a reduction in the difference between men and women's voting turnout have sought to explain why this should have happened. The standard explanation for women's initially higher abstention rates has been Mossuz-Lavau's theory that women underwent an apprenticeship in political participation. Women were affected by socio-cultural influences which distanced them from politics, especially economic dependence on their husband and religious practice. Subileau and Toinet (1993: 106) write:

> Curiously, these arguments are similar to those used by the radicals in the 1930s to oppose women's right to vote. But, if this is true, how can we explain the fact that at least as many women as men voted in the first elections after the Liberation?

Attitudes towards the act of voting may explain why there was little significant difference in turnout even in the immediate post-war period. A survey published in 1954 (Braud 1973: 58) found that 64 per cent of women and only 55 per cent of men felt that they were fulfilling a duty by voting, whereas 28 per cent of men and only 19 per cent of women thought that they were exercising a right (see Table 4.2).

Braud (1973: 58) argued that, although parties and trade unions stressed that voting was a duty, so too did the national education system, the Catholic Church, and secular mores (*la morale laïque*): institutions which exert a powerful influence on women. Sylvia Bashevkin (1984: 85) offers a similar explanation for the small gender gap in voter turnout in the immediate post-war years, arguing that women were encouraged to vote by right-wing and clerical forces exerting a pressure which, although

Table 4.2 Question: When you vote, do you feel that you are . . .

	Men %	*Women* %
Fulfilling a duty	55	64
Exercising a right	28	19
Both	10	5
No response	7	12

Source: Braud (1973: 58).

different to that exerted on men by the labour movement and the left, was only marginally weaker.

Subileau and Toinet (1993: 107–8) also examine the effects of the over-representation of women in the oldest age groups of the population, those most likely to have high abstention rates. These high abstention rates are not necessarily associated with sex, they argue. In the over-75 age group, the proportion of the population on the electoral register was calculated in 1976 to be 113 per cent of the actual population, because the names of deceased voters are not removed immediately. Solitude also seems to be linked to a withdrawal from society and in particular from politics, affecting more elderly women than men. Early studies showed that single women voted less frequently than men, but rarely pointed out that this may be because there are more widows than widowers.

Mossuz-Lavau has attempted to demonstrate a link between women's rising levels of education and their political behaviour, in particular their voting turnout. She states that women's improved levels of education have led to their greater political interest which in turn has produced a higher voting turnout. She points out that, while in 1950, there were only 44,000 women in higher education, out of a total of 125,000, by 1971, women students in higher education outnumbered men (Mossuz-Lavau 1997b: 39). She argues that political interest increases with the level of education, and as women began to remain in education as long as men, the gap in abstention rates disappeared. In a later section, we will examine changes in women's political interest and the relation between this and their level of education. Here, however, it is important to point out that the rise in women's level of education does not correspond to a decline in the gender gap in abstention rates, which, during the period she refers to, remained remarkably stable. Bashevkin (1984: 85) shows that women's political interest increased by twenty percentage points between 1953 and 1978, while men's political interest remained largely unchanged. So while their absolute level of interest in 1978 was still lower than that of men, it had grown significantly since 1953 (83). She explains this increase in terms of social change in the same period, but states that data on electoral abstentionism does not support the same hypothesis, since between 1951 and 1973, there was little change in voting levels of either men or women, and the gender differential remained at 7 per cent (85).

It is important to stress that voting is just one form of political behaviour amongst many. The focus by political scientists on electoral participation has tended to distort its importance in relation to other forms, providing a misleading view of women's political involvement. Vicky Randall (1987: 50) reminds us that the value of voting is often overstated, and that the relationship of voting to other forms of political behaviour is unclear. Sometimes it is portrayed as the first step in a sliding scale of participation and sometimes as a discrete activity. Randall argues that the impact of voting and the individual level of commitment it requires are usually slight and that it is therefore necessary to examine other forms of participation in order to assess the involvement of women.

Interest in politics

A declared interest in politics can be a significant indicator of political participation, although the relation between interest and voting turnout is less clear. While only 24 per cent of citizens who are not at all interested in politics are active, this is the case for 84 per cent of those who are very interested, and this correlation applies whatever the social origins of the individual concerned, overriding some of the other socio-cultural factors which would normally influence levels of participation (Mayer and Perrineau 1992: 34).

In the 1958 French Election Study, for example, the proportion of women professing no party identification was 54.5 per cent, compared with 40.5 per cent among men (Bashevkin 1984: 87). This proportion changed significantly in the two decades following the establishment of the Fifth Republic. In both the 1968 IFOP and 1978 Eurobarometer surveys, approximately 21 per cent of women reported no party identification, less than half the level obtained in 1958. Bashevkin (1984: 85) concludes that this indicates a considerable politicisation of women between 1958 and 1978, and particularly between 1958 and 1968. Data for young women during the same period show that they were relatively interested, aware and as politicised as younger males.

Some more recent surveys suggest that there is a clear gap between men and women's interest in politics, and this gap does not seem to have closed. Eurobarometer measures this periodically by asking men and women whether they discuss political matters with their friends frequently, occasionally or never, and whether they consider themselves close to any political party. It finds that women show a lower level of interest in and attachment to politics than men (see Table 4.3).

These answers are affected by other factors, in particular age, level of education and professional activity (Eurobarometer 1998: 51). Interest in

Table 4.3 Frequency of political discussions in 1983, 1989, 1994, 1996

	April–May 83		*July 89*		*April 94*		*April 96*	
	Men %	*Women* %	*Men* %	*Women* %	*Men* %	*Women* %	*Men* %	*Women* %
Frequently	20	12	18	11	22	14	17	11
Occasionally	57	49	55	48	56	51	60	52
Never	22	37	27	40	21	34	22	36
Don't know	1	2	1	1	1	1	1	1

Source: Eurobarometer (1998), no. 44, 3: 50. Figures for the whole of the EU.

Table 4.4 Question: When you get together with friends, would you say that you discuss political matters frequently, occasionally, or never?

| | Whole of EU | | France | |
	Men %	Women %	Men %	Women %
Frequently	17	11	14.5	10.6
Occasionally	60	52	58.4	56.1
Never	22	36	26.9	32.8
Don't know	1	1	0.2	0.5

Source: Eurobarometer (1998), no. 44, 3: 52. Figures from April 1996.

politics is low among young people, increases in adults and falls again among the more elderly. The difference between the sexes rises consistently with age. In the 15–24 age bracket, 35 per cent of men and 39 per cent of women said they never discussed politics, a difference of 4 per cent. This increases to 11 per cent among 25–39 year-olds and 15 per cent among 40–54 year-olds, reaching its peak at 20 per cent in the over-55 age-group (51). The surveys also show that the higher women's level of education, the smaller the gap between men and women in terms of political interest (51). For France, the gap between men and women is lower than for the EU as a whole (see Table 4.4).

However, this difference in men and women's responses could be due more to the wording of the question than to actual differences in political interest. When the same people are asked about their discussions of 'important social problems', for example, human rights, poverty, the Third World, sexual equality, etc., the replies of men are quite close to their replies on the subject of politics, whereas distinctly more women say they discuss

Table 4.5 Frequency of discussions of political issues and 'important social problems'

| | Discussion of political matters | | | Discussion of important social problems | | |
	Men %	Women %	Total %	Men %	Women %	Total %
Frequently	20	12	16	24	23	23
Occasionally	57	49	53	52	49	51
Never	22	37	30	23	27	25
No reply	1	2	1	1	1	1
Total	100	100	100	100	100	100
Index (from 4 to 1)	2.46	2.13	2.29	2.52	2.43	2.47

Source: Compiled from *Women of Europe* (1984: 43–5).

these problems than say they discuss politics (see Table 4.5). That women discuss 'important social issues' more than 'politics' was confirmed in 1987, when it was found that in Luxembourg, France, the Netherlands, Denmark and Belgium, women discuss social issues more often than men (*Women of Europe* 1987: 41).

Janine Mossuz-Lavau (1995) conducted a qualitative study which aimed to establish whether men and women had different attitudes towards politics. Based on a tiny sample of 28 men and 32 women, its findings cannot be taken as conclusive, but nevertheless provide an interesting contribution to the study of political attitudes. She found (1995: 268–76) that women were more concerned than men with ordinary people (*les gens*) and with finding concrete solutions to political problems. She concludes that women and men have very similar political attitudes, but that women occupy a more limited political space than men, making fewer, if any, references to institutional, economic and European questions and to the trade unions. This is to a certain extent balanced by a greater receptivity to the problems of individuals. Mossuz-Lavau suggests that women are better able than men to relate politics to daily life and to social problems and to make concrete demands, rather than being satisfied with the realm of discourse. She claims that women are more interested in results than processes.

It is not possible simply to state that women are less interested in electoral politics than men, however. The report based on the findings of the Eurobarometer opinion poll conducted in October 1984, as well as previous Eurobarometer surveys, and published in the supplement to *Women of Europe* (1985: 24) states that:

> In general, the findings of the many detailed analyses based on the series of Eurobarometer opinion polls over a period of years show that women and men adopt very much the same attitude to the European Parliament, which enjoys no less credibility . . . among women than among men. It might be said that when women express an opinion it tends to be slightly more favourable than men's.

Knowledge about politics

One factor which is used to measure knowledge about politics is exposure to the news. A Eurobarometer survey, reported in *Women in Europe* (1984: 7) compared the frequency with which respondents claim to watch the news on television, read about politics in the daily newspaper, and listen to news broadcasts on the radio (see Table 4.6). The index for men and women is very similar in the case of television and radio broadcasts. However, women claim to read about politics in the daily newspaper much less frequently than men. There are several possible explanations for this. It could indicate that they are less interested in politics. It could be that

Table 4.6 Exposure to the news in
France (Index from 4 to 1)

Television	
Men	3.36
Women	3.22
Daily Newspapers	
Men	2.41
Women	1.70
Radio	
Men	2.67
Women	2.66

Source: *Women of Europe* (1984: 7).

it is simply easier to combine listening to the radio or television with other tasks. Or the difference could lie in the wording of the question: the question on newspapers is the only one which specifies that the reading is about 'politics' rather than about 'the news'. It is possible that women read the news in a daily newspaper, but do not feel qualified to claim that they read about politics. This suggestion is included in a footnote in the original Eurobarometer survey (June 1983), which states that 'the reference to current politics in the wording of the question may well have magnified the differences or even introduced a topical element'. The Eurobarometer report (June 1983: 50) also points out that when men and women are assigned an information index score, rating their exposure to information from television, radio and the press combined:

> in most countries, there is a gap between men and women which is tending to disappear. Young women are already almost as exposed to the media in Greece and the United Kingdom as are young men, and they are slightly more so in Germany and France.

Attitudes towards women's role in politics

A 1975 survey on socio-political attitudes in the countries of the European Community showed that women continued to be less active in politics than men, to a degree which varied from one country to another. The *Women of Europe* report suggests that this stems from differing perceptions of male and female roles, notably in politics (*Women of Europe* June 1979: 31). The 1977 survey asked men and women whether a much greater representation of women would be good or bad. If the respondent answered that it would bring about an improvement, they were asked whether women MPs would represent a steadying influence; whether greater attention would be paid to women's problems; whether there would be less politicking; or whether new issues would be raised. On average, one man in five and one woman in three replied that things would be better if there were more women in Parliament (40). Asked what difference it would make, the most frequent reply was that new issues would be discussed. The second most frequent reply was that the question of women would be treated more seriously.

The 'Women and Men of Europe 1983' survey (*Women of Europe* 1984: 39) found that for the Community as a whole, men and women do not give very different answers to the questions should politics be left to men, can one have confidence in a woman representative and would more women in Parliament make a difference. However, there were differences between countries. The *Women of Europe* (1984) report categorises them according to their 'progressiveness'. It places the United Kingdom, Denmark, the Netherlands and France among the 'progressive' countries and Germany among the less progressive (see Table 4.7).

Table 4.7 Results by country on women's role in politics and comparison of results for men and women

	Disagree with idea that politics is more a man's business		*Have at least as much confidence in a woman as a member of Parliament*	
	Men %	*Women* %	*Men* %	*Women* %
1 Top countries on the two questions				
UK	79	81	72	70
Denmark	78	80	88	89
Netherlands	74	81	79	82
France	78	75	70	72
2 Countries largely rejecting the idea that politics is a man's business but less confident in women as their member of parliament:				
Greece	78	76	52	58
Italy	75	75	59	64
3 Countries in intermediate position on the two questions:				
Luxembourg	69	62	67	69
Ireland	59	71	60	78
Belgium	54	60	69	76
4 The most reticent country:				
Germany	55	59	54	67

Source: *Women of Europe* (1984: 40).

Political orientation

Throughout the Third Republic suffrage debates, and in the years following women's acquisition of the right to vote, it was widely expected that this would benefit the parties of the right. And indeed, between 1946 and 1967, the gap between men and women's vote for candidates of the right was between 10 and 12 percentage points.

During the 1970s, women's support for the left grew as their support for the centre and right declined (Bashevkin 1984: 94). Between 1973 and 1981, the gap between men and women's vote for candidates of the right had fallen to between 6 and 8 points, and women were moving towards the left more rapidly than men (Ysmal 1995a: 24). This was especially the case for women under thirty. In the 1978 CEVIPOF survey, only 36.8 per cent of this age group expressed a preference for a party of the centre or right, compared with 53.7 per cent of a comparable group in 1968.

The PS gained disproportionately from women's shift to the left, increasing its share of the female vote by approximately fourteen points between 1970 and 1978. The PCF gained slightly, the PSU remained more or less at the same level, and the MRG lost substantially (Bashevkin 1984: 95).

In the 1986 legislative elections, men and women for the first time voted for the left in exactly the same proportions (approximately 44 per cent), and in the first round of the 1988 presidential elections, more women than men supported candidates of the left (51 per cent and 47 per cent) (Mossuz-Lavau 1997b: 36). Women's vote for the left fell below men's in the 1989 European elections, but since 1993, it has been the same or greater than men's (see Table 4.8).

Table 4.8 Vote for the left and right by sex, in per cent

	1946		1951		1965		1967		1973	
	M	F	M	F	M	F	M	F	M	F
Left	65	53	57	47	51	39	44	33	50	42
Right	35	47	43	53	48	60	46	56	47	54
Other	0	0	0	0	1	1	10	11	3	4

	1978		1981		1986		1988		1993		1994	
	M	F	M	F	M	F	M	F	M	F	M	F
Left	53	47	51	44	44	44	49	51	31	32	35	37
Right	44	50	45	52	55	55	47	44	58	55	49	46
Other	3	3	4	4	1	1	4	5	11	13	16	17

Source: (Ysmal 1995a: 24).

Table 4.9 Votes of young men and women
(18–24-year-olds), in per cent

	1995 Presidential	1997 Legislative
Socialist		
Men	19	22
Women	29	34
Front national		
Men	19	19
Women	10	14

Source: Mossuz-Lavau (1997b: 42–3).

The most detailed analyses of women's electoral behaviour have been conducted by Janine Mossuz-Lavau. She divides women's political behaviour since 1945 into three phases, during the course of which women gradually came to vote as much as men, then as much for the left as men, and later, more so (1997b: 35). She refers to the years between 1945 and the end of the 1960s as 'a period of apprenticeship', during which women gradually learnt how to participate. Mossuz-Lavau's second period is the 1970s, which she calls 'a period of take-off'. During this time, women began to vote in the same proportions as men and the gap in left-wing voting fell. The 1980s marked the beginning of a third period, 'a period of independence', during which women continued voting as often as men, especially in the younger age groups, but voted more for ecology parties and less for the FN than men (37).

The 1995 presidential elections also revealed a significant gender gap in voting behaviour in the 18–24 age group. In the first round of voting, 19 per cent of young men and 29 per cent of young women voted for the Socialist candidate, Lionel Jospin. 19 per cent of young men and 10 per cent of young women voted for Le Pen. This was confirmed in the 1997 legislative elections, when 22 per cent of young men and 34 per cent of young women supported Socialist and other left-wing candidates, while 19 per cent of young men and 14 per cent of young women voted FN (see Table 4.9).

Support for green candidates has also been greater amongst women than amongst men since the 1992 regional elections, when 17 per cent of women and 12 per cent of men voted for ecologist candidates. In 1997, 8 per cent of women and 6 per cent of men voted for ecologist candidates (Mossuz-Lavau 1997b: 38).

Explaining women's vote

Although Dogan and Narbonne (1955), Duverger (1955) and Michel (1965) all observed that between 1946 and 1967 women's vote for candidates of

the right was 10–12 percentage points higher than that of men, they attributed this to factors other than sex, in particular religiosity, age and position
in the labour market.

Religion

Religiosity is still strongly correlated with support for the right, but it has
declined dramatically since the 1950s, and is less clearly associated with
women. In the 1950s, women were more religious than men, even if it
could be demonstrated, as Andrée Michel (1965: 74) attempted to do, that
this was the result of social factors rather than a natural propensity. Michel
showed that more girls than boys receive private religious, rather than
state secular, education and that their out-of-school activities reflected this
divide. For example, her study of poor Parisian families found that they
tended to send their sons to *Jeunesses communistes* and their daughters to
catechism classes (Michel 1959: 298).

Changes in the relation between women and Catholicism have affected
voting patterns. In 1952, 52 per cent of women and 29 per cent of men
attended church regularly. Some 40 per cent of women and 18 per cent
of men claimed to pray daily. In the early 1990s, only 9 per cent of the
men and 11 per cent of the women who declared themselves Catholics,
attended church at least once a week and 21 per cent of men and 24 per
cent of women claimed not to have a religion (Mossuz-Lavau 1997b: 41–2).
This is interesting in that it reveals not only the small proportion of the
population who are now practising Catholics, but also that fewer women
claim to have a religion than men. Since there is a correlation between
religiosity and support for the right, the decline both in religiosity in general
and the gap between men and women in particular, has affected voting
patterns.

Age

Age is still a relevant factor. Young women are more likely to vote for
the left and for ecologists than older women, and between the ages of 18

Table 4.10 Vote and age status in 1993 according to CSA exit poll

	18–24		25–34		35–49		50–64		65+	
	M %	*F* %	*M* %	*F* %	*M* %	*F* %	*M* %	*F* %	*M* %	*F* %
Left	28	31	28	34	35	37	27	29	23	19
Right	54	51	54	48	54	51	67	59	71	76
Divers	18	18	18	18	11	12	6	12	6	5

Source: Ysmal (1995a: 27).

and 64, women are less right-wing than men (see Table 4.10). In the over-65 age group, women are more right-wing than men, but the difference is very small. In 1993, 71 per cent of men and 76 per cent of women in this age group supported a candidate of the right (Ysmal 1995a: 27).

Labour market

Women's position in the labour market has changed dramatically since they first acquired the right to vote and has influenced the way in which they exercise this right. Women's weaker support for the parties of the left in the 1950s and 1960s was explained at least partially by the fact that there were fewer female manual workers (*ouvrières*) than male (*ouvriers*), the constituency represented by the traditional left. It was found that when women and men had the same jobs, the same qualifications and were employed in the same sector, then there was no difference in their vote (Michel 1965: 73).

Janine Mossuz-Lavau and Mariette Sineau's (1983) study of women's political participation found that women who worked outside the home were more likely than those who did not to be interested in politics and to vote for the left. This has been confirmed by subsequent studies, including that of CEVIPOF (1988). A SOFRES poll conducted during the presidential elections in 1988 found that: 47 per cent of women employed full-time; 44 per cent of women employed part-time; 40 per cent of women who no longer worked; and 29 per cent of women who had never worked outside the home voted for candidates of the left (Mossuz-Lavau 1997b: 39–40). In 1993, employment outside the home still influenced women's electoral choices: 49 per cent of women employed outside the home voted for the right in 1993, while this was the case for 63 per cent of women who were not employed outside the home (Ysmal 1995a: 25). Women employed outside the home were for the first time significantly less right-wing than men (49 per cent compared with 58 per cent) (Ysmal 1995a: 26).

The influence of employment outside the home was visible once again in the 1995 presidential elections, when 40 per cent of working women

Table 4.11 Vote and employment status in 1993 according to CSA exit poll

	Employed		*Retired*		*Housewives*
	Men %	*Women* %	*Men* %	*Women* %	%
Left	29	35	28	25	22
Right	58	49	64	68	63
Divers	13	16	8	7	15

Source: Ysmal 1995a: 26.

voted for left-wing candidates, as opposed to 28 per cent of those who did not work outside the home. Nineteen per cent of the latter voted for Le Pen (FN), in comparison with 13 per cent of women who worked outside the home, and 24 per cent for Balladur (RPR), as against 17 per cent. In the second round, 49 per cent of women who worked outside the home voted for Chirac (RPR), and 60 per cent of those who did not (Mossuz-Lavau 1997b: 40). These findings were confirmed in 1997. It is clear, then, that working outside the home is linked to a left-wing vote.

Not only do women employed outside the home vote to the left of those who are not and, in particular, have never been employed outside the home, but since the late 1980s, women in employment have voted to the left of men in employment. Colette Ysmal attributes the differences between the political orientation of working men and working women to their different types of occupation. The majority of working women are middle management and *employées* (white-collar and service sector workers), whereas men are more likely to be manual workers, senior management or members of the professions (Ysmal 1995a: 26). Ysmal (1990: 31) suggests that it is not the job itself, but the relation between the work and the worker which influences political attitudes. She proposes the following explanation of the convergence and subsequent divergence of women's and men's vote in the late 1970s and the late 1980s. She states that as women entered the labour market en masse, their voting patterns began to resemble those of men. However, during the 1980s, women's educational attainments increased, while the type of job they occupied remained the same. 'This seems to have provoked more radical political behaviour as the gap increased between their potential and their experience' (Ysmal 1990: 31). In 1988, 64 per cent of female senior managers voted for the left, compared with 46 per cent of their male colleagues (Ysmal 1990: 31). Amongst *employés*, the proportions were 54 per cent and 48 per cent respectively (Ysmal 1990: 32).

Parties

The attitudes of the parties and, since the late 1960s, their conscious attempts to court women voters, have affected women's political orientation.

Michel and Texier (1964: 108) argue that it is not surprising that, at the time they wrote, women's abstention rates were slightly higher than men's, given the ambiguity of both the right and the left in relation to women's rights:

> How can you ask women to differentiate between the left and the right when the former, claiming to be ideologically opposed to the latter, sometimes shows the same indifference or even hostility when it comes to taking concrete steps in favour of women's liberation?
>
> (109)

They suggest that if women voted more for the right than the left, this was not due to their conservatism, but to the attitudes of the respective parties towards women's rights, including, and most significantly at the time, the right to vote and the right to control their own reproduction (108). While the PCF demonstrated hostility towards the idea of legalising contraception, deputies on the right were courting women voters. For a short period during the 1970s, the PCF presented itself as the party of women's liberation, but at the same time, Giscard d'Estaing appointed a secretary of state for the condition of women, and during his presidency, divorce, abortion and anti-discrimination legislation was passed. The PCF's sometimes overt hostility towards women's rights, combined with the right's opportunist courting of women's votes, produced a complex interplay in women's voting behaviour. 'These dual problems of retrenchment inside the PCF, and growing discontent among feminists with the Giscard government provided valuable political opportunities for a third player, namely the *Parti socialiste* (PS)' (Bashevkin 1984: 82). From 1971, the Socialists, under Mitterrand, actively courted female voters. The growing attention to feminist concerns amongst the parties of the left suggests one reason for attitudinal changes amongst women in France in the 1970s (Bashevkin 1984: 82).

The women's movement also affected women's attitudes towards political parties. While the majority of French women were not involved in feminist politics, many became attached to the rights which were won as a result of the actions of the women's movement, and many associated these rights with the left (Mossuz-Lavau 1994: 73–4). The CEVIPOF survey in 1988 showed that 35 per cent of women and only 22 per cent of men were very or quite attached to these rights. Considerable differences exist between women of different generations: 46 per cent of women aged 18–35 were attached to these rights, while this was the case for only 30 per cent of women aged 35–49 and 16 per cent of those over 50 (Ysmal 1995a: 26–7). Mossuz-Lavau claims that this is undoubtedly one explanation for women's support for the PS, which is seen as more likely to defend women's rights than the parties of the right, and for their reluctance to support the extreme right, which explicitly threatens women's rights (Mossuz-Lavau 1994: 74). The FN has been committed to repealing the Loi Veil (legalising abortion in certain circumstances) since 1984, and it has more recently demanded the cessation of social security payments for the cost of abortions. FN activists participate in commando-style attacks on abortion clinics. Le Pen also advocates a *'salaire maternel'* (payment for mothers who stay at home to look after their children). Mossuz-Lavau (1998c) claims that women voters, especially older ones, seem to be put off by the aggressive rhetoric of FN politics.

This cannot explain, however, why women turned away from the left, and specifically the PS, in 1993. Mossuz-Lavau suggests that women held the PS responsible for the economic crisis, of which they were the main victims and whose consequences they had to deal with on a daily basis (1994: 74). Entering the realm of speculation, Mossuz-Lavau writes, 'They may also be more sensitive than men to social inequalities and to poverty, and faced with the inability of the Socialists to eradicate these problems, some of them, in their disappointment, may have decided to withdraw their support.'

She also claims that women, more than men, are sensitive to immorality in politics, judging those involved in political scandals more harshly. This, she claims, explains why women are more likely than men to vote ecologist:

> For some, it was the only alternative to abstention, while feeling that they were supporting a party which had not yet compromised its principles. Moreover, ecologists use a language which women may find more acceptable than the meaningless rhetoric of the other parties, and their concerns (politics of everyday life, local issues) may reflect women's expectations more closely than conflicts around macropolitical issues.
>
> (Mossuz-Lavau 1994: 74)

Mossuz-Lavau (1994: 71) writes (in terms reminiscent of the rational voter model):

> In conclusion, a new type of woman voter has recently emerged: a woman who is happy to vote Socialist and Green (*le rose et le vert*) who will not put up with Jean-Marie Le Pen's xenophobia and aggression, who demonstrates that she is finally able to use her vote as a sanction: the 'no' vote over Maastricht was the first example of this. The relative disaffection with the Socialists in 1993 shows that women can use the means available to punish those who let them down.

Conclusion

The evidence presented in this chapter indicates that the history of women's electoral behaviour and attitudes has been more complex than one of simply catching up with men. Multiple factors have contributed to their voting behaviour and attitudes. If we return to the prediction of the 1955 studies of French women's political participation, according to which women's political behaviour can be expected to become increasingly aligned with that of men as they become more integrated socioeconomically and culturally, we find that this is not exactly what has happened. Rather than becoming integrated into masculine structures, which was predicted, women have come to occupy separate parts of the labour market and education. The labour market, while containing a more equal number of male and female workers, is still markedly gendered. Similarly, women participate in education as much, if not more, than men, and leave with 'better' qualifications, but these are frequently in less socially valued subjects and serve women less well than their similarly qualified male counterparts.

Political participation is influenced by a complex interplay of factors, including the level of education, age, class, attitudes of the parties, the influence of social movements and cultural changes. Sex does not appear to be one of the most important factors.

The study of women's political behaviour is constrained by the definition of 'politics' which is often narrowly focused on organised party politics, and by the readily understandable attraction of political scientists to easily measured voting behaviour. Despite vast quantities of empirical research in this area, the relation between widely different political activities, which include voting and joining a party, is unclear. There are methodological problems with the wording of survey questions, the secrecy of the vote, the causality drawn from correlations and the expectations of the researcher.

One may try to demonstrate that the difference between men's and women's levels of participation has been exaggerated and is closing or disappearing, due, in large part, to social change. On the other hand, one may try to muster evidence to support the view that women do not participate less than men, but rather participate differently, outside conventional party politics, but politically active nonetheless. This will be developed in the chapters which follow.

5 Explaining women's absence from politics

As early as the 1950s, the newly emerging political science was investigating its own version of the woman question: why did women participate less than men? Participation was measured according to certain criteria, commonly arranged on an ascending scale of time and effort. Activities which were included were political interest (defined as discussing politics with friends, following politics in the media etc.), voting, membership of a political party, activism within the party, standing for election, and attaining political office. In France, however, the groundbreaking studies by Duverger (1955), and Dogan and Narbonne (1955) stand out as exceptions rather than the beginning of a trend. Andrée Michel and Geneviève Texier's (1964) detailed critical rereading of the relation between women and politics was the only other significant contribution to this area of research until the much later work of Mariette Sineau and Janine Mossuz-Lavau. However, while individual academics specialising in this area were few and far between, it is a subject which has periodically roused media interest and, at times, provoked detailed analyses in serious newspapers. These provide valuable evidence of the changing nature of the debate around women's political participation and will be examined here along with the academic studies mentioned above.

During the first few years in which women had the right to vote, there was tremendous interest in the difference it would make. First, would women exercise this right and, second, would their electoral choices be influenced by the Church, by their husbands, by the personality of individual politicians . . .? When it became clear that women's voting behaviour was in fact very similar to men's, especially once age had been taken into account, attention began to focus on other forms of participation, where women were apparently no more visible than they had been when they gained the right to vote and to stand for election. This disparity was already evident in 1955 when Maurice Duverger (1955: 125–6) drew the following conclusion from the UNESCO study of women and politics:

> A very clear disparity can be observed between women's participation in elections and their participation in the circle of government

... At the electoral level, women's participation is high: it does not differ significantly from that of men either in terms of content or of the rate of participation ... At the level of government (in the broadest sense), the situation is quite different. Here women's political participation is very low, and it declines even more as one approaches the core of the inner circle. There are few women candidates in elections; even fewer women in parliament; even fewer women ministers and no women heads of government.

In discussing the absence of women from politics, feminist political scientists have found it useful to categorise explanatory factors as those relating to the 'supply side' on the one hand and to the 'demand side' on the other hand (Norris 1993: 308–30).

Supply side refers to those factors which enable and motivate individuals to pursue a political career. They include access to the resources necessary for participation in the political élite: time, money, support networks, political experience and relevant skills. Demand-side explanations refer to the obstacles which individuals encounter which may block or restrict their access to political positions. These include the candidate selection process of the political parties and the broader political climate in the country concerned.

This framework of explanation allows one to highlight the impact of the demand-side factors on women's participation and representation in politics, which traditional political science has ignored in the past. Consideration of demand-side factors means that the blame for women's under-participation and representation in politics is not placed entirely on women themselves, on their alleged lack of knowledge, interest or competence. Instead, it is shifted so that any attempts to change the status quo have to take into consideration the nature and role of political institutions and the prevalent political culture.

While supply- and demand-side explanations constitute a useful framework within which to carry out comparative surveys of women's participation and representation in politics, they make for a general and hence restrictive approach which does not provide easily for single country studies requiring consideration of specific historical, socio-economic and political factors and of the interactions between such factors.

In this chapter, therefore, we have tried to explain women's absence from politics by examining a number of factors which may be categorised as legal-historical, environmental (cultural and socio-economic) and political-institutional and which may be further divided into supply-side and demand-side explanations where it is helpful.

In the French case, considering the first category of legal-historical factors, discussion ought to focus upon four important points in France's history when deliberate legal measures were taken to exclude women from the processes of devolving political power: the time of the establishment of Absolute Monarchy and the reinstatement of the fourteenth-century Salic law (*loi salique*) which prevented women from succeeding to the French throne; the Revolutionary period between 1789 and 1795; the beginning of the nineteenth century when the Napoleonic Code came into force; and the proclamation of 'universal' (male) suffrage in 1848. The legacy of these historical events has been the emergence and prevalence of an aggressive masculine political culture in which women are considered outsiders and in which, furthermore, subsequent legislation has not favoured them.

Second, as far as environmental factors are concerned, the following have been highlighted: first, women's alleged lack of interest, confidence and ambition, offered as an explanation for their under-representation by political scientists and members of the political élite; and second, the gendered social division of labour which has historically meant that the majority of women have devoted their time to home and family welfare, giving them little or no opportunity to gain the resources (time, money and political training or experience) required for effective political participation.

Finally, among the political-institutional factors, the following warrant examination: the type of electoral system and its impact upon party selection procedures, the role of political parties, and the role of the 1970s' women's movement.

Legal-historical factors

France, in 1944, was one of the last three countries within the EU[1] to have granted women the right to vote and to be elected, and today it occupies the last but one position in the league table of EU countries as far as the feminisation of political representation is concerned. These are two significant indicators of the overwhelmingly masculine nature of political power in France and hence of the dismal level of French women's political participation. It is possible to overstate the case for French exceptionalism, however. Siân Reynolds (1996: 207) argues that, once the introduction of universal suffrage is placed in historical context, France was not that late in comparison with other countries. Between 1918 and 1920, women received the vote in twenty-one polities. In France, the Chamber of Deputies voted for full political rights for both sexes in 1919, but this was blocked by the Senate in 1922, and repeatedly in the interwar period. Between 1919 and 1944, many Europeans, both men and women, were denied the chance to vote and, as war approached, other issues appeared more important in France. Nevertheless, Reynolds claims that there 'was a particular form of gender-blindness related to French republicanism, arising from allegiance to a particular model of the republic', and this has been the focus of much recent work by feminist historians exploring the exclusion of women from French politics.

While it is not difficult to find examples of politically powerful women in French history, it is clear that when women stepped into the domain of power prior to 1944, they did so through nomination by a powerful father, husband, or son or through special favours granted by a male leader. The example of such women, it is argued, far from encouraging women today to make rightful claims to sharing power, in fact serves as 'a foil or counter-model . . . supporting the principle: power, real power, has always been masculine' (Viennot 1996d: 51). Furthermore, the belief that politics is a masculine world into which women's entry is legitimised by men's approval and appointment has been deliberately perpetuated from the time of the *ancien régime* in order to contain women within the private sphere because, as Eliane Viennot states, 'history constitutes a strategic domain in which the supremacy of those who rule is legitimised and because those who continue to rule our society are men' (Viennot 1996d: 52).

If women came to be excluded from the political sphere it is because, at one time, their presence within it was significant, and one has to look as far back as the Renaissance period (1480–1520) which, in France, brought large numbers of noblewomen into the public arena, engaging in military, religious, cultural and political activity.[2] One of the legacies of Renaissance Humanism and the scientific revolution was the emergence of what came to be known as the *Grande Cour des dames* (the Great Royal Court of women). The post-Renaissance French Royal Court was unlike those of the late 1400s and early 1500s or those in other parts of Europe when courtiers numbered no more than about a hundred. By the late sixteenth century the French Royal Court came to be composed of almost 10,000 people at a time, including a large contingent of women. The Royal Court served as a vital political instrument used by kings to retain maximum power, and the introduction of women to the Court was a deliberate policy designed to control the nobility.

How were women used to do this? First, of all, the Court was made an attractive place for noblemen to be, so sexual codes of conduct for women were liberalised. In order to ensure that the Court did not become a place of intrigue and conspiracy, the position of women was reinforced through the codification of relations between the two sexes, designed to socialise, verbalise and ultimately neutralise any aggressive anti-royalist attitudes and threats.

Apart from this, women were also used by kings to denounce the rise of the merchant class as an economic force which would ultimately destroy the monarchy.[3] In this way women came to be at the heart of power and privilege until the succession battle of the 1580s,[4] between Henri de Navarre and Henri de Guise, opened up a debate over the Salic law. The call for women to be excluded from the French throne and from political power was launched by an increasingly influential intellectual bourgeoisie allied to Henri de Navarre whose claim to the throne was upheld by Salic law as opposed to that of Henri de Guise based upon direct descendance from Charlemagne through the distaff side.

The eventual triumph of Henri de Navarre (as Henri IV), arguably 'forged and sealed over the question of the illegitimacy of women to inherit the throne' (Viennot 1996d: 58), and culminated not only in the removal of a part of the aristocracy from political power but also in the illegalisation of women's involvement in public affairs.

This history would then, in part at least, explain why, at the time of the Revolution in 1789, when a new social and political contract was being worked out to lay the foundations of a different, more equal society, women were legally excluded from the public arena, not through oversight or simple misogyny but deliberately because they were identified with conservative, counter-revolutionary forces and ideas. When the father (king) was murdered by the sons (revolutionaries), the sisters supporting the father had to be cast aside, thus – '*liberté, égalité, fraternité*'.

Consequently, from the end of the eighteenth century and through the first half of the nineteenth century, an entire corpus of laws was created with the aim of establishing the civic inferiority of women: for instance political power was linked with the power to carry arms, and early laws dismissed women from the army (1793) and banned women from joining political clubs, from attending political meetings and rallies and from gathering in a public place in numbers greater than five (1795).

The Napoleonic Code of 1804 reinforced the idea that women, like minors, should be placed under the care and supervision of their closest male relative. Hence, like minors, women enjoyed protection but not rights. However, unlike minors, they were afforded protection only in return for specific duties related to their role as mothers and wives. These laws were fortified by the construction of a discourse which justified the laws against women on the basis that they were different in nature. Hence, when the huge reference works (encyclopaedias, dictionaries, histories of literature, teaching manuals etc.) of the nineteenth century were produced, the role of women, it would appear, was systematically concealed, distorted or ridiculed.

However, while the republican regimes may have genuinely feared anti-revolutionary forces, they were also faced with the more mundane problems of making new laws and systems work effectively to their advantage. The new leaders had proclaimed democracy easily enough but found that, at every level, it had unleashed fierce competition between groups and individuals for political office and honours on a scale previously unforeseen. Such competition had to be curbed to avoid potential civil war and one way to do that was to restrict the size of the electorate and the number of those who were eligible representatives and leaders. Thus, the principal restrictions based upon sex, property ownership and age were included in all the constitutions from 1793 to 1848.

Following the revolutionary uprisings of February 1848 when the ruling class was forced to abandon suffrage based on property qualifications in order to proclaim 'universal' suffrage, a deliberate decision was again taken to exclude women, for the practical advantage was clear. From February 1848, the electorate had increased from almost a quarter of a million to over nine million (Carpentier and Le Brun 1987: 279), once more raising the spectre of an uncontrolled and fierce contest for power. In these circumstances it was unthinkable that women too should be included. As long as women were excluded, the electorate could always be contained at half its potential size.

There was also, very importantly, a political advantage to be gained from excluding women. The revolution of 1848 had forced the ruling class to surrender a hierarchy based upon horizontal divisions. This lost instrument of rule was, nevertheless, replaced by another one: a hierarchy based upon a vertical division which was intact by virtue of the fact that sexual differentiation was clear, immutable and therefore not open to debate. It can be argued then that retention of this vertical hierarchy until 1944 allowed rulers to undermine solidarity within classes and popular movements, in particular within the working class and the labour movement, to their advantage.

The introduction of 'universal' male suffrage marked a definitive step in casting women as different subjects from the standard (hu)man subject which was represented by and which contributed to the universalism upon which French citizenship is founded.[5] The universality of rights thus became the universality of male rights quite logically and deliberately, and the exclusion of women was not simply part of attempts to exclude the masses.

This exclusion of women from political rights was upheld by the Constitution of 1875 in spite of the fact that an active, at times violent, suffragist movement had emerged by the end of the nineteenth century. The reaffirmation of women's exclusion from politics in 1875, coupled with the growing number of countries in which women's political rights were extended in the early twentieth century, began to expose the peculiarity of the French situation which, in part at least, has arisen from the legal-historical traditions discussed in this section.

The low participation and representation rates of women in France cannot therefore be explained without reference to a history which has created a masculine political culture in which, even today, it is difficult for women to operate politically.[6]

In his UNESCO report, Maurice Duverger (1955) attributed women's absence from sites of decision-making first of all (although not primarily) to male opposition, citing as evidence the historical resistance of male-dominated parliaments to women's suffrage and the continuing resistance of political élites to women's entry into them. He argues (128) that this is because of the highly competitive nature of political élites:

> Giving a place to a woman means taking it away from a man: in these
> conditions, the number of places given to women is reduced to the

minimum required by propaganda. All the evidence gathered on this question in the different countries concurs: the promotion of women in politics comes up against male resistance.

Duverger argues that the exclusion of women from these highly competitive positions is justified by demonstrating that politics is essentially masculine, and that women should only be admitted in exceptional circumstances (128). The traditional argument of women's incompetence is becoming difficult to defend in the face of women's educational and professional attainments, he continues, but it has been successfully replaced by a new justification, known as functional theory. In this version, there is no inequality between men and women, no superiority of one over the other, but a clear division of labour based on their different abilities. Women are no longer limited to the home, but outside the home, they are still confined to family and childcare issues.

Forty years later, Elisabeth Dufourcq, ex-Minister for Research, in the Juppé government of 1995–7 describes a scene in which little has changed:

> [T]he logic of politics is entirely masculine, entirely virile . . . It is also terribly feudal. When a man forms his Macedonian phalanx in order to defeat the enemy, what does he fear? He fears that a woman will not hold out and he fears it intensely. He fears that a woman does not have the talents necessary to stay the course and to use men's arms, that is, the spear, the shield and the lance. We are still at that stage . . . I was told that I was pushed out not due to reasons of competence – when I left, Research was in a better state than I had found it – but because I did not possess the political assets expected of a mayor of a large town.
>
> (Gaspard 1997b: 115)

Environmental factors

Individual and structural factors fall into this category. The former include women's presumed lack of interest and motivation, and the latter relate to the social structures of education, employment and domestic labour. The individual factors are examined first.

Women are not interested in politics

It is often argued that French women are poorly represented in politics because they acquired the right to vote and to stand for election later than women in comparable democracies. Hochedez and Maurice (1997: 86) argue, however, that there is not a straightforward link between the length of time that women have had the vote and the number of them in positions of responsibility. In the United Kingdom, for example, where women have had the vote since 1918, few of them had been elected to the House of Commons until May 1997. Immediately after German women had won the right to vote in 1918, women made up 8 per cent of the German parliament, but in 1984, they were still only 11 per cent. In Scandinavian countries, women's participation in public life increased greatly in the 1970s, even though Finland and Sweden had had fewer than 10 per cent women in their parliaments in the post-war period, and in Spain, where women won the right to vote in 1931, the number of women members of parliament trebled in 1986.

As explained in Chapter 4, early studies of women's political behaviour (in particular, Duverger 1955, Dogan and Narbonne 1955) found that women participated less and were less interested in politics than men. However, the difference was found to be small and was expected to disappear. It was later publications (for example, Alain Duhamel in *Le Monde*, 10 March 1971) which emphasised the difference. It was argued in Chapter 4 that women respondents to surveys may be less willing than men to declare an interest in issues labelled 'political', but are as willing or even more willing than men to claim to be interested in 'important social issues'. It is possible, therefore, that the problem lies with the term 'political'. It was also shown that the gender gap is much smaller in younger age groups and amongst the best educated. The gender gap is smaller in France than in the EU as a whole, and young women in France are more exposed to the media than young men.

During the Third Republic suffrage debates, women's alleged lack of political interest was attributed to their nature (Gaspard 1995: 226). Later, political scientists asked whether it was due to their essential feminine nature or to their social circumstances (Dogan and Narbonne 1955). It was presented as a lack, an insufficiency on the part of women and the discussion focused on the reasons for this insufficiency and whether or not it could be rectified so that women would at some point attain the standard of political interest set by men and unquestionably desirable. Pierrette Sartin (1967), for example, asks:

> How can women allow themselves not to contribute to debates and to be barely involved in decisions concerning housing, education reform, urbanisation, health? How can they believe that the issues raised by the Common Market, by the war in Vietnam, by the Red Guard, by automation, to name just a few examples, are entirely men's issues which do not concern them at all?

Sartin writes:

> It is true that women's political education does not prepare them for a political role. Neither school nor women's magazines direct them towards this area which is often only out of bounds for them because

no-one has been able to interest them in it and make it accessible to them. In this area, as in many others, women lack self-confidence and do not know what they are capable of.

Four years later, Ménie Grégoire (1971) offers similar explanations in *Le Monde*, where she claims that men are not responsible for women's absence from municipal councils, except in the very largest communes. She quotes a mayor who complains: 'We would love to get women out of their kitchens, but it requires, on their part, a sign of interest, however small, in collective life' and slights women 'with an inferiority complex, who resist any form of education – with this limited idea of their role ("it's better to be a mother than a mayor") ("*il vaut mieux être mère que maire*") – with this distorted idea of their responsibilities'.

The blame is laid partly on women themselves for not fulfilling their duties, and partly on their education and on social and cultural expectations which lead them to believe that politics is for men. Duverger (1955: 132) writes, 'they think that politics is mainly a man's thing, because everything encourages them to think this: tradition, family life, education, religion, literature'. Femininity is inculcated into women from birth, and women become dependent on men. And, according to Duverger (1955: 132):

> That is perhaps the main obstacle to full participation in politics. Political activity in a democratic society is an adult activity. It presupposes that he who undertakes it is fully in control of his destiny, that he does not hand over to somebody else responsibility for deciding for him. It is the exact opposite of a paternalistic idea of social relations. Although women are no longer minors in law, they still think like them in many respects and, especially as far as politics is concerned, they accept male paternalism. Men – husbands, fiancés, lovers or myths – mediate between them and the political universe.

Duverger (133) concludes that there is therefore no point trying to increase women's political participation by introducing reform in this area alone. Their low levels of political activity are, he writes, the result of their secondary role in society, which they are taught to accept as natural.

The belief that women are not interested in politics was one of the earliest explanations offered for their under-representation. That is not to suggest, however, that it no longer has any advocates. Elisabeth Badinter (1997: 40), for example, states:

> There are some fields – law, education, media – which women have entered en masse . . . They wanted the power to judge, to educate, to communicate, and this is not negligible, and they got it without asking for special treatment or privileges. Maybe they have no political power because, with a few exceptions, they did not really want it.

We can conclude that it is difficult to prove that women are less interested in politics than men, once the problems with opinion polls and the definition of terms have been taken into consideration. It may be the case, however, that they are less interested in institutional or power politics than men and more interested in seeking solutions to 'political' (social and economic) problems. This may affect their relation to party politics. However, the greater influence on their participation still seems to be structural rather than individual.

The idea that women are less interested in politics than men has been challenged in several ways, first, by attempting to demonstrate that, although it may be true, it is due to social and economic circumstances which are changing and that, as soon as women are as well educated as men and as well integrated into the labour market, the differences will disappear (for example, Mossuz-Lavau and Sineau 1983). The second approach is to argue that it is not women's lack of political ambition or self-confidence which prevents them from participating on the same terms as men, but obstacles which block their path.[7] If these obstacles were to be removed, women's participation would equal men's. The third and most radical challenge to this argument is, however, that it is the definition of political interest and the criteria which have been used to measure it which construct politics as that which interests men and is done by men.

Education and employment

Some commentators argued that women's lack of interest in politics was due to their lower levels of education and employment outside the home. Studies revealed that political interest and voting increased with the level of education attained by women (Duverger 1955: 131). They also showed that women who were employed outside the home were more likely to vote than those who were not (Duhamel 1971). It was expected, therefore, that as they became better educated and more integrated into the labour market, their interest in politics would grow (Gaspard 1995: 226–7). The *Institut français d'opinion publique* (1955: 206) concluded the report of their 1953 survey on women's participation in politics with the following: 'It seems that the increase in women's employment, combined with that of their education and information, will lead to a disappearance of the gap between the sexes.'

Mossuz-Lavau and Sineau (1979), in an early piece of research, found that the main reason for women's under-representation in politics was their absence from the socio-economic élite which provides the political élite. At the time, women made up 38 per cent of the working population, but occupied only a very small proportion of the most powerful economic positions, those from which the political élite is drawn (62.5 per cent of deputies and 34 per cent of departmental councillors were professionals or top managers). This concentration suggests that those who succeed in gaining political office have access to certain resources: time, knowledge, a reputation, and an income sufficiently high to undertake unpaid political activities. Mossuz-Lavau and Sineau (1979) state that it is not surprising that most of the candidates presented by *Choisir* in 1978 were from privileged social backgrounds. Politics is the activity of a privileged minority, and surveys demonstrate that higher in the social hierarchy and correlating with better education, women are more likely to think that politics is relevant to women as well as men.

In 1983, Mossuz-Lavau and Sineau concluded from their research that the single most important factor in whether women enter politics is whether or not they have a job outside the home. They suggested, somewhat optimistically, that since more and more women were entering top jobs, their participation in public politics was sure to follow soon. Although they recognised the existence of men's resistance to women's participation, they argued that its effects are far less significant than women's socio-economic inferiority. Women's employment conditions mean that they do not have the resources to enter politics, including the relevant experience (Mossuz-Lavau and Sineau 1983: 224–5). Women's relation to politics, they conclude, reflects quite accurately their relation to paid employment. Complete economic dependence favours minimal political engagement; women with poorly paid jobs have difficulty breaking into public politics, because they are deprived of the necessary cultural and economic means. It is only good qualifications which will enable women to enter the top professions and thereby become equipped for politics. From this assertion, Mossuz-Lavau and Sineau (1983: 226) draw the conclusion that as women are becoming better and better educated and are obtaining a growing number of top jobs, the future promises a political élite containing a greater number of women.

Women's access to the jobs from which the political élite emerges was therefore an essential prerequisite to their entry into politics. Housewives may have had more time for political activities than those who performed almost all of the domestic chores as well as a full-time job outside the home (part-time work was rare before the 1980s), but evidence suggested they were lacking in other essential resources, including an independent social status, public experience and self-confidence. Further, Delwasse (1982) adds that housewives are economically dependent and therefore less able to take on the financial costs of political activity.

Women now outnumber men in higher education, and girls outperform boys at every level of the education system. Women entered the labour market en masse in the 1960s and now account for 45 per cent of the working population. So why has the improvement in their socio-economic status not affected their presence in sites of political power? First, although numerically they seem well integrated into the education system and the labour market, they are still vastly under-represented in the disciplines and professions which are socially valued and which lead to political office.

Moreover, when they are present in these professions, they are rarely in positions of decision-making. Despite women's educational achievements and despite equal pay and equal opportunities legislation, women are concentrated in a small number of occupational categories and within these categories, in the lowest paid positions. They earn on average 25 per cent less then men. They do not have the same access to the socio-cultural resources which accompany some types of profession or an education in prestigious institutions, notably ENA. During the Fifth Republic, a disproportionate number of the political élite have been educated at this prestigious *grande école*, where women have been under-represented despite the fact that they have never been officially excluded.[8] Although it may seem that women are excluded from sites of political decision-making in particular ('the last bastion of male power'), closer analysis reveals that, despite high-profile media representations of women executives and successful career-women, women in fact occupy very few sites of economic or social decision-making either.

Social division of labour

It is argued that the double shift of employment and domestic responsibilities which women already undertake makes the idea of a triple shift unthinkable. The notion of *disponibilité* (availability) is currently provoking debates and research within the context of the campaign for parity. Studies show that women are still largely responsible for the housework and child-care, whether or not they are employed outside the home (Bihr and Pfefferkorn 1996: 100–23). Few women interrupt their working lives when they have children, and the rapid growth in part-time work has concerned mainly workers over fifty-five and under twenty-five, contradicting claims that it meets the needs of mothers with young children for jobs which enable them to combine work with childcare. Moreover, mothers who leave their families to undertake political activities attract more criticism than fathers who do the same.

The timing of political meetings makes it difficult for those who are responsible for children to attend: 'now, as before, the problem remains unchanged: these ladies rarely have time to be simultaneously with their children and in the office. So as for election meetings . . .' (Bujon 1994). Women are also less able to devote time to informal networking, still an important element of a successful political career.

However, although the idea that women have less time than men is used to explain their lower levels of participation (and there is plenty of evidence to suggest that it makes political participation very difficult), it is clear that, despite the tremendous burden of home, work and politics, many women do combine all three. This demonstrates an overwhelming commitment to political participation which undermines the argument that lack of time offers sufficient explanation for women's absence from politics.

Political–institutional factors

The 1993 election study (*Parité-infos* 1: 1) revealed that there is no scarcity of women candidates, but few of them achieve political office. The authors of this study conclude that this confirms demand-side explanations for women's absence from politics, in other words, political-institutional factors are at play.

The impact of the electoral system

One of the factors which may go some way towards explaining the patterns of women's representation in elected assemblies is that of voting systems. However, the impact that voting systems on their own have on women's representation cannot be assessed easily and the debate surrounding this area of inquiry is far from over.

In the last twenty years, a number of studies (Bogdanor 1983, Castles 1982, Lovenduski and Hills 1981, Rule 1987) have stressed the importance of voting systems, and a certain consensus of opinion suggests that, all things being equal, proportional representation (PR) or mixed-member PR systems with party lists, said to emphasise greater openness, participation and legitimacy, favour the representation of women and other under-represented groups, in contrast with majoritarian systems. The former, it is argued, provide political parties with an incentive to 'gamble' by including women candidates on their lists whereas parties in single-constituency majoritarian systems are likely to present the male candidates who are considered to be the most politically experienced and well known to electors. This would apply particularly to safe seats, with women, if selected at all, being placed in unwinnable constituencies. PR is also said to increase party competition as the access to seats by smaller and less established parties is improved. The increase in party competition, in turn, means that there is a more rapid turnover of seats. A cursory survey of available statistics, relating to countries which are more or less comparable, would appear to support the view that a link exists between the electoral system in place and the number of women elected (see Table 5.1).

For instance, in countries where women account for 30 per cent or more of parliamentary representatives in the lower house or single chamber, a clear picture emerges in which almost only PR systems are in evidence. Differences within this category may be explained by examining particular electoral practices such as how party lists operate. For example, the use of closed lists is more widespread within this category, suggesting that women stand a better chance of gaining representation where they are nominated by their parties. Greater voter choice (where voters are allowed to express preference for one candidate over another or to modify lists), it is often argued, may hinder women's chances of success. However,

Table 5.1 The proportion of women representatives in the lower house or single chamber according to the electoral system in place

Year of last election	Percentage of women	Country	Type of electoral system
1998	43	Sweden	PR (closed list)
1998	37	Denmark	PR (preferential vote)
1998	36	Netherlands	PR (preferential vote)
1997	36	Norway	PR (closed list)
1995	33	Finland	PR (preferential vote)
1998	31	Germany	Mixed (closed list)
1996	29	New Zealand	Mixed (closed list)
1995	27	Austria	PR (closed list)
1996	25	Spain	Mixed (closed list)
1998	22.3	Australia	Majoritarian (preferential vote)
1997	21	Canada	Majoritarian
1995	21	Switzerland	Mixed (preferential)
1994	20	Luxembourg	PR (preferential vote)
1997	18.4	UK	Majoritarian
1997	14	Eire	PR (preferential vote)
1995	13	Portugal	PR (closed list)
1998	13	USA	Majoritarian
1995	12	Belgium	PR (preferential vote)
1996	11	Italy	Mixed (closed List)
1997	11	France	Majoritarian
1996	6	Greece	Mixed (preferential)
1996	5	Cyprus	PR (preferential)

Source: Compiled from Interparliamentary Union Parline Database (1998), accessed 10 November 1998.

it may also be true that where parties are more hesitant about the feminisation of candidatures and where a preferential voting system exists, there is a possibility for voters to modify lists in favour of women candidates. For instance, the index[9] of women-friendly measures adopted by political parties in Finland (0.08) is significantly lower than that relating to parties in Germany (0.70) where a closed list system operates, yet Finland boasts a higher proportion of women representatives in its national parliament which could be attributed to gendered preferences of voters (IPU 1997: 147).

As one moves down the scale, the pattern becomes less distinct. First, PR and mixed-member PR systems continue to predominate in the next category of countries where women's representation varies between 20 and 30 per cent. Second, a number of countries, notably Australia, Canada and the UK, applying majoritarian voting systems manage to achieve women's representation levels of between 18 and 23 per cent and, although such statistics are by no means approbatory, they are respectable in comparative terms, positioning the countries that they relate to in the middle of the league table (Table 5.1). Finally, the electoral systems of countries such as Belgium, Italy, Greece and Cyprus operate according to the rules of PR or mixed-member PR, yet generate much lower numbers of women representatives in their national assemblies.[10]

Once again, when considering such differences, one has to take into account the particular practices of electoral systems which have already been mentioned above. Hence, explanation of the relative success of women under the majoritarian Australian system, as opposed to women's poor representation in Italy may lie in the fact that preferential voting in Australia has favoured women candidates, especially so in winnable constituencies, while Italy's mixed-member system, which only allows PR in 25 per cent of its constituencies, does not sufficiently counteract other electoral hurdles faced by women candidates, for instance, the very slow renewal of seats in the 75 per cent of constituencies where male élites enjoy predominance, and in particular the lack of pre-selection party initiatives in favour of women. On the other hand, in both Greece and Cyprus, where the level of women's representation drops to well under 10 per cent, in spite of the operation of mixed PR and PR systems (with preferential voting) respectively, it is clear that factors other than that of the electoral system must be considered.

From the discussion above it could be justifiably concluded that while there are some links between voting systems and women's representation, other factors which may be equally or more important in explaining women's absence from politics, must not be overlooked.

The French case

Since the establishment of the Fifth Republic in 1958, a majoritarian electoral system based on single member constituencies[11] has operated more or less continuously in France for legislative elections. This system replaced the closed list PR system which had been used since 1945 and was, in turn, replaced briefly between 1986 and 1988. According to Pippa Norris (1987), this alternation of systems has made France a prime case for study of the impact of electoral systems on women's representation. Furthermore, the variety of electoral systems in use in France, depending on the type of election (cantonal, municipal, etc.), and the peculiarity of certain French electoral practices (for example, the system of multiple mandates or *cumul des mandats*) offers greater scope for assessing the impact of electoral systems on women's representation in France.

Table 5.2 shows clearly that the level of women's representation plunged from 5.7 per cent, achieved under PR in the Fourth Republic, to a low of 1.5 per cent when a majoritarian system was introduced in 1958. Conversely, when PR was reintroduced in 1986, more women were elected while in 1988, the return to the pre-1986 majoritarian system brought some setbacks for potential women candidates.

However, it can be argued that PR has only relatively influenced the gender profile of the French National Assembly both prior to and after 1958. First, although the legislative elections of 1958 generated a sharp drop in the number of women deputies, it also appeared to be part of a trend which had started in 1951 when the elections of that year saw the level of women's representation lowered significantly from 5.7 per cent to 3.5 per cent. The reason for this decrease cannot be attributed to the electoral system which had remained unchanged but to other factors among which the following were of foremost importance: the post-war promises, made by the first Resistance-led governments, to improve women's political participation along with their socio-economic status were being abandoned in the increasingly conservative climate of the Cold War; heightened party competition and the constant jostling for power in the short-lived coalition governments, dealing with the 'hard' issues of decolonisation and West European defence against the USSR, meant that women were being edged out of national political life. Furthermore, the 1958 result may be explained also, and perhaps more convincingly, by the electoral crushing of the PCF which had, up until that point, provided by far the greatest number of women deputies.

Second, and this is demonstrated by the figures in Table 5.2, PR may have generated far greater numbers of women candidates, but the increase in candidates did not translate into an increase in the number of women deputies. This is most noticeable in 1986 when legislative elections were held under a PR system. While 1,680 women accounted for a quarter of all candidates that year, only thirty-four entered the National Assembly. This was compounded by the fact that, while at the following legislative elections of 1988 which saw a return to the majoritarian voting system 336 women represented approximately an eighth of all candidates, only thirty-three became deputies. The difference in outcomes of both elections, each held under different voting systems, was negligible where women's representation was concerned (5.9 per cent in 1986 compared with 5.7 per cent in 1988).

The poor results of the PR experiment of the 1980s (and indeed of all elections held under the majoritarian system) as far as women are concerned, have been attributed, most commonly by the major political parties, to the apparent lack of women candidates. This, however, serves as a convenient argument allowing political parties to disregard electoral practices which mitigate against women's equal presence in decision-making assemblies.

For instance, during the 1986 legislative elections held under PR, women did not occupy the list positions which were most likely to produce a positive outcome. Under the closed party list system, the majority of parties were guilty of placing women in the worst list positions or of leaving them out altogether. A survey of the results of the 1986 legislative elections[12] shows that the major parties were the most inflexible as far as candidate positioning was concerned while the more marginal the party, the more likely it was that women figured in greater numbers and in better positions on their lists. Out of the seventy-three women-headed lists, only sixteen were presented by the major parties: eight by the PCF, five by the PS, three by the RPR and none by the UDF. The remaining fifty-seven were presented by the smaller parties including *Lutte ouvrière* (thirteen lists), the *Mouvement pour un parti des travailleurs* (sixteen lists), the *Front national* (nine lists), the *Parti ouvrière européen* (seven lists), the *Verts* (three lists) and various other oppositional groupings and individuals.

Furthermore, of the thirty-four women candidates elected in 1986, the majority (thirty) were placed in positions one to three on their party lists. Of these, twenty-four had already held National Assembly seats previously, while the remaining ten had gained considerable experience in local assemblies or within their party organisations and were therefore considered low-risk candidates by the main parties.

However, as mentioned above, the argument about the unavailability of women candidates is a familiar one and not used exclusively to defend the minor presence of women in the National Assembly following elections fought under PR. Nor is it only French parties which put forward such an argument. In fact, in all countries and under various types of electoral system, the proportion of women candidates has always been considerably higher than the proportion of women representatives while the situation has been the reverse for men. A study of legislative elections in the twenty-nine OSCE (Organisation for Security and Cooperation in Europe) countries reveals that after averaging out results for all the member countries, men account for about 76 per cent of all parliamentary candidates and women for the remaining 24 per cent but that men then go on to make up about 85 per cent of parliamentary representatives while women make up only 15 per cent (IPU 1997: 58).

The figures in Table 5.2 show that in every French election fought since 1945, the same pattern has been reproduced. Traditionally the major parties have been extremely reluctant to place women in winning positions unless there are vacant seats (due to death or retirement) for which a man cannot be found and where a woman is already a well-known personality.

In addition, in France, the principle of separation of powers means that the functions of a minister are incompatible with those of a deputy, so candidates are elected together with a substitute (*suppléant(e)*). This substitute may then be called upon to sit in parliament if the elected candidate becomes minister. The selection of substitutes has been subject to as fierce competition as that of candidates, especially of those likely to become ministers. Potential women substitutes have been kept out by political parties for the same reasons as women candidates. For example, although the 1997 legislative elections produced a greater number of women substitutes than in previous elections, the number of women deputies fell once

Table 5.2 Women's representation in the National Assembly, 1945–97

	Female candidates	Male candidates	Percentage of female candidates	Female deputies	Male deputies	Percentage of female deputies
21.10.45*	281	2,912	9.6	33	586	5.6
2.6.46*	331	2,762	12.0	30	586	5.1
10.11.46*	382	2,801	13.6	35	618	5.7
17.6.51*	384	3,962	9.7	22	627	3.5
2.1.56*	495	5,372	9.2	19	596	3.2
23–30.11.58	65	2,809	2.3	9	586	1.5
18–25.11.62	55	2,172	2.5	8	482	1.7
5–12.3.67	70	2,190	3.2	10	487	2.1
23–30.6.68	75	2,265	3.3	8	487	1.6
4–11.3.73	200	3,023	6.6	8	490	1.6
12–19.3.78	706	4,266	16.5	18	491	3.7
14–21.6.81	323	2,715	11.9	26	491	5.3
16–23.3.86*	1,680	6,804	24.7	34	577	5.9
5–12.6.88	336	2,896	11.6	33	577	5.7
21–28.3.93	1,003	5,139	19.5	35	577	6.1
25.5–1.6.97	1,464	6,360	23.0	63	577	10.9

Source: Compiled from data in Gaspard and Servan-Schreiber (1997: 6–7).

Note: * Denotes elections fought under proportional representation.

ministerial nominations had been made. This was because the majority of women candidates had male substitutes (Gaspard and Servan-Schreiber 1997: 13–14)[13] and of the twelve deputies[14] (seven women and five men) who became ministers, only three (Jean-Pierre Chevènement, Elisabeth Guigou and Dominique Strauss-Kahn) had women substitutes (Gaspard and Servan-Schreiber 1997: 4).

The problem of winnable seats being made available to women candidates is intensified by the peculiarly French practice of *cumul des mandats* (multiple mandates) which has produced the twinned 'incumbent' and 'recognition' effect and which, in turn, has conspired to keep women out of positions of power.

In France, politicians have not been barred from holding mandates consecutively or from combining more than one type of mandate at the same time. The practice of combining political mandates dates from the establishment of the centralised republican state and its tradition which demanded that national policy orientations were reflected uniformly at local level through, for instance, the deputy who was also local mayor. At a socio-structural level, however, the multiplication of mandates helped construct an integrated republican bourgeoisie (*la république des notables*) which, when established at both the national and local levels, was able to exert a strong political influence and resist anti-revolutionary forces.

From these origins and for the reasons outlined above this practice flourished although it became particularly widespread during the twentieth century as a result of the multiplication of seats at different levels (municipal, cantonal, regional, national and European). Thus, during the inter-war period deputy–mayors represented 27–35 per cent of the National Assembly. This figure had increased to between 36 and 42 per cent during the Fourth Republic, 49 and 56 per cent during the period 1958 and 1981, and stood at 51.6 per cent in 1997. Furthermore, the percentage of deputies holding at least one type of local political mandate had risen from 42 per cent in 1956 to more than 70 per cent in the last 25 years. By April 1997, the number of deputies who did not hold any other mandate stood at only 7.3 per cent (Dubois 1997: 8). The growth of this practice has also meant that its original rationale, of maintaining republican unity at local levels, has been replaced so that the majority of deputies who seek a parliamentary mandate for the first time are holders of a local mandate which provides them with useful political training and public recognition and hence serves as a crucial stepping stone to national power.

One of the consequences of the widespread nature of this practice, although a law of December 1985 was passed to curb it, has been the creation of a self-perpetuating, narrow circle of élites which monopolises power and privileges at a number of different levels and which is reluctant to admit newcomers. This has meant that the renewal of seats is extremely slow, as the majority of incumbents are reselected by their parties until retirement or death. It has also meant that the status of the elected representative is strongly identified, historically, with the male *notable* who not only undertook political functions but also exercised a moral, father-like authority and symbolised a benevolent sense of duty which provided the glue of national unity in scattered communities.

Women have found it almost impossible to take on this status because, in order to exercise the (unpaid) functions of the local representative, it is necessary to have a good profession which provides a stable income and a certain amount of organisational autonomy. The profession and the income attached to it give one an elevated social status and imply that one possesses the level of competence (*compétence*) demanded by elective office, while autonomy is required in order to have the time (*disponibilité*) to carry out the functions of elective office. Traditionally, elected representatives have been male, over forty years of age (with a quarter belonging to the over sixty-five age group) and are drawn mainly from the liberal professions or from the civil service (Deljarrie 1997: 12).

This conception of the local representative remained fairly intact until the 1980s when it began to be challenged by younger potential candidates who took a business management, rather than a public service, approach to the job of the local representative. This was especially so after Socialist decentralisation measures of 1982 reinforced the functions of the local representative. From this time, the local representative as benevolent father figure came to be slowly edged out by the younger, 'hard-headed' male for whom the local authority represented an economic enterprise whose books had to be balanced, and whose personal success was strongly tied up with effective economic management. Again, women have found it difficult to take on this role because of their position in the social division of labour generally, but also because for many potential women candidates and representatives, emphasis upon the 'business' approach detracts from the 'people-centred' (*du côté des gens*) one which they appear to favour.[15]

During the early 1990s, women began to demand an improvement in the employment conditions of the elected representative (*statut de l'élu*) so that some of these problems would be alleviated (Deljarrie 1997: 13). The main guarantees sought by women relate first to *disponibilité*, or time available to local representatives to carry out their functions without disrupting their home life, and second, to the question of competence, for which training is necessary, taking into account all aspects of political life, including public speaking, chairing meetings and dealing with and using the media. The example of Sweden, where women's federations within political parties have fought for and succeeded in gaining women-friendly working hours and political training for women, is emphasised.

Clearly then, certain electoral practices prevent women from entering local politics in sufficiently large numbers, and while this remains the case they will be unable to gain recognition in order to promote themselves or other women as parliamentary candidates.

Nevertheless, the 1997 legislative elections represented a turning point. As a result of 30 per cent quotas adopted by the two main parties of the left, the PS and the PCF, and with a real prospect for both of either regaining seats lost in 1993 or of wresting seats from the RPR or UDF, Socialist and Communist women, in relatively high numbers,[16] were for the first time placed in winnable seats. The resulting National Assembly was one in which women accounted for 10.9 per cent of deputies, the highest figure achieved in the history of French legislative elections (see Table 5.2). However, France still occupies the last but one position in the league table of women's representation in the EU, and demands continue to be made for the reduction of multiple mandates and the improvement of the working conditions of elected representatives.

The picture of women's representation, as one moves down from the national to the local level of political power, remains disappointing. Women continue to constitute a minority among mayors (7.5 per cent) and municipal councillors (20.28 per cent) (Gaspard 1998c: 42) and among general councillors (6 per cent) and regional councillors (25.8 per cent) (European Database: women in decision-making website, 1998). The figures for women's representation improve at the regional and municipal levels, where elections are fought under PR and mixed-member PR with preferential voting.[17]

This improvement may be attributed, in part at least, to the type of electoral systems in use at this level. For example, the 1995 municipal elections brought about an increase in the number of women representatives (from 86,549 in 1989 to 108,570), and of the 22,021 newly elected women, almost 19,000 were elected in the smaller municipalities of under 3,500 inhabitants, where preferential voting is permitted and where the weight of party selection is therefore not crucial in the drawing up of lists (Gaspard 1998c: 39–42). It is also true that France has the largest number of municipalities in Europe (36,545) and a record number of municipal councillors which means that political parties, even in the bigger municipalities, can be more 'generous' in presenting women candidates.

Besides, it would be not be an exaggeration to say that less power is seen to be at stake in local politics which explains the higher proportion (between 20 and 42 per cent) of women municipal councillors in the majority of EU countries (*CEMR* 1997: 4).[18] Issues relating to schools, health, road safety and refuse collection are considered by many male politicians to be only one step removed from the concerns that women deal with in their homes and private life. Local politics provides a convenient intersection between the private and public domains but is removed from the brokering of power at national level and is therefore seen as more suited to the pattern of women's domestic commitments, their lesser political experience and assumed levels of competence. For this reason then, parties have been less reluctant to place women on local lists.[19] Yet, even at local level, the better rates of representation and participation are at the lower levels of the hierarchy of local representative and administrative institutions. There are proportionately fewer women mayors than municipal councillors and pro-portionately fewer women heads of regional and general councils than there are women regional and general councillors. This pattern is not, however, peculiar to France.

The role of the parties

The parties play a crucial role as gatekeepers to political office and have been identified by feminist analysts as the main obstacles faced by women (Sineau 1994a, Mossuz-Lavau 1998c, Gaspard 1995). Andrée Michel and Geneviève Texier (1964: 195) were the first to challenge the view of their contemporaries that if women were under-represented in politics, it was because they did not make the effort to join and become active in the parties. Michel and Texier argued that this ignores the question of *why* women find the parties unattractive. They demonstrate the ways in which the parties' agendas have always reflected masculine priorities and the ways in which the parties have failed to support women in some of their most important campaigns, for example the failure of the PCF to support the campaign for contraception in 1956. In their view, then, it is hardly surprising that women (and other oppressed groups) have turned their political energies to organisations other than the parties. They write (1964: 195):

The lack of democracy and information in the parties of the left is the real obstacle to women's participation and to their promotion in politics. The anti-feminism of the parties of the left is evident not only in the hostility of the parties to measures demanded by women, but also in the naming of priorities which are never the same as women's.

More than thirty years later, similar conclusions were still being drawn. Mariette Sineau (1997a: 53–4) finds that the main obstacles to women's success in politics come from the parties and the men in the parties, and Janine Mossuz-Lavau (1998c: 24) is unequivocal in the following assessment:

The main reason today for the problems women have getting elected is the reluctance of many political parties which are male inner circles operating as closed circuits, self-reproducing in their own image and not prepared to take jobs from men and give them to women.

There are several ways in which the parties might restrict women's access to political office. First, they may nurture and reproduce a masculine culture which has its roots in the private/public divide. Gaspard (1995: 225–6) argues that it is not simply a case of women needing time to catch up with men, having gained the right to vote and to be elected relatively recently: women were active in the parties long before they won these rights. Gaspard writes, 'It is not a case of women lagging behind, but rather a case of the organisations lagging behind and failing to take into account social change.'

Second, the parties may be committed to women's representation more on a rhetorical than a practical level. All the parties are currently declaring their commitment to the better representation of women in politics, but an examination of their internal structures reveals that positions of power in the parties are still occupied by men.

Third, party selection procedures may favour men. Selection procedure varies from party to party, but in all the parties, two unwritten rules have blocked women's selection: priority is given to the present incumbent and to well-known local figures. There is no limit to the number of times a politician is re-elected – only the number of posts held concurrently is limited. This makes it difficult for newcomers, and accounts abound of the resistance met by women seeking selection in a particular constituency (see Adler 1993, Halimi 1997). The experience of Florence d'Harcourt (RPR) is well known but not exceptional. D'Harcourt, deputy for Neuilly and hoping to be re-elected for the fifth time in this safe RPR seat, found herself competing for selection with press magnate, Robert Hersant, who had been 'parachuted in' by the party selectorate. Discovering this, a member of the selection committee stated, 'Mme d'Harcourt is well brought up; she will withdraw.'

The influence of party selection procedures on the number of women in elected bodies is demonstrated by cross-European comparisons of the effect of quotas imposed within parties. In Sweden, Iceland and Norway, a formal or informal rule requires all parties to select 50 per cent women candidates. The number of women in the German *Bundestag* rose substantially when the SPD imposed a unilateral quota (Hochedez and Maurice 1997: 88).

In France, the 1993 election study revealed that more women stand as candidates than had previously been thought, but they are rarely selected by the parties which stand the greatest chance of success in any particular constituency. When the PS made a conscious effort to select women for the 1997 election, it found that there was no shortage of potential candidates and that selecting women did not adversely affect the party's result (in fact, the opposite may have been true). The increase in the proportion of women deputies in June 1997 was largely due to the decision of the PS. A similar phenomenon could be observed in the British election in May 1997, when Labour selected 159 women candidates out of a total of 659, raising the proportion of women in parliament from 9.5 per cent to 18.2 per cent.

Finally, infighting between ideological factions in the parties, each of which is usually headed by a man, may take precedence over the representation of women. This has been reported in the case of the PS and the *Verts*. Members of the women's section of the *Verts* attribute the party's failure to respect the principle of parity partly to the power struggles between individuals and between the currents in the party, which tend to take priority. They claim that the idea of 'competence' also plays a part in the preferential selection of men by the party (Comte and Léonard 1993: 6).

Perceiving party selection procedures as an obstacle, many women have sought appointment to government and ministerial posts, rather than election. The problem with this, however, is that it does not have the same legitimacy, and appointees can easily be dismissed, as Juppé so clearly demonstrated in 1995, when he sacked eight of the twelve women ministers he had appointed only six months previously (Sineau 1994a: 192).

The role of the women's movement

In considering the political participation of women, it is important to examine the role played by domestic women's movements in the overall integration of women in the politics of a country. It is often argued that, in contrast to Britain, French feminists were not interested in political rights and there were no suffragists. This is a misrepresentation. The demand for political rights was a constant, although not unanimous theme amongst nineteenth-century feminists (Perrot 1994: 38, Michel and Texier 1964: 180). Siân Reynolds (1996: 174) finds that of the 144 Paris-based women's political organisations between the war, thirty-three were concerned with the suffrage and related causes. In 1919, the lower chamber passed a motion giving women the vote, but it was blocked by the Senate. Between the wars, the suffrage campaign continued, even though pacifism and abortion were at times higher on the feminist agenda than the vote.

During the second wave of French feminism, however, parliamentary politics was of less interest. In the Nordic countries, where 1960s' and 1970s' feminism led to the emergence of various campaign groups (including men), women's sections in parliamentary parties, NGOs and so on, women have found themselves in a larger 'recruitment pool' from which they may be selected for decision-making positions.

In contrast with the feminist movements in the Nordic countries, the second-wave women's movement in France did not believe in working with or within political institutions and organisations. This was because of its origins in May '68, producing a refusal to accept the delegation of power and a preference for direct democracy. Movement feminists rejected the idea of struggling for access to institutions, preferring instead the goal of overturning them. At the same time, however, there were feminists active in the parties, in the trade unions and in other groups and associations (see Chapter 7).

If we refer back to and accept the specific socio-historical circumstances which led to the exclusion of women in France, it is possible to accept also that the same circumstances, along with the ideology and discourse of difference between men and women constructed by men, produced a feminism which was specifically French. The crucial division within it which persisted through the nineteenth and twentieth centuries has been between 'egalitarian feminists' who dismissed the biological differentiation made between men and women and who demanded equal access for women to all domains of public life on the basis of equality between the sexes, and 'differentialist feminists' who had accepted, either for tactical reasons or because they actually believed in them, the difference arguments which locked women into a particular biological destiny.

Differentialist feminists therefore demanded access to areas of public life on the basis that women were different and not inferior to men and that they could contribute something different but equally useful to public affairs. This division has been so persistent and marked that it split the second-wave feminist movement of the 1970s, the MLF, into two camps which seemed incapable of speaking to each other.

The defining feature of the MLF, dominated largely by differentialist feminists, particularly at the peak of its dynamism, was that it believed in autonomy of action. There was never any question of lobbying political parties or government. The MLF called for strict separatist action over issues such as abortion believing that women could only benefit by challenging the basis of patriarchy. For some, then, the absence of women in political decision-making has in part to do with the anti-institutional ideology and actions of the second-wave feminist movement. Mariette Sineau states:

> At the very point when the women's movement, as a social movement, was at its most powerful, the MLF advocated extreme anti-parliamentarianism. It, therefore, carries some responsibility for the current political under-representation of women in France. The presidential election of 1981 caused a late U-turn and a difficult theoretical conversion. But the damage was done.
>
> (Quoted by Gaspard 1997d: 100)

Conclusion

In this chapter, a number of different factors accounting for the absence of women from politics have been examined. The evidence presented favours the conclusion that women are excluded from politics rather than that they exclude themselves, although it is undeniable that a complex interaction of these factors is at play. However, in looking at these factors, the discussion has necessarily been limited to the conception of 'politics' and political activity as presented in traditional social science, and the problem with this conception is that it establishes men as the norm with which women must be compared.

In the next two chapters of this book, we will examine the challenges which have been presented, mainly by feminist social scientists, to the dominant definitions of 'politics' and 'political activity'. In challenging traditional social science, feminists have attempted to redefine the political in order to argue against the prevailing view that women are absent from the public sphere. They argue instead that women, in massive numbers, have not only acted politically, but have also influenced political decision-making in a different way from men.

6 Women's political activity in the ecology movement and coordinations

The events of May 1968 spawned new ideas about political activism. The new movements (such as the *Front homosexuel d'action révolutionnaire*) which emerged in the wake of the student experience of the period and within the ultra-left's sphere of influence, rejected institutions and hierarchies and practised direct democracy. Although women were active in May 1968, they became increasingly aware of the male dominance of the movement and the division of labour within it, which accorded women subordinate tasks, while men took control of debates and strategy. Disillusionment with their role in mixed movements led to the creation of an autonomous women's movement, which, heavily influenced by the ideals and practices of the student movement, represented an alternative to traditional political activity. The women's movement will be examined in detail in Chapter 7. However, not all women abandoned mixed movements, and the aim of this chapter is to examine their participation in 'new social movements'[1] other than the women's movement, in order to demonstrate some of the ways in which women participated in alternative political activities. Two different social movements are considered here: the ecology movement and coordinations.

The expression 'social movement' has been and continues to be used quite loosely. For example, during the strikes of 1995, it was common to see notices in Paris metro stations informing passengers that the normal operation of particular metro lines were disrupted due to 'le mouvement social'. Alain Touraine (1995: 371) states, 'All of us employ the term social movements in such different ways that our debates are often artificial.' However, there exists in the now extensive literature in both English and French a certain consensus around some of the main defining characteristics of social movements.[2] For example social movements are said to be: collective in nature; organised outside established political and corporate institutions precisely because those involved lack regular access to such institutions; and contentious; and their actions, in defence of their particular causes, often generate a political crisis the result(s) of which can vary. These characteristics are shared not only by the older new social movements which emerged in the wake of the May 1968 events but also by the newer new social movements of the 1980s and 1990s of which the coordination is a particular temporary form.

The reason for examining the ecology movement and the coordinations, in this chapter, is that they offer contrasting examples of women's participation in political activity outside mainstream political parties and pressure groups.

On the one hand, women's participation in the ecology movement has taken place on a regular, longer-term basis and has, consequently, eventually been integrated into the formal arena of political activity.

The longer the period over which a social movement operates, the more likely it is to enter formal political or corporate structures. In common with the post-1968 feminist movement, the ecology movement has been caught in the dilemma of straddling two distinct areas of political activity. If it attempts to define an alternative way of acting politically, it finds itself marginalised from mainstream politics. Entering the political system seems the only effective way to exercise any real influence. But by doing this, it has to compromise some of its principles of organisation and strategy. The integration of the ecology movement into the mainstream institutions therefore raises the same questions as the integration of feminism. In 1974, Giscard d'Estaing's government created a Ministry for the Quality of Life and a Secretariat for the Status of Women. Both were obviously responses to the movements which had emerged in French society since 1968. For sceptics from both movements, they constituted attempts to 'recuperate' or institutionalise the movements, thereby removing their radical and subversive edge. The further co-option of ecology and feminism (and anti-racism), by the Socialist government in the early 1980s led to an overall reduction of 'contentious collective action' by the mid-1980s (Tarrow 1998: 3).

The loss of radicalism and contentiousness of any movement has a significant and, arguably, negative impact on women's participation. The section on the ecology movement, below, suggests that as ecology politics have become formalised, the patterns and volume of women's participation and activism within it and allied to it are not that different from those one might detect in mainstream political organisations.

On the other hand, coordinations rely on bursts of militancy, almost always involving new sections of the population, in response to a particular set of socio-economic and political circumstances. Because of their temporary nature, they remain outside established political and corporate institutions.

In the 1980s, as the post-1968 new social movements (and trade unions) were losing their capacity for contentious political action and as the negative effects of neo-liberal economics (austerity budgets, job losses, deregulation of essential services, contraction of the welfare regimes) were being experienced by ever-increasing numbers of people, newer movements, bringing together a broader range of social actors than in the 1970s, began to emerge. One of the most noticeable differences in the profile of the 'newer' social actors was the shift in gender balance. Dalton (1996: 78) notes that although men continued to form the majority of actors in contentious collective action, 'this pattern is changing with a narrowing of gender roles'. Examples of increasing involvement of women (some-times almost exclusively) in such social movements are: the Greenham Common protest camp in Britain, the anti-abortion blockades by American women in the 1990s, and, in France, the nurses' coordination of 1988. The latter forms the focus of the section on coordinations later in the chapter.

The ecology movement

Ecology in France gained public attention in 1974, when René Dumont stood as a candidate for the presidency, and it broke onto the electoral scene in the 1989 municipal elections, when ecology candidates gained on average 8 per cent of the votes. In the European elections of the same year, the list headed by Antoine Waechter won almost 2 million votes (Pronier and Jacques le Seigneur 1992: 9).

Until the Second World War, ecology had been the preserve of natu-ralists, attracting little attention in France. But after the war, and particularly in the 1960s, concern grew about nuclear power and the effects of urbanisation and industrialisation. Protests emerged against pollution and the destruction of natural habitats (Boy 1990: 212). Ecology was not on the agenda during the events of May 1968, and many of the future leaders of the movement were active in the PSU, Trotskyist organisations or the Communist Party. But the events of May 1968 were to influence the movement in terms of organisation and propensity for ideological divisions, and in the utopian visions still embraced by ecologists twenty years later (Besset 1993: 9).

In France, the new associations quickly divided into two tendencies. The first was moderate and environmentalist, rather than ecologist. It was made up of the associations which in 1969 formed the *Fédération nationale des sociétés de protection de la nature* (FNSPN) (Boy 1990: 212). They were led by scientists and worked with public bodies. In 1971 a Ministry of the Environment was created in the Chaban-Delmas government, and this ministry was responsible for the *Charte de la nature* in November 1972. The FNSPN changed its name in 1989, becoming *France Nature Environnement* (Boy 1990: 212).

The second tendency was ecologist, radical and heavily influenced by the ideology of May 1968 (Boy 1990: 213). It comprised many associa-tions and was responsible for numerous demonstrations. Impetus came from the sinking of the *Torrey Canyon* in 1967 and the successful protests against the construction of skiing resorts in the Vanoise in 1969 (Besset 1993: 9, Prendiville 1993: 22). In Alsace, the ecology movement grew in the late 1960s around two particularly active militants, Solange Fernex and Antoine Waechter, and responded particularly strongly to Giscard's announcement of a nuclear power programme in 1970 (Besset 1993: 10). In 1970, Alsace was responsible for one-fifth of the letters and petitions demanding that the *parc de la Vanoise* be saved from plans to construct skiing resorts (*Le Monde*, 7 June 1978: 24). The first anti-nuclear committee was established in Fessenheim, where 1,000 people demonstrated in April 1971 and 10,000 in May 1972. Demonstrations followed at other proposed sites for power stations (Boy 1993: 311). The ecology movement became the site for a May 1968-style anti-nuclear protest (Besset 1993: 10).

The other main area of ecologist protest was the attempt to prevent the construction of a military camp in Larzac (Besset 1993: 10). This campaign became a symbol for non-violent protest against the military and the state. It brought together pacifists, ecologists, the extreme left (Maoists and the LCR), and the alternative left (PSU) in a 6,000-strong protest in November 1971. The struggle continued until 1981, when Mitterrand withdrew the plans, sensing the political significance which they had acquired (Prendiville 1993: 23).

During the 1970s, the ecology movement was dominated by libertarian tendencies, which wanted to find alternative forms of political activity outside the institutions. During the 1980s, electoral politics gradually took hold.

Electoral politics of ecologist organisations

The most powerful of the numerous ecology groups which formed in the early 1970s was *Amis de la terre* (Friends of the Earth) which declared itself 'anti-capitalist, *autogestionnaire* and socialist' and was opposed to structuring, global programmes, alliances, strategic power play and institutional politics (Besset 1993: 10–11). It persuaded René Dumont to stand in the presidential elections in 1974 in order to draw public attention to ecology politics. Dumont's manifesto had little in common with the priorities of the naturalist associations. It talked of the plundering of the Third World, of population growth, self-management within companies, class struggle, the oppression of minorities, the subordination of immigrant workers, consumerism, and women's liberation (Pronier and Jacques le Seigneur 1992: 24). The issues included in this electoral platform indicated clearly its origins in the events of May 1968.

After the election, René Dumont withdrew from electoral politics, and the 3,000 ecologists who met at Montargis to discuss the future found themselves divided. The movement was characterised by divisions between those who supported a national organisation and those who did not, those who considered themselves part of the left and those who dissociated themselves from both the left and the right (Boy 1990: 213). By the 1978 legislative elections, the movement was clearly split into electoralists and anti-electoralists.

Debates raged over whether or not to form electoral alliances, poles forming around Antoine Waechter and Brice Lalonde. A plethora of ecology groups emerged in 1977, on the right, the extreme left and around the *autogestionnaire* and regionalist movements (Boy 1990: 214).

Further divisions arose at the 1979 European elections. Besset (1993: 11) reports that by this time, the movement had entered a retreat into fragmented groups (*hibernation groupusculaire*). Boy's account is more positive. He recounts that the list *Europe-Ecologie*, led by Solange Fernex, represented locally-based ecology against Parisian stars and left-wing tendencies. It centred its campaign on the critique of industrial society and won 4.4 per cent of the vote, the highest ecology score in Europe. This relative success inspired the creation of the *Mouvement d'écologie politique* (Movement for Political Ecology) in 1979, an organisation whose function was to popularise ecology, not gain political power. Its president was Philippe Lebreton (Boy 1990: 214–15).

During the 1980s, the ecology movement, like the feminist movement and all social movements, was faced with the problem of developing a strategy which would enable it to advance its project under a Socialist government. While some advocated working with the Socialist government and attempting to introduce ecologist concerns, others refused to cooperate with a government developing nuclear power. Several attempts were made to create an ecology party, resulting in the creation of *Les Verts – parti écologiste* (the Greens – Ecology Party) in November 1982 (Boy 1990: 215–16).

After achieving disastrous results in elections throughout the 1980s, ecology candidates finally made a breakthrough in 1989, when 1,300 local candidates were elected in the municipal elections, and 9 in the European elections (Boy 1990: 217).

Hainsworth's (1990: 102) assessment of the problems which the *Verts* were facing in 1990 is reminiscent of debates around feminism and electoral politics. They include the question of how to react to the infiltration tactics of former alternative left forces; how to maintain democratic structures as the membership grows; how to balance the 'mediatisation' of certain stars in the movement, and the growing tendency of the *Verts* to turn into a political party, with its opposition to party politics and leadership; how to reconcile the persisting divisions within the movement between leftism and autonomy; and how to avoid the co-option by other parties of green themes. The appointment by Michel Rocard of Brice Lalonde as Minister of State for the Environment can be read either as a concession to the pressure exerted by ecologists or as an attempt to win their voters.

Ecology parties have developed an ideology which reaches far beyond defence of the environment. They have constructed a critique of diverse aspects of the cultural, social and economic structures of industrial societies, including the alienation of non-creative work, the uprooting caused by urbanisation, and overconsumption encouraged by the advertising industry (Boy 1993: 319). Of particular interest here, however, is their critique of the organisation of the state which is seen as centralised, bureaucratic and hierarchical, and their analysis of the 'democratic deficit', which results when an archaic and corrupt party system confiscates state institutions. They argue that the current parliamentary system silences minorities and ignores the demands of unions, groups and associations in civil society. In order to rectify these problems, ecologists propose transforming the electoral system to introduce proportional representation at all levels, an increase in the use of referenda, greater power for local bodies and the participation of immigrants in local elections. The *Verts* remain wary of structure and leaders and value direct democracy and local action.

Women's activism in the ecology movement of the 1960s and 1970s

A search for evidence of women's participation in the ecology movement of the 1960s and 1970s produces more allusions to their activism than details of it. Dependence on the press leads to unbalanced accounts, reflecting what was considered newsworthy at the time, rather than an overview of day-to-day activism. Detailed biographies of particularly active militants can be found, for example, a profile in *Le Monde* (7 June 1978: 24) of Solange Fernex, a prominent force in the Alsatian ecology and anti-nuclear movement. Fernex was Secretary of the Haut-Rhin section of the *Association fédérative régionale de protection de la nature* (AFRPN) and municipal councillor. She stood as substitute to the first ecology election candidate, Henri Jenn, in 1973. In 1974, she led the successful protest against the construction of a lead factory at Marckolsheim and in 1975 joined the anti-nuclear protest at Wyhl, which succeeded in preventing the construction of a power station. However, her 23-day hunger strike with her son and five other protesters against the construction of a nuclear power station at Fessenheim was less successful.

A short biography of Renée Conan appears in *Génération verte* (Pronier and Jacques le Seigneur 1992: 31–2). Conan's first ecological protest followed the *Torrey Canyon* disaster in 1967, but she had already been involved in support for the FLN during the Algerian war, in the Communist Party, and *Amitiés franco-chinoises*. During the events of May 1968, she was active in the CGT, until she met Daniel Cohn-Bendit and became an anarchist. Soon afterwards, she became an ecologist. She became president of the Family Planning Association in Lorient and active in an association promoting organic food. She was involved in the protests at Larzac and Plogoff, and joined *Amis de la terre* in 1975. Conan was elected to the European Parliament in 1989.

While it is important to record such details in order to avoid the obliteration of women's political participation, the history of exceptional individuals cannot provide general conclusions. Were women more active in the ecology movement than in mainstream political parties? Were they more active in the ecology movement than in other alternative social movements? We do not know. We know that some of the major ecological protests were led by women, for example, in 1980, women of the village of Plogoff in Brittany led a 45-day anti-nuclear protest involving 2,400 protesters (Le Borgne 1980: 1). This protest is described by Prendiville (1993: 33) as the last great anti-nuclear protest and the only real victory. There was much violence. Mitterrand withdrew the project in 1981.

The arrival of the Socialists in power in 1981 led to a demobilisation of extra-parliamentary pressure groups, many of whom felt that victory had been won. Not only were the projects for Plogoff and Larzac abandoned, but some of the key figures in the opposition to them were appointed to positions of responsibility: Huguette Bouchardeau became Minister of the Environment and Michel Rolant, CFDT, was appointed head of the new *Agence française de la maîtrise de l'énergie* (Prendiville 1993: 33).

Women's candidacies under ecology banners

In the 1978 legislative elections, three candidates from the *Parti féministe* stood for the alliance *Ecologie 78* in the Paris region: Anne-Marie Vergès, Christine Roux and Gisèle Chaleyat, and seven women and two men from the *Parti féministe* stood as *suppléants* to ecology candidates also in the Paris region (*Le Matin*, 24 February 1978). The *Parti féministe* declared itself opposed to traditional male politics, while aiming to achieve a representation of women in all national and international political bodies in proportion to the gender balance of the electorate. *Le Matin* (24 February 1978) reports that 'while it [the Feminist Party] approves of and sometimes supports Gisèle Halimi's feminist demands, it finds her too political' and that it formed an election alliance with the ecologists because of their 'neither left nor right' stance.

Libération on the same day (24 February 1978) reports the candidacy of Chantal Mamou-Ani and her substitute, Amy Dahan. Mamou-Ani is reported to have said:

> I am feminist and at the same time opposed to the centralised state and nuclear power. I am also in favour of the reduction of the working week, and not only in favour of women's employment rights. In my view, the Choisir candidacies, which are nevertheless the highlight of this election, are too constrained by the traditional framework of 'women's rights'.

Feminists were involved in the attempts to create a minorities list (*liste des minoritaires*) in 1979, along with the PSU and ecology groups. Individual women supported the initiative (Annie Leclerc, Chantal Chawaf, Xavière

Gauthier, Anne Tristan, Leila Sebhar, Hélène Bellour, Michèle Perrein and Maria Macchiochi) (*Libération*, 27 April 1979). Feminists (Colette Auger, Edith Lhuillier) also participated in debates organised by *Amis de la terre* around the creation of a feminist element on this list, but divisions amongst ecologists and amongst feminists made this difficult (*Libération*, 27 April 1979).

Solange Fernex headed the *Europe-Ecologie* list at the 1979 European elections (*Le Monde*, 14 February 1980). *Europe-Ecologie* initially united, on the one hand, ME activists and ecologists who were not attached to any particular organisation (*les écologistes inorganisés*) and, on the other hand, the PSU and MRG. However, the ecologists withdrew, fearing the loss of a separate identity. Friends of the Earth refused to participate (Prendiville 1993: 38).

Women's activism in ecology movements in the 1980s and 1990s

Arc en ciel was a movement which, between 1987 and 1990, brought together ecologists, former members of extreme left organisations, former communists, socialists, and anti-nuclear protesters. It invited feminists to join its attempt to create a new social movement. The feminist collective *Ruptures* and feminists from the *Centre d'initiatives pour de nouveaux espaces de liberté* (CINEL) accepted the invitation. The feminists who were at that time members of the collective *Ruptures* had been active in various left and extreme left organisations: 'As a result of this experience, they wanted to undertake an analysis of politics from the standpoint of feminist women. We decided that, as soon as the opportunity arose, we would present feminist women candidates at elections' (Dental 1996: 65). The *Verts* offered them candidacies in the 1992 regional elections, which they accepted but only as token names too far down the list to stand any chance of election. At the 1993 legislative elections, Monique Dental, of the feminist collective *Ruptures* and *Arc en ciel*, stood in Paris as a *Verts* substitute. Her campaign focused on the right to abortion and contraception, opposition to male violence towards women, and parity in elected bodies. The list won 9.8 per cent of the vote, the highest score obtained by the Greens in Paris and the Paris region (the national score was 11.6 per cent).

Dental was asked again to stand for the *Verts*, this time at the European elections, as *candidate d'ouverture*, non-party activists from social movements who are invited to fill every seventh place on the party's candidate list in order to demonstrate its understanding of politics as a plural convergence of different sectors of society who participate together in the social project. Dental (1996: 67–70) reports that the *Verts* tried to ensure that as many as possible of the *candidats d'ouverture* were women, in order to achieve their goal of *listes paritaires*. This included women from the feminist movement and from other social movements. The enthusiasm of the women's committee within the *Verts* was not, however, shared by the others involved in the selection process, and the two women *candidates d'ouverture*, Anne Zelensky and Monique Dental, moved down the list. Dental (1996: 67–70) describes her encounters with anti-feminists within the *Verts* and amongst the other *candidats d'ouverture*.

Ecology, femininity and feminism

In an article published in *Libération* in 1978, Anne-Marie de Vilaine (1978) describes her experience of a public debate on 'La Nouvelle Politique' with Brice Lalonde, Serge Moscovici, Alain Touraine, Marcel Mousel, Pierre Rosanvallon and Jacques Julliard and includes the text of the contribution she had prepared, but had been unable to give. Vilaine recounts her feelings of unease following professional speakers and adds, 'In any case, it is impossible for a woman who is not at all aggressive to contribute to a somewhat heated political debate' (1978). There are two elements to her critique of the meeting. The first is the explicit critique of the politicking of the dominant members of the meeting, which upset some of the ecologists present. She felt excluded because she was an outsider who did not know how to play the game. The others were experienced professional speakers. The second is the more or less implicit suggestion that this was associated with the fact that they were men. She did not feel aggressive enough to intervene and felt unable to introduce a '*parole féminine*' (women's voice) into a debate which she compared with a boxing match (Vilaine 1978).

The text of her undelivered contribution makes an explicit connection between ecology and femininity. Ecology is an appeal to a non-violent ethics, which aims to bring an end to the rape of the environment and of people. The earth has been raped by men. Consciousness of this and the political fight to bring an end to it is inherently feminine and feminist. Putting ecological concerns on the political agenda is linked to bringing women into politics, both of which are taking place slowly and uneasily. Vilaine (1978) asks, 'Based on these comments, can it not be said that ecology is, to a certain extent, women's politics?'.

Vilaine argues that the repressed other, of which femininity is the epitome, is the stimulus for protest, whether the protesters are ecologists, pacifists or feminists. If women were present in politics, they would introduce new elements:

> The body, emotions, feelings, relations with others, communing with nature, caring about the environment and everything connected with 'private life' that society merely tolerates: the question of relationships, families, children, the elderly. Women would talk about children imprisoned in the tyranny of school hours, disabled by inappropriate childcare and the lack of space. They would talk of the loneliness of

elderly people, mothers' lack of time, the impossibility of affection at the end of a double working day, of the selfishness and intolerance caused by overwork and too much noise. Women, who are responsible for buying 83 per cent of consumer goods, would talk of the depersonalisation of commerce which turns shopping into a daily grind. In short, they would be in a much better position than men to report the process of dehumanisation which they experience daily, since, for them, there is no compensation in the form of power.

(Vilaine 1978)

In many ways, these issues do seem to suggest links between the interests of feminism and ecology, although to suggest that women would automatically bring them into the political arena does not take into account the diverse political views held by women. Some of these concerns are still at the centre of debate within the ecology parties, and the practice of the *Verts*, for example, has been adapted to respond to the lives of the women present at the highest levels of the party (Lipietz 1994). But this is not an inevitable consequence of the presence of women. The recent case of a woman minister who announced that she would not be taking the maternity leave to which she was entitled illustrates the way in which many women politicians have adapted to the rules of the game and left the structures and practices of male politics unchanged.

The ideological links between feminism and ecology were explored in a special issue of *La Baleine*, the journal of the *Amis de la terre*. Sophie Chaveau (1979: 2) claims that women are attracted to a movement which is concerned with the body, the earth, life, cycles, seasons . . . Women's voice, she states, is ecologist, although it has been silenced by electoralism. She asks whether it is still possible for women to participate in the movement, or whether they should abandon it and look elsewhere. Claire Bajard, in the same issue, argues that, because of the way they live and the tasks they perform, women are better adapted than men to a future ecological society:

> There is every chance that they will adapt better to the society which ecologists wish for: non-violent, *autogestionnaire*, non-hierarchical, where job-swapping would be common, where work would no longer be surrounded by a sacred aura and would be limited to what was strictly necessary, where recycling would be the norm.

(Bajard 1979: 6)

In 1979, a tract was circulated announcing the creation of a mixed group '*Ecologie et féminisme*'. It argued that feminism and ecology are inextricably linked: both challenge industrial society; the idea of the domination of nature has much in common with the idea of the domination of women; and the woman-mother has much in common with Mother Nature.

'Ecology must be feminist, otherwise it will contradict itself, perpetuating a form of domination, that of women by men, and consequently legitimising other forms of domination: that of nature by men and of men by other men.'

Anne-Marie de Vilaine states that the link lies, first, in the fact that women and nature have both been oppressed by men for thousands of years (Dialogue des femmes 1981–2: 7). She argues that male scientific and rational thought on which today's society is based, and the centrality of relations of production and consumption, mean that 'private' issues are ignored. Women can only begin to seek access to sites of power if they leave behind their periods, their breasts and their babies. Decision-makers are self-reproducing in their own image. Ecology teaches us that this is wrong: 'the more diverse an ecosystem is, the more resistant it is to agents of destruction' (8).

Françoise d'Eaubonne, in a book entitled *Ecologie/Féminisme* (1978) argues that feminism and ecology *must* work together, since socialism has failed both to bring about a revolution and to fight against nuclear power and genetic experimentation (d'Eaubonne 1978: 13–14). A socialist revolution limited to a settling of scores between two classes of men would not bring about a change in lifestyle which would benefit not only women, but everyone.

In the entry on women in the *Le livre des Verts* (Les Verts 1994: 41–50), it is argued that the women's movement and the ecology movement derive from the same aspirations and the same values, although the assimilation of a 'feminine nature' and ecology is rejected. The two movements both question a society based on growth and inequalities. They value solidarity over competition and refuse to exclude on the basis of difference. They want a better balance between 'work' and 'private life'. The *Verts* write (46–7) 'Finally, peace and environmental protection concern most women, perhaps because their culture means that they love life and want to protect it (and not only because they can create life)'.

The *Verts* support the right to abortion for all women, including minors and immigrants. They support non-sexist education and training for women, giving access to all forms of employment, and the removal of all discrimination against them whether during recruitment or promotion. They advocate the reduction of the working week for all, which would enable the redistribution of domestic labour (*Les Verts* 1994: 47).

It is impossible to tell from the available evidence whether women were more involved in the ecology movement of the 1960s and 1970s than in the mainstream political parties. Only a tiny minority of those who demonstrated at Larzac and Plogoff, for example, belonged to an ecology organisation. A larger number belonged to the extreme left or the PSU (Pronier and Jacques le Seigneur 1992: 219). However, it is clear that women were active in the ecology movement and that a debate took place within the movement around the links between ecology, femininity and feminism.

As part of the movement integrated itself into electoral politics, some of its principles were compromised. But the *Verts*, by including in its statutes a commitment to the equal representation of women and men within party structures and on electoral lists, have attempted to keep the issue of women's access to politics on the agenda. The extent to which the principle is reflected in the actual practices of the party was discussed in Chapter 2.

It has been suggested that women have been particularly attracted to ecology politics for two main reasons. The first argument is that there is a link between ecology and women/femininity/feminism. This link has been variously ascribed to women's experience of motherhood, their closer links with the Earth, with life and nature, and to their social experience of subordination/exploitation/colonisation. The second argument is that women found in the ecology movement a critique of mainstream political parties and a commitment to direct democracy with which they agreed. Nevertheless, it seems that the proportion of women in the membership of the *Verts* is no higher than in other parties, so the question must remain open.

The nurses' coordination of the 1980s

The coordination as a vehicle for social protest was not new to the 1980s and 1990s. Its roots can be traced back to the strike movements of *lycéens* (high school pupils) which took place sporadically during the five years following the events of 1968.[3] It was 'rediscovered' during the 1980s: in 1986 at the time of the student and railway workers' strikes and in 1988 when 90 per cent of French nurses and other health sector workers decided to take to the streets to protest against their wages, working conditions and cost-cutting health budgets. In the 1990s, the coordination was used by a multitude of women associations, gathered under the name CADAC, to fight in favour of abortion, contraception and other rights for women.

The nurses' coordination emerged in March 1988 when an estimated 3,000 nurses (Granger 1988: 16) demonstrated against the Barzach decree (of December 1987), seen to devalue entrance requirements to the nursing profession.[4] The demonstration was followed up by a meeting (of about a hundred nurses from the Île de France region) in April when three commissions (on salaries, professional status, and working conditions) and a national bureau were set up to coordinate nurses' action in favour of their needs and ensuing demands. This coordination was responsible throughout 1988 and most of 1989 for mobilising nurses and their supporters in mass demonstrations,[5] talking to press and government representatives and organising general meetings (*Assemblées générales*) from which emerged a portfolio of demands[6] to put to the government. Although the coordination disintegrated at the end of 1989, the social movement of nurses (strikes and demonstrations)[7] from which it emerged continued sporadically between 1990 and 1992.

A brief definition of the coordination has already been given in Chapter 3. However, some expansion of that definition is required here before an examination of the nurses' coordination takes place. In Chapter 3, a coordination is defined as a temporary form of organisation emerging during periods of social mobilisation in order to represent and organise those belonging to a particular occupational group at national level if possible (Leschi 1996: 167). Three points which are not made explicit in this definition and which are worth noting are: first, a coordination is autonomous and therefore distinct from trade unions or party organisations which may be operating in the same context, at the same time; second, a coordination cannot outlive the social movement from which it springs because if it did, it would change in nature. Very often attempts to transform a coordination into a permanent structure conclude in the demobilisation of the social actors involved and cause the social movement to ebb away. Third, because a coordination represents a particular occupational group, its demands are categorial or exclusive rather than global and it can be argued that this aspect of the coordination can eventually lead to its decline.

In this respect the nurses' coordination of 1988 represented an archetype of the form: it easily set itself apart from the trade unions as a very small percentage of nurses – 5–8 per cent (Rosehill 1988: 29) – were unionised; attempts to transform it into a permanent organisation along trade union lines led to its dissolution in December 1989 and to the subsequent establishment of a corporate representative body by a section of the original coordination; the fact that the coordination represented a specific category of workers with particular demands meant that the question of the nursing body's relationship with other groups of health workers and the linking of demands was left to one side. Although the dynamism of the coordination inspired other groups of workers to take similar action (for example, social workers), the desire of a section of the coordination to build a single broader movement of health workers was unfulfilled. The rift between those who wished to broaden the movement and those who did not also contributed to the coordination's disintegration.

The study of women's participation in the nurses' coordination is interesting in that the latter gives some indication of the way in which power relations can operate when women are in charge and can therefore serve as a lesson for women in future protest movements. In this respect, the nurses' coordination indicated that: women in large numbers – and they represent 85 per cent of all nurses and 93 per cent of state registered nurses (*Infirmières Diplomé(e)s d'Etat*) (Kergoat 1993: 130) – can demand greater representation and power in decision-making sites but that men have to be willing to hand it over; and while the state can be forced to deal with an autonomous adversary outside the accepted arena of parties and trade unions, it has greater power to force change on this adversary than vice versa. This is demonstrated below.

As far as the question of representation and decision-making power is concerned, and contrary to normal practice, women formed the visible majority in all the decision-making sites of the coordination. They were present, in the majority, in general meetings at hospital, regional and national level, in the three national commissions and in regional and national bureaux. For example, on average, 70 per cent of those who attended national bureau meetings, contributing to decision-making, were women (Kergoat 1993: 130). This figure stands out as highly unusual when compared with corresponding figures in party and trade union organisations. However, the representation that women achieved in decision-making, in this case, did not occur naturally just because they formed an overwhelming majority of the profession. In fact, in spite of their large numbers, they had to consciously force themselves to take control from the men who had come to the fore at the beginning of the movement because of their previous experience of contentious action and organisation. One woman activist describes the experience thus:

> At the beginning, in general meetings, coordinations, [national and regional] bureaux meetings, it was always the men who spoke most often . . . later we, that is the women in the bureaux, started discussing this amongst ourselves. This was our battle . . . So then, when men spoke for too long in general meetings, we used to say to them: 'that's enough now, women have the priority!' . . . [W]e became assertive as individuals and as women.
>
> (Granger 1988: 21)

However, the women's determination to take control over their struggle was also matched, to a certain extent, by the willingness of many of the men concerned to hand over power. The male activist's experience is summed up as:

> It's true that during the first stage, the stage of building and structuring the movement . . . we [the men] . . . had experience of militant action in trade unions and the LCR [*Ligue communiste révolutionnaire*], whereas on the whole, this milieu [nursing] had very few militant traditions (trade unionists are mainly men) . . . The result was that it was mainly men who intervened. In the end the women reacted and we realised that if we continued in this way, we would cut ourselves off from the reality of the situation.
>
> (Granger 1988: 21)

The realisation of both women and men that there had to be a rebalancing of power relations between them meant that action was taken to prepare meeting agendas and the sequence of interventions in advance with all proceedings being accurately minuted. Once this process acquired a dynamic of its own, women came to take charge of running meetings, organising demonstrations, and talking to the media and government, and of the coordination in its entirety. Danièle Kergoat (1993: 132) notes that such transfers of knowledge and skills, and ultimately power, are normal within such movements but that they take place mainly between men and sometimes between men and individual women who are seen either as exceptional or particularly deserving. However, what was new and instructive about this situation was that power was transferred to women collectively.

Finally, the study of the nurses' coordination also shows that while the state can be forced to deal directly with an adversary, the result of such an exchange is almost always negative for the adversary.

The nurses' coordination decided, early on in its history, that the state would be the main target of confrontation because it possessed ultimate power to respond to their demands. The coordination therefore bypassed the normal channels of negotiations at hospital and regional authority level. The state or its representatives in government,[8] used to negotiating with recognised social partners (employers and trade unions), refused direct confrontation until the massive demonstration of 13 October which mobilised 100,000 people. However, the government's acceptance to meet with coordination leaders, but only in tripartite meetings with the trade unions, meant that it was able to conclude an agreement (the Evin agreement of 24 October 1988) with the trade unions (excluding the CGT and CGC) which had the capacity of splitting the coordination and the wider social movement. The result of dealing directly with the government, with the trade unions present, was that an internal debate was launched within the coordination. The debate over the question of whether or not the coordination should transform itself into a 'recognised' negotiator led to its eventual disintegration, as disagreements over the importance of the debate itself as well as over the kind of transformation that should take place produced intractable divisions.

However, Kergoat (1998: 127–8) argues that despite the eventual failure of the coordination to extract gains from the state, in its exchanges with the state it refused, for a time at least, to allow the latter to separate women's needs and demands into strict categories of the 'private' and the 'public'. One member of the government's negotiating team confessed that dealing with the nurses was disconcerting as they would talk about day-to-day problems which were moving but which could not be treated within the abstract, codified way that was the norm; governments were not used to dealing with 'slices of life'. Kergoat states that the nurses' exchange with the states' representatives also revealed the contrast between a monolithic power which functioned on the basis of a masculine logic and a plural, female power which was interested in the political rather than in politics. The coordination showed the state and society that there were different ways of dealing with social actors. In addition, the nurses' insistence on confronting the state directly brought into public view a new (female) model of the waged worker, unlike the masculine model portrayed by the trade unions.

Conclusion

This chapter has shown that women's involvement in social movement politics is greater than that suggested by public images. Moreover, the participation of women has raised important questions about the organisation, structures and conduct of social movements and the issues with which social movements are preoccupied. It can be argued that, in doing so, women's involvement in social movements can provide a rich experience from which future movements can learn useful lessons.

7   Feminist politics

Feminists have been active throughout the Fifth Republic, although their ideology and practice have varied considerably during this period. After a lull in the 1950s, French feminism was reactivated during the 1960s, which saw a radicalisation in some women's groups and associations. During the 1970s, a specific manifestation of French feminism, the *Mouvement de libération des femmes* (MLF) became dominant, although other forms of feminism existed alongside it. These continued their activities after the MLF had disappeared in the early 1980s, and other forms of feminist activity had emerged. The frequent representation, especially by the media, of feminism as synonymous with the MLF obscures the diversity of feminist politics in France. Feminist politics is theory and practice which aims to change the power relations between men and women. It includes attempts to achieve equality between men and women, to improve the status of women, and to fight against their systematic oppression by men. A wide variety of strategies can be used to achieve these aims.

This chapter presents the various actors in French feminist politics, their aims, and their strategies. It asks whether feminism offers a different way of doing politics and to what extent we should see this as encapsulated in the type of feminist politics which dominated the 1970s, the *Mouvement de libération des femmes* (MLF). It examines the extent to which the MLF represented continuity or discontinuity in women's political practice; the relation between French feminism and institutional politics; and the extent to which French feminists successfully challenged the definition of the political.

These discussions are situated in the context of rapid social change in the 1950s and 1960s; the influence of the thinking and practice of the new left; and the events of May 1968. It is argued that the MLF did not appear out of a vacuum and that it was not the only expression of feminist politics, but a historically specific manifestation of it. It was preceded by the existence of increasingly radical women's groups campaigning and lobbying for change, as well as providing alternative information and services, for example, concerning contraception. It coexisted with such groups, as well as with women active within political parties and trade unions. And when it had disappeared, such activities continued, along with new initiatives such as refuges for women survivors of male violence.

Women's groups of 1950s and 1960s

It is not possible here to chart all the instances of women's political activity during the Fifth Republic. Duchen has contributed to this in *Women's Lives* (1994) detailing a number of significant groups and associations which, in highly diverse ways, agitated in order to improve women's status, increase their autonomy, or challenge expectations. Duchen's exploration of women's activity from the liberation to 1968 finds that groups, organisations and individuals were discussing women's rights and status and campaigning around specific issues in the 1950s. These included the *Ligue française pour le Droit des femmes* (LFDF), the movement for the legalisation of contraception; women politicians who, from the mid-1950s attempted to force the revision of the civil code onto the political agenda; and women's sections of trade unions and political parties. However, Duchen (1994: 3–4) points out that this did not constitute mass opposition to domesticity nor to women's oppression; instead they were concerned with specific questions and addressed specific audiences. Demands for legislative change were not situated in a coherent theoretical framework.

In the 1950s, groups sought to defend or obtain rights for women. An exceptional few held more radical views which would be recognised as having more in common with contemporary understandings of the term feminist (Duchen 1994: 170). As Sylvie Chaperon (1995) demonstrates, the objectives and strategies of many of them radicalised during the 1960s, as the contradictions between social change and women's status became increasingly evident. Some had close links with mainstream politics, for example, the *Mouvement démocratique féminin* (MDF), which was formed in 1962. Its president, Marie-Thérèse Eyquem, was Minister for Women in Mitterrand's 1965 shadow cabinet, and the future Minister for Women's Rights, Yvette Roudy, was also active in it (Chaperon 1995: 63). The MDF made concrete demands and lobbied parties and those in power. It cooperated with women in the PCF, the trade unions, the family planning movement (*Mouvement français pour le planning familial* (MFPF)), and *Jeunes femmes*. It was responsible for bringing contraception to Mitterrand's attention and for developing feminist consciousness in the non-Communist left. Many women from the MDF joined the new PS in 1969 (Duchen 1994: 171–3).

Feminist consciousness grew during the 1960s, and feminists were active around three major issues: the fight for contraception, labour rights and family policy. The fight for contraception was led by the MFPF which, in 1961, began to provide contraceptives illegally to its members. Its membership soared, it gained the support of women's associations and progressive organisations, and, from 1965, that of some of the most conservative strongholds around this question, including the small conservative organisation, the *Conseil de l'ordre des médecins* (Council of the Order of Doctors) and the PCF. The demand for women's labour rights, including equal pay, shorter hours, retirement at fifty-five and paid maternity leave, was led by the women's sections of the unions and women's professional bodies. Many women's associations were active in the 1960s around family legislation, particularly those which dated from the Third Republic such as the LFDF and the *Conseil national des femmes françaises*. They lobbied members of parliament, particularly women representatives, drafted bills, and campaigned publicly (Chaperon 1995: 64–5).

Research and publications by and about women also increased during the 1960s, although most were situated within a framework which did not question the reality and desirability of the gradual acquisition of equality with men. The demand for subjectivity which emerged from some groups and the work of some individuals was new, however, and was to influence the practice and theory of the MLF of the 1970s. In particular, it brought personal experience, the body and sexuality into the arena of public debate. The idea of a women's culture, unconstrained by phallocentric hierarchies, developed, and this contributed to the democratic ethos of the MLF (Chaperon 1995: 66).

By 1965, the media were showing a growing interest in women's issues, and the publication in 1964 of Andrée Michel and Geneviève Texier's *La condition de la Française aujourd'hui* and in 1965 of the translation of Betty Friedan's *The Feminine Mystique* was a sign of radicalisation (Chaperon 1995: 66). Women's issues began to play a part in election campaigns. In 1965, for example, Mitterrand was the first candidate to declare his support for the legalisation of contraception.

By 1968, then, feminism in France had become more active and more radical. However, despite women's participation in the events of May, they found themselves excluded from sites of decision-making and their demands ignored. Women's issues slid off the political agenda and were barely mentioned in the June 1968 elections. Chaperon (1995: 71) argues that it was the widening gap between the inertia of politicians and the radicalisation of women's groups, accompanied by the influence of American women's liberation which led to the formation of a large movement.

Recent analyses of the links between pre- and post-'68 forms of feminism suggest that, although May '68 had a profound effect on feminist politics, the MLF forms part of a feminist continuum which stretches both backwards and forwards. Chaperon (1995: 72) argues that, although there were major differences between the pre- and post-'68 forms of feminism, there was also a continuity, and the MLF would not have appeared without the gradual changes of the 1960s. Similarly, Duchen (1994: 207) argues that, although post-'68 feminists did not acknowledge the struggles for women's rights which preceded their own struggles, there were connections between the two. Anne Zelensky and Jacqueline Feldman passed through the MDF on their way to creating *Féminin, Masculin, Avenir* (FMA) and the basis of radical feminism, for example, and some of the features which were considered unique to the MLF (informal discussion groups, defiance of the law) can, in retrospect, be identified in earlier forms of feminism. Nevertheless, May '68 marked a new way of conceptualising women's situation, replacing 'condition' and 'emancipation' with 'oppression' and 'liberation'. The women's movement which emerged in 1970 constructed women as women, rather than as mothers, carers or workers. Women who identified with the MLF were acting as women, and this female subjecthood was the basis of their political demands. Individually and collectively, women who participated in the MLF constructed themselves as subjects, challenging the dominance of the male subject at the social, cultural and symbolic level.

The MLF

It is unnecessary here to devote too much space to a description of the MLF in the 1970s, since this has been done elsewhere (for example, Picq 1993, Duchen 1986, Jenson 1996, Allwood 1998). What follows, then, is the briefest of outlines as a context in which to situate discussions of the politics of the movement.

During the 1970s, many women's groups were created, and feminist publications began to appear. Most of this activity went unnoticed by the general public and the media, but what they did notice was a series of high-profile stunts. In 1970, a group of women laid a wreath at the Tomb of the Unknown Soldier at the Arc de Triomphe in memory of one more unknown than him: his wife. In 1971, a declaration signed by 343 women, including many public figures, claiming that they had had an illegal abortion, appeared in the *Nouvel Observateur*. The signatories challenged the state to prosecute them in the same way that it had just prosecuted a teenage girl who had had a back-street abortion. This case, known as the Bobigny trial, in which feminist lawyer Gisèle Halimi acted for the defence, became a focus of the feminist campaign to highlight the injustice of the 1920 law. Reporting these events, the press increasingly referred to the activists as women from the '*mouvement de libération de la femme*', a reference to the American Women's Liberation Movement. Journalists also began to describe the movement as divided into 'tendencies', and this practice has continued, despite the fact that not all groups or individuals can be fitted neatly into the categories which have been imposed on a diverse and changing movement. There are some minor differences in the labels which have been applied to the various tendencies, and this has implications for the analysis of the politics of the movement, as will be seen below.

The main sources on the movement use the following typologies: Jane Jenson and Mariette Sineau (1994: 250) divide the women's movement into 'revolutionary', 'syndicalist' and 'egalitarian' tendencies, claiming that the term 'MLF' applied to the revolutionary mainstream of the movement. Claire Duchen (1986) and Jenson and Sineau (1994: 251) subdivide the revolutionary wing of the women's movement, or the MLF, into three subcurrents: '*Psych et po*', 'class struggle', and 'non-aligned'. The latter is referred to by Françoise Picq (1993: 176) as '*féministes révolutionnaires*' (revolutionary feminists).

During the 1970s, then, the MLF co-existed with other expressions of feminism (syndicalist and egalitarian). We will use the categories 'class struggle', 'revolutionary' (non-aligned) and '*Psych et po*' to describe the different tendencies of the MLF and, after a brief presentation of each of these, examine the politics of the movement.

Class struggle tendency

One of the major divisions within the MLF was the relative importance accorded to the struggle against capitalism and against patriarchy, and this provoked heated debates between the class struggle and revolutionary feminists. For the class struggle tendency, the destruction of capitalism was the priority; for revolutionary feminists, it was the destruction of patriarchy.

Conflicts between class struggle and revolutionary feminists also concerned the organisation of the movement. Whereas the former demanded a structured organisation, the latter were opposed to vertical power structures and traditional forms of political organisation. They were proud of the movement's informal and flexible structure and objected to any attempts to make it more rigid. But there were also problems on an individual level. The women who entered the MLF from the extreme left often experienced intense conflict between their activities within the movement and those within their political organisations, a conflict which, for many women, became debilitating. Neither trusted nor fully recognised by either, they were fighting a difficult battle. By 1976, the pull of these divided loyalties had forced many of them to make a decision to go one way or the other, and the tendency as such disappeared (Duchen 1986: 28–30), even though feminists associated with the Trotskyist *Ligue communiste révolutionnaire* (LCR) continued their activism throughout the 1980s and 1990s.

Revolutionary or non-aligned feminists

Revolutionary, or radical feminists, as they would probably be called today (Duchen 1987: 22 n.), constituted the most active tendency of the MLF in the early 1970s, and were responsible for the highly visible actions which brought feminism into the public eye. However, they are also the most difficult to define. Françoise Picq (1993: 198) writes, 'Strictly speaking, there is no revolutionary feminist "tendency". There is not even a group which meets regularly. It is rather a collection of ideas, whose boundaries are variable and difficult to define.' Groups formed, split and re-formed with some of the same women and some new ones, especially during important campaigns, such as that against rape, when it appeared necessary to present a radical feminist position represented by a specific group.

Revolutionary feminism was influenced by American radical feminism, and had much in common with it. It saw gender as the primary dividing factor in society; women were seen to constitute a sex class; patriarchy, not capitalism, was the main enemy; and separatism was seen as the only effective political strategy (Jenson 1990: 131). The revolutionary feminists were in constant conflict with the class struggle tendency. However, they were divided on many questions, including the issue of sexual difference: whereas some revolutionary feminists wanted sexual difference eliminated, others wanted to accentuate it. They were also divided on the question of sexuality, with lesbian feminists accusing heterosexual feminists of collaborating with the enemy.[1]

Groups which emerged from the revolutionary feminist tendency and outlived the MLF include the *Ligue du droit des femmes*, which, amongst other activities, formed women's aid collectives, including *SOS femmes-alternatives* (offering support to battered women) and *SOS femmes violées* (Remy 1990: 43–4).

Psychanalyse et politique

One of the first feminist groups to form in Paris, *Psychanalyse et politique*, also known as *Psych et po*, maintained a high profile throughout the 1970s. Part of its influence was due to its creation of a publishing house, magazine and bookshops (all called '*des femmes*'). Another reason for its influence was its charismatic founder and leader, psychoanalyst Antoinette Fouque.

Psych et po was intellectually influential. Luce Irigaray, Hélène Cixous and Julia Kristeva all passed through the group, although Cixous was the only one to maintain any long-term relations with it, publishing all her work with '*des femmes*' between 1976 and 1982 (Moi 1987: 4). However, the group was attacked by other feminists for being politically divisive. It was criticised for using inaccessible language which excluded the majority of women. Other feminists also objected to *Psych et po*'s repeated public claims to be representative of the MLF, claims which culminated in 1979 when *Psych et po* registered the name '*Mouvement de libération des femmes*' and the initials 'MLF' as company trademarks, thus preventing anyone else from using them legally.[2] At the same time as writing in the name of the MLF, *Psych et po* considered themselves 'anti-feminist', and their review *Des femmes en mouvements – hebdo* (FMH) constantly attacked the rest of the movement (Kandel 1980). According to Fouque, feminism was a reformist compromise with the patriarchy. What she advocated was a complete overthrow of 'phallogocentrism', the entire masculine tradition of thought.

The MLF and the left

An important influence on the ideology and practice of the 1970s' women's movement was that of the new left, which had emerged in France, as in several other advanced capitalist societies, as a partial response to the political pressures created by rapid social change (Jenson 1982: 14). New left political practice was based on its central ideas of '*autogestion*' (self-management) and opposition to bureaucracy. It emphasised mass action and direct democracy as a means of creating an autonomous, decentralised, self-managed society (Hirsch 1981: 208).

The discourse of the new left opened up a space in which forms of oppression other than class could be theorised and understood (Jenson 1982: 15). However, women active in the organisations of the new left discovered that they were just as oppressed in them as within the traditional left. The conflict between their experience and their developing analysis of patriarchy led them to abandon these organisations in favour of an autonomous women's movement, taking with them an emphasis on democracy and a critique of authoritarianism, hierarchy and bureaucracy. What was original was the analysis of the specific oppression of women by men within patriarchy, a form of oppression which cut through class divisions and was exercised throughout society, including within the left and its organisations.

The origins of the MLF in the extreme left and the close links which it maintained with it meant that the MLF was able to construct a detailed critique of left political practice, which it used to justify the need for a separate and autonomous movement. The foci of this critique were vanguardism, hierarchy and leadership. Feminists active in both the MLF and left organisations brought new issues onto their agendas. Within the MLF, they raised awareness of working-class women and class analysis. Within the left, they raised the issues of women's role in political activism and their absence from political discourse (Jenson 1996: 80). They insisted on the value of subjective knowledge and argued, as will be discussed below, that 'the personal is political', the longest-lasting effect of which was the placing on the political agenda of issues such as reproduction. The fact that many women chose to remain active in left organisations, despite their criticisms of their practice, was symptomatic of an element of unease about the relationship between feminism and politics. They feared that if they abandoned the left in favour of the MLF, they would no longer be involved in the 'big' political issues of the day and would lose the possibility of developing an alternative global feminist perspective. The tension experienced by women attempting to maintain their dual activism came to a head in 1977, and most left either one or the other (Stegassy 1978). But the problem of the MLF's inability to construct a global perspective on all political issues had long-lasting implications. Gendered power relations were at the centre of feminist analysis, and the aim of the movement was to overthrow patriarchy, or the structure of women's oppression by men. The goal of overthrowing the system precluded any possibility of claiming a place within it or engaging with it on its own terms, by, for example, choosing to elect a representative from one party rather than from another. Throughout the 1970s, then, the MLF refused to participate in electoral politics, scorning attempts by politicians to court women voters. An article in *Libération* in 1974, for example, stated the following:

> The candidates for the presidency can make as many competing promises to women as they like. Women will wittily respond: will they abolish domestic slavery, introduce the equal division of childcare, stop men raping women? No! Whatever the result of the election, the patriarchal system will continue. The only way for women to liberate themselves is not by voting but by fighting.
>
> (Quoted in Picq 1993: 204)

And in 1977, a tract in *Le Monde* (23 December) signed by feminist groups[3] stated, 'just as a man on the left does not need to consider which party of the right to vote for, we could only wonder who we were going to vote for if we were not feminists'.

The danger with the wholesale rejection of party politics was one which faced all new social movements: marginalisation and, potentially, impotence. If feminists would not attempt to act in the sites of power, could they exert any real political influence? This was the subject of an interview conducted by Pierre Viansson-Ponté for *Le Monde*, in which Simone de Beauvoir (1978) discusses the difficult relationship between feminism and institutional politics. She criticises the secretariat or delegation for the feminine condition, describing it as a 'mystification' and says that a ministry under a Socialist government would not be better; the left's attitude towards women, she states, was part of the reason for the creation of an autonomous women's movement. When Viansson-Ponté suggests that Beauvoir nevertheless advocates an increase in the number of women candidates for election, she responds 'not really':

> It seems secondary to me. I am not especially in favour of parliamentary representation. I don't really see the point of elections and I can't see what women would do if they were elected other than being token women there too.

However, she concedes that this is a difficult question since women who occupy social, political or intellectual sites of power are more likely to be able to serve other women than those who do not (although this does not mean that they will).

The decision by *Choisir* to present candidates at the 1978 legislative election was motivated by the conviction that none of the parties were really interested in women's issues, and, in particular at the time, abortion and women's place in the labour market (*Choisir: la cause des femmes* 1978). However, this was the only occasion on which they did this, the results were disappointing, and feminists outside *Choisir* showed little interest or support for the move. In contrast to Belgium, which had an active feminist party (*le Parti féministe unifié*), France did not. There is a brief mention of the constitution of such a party in France in *Le Monde* (5 October 1974), and it signed an article in *Le Monde*, 23 December 1977, but appears to have disappeared in that year. A *Parti féministe* presented candidates under the *Ecologie 78* banner at the 1978 legislative elections, expressing criticisms of the politicking of *Choisir* (*Le Matin*, 24 February 1978). Apart from these ephemeral groups, *Choisir* was the closest to a women's party, but wrote in the Women's Common Programme, 'We are not a party and do not want to become one. We want to remain a women's movement.' They also saw themselves as a pressure group with the aim of influencing policy outcomes (*Choisir* 1978: 25). *Choisir* tried to change the system from within, believing that abstention or complete rejection of the system would leave them powerless to change anything. But they believed that other forms of struggle were also important and supported the actions of the MLF.

The personal is political

Amongst the MLF's most valuable contributions to the redefinition of politics was the assertion that 'the personal is political'. The two most important implications of this were, first, that issues previously considered personal were placed on the political agenda (for example, rape and sexual harassment), and, second, that the legitimacy of the public/private divide was brought into question. This attempt to redefine politics took place largely within, or in relation to, the left and extreme left, which was itself claiming that 'everything is political', at the same time as it relegated certain issues to the private sphere or defined them as 'personal' or 'individual'.

The slogan was not without its problems. While it brought new issues onto the political agenda, it also brought the risk of abandoning all public politics in favour only of the personal. Rather than meaning 'the personal is political as well', it was sometimes taken to mean 'only the personal is political'. Picq (1993: 194) states that it was in response to this that a group of feminists began to meet every Thursday specifically to discuss 'outside' issues.

However, Béatrice Slama (1991: 107) argues that feminists did not speak *only* of the personal; they challenged the public/private dichotomy, refusing to be assigned to the private. Slama argues that it was not simply a case of rejecting the sexual division of roles and spheres, nor was it a case of demanding a fairer place within this dichotomy, in other words, the better representation of women in public politics. Rather, continuing the leftist tradition, Politics with a capital 'P' remained suspect and politicking and elections were seen as men's affairs. But *politics* was something else.[4] It was perceived to be at the heart of all social relations, and feminist discourse in the 1970s stressed the political aspect of private life, including abortion, rape, sexual harassment, domestic labour, the relation between spouses, the body and identity. For the first time, the body was at the centre of debate, and women's writing (*écriture féminine*) had a tremendous impact on women's views of themselves and of the world (Slama 1991: 110–13). The novelty of 1970s' feminist discourse lay in the discovery of subjectivity: writing or saying 'I' for the first time, and also in addressing only women for the first time, in contrast to Third Republic feminist publications, for example, which had addressed a mixed readership (Slama 1991: 108).

However, not all women had the same access to subjectivity. Provincial women, housewives and working-class women did not and, within the movement, not everyone had the same opportunity to speak or write, leaving some feeling ignored or marginalised. Radical lesbians, for example, argued that they were invisible within the movement. Individually, they were able to participate, but collectively and politically, they were hardly recognised and often problematised. Lesbian groups were mainly marginalised, and they were faced with the choice between participating in a movement which represented itself as heterosexual, or organising separately, thus risking ghettoisation. Claudie Lesselier (1991: 100) writes, 'This ambivalence and this tension express in a very concrete manner the contradiction between the affirmative demands of a category or an identity and the demand for the deconstruction of the oppressive system of categorisation.'

Eleni Varikas (1996: 145) argues that the expression 'the personal is political' has conveyed more the meaning that within the personal, power relations are involved which lead to the systematic domination of one sex by the other, than it has theorised the relation between these gendered power relations and political power. In other words, it has not told us much about the relation between gender and politics. Varikas (146) writes:

> The strength of this statement (the personal is political) and of the movement behind it clearly resided and still resides in its ability to identify domination in relations which are thought to be part of human nature; in the suspicion with which it views issues and institutions manifestly considered to be outside politics; and in its utopian character. But the general critique of *what is* leaves a blank as far as alternatives are concerned – what *can be* but *is not yet* – the horizon of possibilities from which the utopia draws its strength. A blank which cannot be filled unless lasting links are formed between politics (*le politique*) and Politics (*la politique*).

Varikas (1996) argues that the insufficient theorisation of the links between the political and institutional Politics and the inability to construct a positive alternative has meant that, in recent years, parity campaigners have been able to argue that women's experience in the private sphere justifies the claim for their representation in political institutions, so that their different needs will be expressed and their different perspective heard. She states that this is a curious transformation of the meaning of 'the personal is political'. Varikas argues that the gendered nature of the separate private and public spheres is now represented as inevitable and as a justification for the equal representation of each sex – and its particular needs and perspective – in political institutions.[5]

Reformism and revolution

It is frequently asserted that the MLF was opposed to reformism and that 1970s' feminism was centred on a binary opposition between revolution and reform. Indeed, the aim of the MLF was to subvert or destroy patriarchy, to bring about a revolutionary transformation of relations between women and men. It had no interest in engaging with the state, since it believed that social change would only come about as the result of mass action against capitalism and patriarchy (Jenson and Sineau 1994: 252). However, the revolutionary aims of the movement did not exclude the possibility of seeking legislative reform. The most striking example of this is the campaign for the legalisation of abortion.

Within the literature produced in the 1990s in favour of a law on parity, a simplified history of the relation between feminism and public institutions seems to have gained acceptance. French feminists in the 1970s are said to have viewed traditional politics as patriarchal, bourgeois, and irrelevant. Rejecting the state and its institutions, they are said to have refused traditional methods of lobbying and campaigns for legislative reform. This is somewhat misrepresentative, as has been pointed out by several authors, including Michèle Le Doeuff (1995: 40–1). Le Doeuff (1995: 40) draws attention, quite rightly, to the massive feminist campaign in the early 1970s, in favour not only of repealing the 1920 law prohibiting abortion, but also of passing another law guaranteeing access to abortions to all women, including immigrants. She objects to the representation by present-day campaigners for parity of a stark contrast between the MLF's refusal to engage with the state and to attempt to influence legislation, and the parity campaign's focus on precisely that.

Others have presented the abortion campaign as an exception (for example, Jenson and Sineau 1995: 91), and it is difficult to find another such clear example of willingness on the part of the autonomous women's movement in the 1970s to engage in attempts to bring about legislative reform. Those groups or individuals who did undertake this form of activity

(*Choisir, La ligue du droit des femmes*) were subject to accusations of reformism and co-option.

It is helpful, however, to distinguish between the legislative process and outcome. It can be demonstrated that the MLF rejected institutional politics, refusing to participate in the legislative process. It did not seek to increase the representation of women in parliament, because it rejected the principle of representative democracy. Christine Delphy (1984: 13) claims that the feminist movement was perhaps more opposed to the principle of the delegation of power involved in parliamentary regimes than other extra-parliamentary direct action movements. Historically, the feminist movement rejected any action which recognised the legitimacy of the legislature and opposed all institutions and all processes of delegating the power of citizens. However, the question of whether it is participation in the law-making process or the content of the laws which is rejected is ambiguous. The MLF did attempt to influence legislative outcome. The campaign for the legalisation of abortion was the primary focus of the MLF in the early 1970s and it aimed specifically at achieving legislative reform. So why did the MLF not participate to a comparable extent in subsequent campaigns for legal reform? Delphy (1984: 12) suggests that the lack of feminist interest in laws concerning parental authority, equal pay and divorce which were passed in the 1970s and 1980s can be explained by the fact that movement feminists had not fought for these changes, which had been mooted before the movement had come into existence. She concedes that it is less easy to explain feminist indifference to the 1980 rape law, however, since rape had been placed on the political agenda only by feminist campaigns, and, in contrast to abortion which had received support from large sections of the public, social movements and political parties, it was an issue around which feminists campaigned in isolation. Despite this, feminists were not consulted about the content of the law and did not pay it much attention when it was passed. Delphy (1984: 13) suggests that this is because legal reform was not the main aim of the feminist campaign against rape. However, she insists that feminists in the 1970s and early 1980s *were* interested in the law, as demonstrated by their discussions around the anti-sexist bill, proposed in 1974 by the *Ligue du droit des femmes* and placed on the parliamentary agenda in the early 1980s by Yvette Roudy.

Eleni Varikas (1996: 144) argues that the legislative reforms sought by the MLF were seen as a necessary part of the preparation for the revolution:

> Thus, even when feminist actions aimed to change the law, as was the case for abortion, for free and legal contraception or for the criminalisation of rape, they were primarily viewed as ways of improving the power relation between the sexes with a view to transforming substantially the existing social order which feminism sought not to adapt or rationalise, but, quite simply, to subvert. This explains, for

example, the refusal to consider abortion simply as an effective means of family planning, and the insistence on women's right to control their sexuality, which was the primary condition of their autonomy.

Seeking legislative reform was therefore not necessarily counter-revolutionary. It could operate as a short-term tactic, within a longer-term revolutionary strategy. As Johanna Brenner (1996: 54) argues in her study of feminism in the United States, the distinction between a revolutionary and a reformist approach lies not in whether or not one organises to wrest some concession from the state, but in how that effort fits into an overall strategy: 'Unfortunately, the feminist debate over the state has rarely been posed in this way, but rather as a choice between being outside or inside the state, between working for reforms or working to build alternative institutions.'

In addition to distinguishing between revolution and reform, it is important not to conflate reformism and egalitarianism. It is the failure to distinguish between the two which enables the construction of an unproblematic history of the development of feminism from revolution to reform. However, the actions of the *Ligue du droit des femmes* in particular disrupt this account, at least if the *Ligue*'s radical objectives are recognised. The *Ligue du droit des femmes* was formed in 1974 by Anne Zelensky and others who argued that the only way to bring about certain changes was by using the law. They proposed an anti-sexist law, similar to the anti-racist law of 1972, and sought legislative change on a variety of issues, but within an overall framework which can only be described as radical, not egalitarian, feminism. The *Ligue* fought against the oppression of women by men in pornography, they campaigned around the representation of women in advertising and schoolbooks, they were very active against male violence, and they saw no harm in alliances with men on specific issues. Their reformist actions were situated within a revolutionary strategy, and they saw them as contributing to the overall struggle against women's oppression (Picq 1993: 201).

Their methods were criticised by other radical feminists, but as much for the fact that they formed a legally constituted association as for their pursuit of legal reform. This went against the principles of spontaneity and the rejection of structures and power. It meant entering the logic of institutions and risked contributing to the co-option or appropriation of the movement. Although these issues had already been raised when *Choisir* was formed in 1971, the creation of the *Ligue* was an important moment in the history of the MLF, because it concerned feminists who had been at the very centre of the movement (Picq 1993: 203).

The account of the development within the movement from revolution to reform is dependent on the exclusion from the history of the MLF of such early 'radical reformists', categorising them instead as egalitarian feminists. Duchen (1986) avoids this by stating that within non-aligned feminism (which she distinguishes from class struggle and *Psych et po*) there were those who sought reform as well as those who rejected it. The problem with the catch-all non-aligned category is that it does not convey the importance within the movement of the major split between radical feminists (patriarchy first) and class struggle feminists (capitalism first).

Jenson and Sineau (1994: 253) claim that egalitarian feminists in the 1970s included women in the parties, trade unions, *Choisir* and the *Ligue du droit des femmes*. They argue that one of their defining features was that they sought to achieve equality through legislative reform and that this caused conflict between egalitarian and movement feminists. However, as we have seen, reformism as a strategy does not necessarily have equality as a goal. It is perhaps more helpful to state that the MLF rejected the goal of equality more than it did the strategy of reformism. This does not mean that all MLF feminists ascribed to 'difference' theories. The major split around this question within the MLF was between those who sought to accentuate women's difference, creating a symbolic and cultural space for women to live outside phallocentrism, and those who sought the elimination of the social significance of sexual difference so that all individuals had access to all attributes with no gendered connotations. All rejected the goal of achieving equality with men if this meant aspiring to the masculine norm. As Michèle Bordeaux (1991: 24) writes:

> Equality and its semantic field were not part of the vocabulary of groups in the movement: they talked less of 'equal pay for equal work' than of sharing tasks, less of discrimination than of an end to the sexual division of labour.

Egalitarian and state feminism

There were, however, egalitarian feminists whose aims were very different from those of the MLF. The commitment to equality which Yvette Roudy and Marie-Thérèse Eyquem persuaded Mitterrand to integrate into his policies and practices had little in common with the MLF's analysis of oppression (Jenson and Sineau 1995: 89). Egalitarian feminists were active long before the 1970s, promoting equality for women as citizens, workers and mothers. They were active in the trade unions and parties of the left, and right-wing parties also took up some of the demands for legislative reform, especially those affecting rights within the family. During the 1960s, the discourse of equal rights for women, especially at work, had grown, and was gaining attention from the media and some politicians.

When Françoise Giroud announced at a press conference in October 1974 the aims of the newly created Secretariat for the Status of Women, the *Ligue du droit des femmes* recognised a few of its demands (an anti-sexist law, a commission on advertising, changes in school textbooks), but others were in complete opposition to the *Ligue*'s objectives: eighteen months' maternity leave, quotas for men in state school appointments, but no quotas for women in male-dominated professions (Picq 1993: 174). The aims of the secretariat had little in common with those of the MLF. The secretariat aimed to 'promote all measures which aim to improve women's condition, encourage women's access to different levels of responsibility in French society and eliminate the discrimination which affects women' (Mission du secrétariat d'état à la condition féminine, décret d'attribution, 23 July 1974). Picq (1993: 175) writes:

> The MLF did not want to improve 'women's condition', but abolish it and struggle against an economic and ideological system founded on the exploitation, negation and imprisonment of women. Women's liberation cannot exist in society as it is; it requires a general rethinking of power relations and of the major sexual division of the world.

The conflict between the MLF and state feminism was exacerbated when Mitterrand and the PS came to power in 1981 and established a Ministry for Women's Rights (MWR) under Yvette Roudy. Within the movement there were bitter disputes over whether to organise, whether to cooperate with the Ministry, how to maintain feminist pressure on the new government and whether it was possible to speak with a united feminist voice (Picq 1993: 314–17). At the same time, grants from the Ministry facilitated certain types of feminist activity, for example, the creation of associations around various issues and the organisation of the first conference on women and feminist research in Toulouse in 1982.

For some commentators, the MWR was simply an extension of the secretariat established by Giscard. For others, it was an important change in public policy directed at women. And for a third group, it was a means of co-opting the ideas of the MLF, which it destroyed or replaced. The MWR was created in 1981 and aimed to bring about equality between the sexes, especially in the areas of work and training. The minister, Yvette Roudy, was an egalitarian feminist. The main legislative reforms of the ministry were, first, the Loi Roudy on equality at work (1983), which is considered by most feminists to have failed. The reforms which were proposed in Roudy's bill were far-reaching, but the final text of the law simply set up recommendations, with no obligation to comply and no sanctions for non-compliance. The second important reform was the reimbursement by the state of the cost of abortion (1982). Roudy also proposed an anti-sexist bill, but this was never passed.

Jane Jenson and Mariette Sineau's (1995) analysis of the Ministry's activities during its first year is fairly positive. It had a budget ten times greater than its predecessor and Roudy participated in the weekly meeting of the council of ministers. Women's associations were able to obtain state funding through the Ministry. Information centres on women's rights were established throughout France, and information on subjects such as rights, contraception and research funding was made available. However, the speeches of the President and the Prime Minister on 8 March 1982 were the high point of Mitterrand's feminism and that of the PS. The minister lost her place on the council of ministers, and the budget was reduced.

Amy Mazur's (1995a) analysis of the achievements of the MWR is more negative. She claims that the ministry spent time and resources on publicity campaigns, information services and research, but did not establish permanent structures which could survive a change of government. Its ambitious legislative agenda had little long-term impact because its resources were limited and its position within the hierarchy of the state was marginalised. The Ministry's reforms were more symbolic than material.

Mazur claims that part of the reason for the limited results of the Ministry was its poor relationship with the women's movement, even though Roudy tried to convince all the tendencies of the MLF that they had equal access to state funding and would all be consulted. At a PS meeting on women in February 1978, Yvette Roudy (*Rouge*, 6 Februrary 1978) had stated: 'I do not agree with the external feminist struggle. External women's groups have a strength which we recognise, but we are opposed to their strategy.'

French feminism today

There is no longer a women's movement as such in France. The conditions of its disappearance and the reasons for this are chronicled in Picq (1993) and Allwood (1998). However, feminist activity has not disappeared. Small groups of project-orientated feminists continue to work in specific areas, whether this is solidarity with the women of Algeria,[6] campaigns against genital mutilation (the *Commission pour l'abolition des mutilations sexuelles* (Committee for the Abolition of Genital Mutilation) (CAMS) and the *Groupe de femmes pour l'abolition des mutilations sexuelles* (Women's Group for the Abolition of Genital Mutilation) (GAMS)), or support for women with Aids.[7] Other issue-specific feminist groups are active around male violence towards women (*Association contre les violences faites aux femmes au travail* – Association against Violence towards Women at Work, *Collectif féministe contre le viol* – Feminist Collective against Rape); the defence of the right to abortion and contraception (*Mouvement français pour le planning familial* – Family Planning Association); and the problems faced by immigrant women (*Collectif des femmes immigrées* – Immigrant Women's Collective).

In November 1995, a demonstration organised by the *Coordination d'associations pour le Droit à l'Avortement et à la Contraception* (CADAC) (Coordination of Associations for the Right to Abortion and Contraception), which had formed in 1990 in defence of the right to abortion, attracted 40,000 marchers. One of the outcomes of this demonstration was the creation of the *Collectif national pour les droits des femmes* (National Collective for Women's Rights), which brought together 166 organisations, parties, unions and associations. It organised a national conference on women's rights in March 1997, in which 2,000 women participated.

In addition to these groups and many more which are active around a wide variety of issues, there is also the increasingly visible campaign for parity, which will be examined in detail in Chapter 8.

Conclusion

Did feminism succeed in redefining politics? In terms of broadening the definition of the political, it is undeniable that feminism has had a long-term influence. The impact of feminism on political action and organisation is more questionable. Informal non-hierarchical forms of organisation were difficult to maintain, especially as the movement grew. After a short period of direct democracy in the form of general assemblies, an informal hierarchy emerged, and a small group of Parisian activists clearly dominated the movement, even while denouncing the idea of leadership. The anti-hierarchy, anti-authoritarian mood was affected by the onset of economic crisis, and the arrival of the Socialists in power in 1981 brought further problems. By 1984, there was no longer a women's movement, simply disparate pockets of feminist activity (Picq 1993: 332).

By the 1980s, feminist associations had formed which were involved in more conventional interaction with the state. This had certainly co-existed with the MLF in the 1970s, but it became dominant after the Socialist victory and outlived the movement. Protecting the right to abortion is a particularly good example of the way in which state and movement feminisms have worked together in recent years. Jane Jenson (1996: 104) writes:

> The number of efforts to roll back already acquired rights, whether through cuts in funding, violence or neglect, were impressively high. Equally impressive was the capacity of groups to monitor the situation, act effectively and make use of the links they had within the state. Such examples of successful practice had never been totally absent in the 1970s, but they became more frequent and institutionalised in the 1980s and 1990s, at least in this policy domain.

Feminists had tried to construct an alternative way of doing politics, but this was difficult to maintain and carried the risk of existing in parallel to mainstream politics, on which it had little effect. This raised the question of how to change the system while remaining outside it. Summarising the conclusions of her full-length study *Les femmes en politique*, Mariette Sineau (1991: 200) explores the links between the attitude of 1970s' feminists towards institutional politics and the views of women politicians in the 1980s. Amongst her interviewees, she identifies a widespread critique of the masculine way of doing politics which the majority felt would be changed by the introduction of a critical mass of women into political institutions. Sineau argues that overthrowing masculine political practices was also the aim of the MLF. While women politicians cannot use such subversive strategies, they are profoundly influenced by feminist ideology, which expanded possibilities and afforded credibility to the critique of masculine norms. But most women politicians believe that pressure from within the system is indispensable, even if it could not be effective on its own; this is in contrast to the widespread opposition to participation amongst movement feminists. They also believe that women in politics will bring new issues onto the agenda. Parity campaigners have argued recently that in order to change the system, it is essential to enter it first and change it from within.

8 Increasing women's political representation

From the late 1970s and throughout the 1980s women politicians, feminists, and alternative left and ecology parties made various attempts to increase women's political representation. Since gaining the right to vote and to stand for election, women's representation in the national assemblies had barely increased. Their voting turnout, however, was equal to that of male voters. It was suggested that it was not their lack of will which excluded them from political office, but obstacles which stood in their way. It was therefore argued that measures had to be introduced which would either remove these obstacles or enable women to overcome them. Initially the demands were for quotas for women within party hierarchies and on candidate lists. By the 1990s, the efforts of campaigners and the opportunism of politicians made the media-friendly notion of 'parity' (numerical equality between men and women) a subject for public debate. In contrast to quotas, which are frequently associated with a feminism portrayed as outdated and misguided, parity is supported by a broad spectrum of politicians, all main parties, European organisations, some feminists and intellectuals and a large majority of public opinion. For some, parity is a potential source of legitimacy at a time when many are suggesting that there is a crisis of representation. Whether or not this is true, support for the idea features in a growing number of pre-election speeches and manifestos.

In 1979, the United Nations conference on the elimination of all forms of discrimination against women invited member states to include in their Constitutions or law the principle of equality between men and women and to apply this principle through legislative or other appropriate means, including the introduction of quotas. The Interparliamentary Union, in its 1994 plan of action, accepted positive action including quotas as a strictly temporary measure. In 1995, the signatories of the declaration passed at the world conference on women in Beijing accepted the more radical objective of parity in their decision-making bodies. However, although parity has not been achieved anywhere, very few countries have introduced legislation which could improve women's access to elected bodies. In 1997, the Interparliamentary Union had identified six, only one of which, Belgium, was in Europe (Hochedez and Maurice 1997: 79–80).

A prominent feature of the French debate around parity is the claim that the under-representation of women is exceptionally bad in France, and much has been made of its low position in European and international tables. However, in 1993, when parity campaigners were stressing the exceptionalism of France's poor performance, not one European country had attained parity, although Finland, Denmark, Sweden and Norway all had over 30 per cent in the lower or single chamber (Sineau 1994b: 276). At the bottom end of the scale, France, with 6 per cent women deputies, did not stand out as an exception, but was instead one of seven European countries in which women accounted for 10 per cent or fewer elected national representatives. What is specific to France is, first, the strategy adopted by those who wish to see women better represented, which has focused almost exclusively on a demand for a law or constitutional reform.[1] The second French specificity is the terms of the debate which has surrounded the issue, which centres largely on the relation between parity and universalism.

The first part of this chapter is an overview of the numerous attempts which have been made to increase women's presence in politics. It is demonstrated that there is now a broad consensus around the principle of increasing the number of women in politics, but there are two contentious issues arising from it. The first is whether or not it would make a difference. This has important strategic implications for feminism. If parity would not advance the feminist project, then feminists should not devote all their energies to this single goal. The second is the more pragmatic concern of how the principle should be translated into practice. Both of these debates are examined later in the chapter.

Attempts to improve women's political representation

Monique Pelletier, minister for the family and 'women's condition' was the first to propose the introduction of a quota in 1979, when she suggested that, in municipal elections in towns with a population greater than 2,500, at least 20 per cent of the candidates should be women. This was translated into a bill presented in November 1980 by the Prime Minister, Raymond Barre. Constitutional experts had advised that a quota for women would probably be deemed to breach the spirit of the Constitution, which guarantees equality between the sexes. The bill therefore stated that neither sex could have fewer than 20 per cent of the places on each list. It was passed by a large majority of the National Assembly (439 votes against 3), but the parliamentary session ended before it could be debated in the Senate (Loschak 1983: 131).

The next attempt to introduce quotas was contained in an amendment to a bill on municipal election reform proposed by Gisèle Halimi and passed by the National Assembly with a majority of 476–4 with 3 abstentions. It was this vote which was famously overturned by the Constitutional Council in 1982. The ruling and its implications for further attempts to increase women's representation are discussed later in this chapter.

A commitment to the participation of women in politics led to the adoption of voluntary measures by parts of the alternative left. *Arc en ciel*, a movement which, between 1986 and 1990 attempted to unite members of the extreme left and left-wing ecologists, introduced parity into its internal organisation, and this was carried on by its successor organisation, *Alternative Rouge et Verte*. In 1988, the *Verts* also included in their statutes the principle of parity in the distribution of responsibilities and the selection of candidates for election. In 1989, they presented a list for the European elections on which every other candidate was a woman.

A variety of demands had been voiced in other European countries, ranging from appeals to the parties to calls for absolute parity by, for example, the 300 Group established by Lesley Abdela in the United Kingdom (*Women of Europe*, 27 June 1988: 50). European institutions, including the Parliament and the Commission, began to debate the question of women's place in politics in the early 1980s, and, in 1989, the Council of Europe introduced the concept of *démocratie paritaire*. A true democracy, they stated, would ensure the full representation of each sex as a sex. Following the Council of Europe, in April 1992, the EC Commission created a network of experts around the subject 'women and decision-making'. At their first meeting, they established parity as their main objective. On 3 November 1992, a declaration was signed in Athens by women in positions of political responsibility. It included the sentence 'Democracy requires parity in the representation and administration of nations' (Gaspard 1994: 35). Simone Veil and Edith Cresson signed for France. In March 1995, a conference took place in Dublin on strategies for promoting women in decision-making, and in May 1996, there was a conference in Rome on women for the renewal of politics and society. The equality of men and women in decision-making is one of the six objectives of the fourth programme of action of the European Commission (1996–2000).

In France, a campaign for parity began to gather momentum in 1992, with the publication of a book which soon became the reference work of the new movement: Françoise Gaspard, Claude Servan-Schreiber and Anne Le Gall's *Au pouvoir citoyennes!* (1992). The aim of the book was to plead the case for parity and to gather support for a campaign in favour of it. The aim of the campaign, as stated in this book, was to insert the following text into the Constitution: 'elected bodies at the local and national level are composed of an equal number of women and men' (10).

Two associations were formed in 1992, *Parité* and *Parité 2000*. By March 1993, many new groups and organisations were forming with the aim of bringing about a change in the constitution which would enforce parity

(Chombeau 1993: 9). These included *Elles aussi* and *L'Assemblée des femmes* (Trat and Vigan 1993/4: 11–12). A network was created in an attempt to facilitate the exchange of information between the numerous groups and to coordinate the organisation of demonstrations and meetings. During 1993, the network organised a round table in the National Assembly on 8 March and a demonstration outside parliament on the first day of the Balladur government a month later. It launched the newsletter *Parité-infos*, which publicised the movement's activities until December 1997, and coordinated the *Manifeste des 577*, a petition published in *Le Monde* on 10 November 1993, supporting the introduction of parity into political institutions by means of a new law. It was intended to be signed by 289 women and 288 men, the number of male and female deputies there would be in the National Assembly, if it operated according to the principle of parity. In fact, the number of signatories quickly exceeded the original target (Gaspard 1994: 35–6). A new network, *Demain la parité*, formed in 1994 and by 1997 claimed to have more than two million members (*Parité-infos*, no. 18, June 1997: 3).

Parity made its first prominent mainstream appearance in the run-up to the 1994 European elections. Six *listes paritaires* (candidate lists on which men and women featured alternately) were finally presented, including that of the *Verts* (following the practice they established at the 1989 European elections), Jean-Pierre Chevènement (former leading light on the left of the PS, and founder of the *Mouvement des citoyens*) and Michel Rocard, first secretary of the PS, after a surprise announcement in October 1993.

Also in 1994, several bills were presented to the National Assembly proposing the introduction of parity or measures which would improve the representation of women. The first two were presented by the *Mouvement des citoyens*. The bill of 23 March 1994 aimed to ensure equal access to political office for men and women. It demanded constitutional reform and a referendum to bring this about if agreement between the National Assembly and the Senate could not be reached. Its single article stated 'A fifth clause is added to article 3 of the Constitution: "The equal access of women and men to political office is ensured by parity".' The same deputies presented a second bill on 24 March 1994, with the same goal, but this time specifying details according to the type of election. In single candidate majority elections, each party would select an equal number of male and female candidates in each department and, where there were lists of candidates, each list would feature men and women alternately (Mossuz-Lavau 1998c: 46).

The Communist group presented a bill on 13 April 1994, stating that the equal representation of men and women in public life is a major contribution to democracy and to society. The bill demanded the introduction of proportional representation for all elections, improved conditions for elected representatives and the presentation of an annual report to parliament on the progress which had been made towards parity in political institutions and public and private sites of decision-making. A second bill was presented by the Communists on 18 January 1995, this time before the Senate, and a third, in November 1996, proposed the insertion in article 3 of the Constitution of the words, 'Parity between women and men in public life is a condition of the development of democracy' (Mossuz-Lavau 1998c: 47–8).

UDF deputies, Nicole Ameline and Gilles de Robien, also presented a bill on 24 June 1996. It proposed the insertion of the following text in article 3 of the Constitution: 'The law can limit the proportion of candidates of the same sex on candidate lists in an election' (Mossuz-Lavau 1998c: 48). More limited than the MDC and Communist bills, the UDF bill aimed to permit the introduction of quotas, rather than parity, and only at elections with candidate lists.

Finally, although the *Verts* were not at the time represented in parliament, they published a constitutional reform bill according to which 'deputies in the National Assembly are elected by direct suffrage according to the principle of parity between men and women' (Mossuz-Lavau 1998c: 48).

By the presidential elections of 1995, almost all parties and presidential candidates felt it wise to be seen to be in favour of an increase in the number of women in parliament. Pre-election declarations were heard from all candidates except Arlette Laguiller (Mossuz-Lavau 1998c: 53). Only Le Pen declared his opposition on the grounds of the indivisibility of the French people. Robert Hue and Dominique Voynet declared their support for a law imposing parity. Edouard Balladur proposed a change to the Constitution to introduce a quota of 30 per cent for women at list elections. Lionel Jospin declared his intention to move towards parity, and Jacques Chirac stated 'Clear objectives need to be fixed as regards the representation of women. As far as I am concerned, this can only mean parity' (Mossuz-Lavau 1998c: 53). At the same time, although he declared his support for *de facto* quotas, he expressed concerns about *de jure* quotas, which, he claimed, meant that candidates were chosen not for their achievements, but because of their sex. He argued that this would provoke claims for quotas from religious and ethnic communities. Chirac declared his support for a mechanism which would link the public financing of parties to their selection of women candidates, an *Observatoire de la parité*, and a commission to consider other possible measures. Only the *Observatoire* came to fruition after his election as president. Commissioned by Alain Juppé, the *Observatoire* was to report on parity in all areas. The sub-group concerned with parity in politics was headed by Gisèle Halimi, and her report was submitted to the Prime Minister in January 1997. The report suggests various ways of improving women's representation in politics, including financial incentives for parties which increase the number of women elected, encouraging mixed electoral tickets (deputy and substitute of opposite sexes), and a revision of the Constitution by referendum. In March 1997, the report was the subject of a debate without a vote in a half-empty National Assembly dominated by the right. During this debate, Juppé said:

> I am in favour of changing our Constitution in order to permit laws introducing temporary measures, lasting for example for ten years, which would encourage women candidacies in list elections, which are the only type of election which could adapt easily to this logic. This measure, applicable for a clearly defined period, would enable the generation of women which our political sphere needs so badly to emerge at the municipal, regional and European level. I am convinced that, having completed a political apprenticeship at these levels, women would then have all the skills necessary to fight single-member elections successfully.
>
> (Quoted in Mossuz-Lavau 1998c: 59)

The suggestion in this speech that women politicians might be capable of national office after a ten-year apprenticeship in local politics, coupled with Juppé's sacking of eight of the twelve women ministers six months into his first government, did not improve the image of the right at a time when public opinion was becoming increasingly favourable towards the better representation of women in politics. The PS, judging the mood of the electorate more accurately, made an unexpected and successful decision to raise the number of women candidates selected for the next legislative elections, due in 1998, but called unexpectedly in May 1997.

Parity was still enjoying a high profile in the media, and the efforts of parity campaigners and women politicians committed to the cause ensured that it would be an issue in the forthcoming elections. On 6 June 1996, *L'Express* published a 'Manifesto for Parity', signed by ten women politicians from across the political spectrum, and calling for the progressive introduction of parity. The proposed stages included voluntary quotas within the parties; the limiting of the *cumul des mandats*; linking party funding to efforts to advance parity; ensuring the appointment of women to positions of responsibility in the state and the government; and finally, the possibility of changing the Constitution through a referendum.

In September 1996, the PS voted to reserve 165 constituencies for women candidates (Sineau 1997b: 136), and 17 per cent of successful PS candidates were women (Mossuz-Lavau 1997a: 457). This unilateral move by the PS was popular with the electorate. Not only did the women candidates not lose the party votes, as some had feared, but they may have done better than male candidates, given that many of them were unknown and were fighting more difficult seats. The 1997 election was a watershed in terms of women's representation, which increased in the National

Assembly from 6 per cent to 10.94 per cent, mainly due to the actions of the PS.

The regional elections of spring 1998 saw a dramatic increase in the number of women candidates selected and elected, even though no measures had been introduced to force the parties to bring about this change (Sineau 1998b: 13). The number of women candidates rose from 27 per cent in 1992 to 37 per cent in 1998, and the number of women elected rose from 13 per cent to 26 per cent. The proportion of women candidates selected by each party on the left was 43 per cent for the PCF, 39 per cent for the PS, and 35 per cent for the *Verts*. The proportions on the right were astonishingly similar: 34 per cent for the RPR and 32 per cent for the UDF. It was the PS, however, which placed its women candidates in the best positions on its lists, so that 35 per cent of those elected were women. For the *Verts*, this figure was 34 per cent, for the RPR 27 per cent, the PCF 26 per cent, the UDF 23 per cent and the FN 17 per cent.

The cantonal elections were quite different, however. The proportion of women candidates was 15 per cent (13 per cent in 1994) and of women elected, 8 per cent (from 5 per cent). Mariette Sineau (1998b: 13) attributes this difference to the type of voting system. The regional elections take place according to a proportional representation list system, allowing the central party to determine the content of the list. The cantonal elections, however, are single-candidate majority elections, which favour local personalities against the central party. Sineau argues that this demonstrates that, unless there are rules coercing the parties, single-member majority elections do not favour the election of women.

The competitive climate created by the cohabitation of a left-wing prime minister and a right-wing president has engendered a battle for the title of 'political moderniser'. The main elements of the process of modernisation are presented as the removal of the *cumul des mandats*, the reform of the mode of election of the Senate (more senators elected by proportional representation and a change in the electoral college), and an increase in the number of women in politics. Jospin's election platform included a commitment to increasing women's representation, and Chirac, in a speech at Rennes, 4 December 1998, declared: 'opening up political life is one of the most pressing needs of our time . . . I hope that constitutional reform favouring the access of women to posts of political responsibility will come about as soon as possible' (*Le Monde*, 6–7 December 1998). As a result of their eagerness to be seen to support the increase in women's representation, Jospin and Chirac have found themselves pursuing the same goal and have thus sought compromise and agreement with each other in order to see it through parliament.

By June 1998, Jospin and Chirac had agreed on the text of a bill modifying article 34 of the Constitution. It read, 'the law can determine rules favouring the equal access of women and men to political, professional and social responsibilities' (*Le Monde*, 17 June 1998). The council of ministers opposed this, however, on the grounds that social and professional equality were already assured by the preamble of the Constitution, so on 17 June, the council of ministers agreed to the modification of article 3 instead, thus restricting the reform to elections and appointments to public office (Bacqué 1998). The agreed text, which was presented by the Minister for Justice, Elisabeth Guigou, read, 'the law favours the equal access of women and men to political office'. The aim of the proposed reform was to prevent the Constitutional Council overthrowing any laws which might be passed on parity in a repeat of its 1982 ruling.[2] Despite the disappointment of some deputies and campaigners with the term 'favours' rather than 'guarantees' (for example, Catala 1998, Gaspard 1998a), the Bill was met with largely favourable reactions by the main parties (*Le Figaro*, 18 June 1998), and by the general public (*Libération*, 18 June 1998). A poll conducted on 5 and 6 February 1999 found that 75 per cent of those asked favoured a referendum (20 per cent against, 5 per cent don't knows). Asked how they would vote if this referendum took place, 80 per cent said yes, 11 per cent no, and 9 per cent didn't know (*L'Evénement du jeudi*, 11 February 1999: 85).

Having been modified by the National Assembly's legal committee, chaired by PS deputy Catherine Tasca, the Bill was passed unanimously (with one abstention) by the National Assembly on 15 December 1998. It inserted into article 3 of the Constitution (on national sovereignty) the following text, 'The law determines the conditions in which the equal access of women and men to political office is organised'. The only opposition to the Bill during the debate in the National Assembly was voiced by Didier Julia (RPR) and François Goulard (DL).

The Bill was the result of negotiation and compromise between the Prime Minister and the President. In particular, Chirac had argued that the term 'parity' should be removed in order to make the reform more acceptable to the opposition. He also requested that the word 'favours' should replace the 'guarantees', initially proposed by Jospin (Bacqué 1998). During a period of cohabitation, compromise is essential if the Constitution is to be changed, as this requires agreement between the prime minister and the president. The National Assembly and the Senate must also agree, each passing the same text, which must then be approved by three-fifths of a special Congress of both houses which meets at Versailles. Despite the agreement of the President and the Prime Minister, agreement between the National Assembly (with a left-wing majority) and the Senate (with a right-wing majority) proved more difficult to achieve.

At its first reading in the Senate, on 26 January 1999, the Government Bill was rejected. An alternative text was proposed and passed (164 RPR–UDF–DL votes to 113 PS–PCF votes) (*Libération*, 27 January 1999: 13), modifying article 4 of the Constitution, which concerns the role of the parties: 'The parties favour the equal access of women and men to electoral mandates and appointed posts.'

During the debate in the Senate, the main arguments which were voiced against the Government Bill were, first, that it was a means of introducing proportional representation through the back door, an accusation flatly denied by Jospin (*Le Monde*, 11 December 1998). Second, numerous references were made to the position taken before the Senate's laws committee by Elisabeth Badinter and reiterated by her husband, Socialist senator Robert Badinter, according to which parity endangered republican universalism. The press made much of the fact that the Senate was able to draw on the arguments of a left-wing intellectual and senator in order to support its opposition to the Bill. The third main argument, which follows on from the second, was that it would open the door to demands from 'other minorities'. These issues are examined in detail later in this chapter.

The majority of senators prefaced their objections to the Bill with a declaration of their profound support for the goal of increasing the number of women in French politics. Christian Bonnet, former minister of the interior, RI (Républicains Indépendants), for example, stated (*Le Monde*, 28 January 1999), 'My cultural revolution took place a long time age. My [female] substitute [*suppléante*] had two periods of office as a deputy while I was a minister.'

Although there were calls for a referendum as an alternative means of bringing about Constitutional reform without the agreement of the Senate, Chirac preferred to try to obtain this agreement. At the Bill's second reading in the National Assembly, 16 February 1999, the same text was passed as before. Chirac went to great lengths to rally the parliamentary right around his own position so painstakingly negotiated with Jospin. He was successful: the Senate finally passed the original government bill ('the law favours the equal access of men and women to elected mandates and appointed posts') on 4 March 1999 by 289 votes to 8 (*Le Monde*, 6 March 1999) as well as inserting into article 4 that the parties contribute to the application of parity. A Congress of both houses was held at Versailles on 28 June 1999, when this text was passed by 741 votes to 42[3] (*Le Monde*, 30 June 1999).

The rhetoric of parity has been widely embraced by politicians on the left and the right, who publicly deplore the absence of women from politics and make statements of varying credibility about the need for change. In the view of some commentators at least, electoral pragmatism is motivating these actions, which might turn out to produce more in the way of political rhetoric than tangible benefit. There is no doubt, for example, that the frenzied activity around parity during the campaign for the 1994 European elections was associated with the fact that the stakes are lower for European than for national elections, and Alain Juppé's decision to include twelve women in his first government is described by Mariette Sineau (1995b: 2–3) as an election gimmick. The women were excluded from the 'serious' ministries and real sites of power,[4] and eight of them were dropped in a reshuffle only six months later. Jospin's commitment to women's rights may be just as superficial, as was argued in Chapter 2.

Public opinion has clearly been much more favourable to parity than politicians, whose own interests are at stake. In 1994, an IFOP/Ministry of Social Affairs poll found that 62 per cent favoured the introduction of parity in the Constitution. In 1996, 71 per cent of those polled by IFOP for *L'Express* were in favour of parity, and 82 per cent were in favour of a referendum (*Libération*, 18 June 1998). In contrast to the overwhelming public support, deputies were found to be more reticent. A survey carried out by *Le Monde* (Biffaud and Roland-Lévy 1997: 6) revealed that the majority of the 312 deputies (out of 576) who responded to the question-naire were opposed to the introduction of parity in the Constitution, the imposition of quotas within the parties, and to a referendum on these questions. The survey was conducted before the 1997 elections, when there was a right-wing majority. The 128 RPR deputies therefore had a strong influence on the results, even though Alain Juppé was in favour of quotas and 'not opposed' to a referendum. The 108 UDF deputies who responded were also largely opposed to parity, although 38 per cent favoured quotas. Of the 38 Socialist deputies who responded, 33 supported quotas, but the majority were opposed to constitutional reform and to a referendum. All the Communist deputies were in favour of constitutional change and opposed to a referendum. Of the 32 women deputies, all of whom responded (17 RPR, 8 UDF, 4 PS, 2 PC, 1 *République et liberté*), more than twenty rejected all three suggestions. Only the four PS women supported them all.

With the exception of the FN, very few public figures are willing to expose themselves as opponents of the better representation of women. On a superficial level, there is consensus around the idea that introducing more women into politics is a good thing, although this is often qualified with concerns about their ability to do the job properly. Jean-Claude Gaudin, for example, influential in the UDF selection process, has said, 'It is difficult to free up places for women of quality, but it is also diffi-cult to find women of quality. Quantity is one thing, quality is another' (*Le Point*, 8 March 1997). As was argued in Chapter 5, it is difficult to substantiate the claim that suitable women candidates do not exist, nor that the introduction of parity would see women achieve political office 'simply because they are women'. As Janine Mossuz-Lavau (1999) contends, women, who now outnumber men at university and make up 45 per cent of the working population, no longer need to prove their competence; they simply need to have the barriers removed which prevent them from exercising it.

There is little debate around the principle of increasing women's polit-ical representation. However, two questions have proved more contentious. The first is whether parity would make a difference and the second is what mechanisms, if any, should be introduced in order to bring about this increase. Each of these is examined here in turn.

What difference would parity make?

Excluding those whose primary motivation is to enhance their own political standing, supporters of parity can be divided into those who believe it would make a difference and those who believe that, whether or not it would make a difference, it would be fairer and is therefore a goal worth pursuing. Justifying support for parity on the grounds that it would make a difference is more contentious than arguing simply that it would be fairer. Areas in which it has been suggested that a difference could be made are the political agenda, policy outcomes, the style of politics, the public perception of women's roles and women's share of power. These will be examined here, with studies from other countries providing some indication of whether or not these outcomes could be expected.

Political agenda and policy outcomes

Would the equal representation of men and women mean that different issues would be brought onto the agenda and different decisions made? And if so, would this mean that women's interests, if there is such a thing, would be better represented?

It is difficult to ascertain whether the policy agenda would be affected. Drude Dahlerup's (1988: 291–2) study of Scandinavian politics, where women's presence in elected bodies has exceeded 30 per cent for many years, shows that 'women's issues' feature more on the political agenda than previously and have been placed there by women politicians. However, she states that it is difficult to isolate the effects of the presence of women politicians from action outside the formal political arena, and that it is therefore not clear that the presence of women in parliament has been responsible for the change.

Eliane Viennot (1996b: 185), active parity supporter, suggests that different issues, such as abortion, contraception, domestic violence and unemployment would be brought to the political agenda and that these issues would be recognised by the electorate as being closer to their own everyday concerns. This view is shared by many of the respondents in Janine Mossuz-Lavau and Anne de Kervasdoué's (1997: 161) recent study. The argument that women would make a difference to policy outcomes seems to rely heavily on a gut feeling that parity would surely have some effect. This conviction is strongest around the issues of abortion and violence. Eliane Viennot (1994: 71), for example, states that there would surely not be commando-style raids on abortion clinics if women were in power, and Françoise Gaspard and Claude Servan-Schreiber (1993: 2) have claimed that it is inconceivable that a legislature comprising a significant number of women would ever have debated the criminalisation of the practice of abortion on oneself. They argue that this is evidence that women have different political interests to men and that these interests are not being adequately represented by a male-dominated parliament. Marie-Victoire Louis' (1994: 43) analysis of the parliamentary debates around the new Penal Code leads her to the conclusion that, with the exception of the debates on abortion, only women representatives defended women's rights.

Sydney Verba's (1990: 561) examination of the impact of women in American politics, however, finds that on all issues around which there has been strong political activity on the part of women in the United States (suffrage, prohibition, the Equal Rights Amendment) there has also been strong opposition by women. In France, women are certainly active in anti-abortion activities, and Lesselier and Venner's (1997) study of women on the extreme right demonstrates that the 'women's interests' they claim to represent are often far removed from those understood by feminist parity campaigners. Women representatives cannot even be expected to support measures aimed at increasing women's representation. Twenty of the 32 women deputies who responded to the survey conducted by *Le Monde* (Biffaud and Roland-Lévy 1997: 6) were opposed to all three of the suggestions offered: writing parity into the Constitution; introducing quotas within the parties; and holding a referendum on these questions. Only the four PS women supported all three suggestions.

The minority presence of women in national assemblies may affect the policy issues which they support publicly. It is possible that the few women who are elected are those who do not support 'women's issues' or that they do not support these issues while they are present in such small numbers. The idea of a threshold, usually placed at around 30 per cent, beyond which women would constitute a critical mass and begin to make a difference to politics has held a certain appeal for commentators on this issue. Drude Dahlerup (1988: 296), however, argues that it is not a critical *mass* which makes a difference, but critical *acts*. In other words, what is important is not how many women are present, but how many of them are prepared to, or able to, act in a way which improves the status of women. It seems more likely that an increase in the number of women who identify politically as women and seek to represent the group's interests would make more of a difference than an increase in the number of women alone. In fact, it is possible to imagine a scenario in which three hundred women entered parliament, but did nothing to change the functioning or ideological content of the political process (Le Doeuff 1995: 26). Campaigners for parity need to consider whether their goal is simply the physical presence of a number of women equal to that of men or whether they want this to produce certain outcomes.

Representation

Whether or not parity is advocated on the grounds that it would produce a more representative democracy depends on one's conception of representation. There are two main views. According to the first, the elected representative acts in what he/she perceives to be the best interests of the electorate. It is unnecessary for there to be any resemblance between representatives and voters other than a shared belief that the latters' interests are best defended by the former. According to the second view, the elected body should reflect the diversity of its electorate. Representatives are elected by constituents and are accountable to them.

In the French tradition of representation, sovereignty emanates from 'the people', which is not a sociologically and culturally diverse population, but an undifferentiated unit. French institutions do not derive their legitimacy from the fact that their members are a representative sample of the population. It is the elected body as a whole which represents the people as a whole. Deputies do not represent their constituency, but are members of the representative body. Representatives are not elected to act as delegates of the voters and are not accountable to them. Instead, they act in what they believe are the best interests of the people (Millard and Ortiz 1998).

It is interesting to note that Lionel Jospin, in the speech he gave at the special Congress of the National Assembly and the Senate at Versailles in June 1999 (http://www.premier-ministre.gouv.fr/PM/D280699A.HTM, accessed 9 October 1999) ardently defended the type of representation which expects the representative body to reflect its electorate. He states:

> We must act to ensure that our representative democracy is as true a reflection as possible of the electorate so that our fellow citizens feel closer to their elected representatives who resemble them more and so that our democracy, profoundly renewed through its feminisation, becomes more dynamic, livelier and more imaginative.

In this view, however, the only way in which elected representatives would resemble their voters is in their sex. No mention is made of other differences between voters and the political élite.

Parity is advocated by those who believe that women should be able to exercise their right to participate in the body which represents the will of 'the people' or 'the nation' and also by those who believe that women should be present in the representative body in order to represent 'women's interest'. This latter position is the most difficult to reconcile with the view of representation outlined above and also raises the question of whether groups can be adequately represented only by their own members. If this is the case, it is difficult to deny the claims to representation of all groups. Unless representatives are accountable to their electorate, however, there is no assurance that a woman, simply because she is biologically female, will represent the interests of other women, and this lack of attention to what women would do once present in decision-making bodies worries left-wing feminist theorists such as Michèle Le Doeuff (1995) and Eleni

Varikas (1995b). Varikas (1995b: 100–1), for example, is particularly critical of the idea that feminists should support parity on the basis that women are best represented by women, regardless of political programme or policy objectives:

> Since when has feminism been transformed from a project for the self-emancipation of women – a political project to be constructed – into an ideology which says that women are always right? Since when have we converted our confidence in the liberating dynamic of such a project into confidence in the *intrinsic* ability of women (*all women*) to pursue better policies than men (all men)?

Women do not express themselves *as women* on every question, because they never form part of only one group, and their loyalty to a certain group varies according to the question. Françoise Collin (1996b: 107) suggests that the equal representation of women in elected bodies should be accompanied by a project, or at least a minimal charter, committing the women elected to the support of women's rights. This is only a partial solution, however, given the numerous possible interpretations of women's rights and interests. Furthermore, Collin states that the relation between equality of representation and equality of rights and interests for all needs to be examined more closely, '[s]ince starting with parity in representation seems to presume that democracy comes from above' (Collin 1996b: 107).

So do women constitute an interest? Can they be shown to constitute a coherent category whose views differ from those of men? Studies in other countries have revealed that in most areas, including 'women's issues', women's views overlap with men's, and divisions between parties are clearer than between men and women of different parties (Lovenduski and Norris 1993: 6). However, Lovenduski and Norris' study of British politics shows that, although party is the most important factor, gender does make a difference to policy interests, political activity and support for women's rights (Norris 1996: 103–4). There is also some evidence to suggest a gender gap in attitudes towards the environment, welfare and military spending (Sineau 1992: 488).

In conclusion, we might suggest that women probably do constitute an interest different from men, even if this is very heterogeneous and cut through by many other divisions. But there is little evidence to support the argument that more women in parliament would better represent this interest. It can be argued that women representatives will not *worsen* women's status and that the representation of the diversity of women's views is as necessary as the representation of the diversity of men's views. It would rectify an injustice and undoubtedly be of symbolic significance. However, it falls short of the demands of feminist theorists on the left, who seek a more radical overhaul of the democratic process. This is examined in more detail in Chapter 9.

Style of politics and access to power

Parity campaigner, Eliane Viennot (1996b: 185), suggests that if parliament were composed of equal numbers of men and women, it would conduct its affairs differently. For example, she claims that there would be no more all-night sittings. Others suggest that politics would be more cooperative, less ritualised and less competitive. In her study of Scandinavian politics, Drude Dahlerup (1988: 288) asserts that the political culture has become less formal. She states that this may be directly due to the growing numbers of women in politics, or it may be due to the presence of Socialist and Green parties, in which women have played an important role.

While some studies (Thomas 1994, Verba 1990) suggest that, below a certain threshold, at least, women politicians 'act like the boys', it is still possible that this might change if a significant number of women were present. Sue Thomas (1994), for example, found that, while most of the American women politicians she included in her study did play by the rules, they were in favour of systemic reform, and might be more willing to act on this if there were more of them. However, the evidence is inconclusive, much of it being anecdotal and often heavily influenced by preconceptions of gender-appropriate behaviour.

Supporters of the parity campaign argue that the initial implementation of parity in elected assemblies would act as a model for other organisations, promoting change in society as well as in politics (Gaspard 1996: 28, Viennot 1996b: 185). Concerns that this is not necessarily the case are expressed by Florence Montreynaud (1996: 187), who argues that in Sweden and Norway, the presence of women in political bodies has not led to a correspondingly high presence in important sites of economic power. Montreynaud states that 'when women enter a particular sphere, power tends to drain away, and today, power is economic rather than political'. Others share the concern that focusing on the national legislature does not target the real sites of power in contemporary France. Without undermining the importance of equal representation in parliament, these critics stress that this must not ignore far more important sites of economic power and that it must be viewed within the context of a shift in power from parliament to the executive and from the nation-state to supranational organisations. Françoise Collin (1996b: 103), for example, asks:

> Are we not, as usual, demanding access to sites which have been deserted, sites of symbolic rather than actual power? Where is the real political power in France today, with the increase in presidential power, the relative dependence of the judiciary on the executive – and/or on the president – and the weakening of the legislature? And where is the real power in the international, European or global context? A spot of good old Marxism and a reference to economics would not go amiss here.

In summary, then, parity would bring an equal number of women into the political élite. This would have symbolic significance and might bring about changes in the policy agenda, policy outcomes and the political culture. However, it would not on its own address the problem of the differential access of social categories to the resources necessary for political activity and would not guarantee women's greater access to sites of real power.

How should women's representation be increased?

When women won the right to vote and to stand for election, it was widely expected that their presence in elected bodies would gradually increase as they acquired the necessary skills and experience. By the fiftieth anniversary of universal suffrage in 1994, it was clear that this was not going to happen: in 1945 there were thirty-three women deputies; in 1994, there were thirty-four. It was therefore fully justifiable to argue that change was not going to occur 'naturally' and that action was necessary in order to bring it about. Gaspard, Servan-Schreiber and Le Gall's (1992) *Au pouvoir citoyennes!*, made a clear and simple demand for the insertion of parity into the Constitution, and they rallied support around this demand. The intervention of feminist lawyers in the debate raised technical questions about the chances of success and about the relative advantages of constitutional and legislative reform. The campaign for parity undertook a major strategic review at the 1998 Toulouse conference, where Françoise Gaspard introduced the bill she was about to present to parliament. Interestingly, this bill proposed, first, the presence of at least one-third of candidates of each sex on lists at the next municipal, regional and senate elections conducted under proportional representation, and, second, the aim of presenting candidates according to parity at all subsequent elections, including the forthcoming European elections. Admitting that this proposal falls short of the principle of parity, Gaspard nevertheless denied that it was a U-turn on quotas (Millard 1998: 269). The open discussion which took place at the Toulouse conference centred on pragmatic measures for achieving success as soon as possible, and addressed the question of how to ensure that a law on parity would be more effective than the 1983 law on professional equality. Much of the debate centred on the 1982 ruling of the Constitutional Council, which was seen as a major obstacle to the introduction of legislation aimed at increasing women's representation.

1982 ruling of the Constitutional Council

In 1982, Gisèle Halimi proposed an amendment to a government bill on municipal elections, to the effect that no more than 75 per cent of the candidates on any list should be of the same sex. The Constitutional Council ruled that this was unconstitutional, invoking article 3 of the

Constitution and article 6 of the Declaration of the Rights of Man and the Citizen (despite the fact that the latter dates from a time when women had neither the vote nor the right to stand for election). Article 3 of the Constitution states that national sovereignty belongs to the people and must be exercised by them directly or through their representatives. It may not be exercised by a section of the people. Article 6 of the Declaration of the Rights of Man and the Citizen states that 'all citizens are equally eligible for all public functions, posts and appointments, according to their ability and with no distinction other than their qualities and their talents'. The Constitutional Council ruled that all citizens have an equal right to stand for election, and that it is unconstitutional to divide voters or candidates into categories.

Although in French law, precedents are not binding, there was a broad consensus amongst politicians and lawyers that the 1982 ruling would exert a strong influence, and that a law on parity would be overturned for the same reasons as Halimi's amendment. Parity campaigners were therefore faced with a choice of strategy: they could attempt to challenge the ruling, by presenting a bill in which it was argued that parity is not unconstitutional; they could hope to avoid the Constitutional Council, which can only consider the constitutionality of a law if asked to do so by sixty members of parliament, the president, the prime minister, or the presidents of each house; or they could try to change the Constitution.

There was a case to be made for the constitutionality of parity. It could be argued that parity is not opposed to the principle of equality. On the contrary, it is the epitome of equality. It is a means of translating into reality the principle of equality which is guaranteed in the preamble of the Constitution. It could also be argued that parity does not create categories; it simply ensures that both of the components which make up humanity have an equal share in decision-making. It could be argued that parity does not contravene the principle of the freedom to stand for election. Given that in 90 per cent of cases, this results in the election of one category of citizens – men – it is likely that something is interfering with the freedom of women candidates. Some would argue that it is the role of the law to ensure that conditions of access are equal, and if this were the case, one could expect a much more equal distribution of seats between men and women. Finally, it could be argued that the Constitutional Council ignored constitutional texts which seem to support the case for parity (Kriegel 1996: 377). For example, no reference was made to article 1 of the Declaration of Rights, which states that social differences can only be based on the common good, nor to the preamble of the Constitution of 1946, which states that 'The law guarantees equal rights between men and women in all areas'. Parity supporters also invoke international treaties, which take precedence over national laws in the hierarchy of legal texts. The New York Convention is the most frequently cited, although feminist lawyer, Danièle Loschak (1996: 47) contends that it is of limited use for two reasons. First, although it insists on the removal of all legal discrimination against women, this has already been done in French law. Second, although it permits positive discrimination, it does not require it. Furthermore, the Constitutional Council does not see it as its role to examine the accordance of new legislation with international treaties; this is the role of the Council of State.

In effect, the campaign for parity was overtaken by events. While internal debates were still taking place about the relative merits of constitutional and legislative reform, Jospin and Chirac, noting the political opportunism of acting on this issue, both backed a constitutional reform bill which they then pushed through the necessary parliamentary processes.

The Constitutional Reform Bill 1998

This Bill was intended to prevent a repeat ruling by the Constitutional Council should a law on parity be passed in the future. The Bill itself was very different in content to that which had been demanded by parity campaigners, and was therefore not celebrated by them as a victory. Françoise Gaspard (1998a), for example, claimed that the constitutional reform bill was superfluous, adding nothing to the guarantee of sexual equality already stated in the preamble of the Constitution and the 1979 UN Convention on the elimination of all forms of discrimination towards women, which permits temporary positive action measures in public life.

The Bill was enough, however, to provoke criticism from those opposed not to the principle of the better representation of women, but to the introduction of parity into the law. Against the current of public opinion, a number of prominent women intellectuals declared their opposition to constitutional reform (see, for example, *L'Express*, 11 Februrary 1999, *Le Monde*, 6 February 1999, *L'Evènement du jeudi*, 4 February 1999, *Le Nouvel Observateur*, 14 January 1999). Their case was based on the argument that the recognition of sexual difference in the Constitution was contrary to the principle of universalism. The opposition between universalism and particularism had been at the centre of the debate on parity throughout the 1990s, although until February 1999, it had not correlated neatly with anti- and pro-parity positions, since the aim of the campaign – to bring about the equal representation of men and women in politics – could be supported by those who wanted to eradicate the social difference between men and women as well as by those who wanted to accentuate it. However, the debate which took place in the media around the parliamentary readings of the Constitutional Reform Bill in February 1999 polarised around universalist opponents and differentialist supporters of legally imposed parity.

In a prominent and controversial article published in *Le Monde*, Sylviane Agacinski (1999) claimed that the support French women have shown for the idea of parity demonstrates their agreement with the 'difference' position, in other words, their belief that sexual difference should be recognised, not eradicated. She argues that the discourse of universalism obscures the fact that the 'universal' is masculine and claims that parity will force the recognition of the duality of humanity.

Elisabeth Badinter (1999a: 84) holds that the insertion of parity into the Constitution would contradict the principle of abstract universalism, according to which all citizens are equal, and sex, age, colour, physical ability and all other markers of identity are, or should be, irrelevant to an individual's public life. Naming sexual difference would reinforce it at a time when it was becoming increasingly blurred in society. It would suggest that there are two perspectives on the world, masculine and feminine, whereas, in fact, there are multiple feminine points of view, and masculine and feminine virtues belong to both sexes.

The problem with emphasising the dual nature of humanity is that it suggests that biological difference is the pertinent factor. If parity advocates deny this, arguing that sexual difference is socio-historical, then it is difficult for them to deny the legitimacy of other claims for representation, and this is something they seem determined to do. Elisabeth Badinter (1999b: 89) criticises parity campaigners for refusing to recognise the validity of claims of other categories, stating:

> To those who present a critique of the masculine universal, I say that they are wrong: they should develop a critique of the masculine, white, Catholic, judaeo-christian universal, since it is absolutely essential that the Republic should open up to all others.

Badinter opposes measures which draw attention to differences, rather than minimising their relevance. She claims that her ideal is an inclusive universal. However, she does not suggest how this can be achieved without the explicit recognition of differences and the implementation of corrective measures aimed at bringing it about. Simply ignoring or denying the existence or relevance of these differences in the name of the abstract universal has obscured the way in which women are excluded, parity campaigners claim.

Eliane Viennot (1994) and others from the parity campaign argue that, far from accentuating women's difference, parity is a fight for the elimination of sexual difference as a major factor in the identity of individuals. Even if it necessitates a preliminary stage in which difference is recognised, at the end of the process, women will come to be seen as being equally as capable of running the country as men, and there will be no political, social or symbolic difference between men and women. In order for women to become equal to men, we must first admit that they are not. She writes (1994: 86):

One day, no doubt, when 'man' and 'woman' no longer make a difference (politically, socially or symbolically), the law will no longer serve any purpose and it can be dropped. But this stage is essential. In order for women to become equal to men, it must first be admitted that they are not. Rather than having a Constitution which declares sexual equality, we need a law which brings it into practice.

In an attempt to counter suggestions that the demand for parity would lead to demands from other under-represented groups, many parity campaigners claimed that the demand for women's representation was different from all other claims for representation, since sexual difference is fundamentally different from differences between social categories.

The main points of the argument, which have been variously and not always clearly expressed, are that humanity comprises two sexes, and that they should share equally in decision-making (Agacinski 1998: 155); that women do not constitute a social category, because they are present in all social categories (*Parité-infos*, no. 0, March 1993: 5, Gaspard 1997a: 123); and that sex is different from all other categorisations, because it is immutable and is the only one recognised by French law and noted on the birth certificate (Gaspard 1997a: 123). These arguments inevitably suggest that parity is based on an acceptance that there is a fundamental difference between men and women, a position which many feminists refuse to accept.

In addition, the naming of the sex category 'women' risks homogenising women's diverse interests and needs. Although it is true that women share certain material conditions and historical experiences, they do not constitute a homogeneous group with a single interest; they form a diverse category cut through by other social divisions. On the other hand, not naming the category 'women' risks leaving women's exclusion hidden behind the discourse of universalism, and ignoring policy needs which are gendered, even if they are not shared by all women. The feminist debate around these questions is examined in detail in Chapter 9.

In the same way as in 1982, then, it was argued that the change brought about by the Constitutional Reform Act would contradict republican universalism by dividing the people into categories. The creation of categories of citizens would inevitably lead to demands from other categories: 'Following the deplorable example of American society, it would mean the break-up of the body politic' (Terré 1998).

In fact, the content of the Act was very vague and left much open to interpretation. It does not stipulate whether the aim is to achieve equality of means or equality of results, so a future legislature could interpret it in either way, with very different outcomes. A central issue was whether it is legitimate to divide potential candidates into categories in order to ensure equality of representation, or whether equality of opportunity is the best that can be achieved under French law. Gaspard (1998a: 13) argues that the law already permits categorisation in order to achieve particular outcomes. For example, tax laws differentiate between citizens in order to reduce inequalities and, in the case of elections, rules exist which ensure or restrict the election of certain categories, for example, residents of the constituency, French nationals and certain age groups.

Opponents of the Bill argued that it would interfere with the freedom of the voter, who would be forced to vote for at least 25 per cent women candidates. Gaspard (1997a: 121) counters that the voter is not free to choose a candidate, but must vote for one who has been selected by a party. The freedom of the voter is therefore already limited. Gaspard writes:

> The only thing that would change if parties were forced by law to select as many women as men is that there would be more female candidates. It is therefore not the voters whose freedom would be compromised, but the parties and their apparatus. Moreover, it is paradoxical that those who invoke this argument claim that the solution to the scarcity of women in elected bodies lies with the parties themselves: it is precisely because the parties find it so difficult to change that it is worth forcing them to do so.

In addition, Loschak (1983: 134) argues that there is a much stronger argument that the freedom of the voter to vote for the candidate of their choice is limited by blocked lists, a practice whose constitutionality has never been questioned.

One of the main debates was around the relative merits of changing article 3 on national sovereignty or article 4 on the role of the parties. Universalists, the most prominent of whom were the Badinters (Badinter, Robert 1999, Badinter, Elisabeth, 1999a, 1999b), who opposed the introduction of parity on the grounds that it threatened the unity of the French people, had no objections to its inclusion in article 4. Robert Badinter (1999) concedes that, although in law, all eligible citizens have the right to stand for election, in reality, it is the parties which select candidates. It is therefore their responsibility to bring about parity, and this can be enforced by modifying article 4 of the Constitution. In response to this argument, Janine Mossuz-Lavau (1999) asks whether the inclusion of sexual difference in article 4 is less of a threat to universalism than its inclusion in article 3, simply because this article concerns the parties and not national sovereignty.

The fourteen women intellectuals who spoke out against the version of parity contained in the Constitutional Reform Bill (*L'Express*, 11 February 1999) proposed alternative measures including the elimination of the *cumul des mandats*, changing the times of political meetings, modifying article 4 instead of article 3, and focusing on the sharing of domestic labour and childcare. It seems that such a combination of measures is necessary if effective change is to be brought about.

A report on the technicalities of parity was submitted to the Prime Minister on 8 September 1999 by Dominique Gillot, General Reporter of the *Observatoire de la parité* since January 1999. It proposes that in the 2001 municipal elections, women's representation should reach 40 per cent. In the 2007 regional, European and municipal elections, it should reach 50 per cent. Any list not meeting this requirement would be disqualified. However, communes with fewer than 3,500 inhabitants (34,000 out of 36,000 and one-third of the population) would be exempt, because they have a different voting system, allowing voters to remove names from candidate lists and add new ones to them. For legislative elections, Gillot proposes the creation of a special fund accessible only to parties with 40 per cent women candidates. The amount available would depend on the votes obtained by these candidates. She also proposes some secondary measures, including limiting the number of mandates which can be held at any one time and improving the working conditions of elected representatives so that they better meet the needs of women.

The Government Bill, tabled in December 1999, requires the parties to include 50 per cent women on lists in elections under PR, beginning with the municipal elections in 2001. It does not stipulate where on the lists women should appear. In legislative elections, parties which do not respect parity will be penalised (*Le Monde*, 9 December 1999). The successful implementation of these measures and their correlation with feminist demands are largely dependent on political will and need to be carefully monitored.

9 Parity, democracy and citizenship

During the 1990s, the idea that democracy or representation was in crisis attracted much attention in journalistic and academic debates. The main indicators of this crisis included the growing gap between the concerns of the French people and the political élite, repeatedly demonstrated by public opinion polls;[1] rising abstention rates; the failure of the parties to recruit new members; and public disaffection with a political class in which scandals seemed endemic.[2]

Some of these claims can be qualified, in particular the suggestion that abstentionism is on the increase. It is true that between 1988 and 1992, record levels of abstention were reached at several elections, but the number of elections held during this period, combined with the issues on which campaigns were run, contributed to this exceptionally low turnout (Chagnollaud 1993: 436). Moreover, Subileau and Toinet (1993: 193) find that less than 1 per cent of the French electorate abstains habitually and, even when combined with those who are not on the electoral register, the total proportion of the potential electorate which never participates in elections is less than 3 per cent. One-third of the electorate votes at every election and two-thirds vote at most.

The decline in participation in traditional forms of activity is said to be accompanied by a rise in 'alternative' movements, such as anti-racist, humanitarian and human rights demonstrations and organisations and new forms of political lobbying (Perrineau 1997: 18–21). This is interpreted as a sign that French citizens are not becoming less political, but that the political system is failing to respond to their demands. What they want is a more participative democracy (Rémond 1993: 207–8).

The democracy in crisis discourse has stimulated reflection on what democracy could be. The most popular calls for improvement include the introduction of an age limit of 75 for candidates; the abolition of the *cumul des mandats*; and the reform of the voting system (Rozès 1997: 507).

The introduction of women into the political élite is claimed by some to be a way of bridging the gap between the people and an increasingly distant élite. The prevalence of the discourse of crisis at the time of the launch of the parity campaign resulted in its claim that the exclusion of women was a symptom of this crisis and that parity would contribute to its solution.

In the early days of the campaign for parity, pragmatic concerns seemed to take precedence over the theoretical issues raised by this demand. Eliane Viennot (1993: 5), in a report on the conference organised by *Choisir* at UNESCO on 3–4 June 1993, stated that the most important thing at the time was the introduction of a law enforcing parity in elected institutions; the theory could come later. She reports an agreement amongst all the international representatives that parity *must* be introduced institutionally, regardless of the debates, conditions, and other considerations.

The campaign is still driven by a 'realist' pressure, which insists on the simplicity, justice and cross-party attractiveness of the principle of parity. While the individuals involved may perceive parity as a far more ambitious goal, which should be pursued in all areas of decision-making and all sites of social, political and economic power, the main force is pragmatism and commitment to the single aim of the campaign. Alongside this, and intertwined with it, is a 'utopian' pressure, which insists that the problem is rooted much more deeply than a gender imbalance in the political élite, and that a fundamental reworking of democracy and citizenship is necessary if parity is to improve women's lives. By examining the theories which have emerged from this claim, we can draw some conclusions about the extent to which the introduction of a law on parity would improve the status of women as citizens and their opportunity to participate fully in politics and civil society.

The demand for parity was originally based on the argument that women had been (inadvertently) omitted from democracy and that, once this was corrected, democracy would be truly democratic. Women's presumed proximity to 'everyday concerns' was frequently used to support the argument that a *démocratie paritaire* would not suffer the same problems of lack of representation as the current version. However, while the slogan 'a democracy which excludes half of the population is not a democracy' had a winning simplicity, critics countered that women could not simply be added on to an inherently flawed system. While this may give the impression of political equality, the problem of women's citizenship is more deeply rooted, they argued.

The processes and justifications for women's exclusion from democracy thus became an important area of feminist research. These were traced back to the Revolution and the Enlightenment thought which inspired the construction of the republic. Key concepts such as universalism and the public/private divide have been explored in order to demonstrate how and why women's citizenship has developed as it has. This chapter examines these explorations and the suggestions for the transformation of women's citizenship which have emerged from them. It then considers the extent to which parity could contribute to this transformation.

What is citizenship?

One of the main problems with any analysis of citizenship theories is defining terms. Citizenship has always been a slippery concept, its meaning the subject of competing discourses. Many commentators draw on T.H. Marshall's seminal work from the 1950s, in which he defines citizenship as 'a status bestowed on those who are full members of a community. All who possess the status are equal with respect to the rights and duties with which the status is endowed' (Marshall 1950: 28–9). Marshall divides these rights and responsibilities into three categories: civil, political and social. Civil citizenship is the recognition of a civil society which is distinct from the state and which constitutes a sphere of liberty for the individual. Civil rights are defined in terms of freedoms: the freedom of speech, the freedom to own property and sell one's own labour, for example. Political rights include the right to participate directly or indirectly in government. Social rights respond to the inequalities generated by civil liberties (Jenson and Sineau 1995: 15–17).

The advantage of Marshall's approach is that it enables citizenship to be theorised as a multi-layered construct, and the focus on membership of a community allows it to operate at a local, national and transnational level (Yuval-Davis 1997: 69–70). Ruth Lister (1997a), however, highlights the limitations of Marshall's liberal rights approach to citizenship which interprets it as a status, rather than an act. She attempts to achieve a synthesis of the positive aspects of this approach with those of the civic republican tradition, which emphasises participation as a defining feature of citizenship. The theories which are examined here are based on diverse conceptions of citizenship, many of them focusing primarily on rights. However, as will be seen later in this chapter, this perception is being challenged as French feminist citizenship theories develop.

Citizenship and universalism

Much of the literature on women's citizenship in France since the Revolution focuses on their access to, or exclusion from, rights which have been misleadingly declared universal. It attempts to identify the processes of, and justifications for, women's exclusion from these rights. Feminists have argued that, while the principle of universalism has played a central role in the political ideology of modern citizenship, women are not citizens in the same way as men. The declaration of universal rights did not mean that these rights were accessible to everyone. The categories which had access to 'universal' citizenship were restricted and have been the subject of much debate and negotiation since the Revolution, as has the nature of the rights themselves (Hunt 1996: 23). Condorcet was very much in the minority when he stated:

It would be difficult to prove that women do not have citizenship
... Men's rights result only from the fact that they are sentient
beings, capable of acquiring moral ideas and reasoning on these ideas;
thus women with these same qualities necessarily have equal rights.
Either no individual of the human race has real rights or all have
the same.

(Quoted by Vogel 1994: 21)

Women's exclusion at the Revolution was facilitated by the creation of
a separate public and private sphere, with which men and women were
associated respectively. This separation was justified through naturalist
ideology derived from Enlightenment thought, and in particular that of
Jean-Jacques Rousseau. Women, who were associated with nature, reproduction and the family, constituted a separate category with a specific role
in democratic life. They were responsible for maintaining moral standards,
and this was done in the private sphere. Men, who were associated with
reason, were responsible for making laws, and this took place in the public
sphere (Fraisse 1997: 9).

Much feminist work in this area has concentrated on exposing the gap
between the theory of universality and the practice of specificity. Eleni
Varikas (1995a: 146), for example, argues that the general law 'applicable
to everyone, known by everyone and made by everyone' established the
duties of citizens, but not their rights. These were not accorded univer-
sally, but instead to certain categories of citizens through specific laws.
Laws which have applied specifically to women have been situated within
a logic of protection or special measures, rather than universal human
rights. Women's needs and interests were not seen to stem from membership of a common humanity, but from membership of a separate and
homogeneous category with specific rights and responsibilities. Universal
citizenship, then, applied only to men. Women were constructed as a separate category, their difference justified by naturalist ideology.

Some feminists have attempted to demonstrate that, far from being an
accidental omission from universalist ideology, the exclusion of women
was an essential part of the construction of a cohesive and homogeneous
public body of citizens. The equality of autonomous rational subjects within
the public sphere seemed to require their sameness, a sameness which
would be jeopardised by the presence of sexual difference, a powerful
symbol of all difference (Fraisse 1997: 8). So women were excluded from
the public sphere, rendering it homogeneous in that all citizens had in
common the fact that they were not women (Scott 1996: 3). Hirata,
Kergoat, Riot-Sarcey and Varikas (1994: 117) write:

The exclusion of women was the condition and the symptom of the
construction of a homogeneous body which was necessary in order
for the modern state to reduce – to the singular – the multiplicity of

humanity. Women are the sign of this multiplicity, and since this sign is visible, it cannot be ignored.

Fraisse (1997: 9) imputes a sense of political will to this decision to exclude women who, from the outset, represented a threat to the homogeneity of the body of citizens, and whose potential sameness or equality provoked fears that love would no longer be possible if sexual difference were removed.

In the private sphere, women were subordinated to the male head of household, who alone existed politically. The subjection of women in the private sphere, it is claimed, was essential to the creation of the modern state, guaranteeing the commitment of citizens to the general interest. The status of men as members of the sovereign and heads of family ensured the transmission of wealth, which is a condition of the renewal of the political community. For women, it meant dependence on an individual man and, as protective measures were introduced to meet their presumed specific needs and interests, on the state (Varikas 1995a: 149–56). As Carole Pateman's (1988) influential work on the sexual contract argues, the advent of democracy brought about the transformation of the hegemonic power relations in society from a patriarchy to a fraternity, in which men have the right to rule over women in the private domestic sphere, but agree on a social contract among themselves within the public political sphere. Pateman argues that women were not excluded accidentally, but as part of a new regime based not on universal rights, but on the rights of man. Since the social contract presupposes a sexual contract which subordinates women, women cannot simply be added on to democracy.

Universalism and parity

As was shown in the previous chapter, universalism is frequently invoked in order to justify opposition to the idea of parity. Parity, it is claimed, would distinguish between categories of citizens, and this is contrary to the principle of universalism, according to which all citizens are equal and, in political terms, the same. Parity would thus destroy one of the very bases of democracy. These arguments are not new. They featured prominently in debates around women's suffrage in the Third Republic (Sineau 1997b: 123) and, in 1982, justified the Constitutional Council's decision that the introduction of quotas was unconstitutional. Mariette Sineau's (1995a: 519) interviews with politicians and members of the legal profession reveal a dominant interpretation of universality which fiercely opposes the division of *le peuple* (the people) into categories. Equality is assured by the political irrelevance of differences, and to attach political significance to membership of a certain community is dangerous to the cohesion of the nation. The assimilation of citizens regardless of their differences is opposed, favourably, to the horrors of communitarianism (Sineau 1997b: 123).

Attempts to explain the late acquisition of political rights by French women, which is sometimes presented in a reductionist manner as 'citizenship', often claim that this is due to the influence of universalism. Pierre Rosanvallon, for example, writes, 'women were deprived of the vote because of their specificity, because they were not real abstract individuals, because they were too affected by factors determined by their sex' (quoted by Reynolds 1994: 6).

Siân Reynolds (1996: 208–11), however, claims that analysis of the parliamentary debates between the wars shows that universalism and the case for women's rights are not incompatible. She challenges the view that the exclusion of women from political rights was determined by the impossibility of their inclusion within republican logic and argues that political pragmatism played an important role. Worries about the falling birth rate and fears that women would vote for the clergy had more of an influence on the strong resistance to women's suffrage than did a commitment to universalism (Reynolds 1994, Knibiehler 1996: 22). Joan Scott (1996a: 2) also argues that universalism did not have to mean sameness. In the Encyclopedia (1755), the individual is defined as a unique being, different from all others. Scott argues that if the idea of infinite differences had been retained in democratic thought, the universal would have been inclusive, not exclusive (Scott 1996a: 2). This suggests that universalism does not need to be abandoned in order for women's citizenship to be achieved. Since the majority of second wave French feminists have been attached to universalism (Collin 1992), this provides an opportunity for them to rethink women's citizenship within a universalist framework, and this is why three of the four approaches to citizenship discussed below retain, yet modify, the universalist tradition.

How can women achieve citizenship?

French feminists have taken four main approaches to this question, although these positions overlap and are in constant dialogue. The first is a call for 'true' universalism which is sexually undifferentiated and demands access for women to autonomous rational subjectivity. The second approach is to demand a universalism which recognises sexual difference. The third approach is a recognition of the differences between men and women, resulting in a true and specific citizenship for women. The fourth approach is the search for a universal citizenship which can recognise multiple differences while maintaining a sense of membership of a community.

Advocates of the first position are unlikely to oppose the principle of the equal political representation of men and women, but they do not subscribe to the notion that women are better able to represent women's interests than men. Their aim is to see women obtain the status of autonomous rational subjects able to represent the universal on the same terms as men. This implies the extension of equality to all areas of public and private life, and much of the work in this area has centred on the need to achieve women's independence from their familial status and attach citizenship to the individual. This position is in the tradition of 'equality' or 'sameness' feminism, exemplified by the radical feminist journal of the 1970s, *Questions féministes* and its successor, *Nouvelles questions féministes.*

The second approach, and this is taken by some of the most prominent parity campaigners (Gaspard and Servan-Schreiber 1993, Halimi 1994a, 1994b), argues that the collectivity, whose interests are encapsulated in representative democracy, is comprised of two genders, who should contribute equally to decision-making. Gaspard and Servan-Schreiber (1993: 2) state that parity challenges the idea that representative democracy transcends the interests of individuals:

> Together, women and men combine to define and perpetuate the species. Together, they should combine in equal numbers to organise communal life. Not in the name of the difference of one sex in relation to the other, but in the name of their dual participation in the human race.

In a paper which has been both influential and hotly debated by those concerned with parity, Elisabeth Sledziewski (1993) argues that women should be included in human rights with explicit reference to sexual difference. She claims that naming sexual difference is the only way to eliminate its pertinence and to remove the discriminations produced by a false universalism which denies the possibility of inequalities by declaring that rights are equal and universal. Sledziewski (1993: 30) writes:

> In contrast to the belief that all men have rights, but that women can neither use them in the same way as men, nor benefit from them as widely, it seems necessary to state that human rights are those of men and women and that this biological difference cannot legitimise the construction of two separate regimes for exercising one's rights. Individuals of both sexes must be able to assert their difference and their equality within carefully separated categories. In order to achieve this, it must be guaranteed that sexual difference and joint access to rights are not mutually exclusive.

Sledziewski argues that the sexes are different and that one sex cannot be assimilated into the other. She insists that gender is not a social category, but a physical fact of the human race, and democracy needs to recognise the dual nature of humanity. In order for the decisions made in representative institutions to be representative of humanity, they must be made by the two sexes together. By arguing that parity would render democracy more democratic, Sledziewski is adhering to a notion of representative bodies reflecting the composition of the electorate. But by stating that sex is not a social category, but a physical fact, she is dismissing at least some claims for representation by other groups (the working class, ethnic minorities). Sledziewski's arguments suggest some kind of essence which women share *as women*, and this would be included in a new two-gendered definition of the universal.

Women's essential difference is the basis for Irigaray's demands for a separate and specific citizenship for women, and this constitutes the third approach to citizenship. The goal is not to enter institutions created by and for men, she argues, but to achieve women's sovereignty as *citoyennes*. This would involve the recognition of their difference and a rejection of neuter citizenship. Irigaray (1994: 107) writes:

> Before we try to enter institutions whose democratic nature needs rethinking, the first thing which it is necessary and totally legitimate to demand is the right to civil majority, the right to represent oneself, before demanding the right to represent others, whilst lacking the legal criteria for an identity of one's own.

Irigaray argues that all women should have the right and the duty to exist as women. This necessitates rewriting the law in order to emphasise that the universal is dual, feminine and masculine. She writes (1994: 108):

> A community composed of male and female sovereign citizens – the accomplishment of democracy – would be a great achievement for women, an achievement which would respect the first victories of women's struggles for liberation. Certainly, this neither implies nor promises any form of power. But democracy cannot be founded on power, even if this is shared, unless it is the power to be oneself: a woman *or* a man, and to share this right to exist in a community made up of women *and* men. Democracy begins with a relation of civility, guaranteed by rights between men *and* women, between male citizens *and* female citizens, between all male citizens *and* all female citizens.

The fourth approach which French feminists have taken aims to redefine the universal such that it can include multiple differences. This has the advantage of not homogenising the categories 'men' and 'women', ignoring the differences within these categories. One of the main problems of citizenship (and the issue of parity has undoubtedly provided a further stimulus to the debate around this question) is how to make room for differences or multiplicity while still retaining a sense of shared destiny or membership of a (national) community. Feminists (Pisier and Varikas 1997, Collin 1995, Hirata, Kergoat, Riot-Sarcey and Varikas 1994) who adopt this position argue that replacing a falsely neutral abstract universal with a two-gendered universal is not the solution. Parity would hide the heterogeneity within the categories men and women and would be a representation of *some* women, while claiming to represent them all. Parity would legitimate the historically constructed difference between men and women and divide the political élite into two socially distinct sexes, obscuring the differences within these categories:

> Demanding parity within the rules and codes which have excluded women and which have served not men, but *some* men, means risking endorsing the historically constructed social and political difference between the sexes; it means accepting the division of the polity into two socially distinct sexes and obscuring once again the differences amongst women themselves and the multiplicity of their positions; finally, it means implying that women can only enter politics as members of a homogeneous group. In short, it means reproducing the masculine liberal model, without introducing the slightest change to precisely the conditions which led democracy into a dead end. In this view, the potential for individuals to make a significant contribution to politics, the defining feature of citizenship, would remain blocked.
>
> (Hirata, Kergoat, Riot-Sarcey and Varikas 1994: 118)

Eleni Varikas (1995a: 160) argues that sexual difference is a historical construct, not a basis for citizenship. It is not 'women's citizenship' which needs to be examined, but simply 'citizenship', 'that is, the search for principles which base autonomy on the mutual recognition of the specificities which make up the universal'. And according to Françoise Collin (1995: 73), democracy should reintegrate humanity not as an abstract concept, but in all the plurality of its existences, with a migrant and multilingual citizenship.

Proposals for a democracy which would recognise multiple differences are at the centre of many Anglo-American debates on citizenship (for example, Lister 1997a, Mouffe 1992, Vogel 1991, Walby 1997: 166–79, Yuval-Davis 1997: 68–92). Feminism and anti-racism have challenged the notion of citizenship and forced an examination of the potential tension between its traditional emphasis on universality and integration and a more pluralist approach, based on a recognition of diversity and difference (Lister 1990: 453). A major problem for French theorists arguing for the recognition of multiple group identities and their collective demands is the strength of the republican resistance to communitarianism. Yves Déloye (1997: 44), for example, asserts that debates around multiculturalism and parity are fuelling a growth in identity discourses in a country which previously resisted group identities by depoliticising differences. He expresses fears that this could endanger universalism and the protection of the individual against membership of a community.

Michel Wieviorka (1997: 5–6), in the introduction to an edited volume on multiculturalism states that this debate is practically impossible in France, where it is seen to endanger political life and institutions. Particularisms are confined to the private sphere and all identity-based or communitarian demands are rejected and criticised. He identifies an unconditional defence of the 'republican model of integration', an expression used since the mid-1980s to refer to two distinct logics. The first attempts to eliminate cultural differences, while the second is more tolerant of them. However, they are expected to respect the rules of the republic, which is seen as the best defence against intercommunity tensions, violence, political and cultural fragmentation and the destruction of democracy. As Danilo Martuccelli (1997: 69) writes in the same volume, 'the appeal to the republican tradition always serves as a support for the demonisation and the repression of any identity-based demands'. Wieviorka (1997: 6) claims that this is often accompanied by stereotypical representations of immigrant populations and scorn for American debates around multiculturalism and political correctness. The contributors to Wieviorka's edited volume argue that the recognition of cultural diversity does not necessarily weaken democracy, and what is needed is a way of articulating, on the one hand, universal references to the law and to reason and, on the other hand, respect for cultural particularisms, even when they are expressed in the public sphere.

The work of Wieviorka and his colleagues, together with the feminist theories referred to above as the fourth approach, provide evidence that there is now a definable current of academics in France who, despite the resistance, are attempting to achieve a satisfying synthesis of universalism and multiculturalism.

Conclusion

Parity on its own would not necessarily address some of the main problems with contemporary democracy, such as the growing disillusionment with the system of representation. It has been demonstrated that women's exclusion from citizenship was not an oversight which was gradually corrected, leaving only the number of women representatives to rectify through parity. Instead, numerous theorists have argued that the construction of democracy was dependent on the exclusion of women and that the addition of a female élite will not change a fundamentally gendered system.

At the level of strategy, adding women to an already existing structure is the more realistic option, and much of the parity campaign has been focused on the single outcome of numerical equality in representative institutions. However, a growing critique of the insufficiency of this aim is leading, on the one hand, to scepticism about the appropriateness of parity as a goal and, on the other hand, to the extension of the concept of parity to more far-reaching changes in politics and civil society.

Some theorists are calling for more locally-based active citizen participation as a means of bringing about a more democratic democracy, 'a truly different conception of what it is to be a citizen and to act as a member of a democratic political community' (Mouffe 1992: 377). These include contributors to *Cahiers du féminisme*, the philosopher Françoise Collin, and activists and intellectuals within various parts of the left and the *Verts*. According to this view, citizenship is more than a collection of rights. It involves civic activism and political participation by citizens who are equal (Mouffe 1992: 377). It refers not only to institutional aspects, but to individual freedom and autonomy in decision-making. Focusing on civil society would enable these social aspects of citizenship to develop (Touraine 1994) and would allow democracy to work from below, rather than imposing it from above through parity in elected institutions (Collin 1996b: 103). Denis Berger (1996: 11), for example, writes,

> at all levels, from the workplace to the school, in the relations between men and women, everyone must be given the means to take control of their own affairs and to keep a check on their delegates in the various institutions.

For many French feminists, in common with their Anglo-American counterparts, it is not just civil society which needs to change, but specifically domestic life (Fraisse 1997: 16, Pateman 1989: 218). Women's citizenship is affected not only by their participation in public politics and their position in the labour market, but by gender relations within the family. It is argued that women would not have an equal share of power even after the introduction of parity, unless these gender relations were transformed (Louis 1996: 161). Ruth Lister (1990: 464) has summarised these arguments particularly well:

> Women's position as the economic dependent of a male partner; as double-shift worker juggling the responsibilities of paid employment and caring work; or as a welfare benefit recipient struggling to raise children in poverty or to manage on an inadequate pension, is incompatible with the full exercise of the social and political rights of citizenship. If women are to be fully integrated into full democratic citizenship, radical changes in personal and domestic life are required. The same applies to the organisation of paid employment and state provisions, so as to reflect the value to society as a whole of caring work, whether it is done in the private or the public sphere.

The redefinition of citizenship must therefore encompass the political, private and domestic spheres.

Parity does not address the problems of other inequalities, and the claims for representation of other excluded groups, in particular foreign residents and the working class. Josette Trat (1996: 16) argues that prioritising one aspect of an individual's identity (their sex/gender) over other aspects which are equally important to them and which intersect in different ways, raises a number of problems. She argues that political institutions should not be the exclusive, or indeed, primary focus of feminist action.

In response to this criticism, parity campaigners have argued that the aim of their campaign is not to correct all the inequalities in contemporary French society, but simply to bring about equality between men and women in elected institutions. They argue that the campaign for parity does not have to be opposed to other attempts to improve the representation of foreign residents, sexual minorities, etc. Supporting parity does not exclude the possibility of fighting for other transformations in the functioning of representative democracy (Gaspard 1996: 23). Eliane Viennot (1996b: 184) writes:

> I think that the limits of parity need to be taken on board. We need to state clearly that it does not aim to bring about equality between human beings, but between men and women. This is enough to legitimise parity, but it is not enough to satisfy all those, including us, who hope to change the world. The struggle for parity will not replace struggles for justice, and we should certainly not reject one in the name of the other.

The question of why women should have a claim for representation but not other oppressed groups who have been excluded from traditional party politics is a difficult one, and one which highlights the problematic relation between feminism and the left in France. While there does not seem to be a coherent case for parity which does not lead one to ask why other oppressed groups should continue to be marginalised from politics, feminists cannot fall for the worn promise that everything will be fine after the revolution. The odd exasperated comment by an advocate of parity responding once again to this question stresses that the parity campaign cannot do everything, and should not be criticised for failing to achieve what it never set out to achieve. And this seems more honest than the somewhat tangled argument that women do not constitute a category, therefore parity would not set a precedent for any other claims for representation.

One of the strengths of the discourse on parity, but at the same time one of its weaknesses, is the diversity of meanings which can be attributed to it. While this has meant that politicians of almost all parties have been able to jump on the bandwagon without necessarily endorsing the same aims as the campaigners, it has also meant that parity could be used to promote far more radical change throughout politics and civil society. While some leading campaigners remain firmly attached to the original aim of the campaign, others have found a framework for thinking about all kinds of equality and power sharing. It is true that parity is not a novel idea. It does not radically change feminist thought, parts of which have always striven to achieve equality – with or without the recognition of difference – in politics, society and the family. But for some theorists, parity does act as a coherent framework within which these projects can be pursued.

However, the danger of focusing on parity in order to resolve problems of citizenship is that it risks conflating citizenship and political rights, deflecting attention from social citizenship which has long been the focus of many feminist demands. As Jenson and Sineau (1995: 18) state, social rights are less clearly linked to the individual than political and civil rights. They were constructed within the concept of fraternity, and took men as their reference. Social policies were aimed at male workers and 'their' families, which were perceived as the basic social unit. Policies which were directed at women were seen not as universal rights, but protective measures or privileges for a specific group of citizens. 'Privileges' which women have gained, such as maternity leave and family allowances, have been presented as pro-natalist or protective measures, rather than rights. Women's social rights have more to do with their familial than their individual status, or they derive from their membership of a category, such as workers, where rights are modelled on the demands of the male worker (Jenson and Sineau 1995: 21). It is for this reason that social citizenship has been the focus of much feminist struggle for equality through calls for the separation of women from the family and for rights to be linked to the individual (Jenson and Sineau 1995: 14).

By focusing on the insertion of a female élite into political institutions, parity risks missing the question of what difference this would make to *all* women and their access to the resources necessary to exercise their rights, for example, money and time. While it is important to expose the exclusion of women from citizenship, and the parity debate has helped to do this, focusing exclusively on representation will not bring access to citizenship to the majority of French women. As a principle applied more widely, however, parity has much to offer. Fraisse (1997: 16) writes, 'Parity is attractive if it also means economic parity and domestic parity. Parity is the sharing of power, and power can be shared everywhere: in the domestic, civil, economic and political arenas.'

Finally, while it may have helped to revitalise a flagging feminist movement, it is important that it does not end up replacing it.

Conclusion

The first part of this book demonstrates that women are active in all areas of mainstream politics: as voters; as members and activists of political parties and trade unions; as candidates for election; and as elected representatives and appointed officials. However, it also demonstrates that they are grossly under-represented in sites of decision-making, whether this is within the parties and the unions; or within parliament, government and the state bureaucracy. In this, France is not exceptional, as was noted by Duverger as early as 1955 (1995a: 125–6) and can be seen in comparative studies such as Norris (1993). The analysis, in Chapter 5, of the explanations which have been offered for this under-representation in sites of decision-making shows that a number of factors combine to produce this exclusion. These include the legacy of historical events and the emergence of a masculine political culture; women's restricted access to the resources necessary to political activity; and the role of the political parties.

It is clear that, if these are the factors which contribute most to women's absence from political decision-making, the problem will not be solved without conscious intervention. Simply waiting for women to catch up with men after their late acquisition of political rights is unlikely to bring about an increase in their presence: almost fifty years after French women won the right to stand for election, their presence in the National Assembly was unchanged (Sineau 1994b: 281).[1] Notions of a 'natural evolution' or of 'political apprenticeship' therefore seem misplaced.

Women's access to political office has not reflected the dramatic social change which has taken place since the 1960s. Women's mass entry into the labour force and higher education, their acquisition of civil rights equal to those of men and their increased control over their own fertility have not removed the obstacles which prevent their entry into public politics. It is therefore justifiable to argue that, if women's presence is to be increased, active measures need to be taken.

In a report for the European Commission, Monique Leijenaar (1996: 30) presents a list of strategies which could be employed by governments and parties in order to increase the number of women in institutional politics. When compared with the limited focus of the French parity campaign, the range of suggested actions is striking in its variety. Government strategies which focus on 'individual obstacles' (those relating to the women seeking office or who could seek office) include public information campaigns, the training of women, and the provision of childcare for elected women. Equivalent party strategies include training and campaigns to attract women members. Government strategies which focus on institutional obstacles include data bases of potential women candidates, funding for women's groups within the parties, quotas for public appointments, and legislation on quotas. Party strategies focusing on institutional obstacles include changing selection procedures and criteria, data bases of women party members, quotas for internal structures within the party and for elections, alternation of men and women candidates on party lists or all-women lists. These measures, argue Leijenaar, need to be combined with those which raise public awareness and with campaigns which exert constant pressure on politicians and parties and encourage voters to vote for women. The European Network of experts 'Women in Decision-Making' has recommended that one of the main priorities of all the member states should be the elaboration of a 'national political plan' which aims to create a balance between women and men in decision-making within five years. This would contain a list of coherent and concrete measures which the government would put into action, including access to education and the labour market, raising awareness of women's competence, creating a pool for recruitment and making the parties introduce quotas as a temporary measure. Leijenaar states (1996: 56) that in order for such a plan to succeed, it would require a favourable political climate and budgetary and administrative support. As well as the parties, women's organisations have an important role in creating a positive attitude towards power-sharing between women and men. Leijenaar (1996: 56) states that most EU countries have the political will to increase the participation of women in decision-making, and this is indeed the case for France. Although constant pressure is necessary in order to ensure that concrete change is brought about, it seems likely that measures will be introduced which will increase the presence of women in French political institutions, although not necessarily achieving parity.

One of the reasons why parity is expected to produce some positive results is its popularity. This popularity could be explained, first, by the fact that it is fairly harmless. It simply means that the political élite will eventually be made up of equal numbers of men and women. This is not a particularly threatening prospect to the general public, with whom it has been much more popular than it has with male politicians, who are directly and personally threatened. Second, at a time when the political élite is increasingly found to be out of touch with the electorate, there is a widely held belief that women are closer to the daily life of the people and more concerned with everyday matters. Parity, then, is part of a call for a more responsive political élite.

Finally, as was argued in Chapter 8, opposition to parity may be weak because national representative bodies are no longer particularly powerful institutions. As decisions in a growing number of policy domains are now determined by supranational institutions at European and other levels, national policy-making processes have a correspondingly narrower room for manoeuvre. It is pertinent to ask, therefore, what role women play in the G7 summits, and in decision-making positions in the World Bank and the International Monetary Fund.

In France, parity is of undeniable symbolic importance and may well produce concrete change. If the idea of parity can be extended and applied to other sectors, including national representation in supranational institutions, sites of economic decision-making and the domestic sphere, it could stimulate far-reaching change which would have an impact on the lives of many women.

However, the relation between women and politics cannot be contained in the concept of parity, however broadly it is defined. The presence of biological women will not necessarily ensure that women's interests are better represented, nor that women's rights are advanced. What is needed is not simply the presence of women, but the presence in sites of decision-making of women who are committed to advancing women's rights and representing women's interests *combined with* pressure from outside parliamentary politics. If the pressure from outside is limited to a campaign whose objective is to achieve numerical equality between men and women in elected, and, more recently, non-elected, institutions, it is not clear that programmatic change will come about. This is why it is important that the campaign for parity does not obscure other feminist activities outside mainstream politics.

Legal rights do not on their own ensure that women have the opportunity to exercise them. The right to stand for election does not alter the fact that women are not selected as candidates by the main parties for winnable seats. The right to abortion does not alter the fact that access is restricted by factors such as the closure of units due to cuts in the health service, the shortage of doctors willing to perform abortions and the actions of anti-abortion activists. And political rights are worthless if domestic oppression – through violence or economic dependency – makes it impossible to exercise them. The current interest in parity has distorted the picture of women and politics, focusing on élites and on participation in mainstream politics, and ignoring women's struggles over reproductive rights, housing, and employment rights, to name but a few of their recent concerns. The inability of individual citizens to take control of their own lives will not be solved by the addition of women to a political élite which is seen as distant and isolated. New social rights and grass roots activism are necessary in order to achieve full citizenship for all.

It is possible, through a study of participation, to prove that women are politically active and that their activity has been ignored, minimised or distorted by other studies and in particular by the narrow definition of the term 'political participation'. Once political activity is defined more broadly to include participation in associations, coordinations, demonstrations, attempts to raise awareness, to place new issues on the public agenda and redefine old ones, and to influence policy outcomes, it is found that women are involved in these activities, not just as participants, but increasingly as decision-makers. This suggests that they are excluded from traditional organisations, in particular, parties and trade unions, or that they choose alternative forms, or a mixture of both. However, it is still possible to ask whether women are simply busying themselves on the margins, occupying spaces that men are not interested in because they are devoid of influence. Is it in the margins or in formal mainstream politics that women can make a difference? The answer is both at the same time. It is absolutely necessary for women to participate in mainstream as well as alternative politics, since politics affects everyone, but also affects women differently because of their position in the labour market and their primary responsibility for the care of children and elderly and disabled relatives, for example. Pressure for change needs to come both from within and outside the traditional political arena.

Feminists have not always sought to increase the presence of women in political institutions, but they seem to be increasingly willing to engage with the state, in order to advance their aims. This is an international trend. In the introduction to a study of women and politics in 43 countries, together covering three-quarters of the world's population, and systematically chosen to represent a variety of political systems, levels of economic development and regions, Najma Chowdhury and Barbara Nelson (1994: 14) report that:

> the political and legal rules of the game, defined by access to political institutions and as critiques of systems or processes, are featured in nearly half the country chapters . . . In a notable change from a decade ago, chapter authors report an increased pragmatism on the part of feminists in democratic regimes who, while retaining concerns over the potentially co-opting character of working within parties and governments, are much less willing to turn their backs on the state as an arena of activism.

An effective feminist politics needs to engage on all fronts, both within and outside the institutions, from the grass roots as well as from above.

Whereas the exclusion of women from politics is not specific to France, the centrality of the construct of republican universalism and the resistance to the representation of social categories is. In the French version of universalism, all are equal before the law, and differences belong in the private sphere. However, this does not leave space for a debate on differences and resulting discriminations and inequalities. Equality of opportunity rarely leads to equality of outcome. This applies to the number of women elected to representative bodies, as it does to the presence in all areas of public life of all excluded or under-represented groups. Parity may have opened up a space in which these issues can be debated, but it is clear that resistance is strong, and that pressure for a reformulation of citizenship needs to continue.

Notes

Introduction

1 Of the 900 parliamentarians gathered at Versailles, forty-two voted against and 741 voted in favour of the constitutional reform. Forty-eight abstained. (http://www.liberation.com/quotidien/semaine/990629marm.html, accessed 5 July 1999).

2 Other countries with more than 40 per cent women candidates were Austria 49.7 per cent, Sweden 43.7 per cent, Spain 41.5 per cent. The lowest proportion of women candidates was found in Italy 18.6 per cent, Luxembourg 25.4 per cent and the United Kingdom 26.8 per cent. The EU average was 36 per cent. (http://nt.oneworld.nl/ewlobby/en/action/campagnes/electedwomen 130699.html, accessed 16 September 1999).

3 'Mainstreaming' is defined by Rees (1998: 191) as 'a paradigm shift in thinking towards the development of policy and practice. It requires being able to see the ways in which current practice is gendered in its construction, despite appearing to be gender-neutral.' This definition is discussed by Rees in her work *Mainstreaming Equality in the European Union* (1998: 191–4).

4 A survey of the standard student texts on French politics reveals little about women.

5 Publications which resulted from this approach include Riot-Sarcey (1995) and Viennot (1996d).

6 The press cuttings service at the FNSP is excellent and has constituted an indispensable source of material. However, the page numbers of the cuttings are rarely recorded, and can therefore not be included in the references in this book.

7 This has been begun by Catherine Quiminal, in the area of ethnic minority women's activities in associations. The existence of postgraduate research projects in related areas suggests that the information available is on the increase.

8 In this instance, the term 'ethnic minority' is taken to mean people of non-European birth or descent, whether French nationals or not. It includes: Maghrebians, sub-Saharan Africans, Turks, non-Europeans from the DOM-TOM.

9 All those who are not born in France even though they may have subsequently obtained French nationality.

10 Those who do not hold French nationality.

11 Children born in France of immigrant or foreign parents.

12 These relations are at the heart of feminist theories of the State. See Watson (1990) and Waylen and Randall (1998).

1   Women and the state

1 See for example, Pateman, C. (1970), Bourque, S. and Grossholtz, J. (1974).
2 In the early years of the ministry's existence almost all associations applying for state financial aid were successful in having direct contact with ministry officials and in obtaining grants.
3 On the level of political commitment, the Amsterdam Treaty recognises equality between men and women as a fundamental objective of the EU and in 1996, the EU Council of Ministers recommended actions in favour of achieving a balanced participation between men and women in decision-making sites. Furthermore, EU institutions have set up structures specially responsible for equality issues, e.g. the European Parliament's Women's Rights Committee, the Group of Commissioners on Equal Opportunities, the Equal Opportunities Unit and so on.
4 At an international level, the organisation of events such as the 1995 Beijing conference on women, has highlighted the question of women and decision-making.
5 For a comparative analysis of such (selected) feminist theory see Nash (1998: 45–57). Nash discusses the work of Anne Phillips, Iris Marion Young and Chantal Mouffe.
6 Waylen and Randall's *Gender, Politics and the State* (1998), represents one of the few attempts to provide an overview of the relationship between women, politics and the state at both theoretical and empirical levels.
7 The works cited in this chapter form a small part of the available literature.
8 These are higher education establishments which recruit students by a specialist competitive exam and which enjoy a high reputation in terms of education and social prestige. Two of these, the *Ecole polytechnique* and the *Ecole des mines*, were closed to women until 1964. Others, where women have been accepted since 1945, have remained male bastions to the present. For example, women have rarely formed more than 10 per cent of the total enrolment figures of the most prestigious engineering schools (Terrail 1995: 588). Two of the most 'mixed' schools are the *Ecole nationale d'administration* (ENA) and the *Ecole normale supérieure* (ENS)) where today women account for approximately 40 and 50 per cent of the yearly admission figures respectively (http://www.fonction-publique.gouv.fr/lac...andsdossiers/rapportcolmou/sommaire.html; http://www.ens.fr/concours/rapports/rapports.html).
9 The strengthening of the state technocracy coupled with the elected status and powers of the President was accompanied by a serious weakening of legislative powers.
10 Women's vote for the left's presidential candidate had increased from 39 per cent in 1965 to 49 per cent in 1981 (Chagnollaud 1993: 452).
11 The legislative elections of 1986 were fought, exceptionally, under a proportional representation system and consequently led to the selection of more female candidates across the political parties. The number of women elected to the National Assembly rose to 5.9 per cent in 1986.
12 No distinction is made here between *secrétaire d'état* (junior minister with specific responsibilities who does not attend cabinet meetings unless invited but reports to a minister), *ministre délégué* (minister who attends cabinet meetings when items relating to his/her ministerial brief are on the agenda) and *ministre (à portefeuille)*, sometimes known as *ministre d'état* to signify enhanced position of the holder of the title or of his/her office (equivalent of UK secretary of state and member of cabinet). For the purposes of this chapter, *secrétaire d'état* is translated as junior minister, *ministre délégué* as minister and *ministre* as senior minister.
13 Dienesch participated in Gaullist government from 1968 to 1978.

14 Ploux was appointed to the post of Junior Minister for Education.

15 An exception to this might be Marie-France Garaud. In her essay, *Les femmes politiques*, Laure Adler (1993: 157–63) highlights the role played by Garaud as Pompidou's private advisor. However, even in this instance one is given the impression that Garaud's role was very much dependent on that of Pompidou's other close advisor, Pierre Juillet, who had appointed her in the first place.

16 This quote is attributed to Pompidou. See Adler (1993: 156, 157).

17 Yvette Roudy achieved secretary of state status in May 1985.

18 Nicole Questiaux's ministry for National Solidarity had been done away with in the government reshuffle of March 1983.

19 The other three were Lucette Michaux-Chévry (Junior minister for Francophony), Michèle Alliot-Marie (Junior Minister for Education) and Nicole Catala (Junior Minister for Professional Training of Teachers).

20 The three senior ministers were Martine Aubry (Employment and Professional Training), Edwige Avice (Cooperation and Development), Frédérique Brédin (Youth and Sport) while the posts of minister were held by Catherine Tasca (Francophony) and Elisabeth Guigou (European Affairs).

21 Edwige Avice was not included in the Bérégovoy team. Instead Marie-Noëlle Lienemann was brought in as Minister for Housing.

22 For example, in 1995, twelve women were invited to join Alain Juppé's government only for eight of them to be unceremoniously dismissed after six months. Françoise Giroud (ex-minister and writer), commenting at the time, remarked, 'Having served the glory of the prince, they were becoming burdensome . . .' (Guigou 1997: 139). Juppé himself did not pretend to look for reasons explaining his action: 'I could dismiss them because I appointed them,' he stated (ibid.).

23 Prior to 1946 women could only enter the civil service if their presence was justifiable in terms of serving the state's interests and, in the case of married women, if their husbands allowed it. It was believed that women were unsuited to long service required by the state because of their role as mothers. Furthermore, they were accused of being unable to apply method, constancy and a sense of service because of their 'tendency to privilege their personal life over public affairs' (http://www.fonction-publique.gouv.fr/lac...andsdossiers/rapportcolmou/letatdeslieux.html, accessed 30 June 1999).

24 The state civil service (*fonction publique d'état*) is one of three branches of the civil service (*fonction publique*). The other two branches are: the provincial civil service (*fonction publique territoriale*) and the health sector civil service (*fonction publique hospitalière*).

25 An administrative area for the organisation of state education services.

26 The Inspectorate of finance (*l'Inspection générale des finances*) can audit or investigate any area of public finance including state-owned companies.

27 The *Conseil d'état* advises the government on bills and ordinances and acts as a court of appeal in state administrative cases.

28 The *Cour des comptes* audits national public expenditure.

29 The voting method varies according to the size of the council. In municipalities of under 3,500 inhabitants, a majoritarian, preferential two-round system is used. In municipalities of over 3,500 inhabitants, a mixed proportional two-round system is operated whereby a party list which obtains more than 50 per cent of the vote is allocated 50 per cent of available seats while remaining seats are divided amongst other parties in proportion to votes obtained. The inhabitants of Paris, Lyon and Marseille elect not only one council for their respective cities but also one council per city district (*arrondissement*).

30 For example, refuse collection and street maintenance, pre-school and primary education, leisure facilities.

31 For instance maintenance of roads, housing, schools and other infrastructure according to a pre-set economic plan.

32 This section does not include a survey of women in departmental councils as this layer of local government is peculiar to France. Most data on women contained in comparative studies of local government in the EU for instance focus on municipal and regional authorities.

33 William Guéraïche (1992: 22) cites the case of statistics relating to the municipal elections of 1947 and 1953 which indicated that 250 and 300 women respectively were elected. He doubts the validity of such exact round figures and suggests that they could have been made up.

34 This league table (CEMR 1998) is constructed on the basis of data which is incomplete but on average, within the EU, one out of five elected municipal representatives is a woman (Giscard D'Estaing 1998).

35 The PS and PCF committed themselves to a quota of 50 per cent whereas the RPR and UDF gave way to one of 30 per cent.

36 All figures quoted have been compiled from Vidal (1998), *Le Mini-Guide: La France des régions*, 9–120.

37 Each regional council establishes commissions to deal with specific aspects of regional planning, development and management. For example, transport, education and training and so on. The number of commissions in operation varies according to the needs and resources of the region.

2   Women and the political parties

1 Readers seeking such an analysis should turn to one of the many texts on this subject, for example Chagnollaud (1993), Borella (1990), and Bréchon (1998). Texts in English include Cole (1990), Hall, Hayward and Machin (1994: Chapter 2), and Morris (1994: 107–52).

2 An exception is the excellent study by Subileau, Ysmal and Rey (1999) on the sociology of the PS.

3 Michèle Alliot-Marie's election as president of the RPR in December 1999 is exceptional.

4 Its membership declined from 700,000 in the 1970s to 200,000 in 1990. However, the decline in its share of the electorate was even more dramatic: 15.4 per cent in the presidential elections of 1981, 6.9 per cent in those of 1988; 16 per cent in the 1981 legislative elections, 9.7 per cent in 1986, 11.2 per cent in 1988 and 9.2 per cent in 1993. It won 6.8 per cent of the vote in the 1999 European elections.

5 Founded in 1972, it made its electoral breakthrough at the 1984 European elections, when it won 11.1 per cent of the votes cast and maintained this proportion of the vote fairly consistently until the split between Le Pen and Mégret in 1998. In the 1999 European elections, Le Pen's list won 5.7 per cent and Mégret's 3.28 per cent of the vote.

6 The *Verts* was created in 1984 and made its electoral breakthrough at the 1989 European elections when it won 10.8 per cent of the vote. At the 1992 regional elections, this fell to 6.9 per cent, due to the appearance of GE. In March 1993, the candidates who stood under the label '*Entente écologiste*' (*Verts* and GE) won 7.9 per cent of the vote. In the 1999 European elections, the *Verts* list, headed by Daniel Cohn-Bendit, won 9.7 per cent of the vote.

7 Candidates which cannot easily be categorised as belonging to a particular organisation.

8 *Lutte ouvrière* is the biggest Trotskyist organisation, which first presented candidates for election in the early 1970s. In 1974, Arlette Laguiller stood for the presidency, receiving 2.33 per cent of the vote and she has been standing at all national elections since then.

9 The LCR is another of the numerous Trotskyist movements in France. It presented a joint list with *Lutte ouvrière* at the 1979 and 1999 European elections, headed by Arlette Laguiller and Alain Krivine. Feminists have been active in the movement since the 1970s, and it claims that 30 per cent of its members are women (LCR 12 October 1999).

10 The PSU, which was founded in 1960, was also influenced by feminists within the party. In 1974, it was weakened by the departure of many of its leaders, including Michel Rocard, who joined the new PS, and in 1989 it became *Alternative rouge et verte*, which described itself as socialist, feminist, *autogestionnaire* (self-managed), ecologist and internationalist (Borella 1990: 226).

11 Barzach had criticised the party leadership and its failure to oppose clearly the *Front national*.

12 Arlette Laguiller, Armonie Bordes, Roseline Vachette and Chantal Cauquil. Alain Krivine (LCR) was also elected.

13 Its leader is Christine Marne (RPR), president of *Femmes pour la France*. The organisations involved include *Femmes Avenir*, whose president is Noëlle Dewavrin (RPR) regional councillor for Pas-de-Calais, and *Femmes du PPDF*, the Giscardian part of the UDF (*Le Figaro*, 27 December 1996: 6).

14 Readers seeking such an analysis could turn to Stetson (1987), Jenson and Sineau (1995), Lesselier and Venner (1997).

15 For example, Marchais at a meeting of Communist women in Paris, 8 March 1974, reported in *L'Humanité* (9 March 1974)

16 A payment to women who stay at home to look after their children.

3 Women and the trade unions

1 In 1896 French women made up 35.2 per cent of the working population. By 1994 this figure had risen to 44.7 per cent (INSEE 1995: 115).

2 The CFDT was founded in 1964 when a majority grouping within the *Confédération Française des Travailleurs Chrétiens* broke away in disagreement over the continued identification of the trade union with Christianity. The much diminished CFTC continued as a legally recognised trade union organisation.

3 This idea was expressed as far back as the late 1880s, by Guesdistes, within the FNS (*Fédération Nationale des Syndicats*).

4 This chapter focuses on the post-1958 period although some historical background relating to the Fourth Republic period is included here. For more detailed examinations of the place and role of women in trade unions prior to this period, see the following works: Colin (1975), Guilbert (1966), Zylberberg-Hocquard (1978).

5 As figures are not available one has to rely on personal impressions of those closely involved with the trade union movement. Madeleine Colin was responsible for women's issues within the CGT, after the war.

6 Danguy, a keen supporter of the CFTC's women's unions (*syndicats féminins*) set up before the First World War but phased out after 1945, was chosen by the union's general secretary to form part of his deputising team. She resigned in 1948.

7 For an excellent account of how women were persuaded to embrace motherhood and family life see Duchen (1994), Chapters 3 and 4.

8 *Antoinette*, which in 1955 replaced the CGT's *Revue des femmes travailleuses*, was lightweight in terms of social and political content. Its editors had preferred to present a more traditional type of women's magazine.

9 A coordination may be defined as a temporary form of organisation which emerges during periods of social mobilisation to organise and represent people

belonging to a particular occupational group in collective action, at national level if possible (Leschi 1996: 167).

10 The presence of trade union women's commission representatives caused some acrimony as commissions were officially union structures, whereas the coordination of workplace women's groups saw itself as part of the autonomous women's movement. See *Rouge* (14 June 1977: 2).

11 See in particular Zylberberg-Hocquard (1978) and Maruani 1979).

12 From 1975, women were the major contributors to growth in the labour market: between 1975 and 1990, out of 3.3 million labour market entrants, three million were women and by the mid-1980s, any growth in the labour market was almost solely attributable to women (Letablier 1995: 108).

13 The CFC, which had been established within the CFTC in 1945, continued to exist in the new CFDT.

14 *Autogestion* was defined as an ideal of socialism extending to the whole of society which would lead to 'the end to exploitation, the disappearance of opposing classes, the abolition of wage-labour, the attainment of democracy' (Parti Socialiste 1972: 63).

15 See Maruani (1979), Tozzi (1982), Gibbon (1989).

16 There is a certain amount of confusion about the acceptance of quotas during this period. In 1978 Laot talked about a 15 per cent quota being imposed, at all levels of decision-making, by the union leadership (Evin 1978a: 50) but this is not backed up by any other mention of this issue.

17 All nine of the new posts went to women, taking the total number of women in the national bureau to ten.

18 CFDT-Information (1979); CFDT-Fédération des banques (1980).

19 The main idea of *recentrage*, launched by the General Secretary, Edmond Maire, in 1976, was that the union had engaged for too long (since 1968) in ideological discourse, centred round the concept of *autogestion* and had to 'return to reality'. What that reality was and how to achieve it were subject to enormous debate and conflicting interpretations.

20 It is not possible to show a statistical evolution of women's representation in decision-making positions as figures were collected by the union in an *ad hoc* fashion until very recently. Furthermore, such figures have never been presented in a single document but are to be found buried in various texts.

21 Women's membership is cited here as standing between 600,000 and 700,000 which, out of a total membership of about 2 million, represents 25–35 per cent.

22 Chardin states that 50 per cent of the CGT's new members in 1973 were women who were inspired to join following high-profile women workers' strikes at Nouvelles Galeries in Thionville, Lip and at textile works at Cerizay.

23 Demands were related to the following issues in the order listed: increase of the minimum wage and equal pay for equal work, conditions of work, reduction of the working week, lowering of retirement age, women's right to work, equal access to training, promotion and posts of responsibility, social rights for working mothers and the recognition of 'the social character of motherhood', the right to advice on sexuality, contraception and abortion and to free contraception and abortion on demand.

24 For extracts of delegates' interventions at the conference, see Rogerat (1978).

25 'Workerist' or '*ouvriériste*' describes the attitude of those who believe first, that only the working class is capable of leading a movement for socialist change and second, that the independent interests of the working class outweigh those of any other grouping or class at all times.

26 For instance, in 1979–80 the first known action, in France, was brought and won by CFDT activists against the head of personnel at the Tours-based Manufacture Tourangelle de Confection, for making sexual advances towards

a woman employee. The mobilisation of workers and branch officers by women trade unionists over this type of issue could not have taken place before the 1970s.

27 The term 'social partners' refers to the representative organisations of management and labour.

28 For an account of the campaigns waged by ETUC's Women's Committee to acquire better representation for women in trade unions and in the European Social Dialogue, see Cockburn (1997).

29 The conservative-leaning CGC mainly represents salaried workers whose jobs demand a high level of education and/or include a managerial role.

30 The left of centre FO, formed in 1948, as a result of a split within the CGT, constitutes the third largest French trade union today.

31 Only 30.5 per cent of working women form part of the aggregate occupational categories *cadres et professions intellectuelles supérieures* (senior management and intellectual professions) and *professions intermédiaires* (intermediary professions) compared with 60.5 per cent in the categories *employés* (commercial and service sector employees) and *ouvriers* (manual workers) (INSEE 1995: 121).

32 A national meeting on women's rights, the *Assises nationales* in Paris, brought together representatives of 166 organisations including trade unions on 15–16 March 1997. The challenge to delegates was to draw up an accurate record of women's rights achievements and failures and to use the meeting to launch further action and activism in favour of women's rights.

33 The strategy of 'combative unionism' stands in opposition to that of 'proposition force unionism' ('*syndicalisme de proposition*') which the CFDT has adhered to since the early 1980s and which the CGT paid lip-service to for a short period in the early to mid-1980s. Proposition force unionism represents the move away from defensive unionism which engages in protest and demonstrations against employment policies and plans which are seen to work against workers' interests. Instead, proposition force unionism engages with employers in making 'constructive' proposals which would allow companies to operate whilst remaining 'socially responsible'.

34 The period 23 June 1981 to July 1984 saw the participation of four Communist ministers (of Transport, Civil Service, Health, Professional Training) in the Socialist government of Pierre Mauroy.

35 Such a policy would ensure that: women are made aware of the duties that positions of responsibility entail; women activists who are willing to take on such positions are 'spotted'; a mentoring system is set up for women who accede to posts of responsibility; the parameters of such posts are clearly defined.

36 These calculations are based on information relating to the current membership of these structures. For the national executive commission see http://www.cfdt.fr/dexorga.htm, accessed 24 August 1999. For the national bureau see http://www.cfdt.fr/reseaubn.htm, accessed 24 August 1999.

37 In 1994 and 1997, questionnaires were sent out to 22 union regions and 21 union federations by the national commission for women. Responses were received from 16 regions and 15 federations.

38 This figure is calculated on the basis of information supplied that there are 200,000 (Duchesne 1997: 47) women members in the CGT out of a membership total of 640,000 (http://www.cgt.fr/01confed/conf1.htm).

5 Explaining women's absence from politics

1 The other two being Italy and Greece which granted women voting rights in 1945 and 1952 respectively.

2 For further reading see Haase-Dubosc, D. and Viennot, E. (1991).

3 Influential women at the Royal Court had engaged in a long-running literary argument (*la Querelle des femmes*) throughout the sixteenth century, against a growing urban intellectual bourgeoisie, over the role of women in culture and society. While the *Querelle des femmes* was subsequently interpreted as a purely literary argument, it was representative of the tension caused by the presence of women in the political sphere.

4 The battle of succession to Henri III had opened up as the latter, third of four children of Catherine de Medici, had no children and because the last son of Catherine de Medici had died.

5 The gendered nature of the concept of universalism is examined in more detail in Chapter 9.

6 Adler (1993) is a catalogue of descriptions by women in politics of the difficulties which they have encountered, as is the slightly older study by Sineau (1988).

7 This is the approach taken by most feminist analyses since the early 1990s, especially those of Mariette Sineau, Janine Mossuz-Lavau and Françoise Gaspard.

8 Created in 1945, ENA was 90 per cent male until the 1970s and in 1997 was still 75 per cent male (Sineau 1997a: 46).

9 If an unweighted index of four major measures (calling meetings at times when women with family responsibilities can attend; establishing a meetings timetable to enable women to plan their commitments; providing a crèche; establishing a women's section) that political parties can take is constructed, then it is possible to make a crude comparison of different levels of achievement where a score of 1.00 indicates that all measures have been adopted by all parties and a score of 0.00 shows that no measures have been adopted by any of the parties.

10 It should be noted that the gap between women's representation rates in Australia, Canada and the UK and those in Italy, Belgium, Greece and Cyprus may be exaggerated due to the fact that elections have taken place very recently in the first three countries and appear to confirm an upward trend in women's representation rates while figures relating to the last four countries are less recent and do not reflect results if elections were to take place today.

11 According to this system, voters choose one candidate in each constituency. If a candidate receives more than 50 per cent of the votes in the first round of the election, she or he is elected, otherwise an outcome is produced in the second round where candidates gaining less than 12.5 per cent of the votes are knocked out of the electoral competition and the person achieving the highest score is elected.

12 All figures quoted have been calculated from a close reading of the results of the 1986 elections as set out in *Le Monde Dossiers et Documents* (1986), 'Les élections legislatives du 16 mars 1986', 75–111.

13 It has been difficult to obtain figures relating to the gender profile of all substitutes but of the sixty-three women finally elected to the National Assembly, only three had women substitutes.

14 The remaining members of the Jospin government were drawn either from the ranks of senators or were ministers without an electoral mandate.

15 The few studies on the impact of women's representatives in local decision-making, suggest that while the strict administrative management of local authorities leaves little place for gendered differences in policy priorities, women nevertheless place greater emphasis on the relationship between those elected and the electors. See Rieu (1998: 94).

16 If one excludes the election of 1986, fought under PR and therefore generating a higher number of women candidates than previous elections, then the 1997 election produced the highest number of women candidates and deputies to date.

17 Regional elections, held every six years to elect members of regional councils are fought under PR. Municipal elections, also held every six years, are mainly fought under a mixed-member PR system except in municipalities of under 3,500 inhabitants where councillors are elected under a majoritarian system in which preferential voting is allowed. In municipalities of over 3,500 inhabitants, councillors are elected under a PR system without a preferential vote.

18 The exceptions are Eire (14.3 per cent), Portugal (11.1 per cent), Luxembourg (10.3 per cent) and Greece (3.6 per cent).

19 The higher proportion of women MEPs in all EU countries (average 36 per cent) can also be explained by the fact that not only is PR used in the majority of member states but also because the decision-making powers of EU institutions are not seen to be as important as those at the national level.

6 Womens political activity in the ecology movement and coordinations

1 Many of the post-1968 social movements to which the label 'new' was eventually applied, in fact marked a resurgence of previous ones. This could be said of the women's liberation and ecology movements which sought, respectively, to revive earlier initiatives to safeguard and extend women's rights and to protect the environment. The students' movement of 1968 can, however, be called 'new' as it emerged in response to a specific political conjuncture: the Vietnam War and an inflexible, authoritarian political regime in the case of France.

2 For useful and accessible discussions of (new) social movements, see Lyman (1995), Neveu (1996), Scott (1990), Tarrow (1998).

3 For a brief history of the coordination as a particular form of social movement see Leschi (1996: 163–7).

4 The Chirac government's preferred solution to the problem of under-recruitment in nursing was to open up the profession to more generally qualified categories such as 'high level sports specialists' rather than to address questions of low salaries and poor working conditions.

5 The three largest demonstrations took place on 29 September, 6 and 13 October 1988. On these three occasions 20,000, 50,000 and 100,000 people respectively filled the streets of Paris (Granger 1988: 16).

6 See Granger (1988: 15) for a summary of nurses' demands.

7 Danièle Kergoat (1993: 126) makes and emphasises this distinction between the nurses' coordination and nurses' social movement, not only because of the different time periods covered by each but because, she argues, the analytical and conceptual tools used to study them are not the same.

8 It should be noted that the legislative elections of 1988 resulted in a change of government in May of that year. The government of the right which had cohabited with a left presidency since 1986 was replaced by a Socialist administration. The latter, though more sympathetic to the nurses than the former, was as reluctant to deal with them directly.

7 Feminist politics

1 This led to the split of the *Questions Féministes* collective in 1980.

2 For a history of *Psych et po*'s appropriation of the movement's name, see *Chroniques d'une imposture: Du mouvement de libération des femmes à une marque commerciale*, Paris: Tierce, 1981.

3 The *Parti féministe unifié*, the *Ligue du droit des femmes*, *SOS femmes-alternatives*, *Féministes radicales* and the *Groupe Liaison du 13e*.

4 The difference in French is between *la* politique – electoral/party politics, and *le* politique – equivalent in English to 'politics with a small "p"', meaning all power struggles.
5 This argument is explored further in Chapters 8 and 9.
6 See, for example *Clara Magazine*, no. 33, March 1995 dossier and issues of *Cahiers du féminisme*.
7 See the special issue on Aids of *Cahiers du féminisme*, no. 65, été 1993.

8   Increasing women's political representation

1 In 1994, Italy imposed quotas for all lists in municipal and regional elections and parity for all lists for the part of the National Assembly elected by proportional representation. However, the Italian Constitutional Court overturned these texts (Gaspard 1998a: 27). Belgium passed a law in 1994 which will come into full force at the end of the century, according to which no more than two-thirds of candidates can be of the same sex. However, it does not specify where on the list women should appear, and in the first elections held after the law was passed, only 19 per cent of successful candidates were women (*Libération*, 16 February 1999: 3).
2 Confirmation that this was probably necessary was provided in January 1999, when the Constitutional Council overturned the law introducing parity in regional elections which had been passed in June 1998. The law had stated that, 'each list ensures parity between male and female candidates'.
3 The three-fifths majority necessary to pass the text required the vote of 470 members.
4 Sineau reports that in the first Juppé government, women represented (in descending order of responsibility) 15 per cent of '*ministres à part entière*', 0 per cent of '*ministres délégués*' and 57 per cent of '*secrétaires d'Etat*'. In the second Juppé government, women were 6.2 per cent of '*ministres à part entière*', 9 per cent of '*ministres délégués*' and 40 per cent of '*secrétaires d'Etat*'.

9   Parity, democracy and citizenship

1 For example, 62 per cent of respondents in a SOFRES poll in 1996 thought that politicians do not listen to the people (Courtois 1996). Further, although 69 per cent situated themselves on a left–right scale, 62 per cent thought that this division no longer applied to positions held by politicians. 54 per cent of the population thought that democracy was working badly and 67 per cent did not feel represented by any party (Rozès 1997: 507).
2 In 1996, 60 per cent of those polled by SOFRES thought that politicians are 'fairly corrupt' and only one-third thought that they were 'fairly honest' (Courtois 1996).

Conclusion

1 5.7 per cent in 1945, 5.7 per cent in 1993.

Bibliography

Abadan-Unat, Nermin (1987) 'Summary of main results', in *The Future of Migration*, Paris: OECD.

Abélès, Marc (1997) 'Ecology, political action and discourse', in Perry and Cross (eds) (1997): 217–33.

Adler, Laure (1993) *Les femmes politiques*, Paris: Seuil.

Agacinski, Sylviane (1998) 'L'universel masculin ou la femme effacée', *Le Débat*, 100, mai-août: 149–57.

Agacinski, Sylviane (1999) 'Contre l'effacement des sexes', *Le Monde*, 6 février: 1, 14.

Allison, Maggie (1994) 'The right to choose: abortion in France', *Parliamentary Affairs*, 47, 2, April: 222–37.

Allwood, Gill (1995) 'The campaign for parity in political institutions', in Knight, Diana and Still, Judith (eds) *Women and Representation*, Nottingham: WIF Publications: 7–20.

Allwood, Gill (1998) *French Feminisms: Gender and Violence in Contemporary France*, London: UCL.

ANEF (Association nationale des études féministes) (1998) *Les féministes face à l'antisémitisme et au racisme*, printemps-été, Toulouse.

Angeli, Verveine (1995) 'Mise en condition', *Cahiers du féminisme*, 71/72: 26–8.

Appleton, Andrew and Mazur, Amy (1993) 'Transformation or modernisation: the rhetoric of gender and party politics in France', in Lovenduski and Norris (eds) (1993): 86–112.

Association Parité website (statistics) http://members.aol.com/pariteasso/STAT. HTM, accessed 11 February 1998.

Aubry, Chantal (1998) 'La parite ne suffira pas à garantir l'égalité aux femmes', *La Croix*, 15 déembre.

Aulagnon, Michelle (1997) 'Le gouvernement crée un poste de déléguée interministerielle aux droits des femmes', *Le Monde*, 16–17 novembre.

Aulagnon, Michelle (1998) 'Les femmes immigrées cherchent à s'insérer dans le monde du travail', *Le Monde*, 20 mars: 10.

Bacqué, Raphaëlle (1998) 'Egalité ou "parité" entre les hommes et les femmes?', *Le Monde*, 15 décembre.

Badinter, Elisabeth (1997) 'Nous ne sommes pas une espèce à proteger', *Le Nouvel Observateur*, 23–9 janvier: 38–40.

Badinter, Elisabeth (1999a) 'Un remède pire que le mal', *Le Nouvel Observateur*, 14 janvier: 84.

Badinter, Elisabeth (1999b) 'La parité est une régression', *L'Evénement du jeudi*, 4 février: 86–9.

Badinter, Robert (1999) 'On ne peut parler de parité qu'au niveau des candidatures', *Le Monde*, 14 février.

Bajard, Claire (1979) 'La femme porteuse de l'avenir', *La Baleine: Journal des amis de la terre*, special issue on *Femmes*, 41, janvier: 6.

Bari, Dominique (1996) 'Brigitte ou l'invitation à être communiste et féministe', *L'Humanité*, 19 novembre: 13.

Barroux, Rémi (1999) 'Les femmes dans le front', Ras-l'front website, www. Globenet.org/RLF/publications/publi-pref/chap10.html, 12 October, accessed 20 October.

Bashevkin, Sylvia B. (1984) 'Changing patterns of politicization and partisanship among women in France', *British Journal of Political Science*, 15, 1: 75–96.

Bataille, Claire (1978) 'Femmes et organisations politiques', *Rouge*, 1 juillet, FNSP press cuttings file FR108.

Bataille, Phillippe and Gaspard, Françoise (1999) *Comment les femmes changent la politique et pourquoi les hommes résistent?* Paris: La Découverte.

Batiot, Anne (1986) 'Radical democracy and feminist discourse: the case of France', in Dahlerup, Drude (ed.) *The New Women's Movement: Feminism and Political Power in Europe and the USA*, Thousand Oaks, California: Sage, 85–101.

Beauvoir, Simone de (1978) Interview in *Le Monde*, 11 janvier: 2.

Belden Fields, A. (1986) '*Liberté, egalité et surtout fraternité?*: the struggle over women's liberation in the French Communist and Socialist Parties', *Polity*, 18, part 4: 553–76.

Bell, David (1995) 'Introduction: French politics and political science: out of the mainstream', in Bell, David (ed.) *France*, Aldershot, Brookfield, Singapore, Sydney: Dartmouth Press: xiii–xxxii.

Bell, David and Criddle, Byron (1994) *The French Communist Party in the Fifth Republic*, Oxford: Clarendon.

Bennahmias, Jean-Luc and Roche, Agnès (1992) *Des verts de toutes les couleurs: histoire et sociologie du mouvement écolo*, Paris: Albin Michel.

Berger, Denis (1996) 'Impasse de la République' *Futur/Antérieur*, 38, 'Les failles de la démocratie': 11–21.

Besnier, Frédéric (1997) 'Le mouvement pour la parité à la croisée des chemins', *Parité-infos*, 18, mars: 2–4.

Besset, Jean-Paul (1993) 'Le grand saga des écolos', *Politis: le mensuel*, 10, mars: 6–13.

Biffaud, Olivier and Roland-Lévy, Fabien (1997) 'Le gouvernement envisage des "quotas" féminins aux élections', *Le Monde*, 8 mars: 6–7.

Bihr, Alain and Pfefferkorn, Roland (1996) *Hommes/Femmes l'introuvable égalité*, Paris: Les éditions de l'atelier/Editions ouvrières.

Bogdanor, Vernon (1983) *Democracy and Elections: Electoral Systems and their Political Consequences*, Cambridge: Cambridge University Press.

Bordeaux, Michèle (1991) 'Les retombées juridiques du mouvement féministe', in *Groupe d'études féministes de l'université Paris VII (GEF)* (1991): 207–22.

Borella, François (1990) *Les partis politiques dans la France d'aujourd'hui*, fifth edition, Paris: Seuil.

Bouchardeau, Huguette (1978) 'Les femmes des autres', *Tribune socialiste*, 22 juin, FNSP press cuttings file FR108.

Bouchardeau, Huguette (1980) 'Je m'estime autant participant au mouvement des femmes qu'au PSU', Interview in *Que faire aujourd'hui?*, 8 octobre: 22–3.

Bouchardeau, Huguette (1993) 'Un parcours politique' in Riot-Sarcey (ed.) (1993): 51–8.

Bouchardeau, Huguette, Goueffic, Suzanne and Thouvenot, Geneviève (1981) *Pour une politique des femmes par les femmes, pour les femmes: les propositions du PSU*, Paris: Syros.

Bourque, Susan and Grossholtz, Jean (1974) 'Politics, an unnatural practice: political science looks at female participation', *Politics and Society*, 4, 2: 225–66.

Boy, Daniel (1990) 'Le mouvement écologique', in Borella (1990): 211–18.

Boy, Daniel (1993) 'Les écologistes', in Chagnollaud (1993): 310–28.

Boy, Daniel and Nonna, Mayer (1997) 'Que reste-t-il des variables lourdes?' in Boy, Daniel and Nonna Mayer (eds) *L'électeur a ses raisons*, Paris: Presses de Sciences Po: 101–38.

Braithwaite, Mary and Byrne, Catherine (1993) *Les femmes et la prise de décision dans les syndicats*, Brussels: CES (Confédération Européenne des Syndicats).

Braud, Philippe (1973) *Le comportement électoral en France*, Paris: Presses Universitaires de France.

Bréchon, Pierre (1998) *La France aux urnes*, Paris: La documentation française.

Brédin, Frédérique (1997) *Journal de bord*, Paris: Fayard.

Brenner, Johanna (1996) 'The best of times, the worst of times: feminism in the United States', in Threlfall (ed.) (1996): 17–72.

Broussine, Georges (1997) 'Un lien très fort unit Jacques Chirac et les jeunes', *La lettre de la Nation*, 1486, 11 mars: 1–2.

Brulé, Michel (1998) 'Les deux visages de la Ve république', *Sociétal*, 22, septembre: 4–7.

Bujon, Stéphanie (1994) 'Elles ont voté, il y a 50 ans', *Le nouveau Politis: l'hebdo*, 21 au 27 avril: 12.

Cacheux, Denise (1996) Contribution to seminar 'Actualité de la Parité', *Projets féministes*, 4/5, février.

Cahiers du communisme (1995a) 'Gagner les femmes à utiliser le vote Robert Hue', Dossier, 71, 2, février: 26–41.

Cahiers du communisme (1995b) 'L'engagement de tous les communistes pour le vote de Robert Hue', 71, 3, mars: 21–7.

Carby, Hazel (1992) 'The multicultural wars', in Dent, G. *Black Popular Culture*, Seattle: Bay Press.

Carpentier, J. and Le Brun, F. (eds) (1987) *Histoire de France*, Paris: Editions du Seuil.

Castles, Francis (1982) *The Impact of Parties: Politics and Policies in Democratic Capitalist State*, London: Sage.

Catala, Nicole (1998) 'L'illusion de la parité', *Libération*, 29 juin: 6.

CEMR (1997) 'Statistics on women's participation in political life', *CEMR-INFOS (Elected Women's Issues)*, 2: 3–6.

CEVIPOF (1990) *L'électeur français en questions*, Paris: Presses de Sciences Po.

CFDT 'Les études générales de la CFDT', http://www.cfdt.fr/etudes.htm, accessed 24 August 1998.

CFDT-Information (1979) *Travailleuses, combat pour une libération*, Paris: CFDT.

CFDT-Fédération des banques (1980) 'La longue marche des femmes', *Bulletin Fédéral*, 109.

CGT (1973) *Les femmes salariées* (Travaux de la Ve conférence nationale des 17 et 18 mai 1973), Paris: Editions Sociales.

CGT (1978) *La CGT et les femmes salariées*, Paris: CGT.

CGT (1985) 'Declaration de la Commission Exécutive confédérale du 2 mai 1985', *Le Peuple*, 1201: 12–17.

Chagnollaud, Dominique (1993) *La vie politique en France*, Paris: Seuil.

Chaperon, Sylvie (1995) 'La radicalisation des mouvements féminins français de 1960 à 1970', *Vingtième siècle*, 48, octobre/décembre: 61–75.

Chaperon, Sylvie (1998) 'Les voies politiques de la parité: débats', in Martin (ed.) (1998): 261–4.

Chardin, Patrick (1973) 'Lorsque les femmes s'éveilleront', *Combat*, 15 novembre.

Charzat, Gisèle (1972) *Les françaises sont-elles des citoyennes?*, Paris: Denoël.

Chaveau (1979) 'Femmes ecologie', *La Baleine: Journal des amis de la terre*, special issue on *Femmes*, 41, janvier: 2–3.

Choisir: la cause des femmes (1978) *Le programme commun des femmes*, Paris: Bernard Grasset.

Chombeau, Christiane (1988) 'La convention socialiste sur les droits des femmes', *Le Monde*, 15 mars.

Chombeau, Christiane (1993) 'La représentation des femmes en politique', *Le Monde*, 8 mars: 9.

Chowdhury, Najma and Nelson, Barbara (eds) (1994) *Women and Politics Worldwide*, New Haven and London: Yale University Press.

Christy, Carol A. (1987) *Sex Differences in Political Participation: Processes of Change in Fourteen Nations*, New York, Westport, London: Praeger.

Cléo, Michèle and Vinteuil, Frédérique (1982) 'Des "psychanalyse et politique" au "MLF" (déposé)', *Rouge*, 2–8 avril.

Cockburn, Cynthia (1997) 'Gender in an international space: trade union women as European social actor', *Women's Studies International Forum*, 20, 4: 459–70.

Cole, Alistair (ed.) (1990a) *French Parties in Transition*, Aldershot, Brookfield, Hong Kong, Singapore, Sydney: Dartmouth Press.

Cole, Alistair (1990b) 'The evolution of the party system, 1974–1990', in Cole (ed.) (1990): 3–24.

Colin, Madeleine (1975) *Ce n'est pas d'aujourd'hui . . . femmes, syndicats, luttes des classes*, Paris: Editions Sociales.

Collin, Françoise (1992) 'Théories et praxis de la différence des sexes', *M*, 53–4, avril/mai: 5–9.

Collin, Françoise (1995) 'L'urne est-elle funéraire?', in Riot-Sarcey (ed.) (1995): 45–75.

Collin, Françoise (1996a) 'Mythe et réalité de la démocratie', in Viennot (ed.) (1996d): 25–35.

Collin, Françoise (1996b) Contribution to seminar 'Actualité de la parité', *Projets féministes*, 4/5, février.

Colmou, Anne-Marie (1999) *L'encadrement supérieur dans la fonction publique: vers égalité entre hommes et femmes. Quels obstacles? Quelles solutions?* (Rapport Colmou), Paris: Ministère de la fonction publique, de la réforme de l'Etat et de la décentralisation. http://www.fonction-publique.gouv.fr/lac and dossiers/rapportcolmou/sommaire.html, accessed 30 June 1999.

Combes, Maurice (1965) 'La condition de la femme aujourd'hui', *Tribune socialiste*, 6 février.

Commission Femmes du Parti Communiste Français (1999) Personal correspondence, 4 November.

Comte, Francine and Léonard, Bernadette (1993) 'Pratique de la parité: l'analyse des vertes ne fait que commencer', *Parité-infos: Lettre d'information sur le mouvement pour la parité hommes/femmes dans la vie publique*, 2, juin: 6.

Conseil d'Etat (1996) *Rapport public 1996 sur le principe d'égalité*, 48, Paris: la documentation française.

Cook, Alice, Lorwin, Val and Kaplan, Daniel (1992) *The Most Difficult Revolution: Woimen and Trade Unions*, Ithaca and London: Cornell University Press.

Coote, Anna and Patullo, Polly (1990) *Power and Prejudice: Women and Politics*, London: Weidenfeld and Nicolson.

Coquillat, Michèle (1983) *Qui sont-elles?: Les femmes d'influence et de pouvoir en France*, Paris: Editions Mazarine.

Courtois, Gérard (1996) *Le Monde*, 17 October.

Courtois, Gérard (1999) 'Majoritaires dans la fonction publique, les femmes deviennent rares aux postes de responsabilité', *Le Monde*, 18 February. http://www.lemonde.fr/actu/societe/parite/articles/180299/femmes.htm, accessed 28 February 1999.

Cresson, Edith (1998) 'La situation des femmes n'a pas progressé', in Martin (ed.) (1998): 11–14.

Cunnison, Sheila and Stageman, Jane (1993) *Feminizing the Unions: Challenging the Culture of Masculinity*, Aldershot: Avebury.

Dahlerup, Drude (1988) 'From a small to a large minority: women in Scandinavian politics', *Scandinavian Political Studies*, 11, 4: 275–98.

Dalton, Russell (1996) *Citizen Politics in Western Democracies*, Chatham, New Jersey: Chatham House.

Dean, Jodi (ed.) (1997) *Feminism and the New Democracy: Resiting the Political*, London: Thousand Oaks; New Delhi: Sage.

D'Eaubonne, Françoise, (1978) *Ecologie/Féminisme: Révolution ou mutation?*, Paris: Editions ATP.

Debbasch, Charles and Daudet, Yves (1992) *Lexique de termes politiques*, Paris: Dalloz.

Deljarrie, B. (1997) 'Le statut de l'élu local: fonction élective et professionnalisation', *Après-demain*, 399: 12–14.

Déloye, Yves (1997) 'Les incertitudes de la citoyenneté', *Les cahiers français*, 281, 'Citoyenneté et Société', mai-juin: 39–44.

Delphy, Christine (1984) 'Les femmes et l'Etat', *Nouvelles questions féministes*, 6–7: 5–20.

Delphy, Christine (1988) 'Le patriarcat: une oppression spécifique', in Centre fédéral FEN, *Le féminisme et ses enjeux*, Paris: Edilig: 157–80.

Delphy, Christine (1996) 'The European Union and the future of feminism', in Elman (ed.) (1996): 147–58.

Delwasse, Liliane (1982) 'Les femmes en politique', *Le Monde*, 7 mars.

Dental, Monique (1996) Contribution to seminar, *Projets féministes*, 'Actualité de la parité', *Projets féministes*, 4/5, février.

Desbois, Josette (1979) 'Le PC reconnaît le "mouvement en avant des femmes" mais surtout pas un mouvement autonome', *Rouge*, 4–10 mai, FNSP press cuttings file FR108.

Dialogue des femmes (1981–2) 'De la nécessité du dialogue entre les femmes et des maladies infantiles du féminisme', Paris, Tome 2.

Dietrich, François (1988), 'Les racines d'un mouvement', *Cahiers du féminisme*, 47: 24–6.

Dogan, Matteï (1955) 'L'origine sociale du personnel parlementaire français élu en 1951', in Duverger, Maurice *Partis politiques et les classes sociales*, Paris: Armand Colin.

Dogan, Matteï and Narbonne, Jacques (1955) *Les Françaises face à la politique*, Paris: Armand Collin.

Doumit el Khoury, Arlène (1997) 'Féminisme, avez-vous dit?', *Vacarme*, 4–5, septembre/novembre: 54–8.

Dubois, J-P. (1997) 'Le cumul des mandats', *Après-demain*, 399: 7–11.

Duchen, Claire (1986) *Feminism in France: From May '68 to Mitterrand*, London and New York: Routledge.

Duchen, Claire (1987) *French Connections: Voices from the Women's Movement in France*, London: Macmillan.

Duchen, Claire (1994) *Women's Rights and Women's Lives in France 1944–68*, London and New York: Routledge.

Duchesne, Françoise (1997) 'Le défi de la mixité', *Le peuple*, 1457: 45–7.

Ducol, Claudine (1978) 'Des luttes des femmes', *L'Humanité*, 22 juin, FNSP press cuttings file FR108.

Ducrocq, Françoise (1985), 'The women's liberation movement in socialist France: four years later', *MF*, 10: 61–77.

Ducrocq-Poirier, Madeleine and Thibault, Marie-Noëlle (1988) *Les Femmes de la CSN (Québec) et de la CFDT (France) et le féminisme*, Paris: ATP-Femmes/CNRS.

Duhamel, Alain (1971) 'Les femmes et la politique', *Le Monde*, 10 mars.

Duverger, Maurice (1955a) *La participation des femmes à la vie politique*, Paris: UNESCO.

Duverger, Maurice (1955b) *The Political Role of Women*, Paris: UNESCO.

Ecole Normale Supérieure, 'Rapports', http://www.ens.fr/concours/rapports/rapports.html, accessed 2 November 1999.

Ehrmann, Henry W. and Schain, Martin A. (1992) *Politics in France*, fifth edition, New York: Harper/Collins.

Elman, R. Amy (ed.) (1996) *Sexual Politics and the European Union: The New Feminist Challenge*, Oxford: Berghahn Books.

Ephesia (Conseil scientifique de la mission de coordination de la 4e conférence mondiale sur les femmes) (ed.) (1995) *La place des femmes*, Paris: Editions de la Découverte.

Eurobarometer (1983) 19, June: 42–52.

Eurobarometer (1985) 24, December: 43–51.

Eurobarometer (1995) 42, spring: 74–8.

Eurobarometer (1998) 44, 3: 51–69.

European Database: Women in Decision-making, 'Details: Elections', http://www.db-decision.de/english/Wahl.htm, accessed 24 July 1998 and 1 March 1999.

Evin, Kathleen (1978a) 'La lutte sur deux fronts', *Le Nouvel Observateur*, 12 juin: 50.

Evin, Kathleen (1978b) 'La politique ne "les" intéresse pas . . .', *Le Nouvel Observateur*, 26 juin: 28.

Eyquem, Marie-Thérèse (1978) 'Le PS et les femmes', *Le Monde*, 16 juin.

Favoreu, Louis (1996) 'Principe d'égalité et représentation politique des femmes: la France et les exemples étrangers', in Conseil d'Etat (1996): 395–407.

Flammang, Janet (1984) *Political Women: Current Roles in State and Local Government*, Beverly Hills: Sage.

Folloni, Sonia (1984) 'Les mauvaises coups', *Rouge*, 1103: 10.

Fontenay, Elisabeth (1999) 'L'abstraction du calcul contre celle des principes', *Le Monde*, 25 février: 16.

Fouque, Antoinette (1982) Interview in *Le Quotidien de Paris*, 709, lundi, 8 mars: 7.

Frader, Laura (1996) 'Women and French unions: historical perspectives on the crisis of representation', *French Politics and Society*, 14, 4: 23–36.

Fraisse, Geneviève (1989) *Muse de la raison*, Paris: Alinéa.

Fraisse, Geneviève (1997) 'La démocratie exclusive: un paradigme français', *Pouvoirs*, 82, 5–16.

Fraisse, Geneviève (1998) 'La parité n'est pas l'égalité sociale', *Libération*, 29 décembre: 5.

Freedman, Jane (1997) *Femmes politiques, mythes et symboles*, Paris: Harmattan.

Gaëlle, Lucy (1996) 'L'emploi des femmes sous le choc de la déréglementation', *Cahiers du féminisme*, 79/80: 4–6.

Gaëlle, Mirabel (1995) 'Déréglementation, flexibilité, humiliations', *Cahiers du féminisme*, 71/72: 29–33.

Gaspard, Françoise (1994) 'De la parité: genèse d'un concept, naissance d'un mouvement', *Nouvelles questions féministes*, 15, 4: 29–44.

Gaspard, Françoise (1995) 'Des partis et des femmes', in Riot-Sarcey (ed.) (1995): 221–42.

Gaspard, Françoise (1996) Contribution to seminar 'Actualité de la parité', *Projets féministes*, 4/5, février.

Gaspard, Françoise (1997a) 'La parité: pourquoi pas?', *Pouvoirs*, 82: 115–25.

Gaspard, Françoise (ed.) (1997b) *Les femmes dans la prise de décision en France et en Europe*: Paris: Harmattan.

Gaspard, Françoise (1997c) 'La République et les femmes', in Wieviorka, Michel (ed.) (1997): 152–70.

Gaspard, Françoise (1997d) 'Les Françaises en politique au lendemain des élections législatives de 1997', *French Politics and Society*, 15, 4, Fall.

Gaspard, Françoise (1997e) 'Résultats des élections législatives: les femmes symboles du renouveau politique', *Parité-infos*, 18, juin: 4–8.

Gaspard, Françoise (1998a) 'La parité, principe ou stratégie?', *Le monde diplomatique*, novembre, 26–7.

Gaspard, Françoise (1998b) 'Proposition de loi tendant à instaurer la parité femmes/hommes dans les assemblées élues', in the programme of *La Parité enjeux et mise en œuvre*, Colloque international, Université de Toulouse-Le Mirail, 6–7 février: 13–16.

Gaspard, Françoise (1998c) 'Assessment: women elected representatives in French municipalities', in CEMR, *Men and Women in European Municipalities*, Paris: CEMR: 35–42.

Gaspard, Françoise and Servan-Schreiber, Claude (1993) 'De la fraternité à la parité', *Le Monde*, 19 février: 2.

Gaspard, Françoise and Servan-Schreiber, Claude (1997) 'Elections législatives des 25 mai et 1er juin 1997: les femmes dans la compétition électorale en France', *Parité-infos* (special issue).

Gaspard, Françoise, Servan-Schreiber, Claude and Le Gall, Anne (1992) *Au pouvoir citoyennes!*, Paris: Seuil.

Gauthier, Nicole (1998) 'La parité s'invite dans la constitution', *Libération*, 18 juin: 2–3.

Gautier, Arlette and Heinen, Jacqueline (eds) *Le Sexe des politiques sociales*, Paris: Côté-Femmes.

Gibbon, Margaret (1989) 'The trade unions and women workers after 1968', in Hanley, David N. and Kerr, Anne P. (eds) *May '68: Coming of Age*, London: Macmillan.

Gilson, Martine (1997a) 'Le pari de Notat', *Le Nouvel Observateur*, 1693: 28–9.

Gilson, Martine (1997b) 'Quand le temps partiel est subi', *Le Nouvel Observateur*, 1716: 11–12.

Giscard d'Estaing, Valéry (1998) 'Foreword by the president of the CEMR', in CEMR, *Men and Women in European Municipalities*, Paris: CEMR.

Githens, Monica, Norris, Pippa, and Lovenduski, Joni (1994) *Different Roles, Different Voices*, New York: Harper/Collins.

Gouvernement français, 'Composition du gouvernement', www.premier.ministre. gouv.fr/GOUV/PMGVT.HTM, accessed 17 November 1999.

Granger, Anne-Marie (1988) 'Infirmières: la tornade blanche', *Cahiers du féminisme*, 47: 13–23.

Granger, Anne-Marie and Jersey, S. (1988) 'Vingt ans aux chèques: militer au féminin', *Cahiers du féminisme*, 45: 23–6.

Grégoire, Ménie (1971) 'Les femmes et les élections municipales', *Le Monde*, 1 février.

Groupe d'études féministes de l'université Paris VII (GEF) (1991) *Crises de la société: féminisme et changement*, Paris: Revue d'en face, Editions Tierce.

Guéraïche, William (1992), 'Women in French political life, from the liberation to the 1970s: essay on the distribution of power', doctoral thesis, University of Toulouse-Mirail.

Guigou, Elisabeth (1997) *Etre femme en politique*, Paris: Plon.

Guilbert, Madeleine (1966) *Les femmes et l'organisation syndicale avant 1914*, Paris: Editions CNRS.

Guillaumin, Colette (1998) 'La confrontation des féministes en particulier au racisme en général: remarques sur les relations du féminisme à ses sociétés', in ANEF (1998): 7–14.

Haase-Dubosc, Danièle and Viennot, Eliane (1991) *Femmes et pouvoirs sous l'ancien régime*, Paris: Rivages.

Hainsworth, Paul (1990) 'Breaking the mould: the Greens in the French party system', in Cole, Alistair (ed.) (1990b): 91–105.

Halimi, Gisèle (1981) 'Quel président pour les femmes?', *Le Monde*, 9 mai.

Halimi, Gisèle (ed.) (1994a) *Femmes: moitié de la terre, moitié du pouvoir*, Paris: Gallimard.

Halimi, Gisèle (1994b) 'Plaidoyer pour une démocratie paritaire', in Halimi (ed.) (1994): 11–22.

Halimi, Gisèle (1994c) 'Egalité-Parité', *Le Monde*, 22 avril: 2.

Halimi, Gisèle (1997) *La nouvelle cause des femmes*, Paris: Seuil.

Hall, Peter A., Hayward, Jack and Machin, Howard (1994) *Developments in French Politics*, Basingstoke and London: Macmillan.

Heinen, Jacqueline and Trat, Josette (eds) (1997) 'Hommes et femmes dans le mouvement social', *Cahiers du Gedisst*, 18, Paris: L'Harmattan.

Helft-Malz, Véronique and Lévy, Paule (eds) (1996) *Encyclopédie des femmes politiques sous la Ve République*, Paris: Editions Patrick Banon.

Hirata, Helena, Kergoat, Danièle, Riot-Sarcey, Michèle and Varikas, Eleni (1994) 'Parité ou mixité', *Politis: la revue*, 6, février, mars, avril: 117–18.

Hirsch, Arthur (1981) *The French New Left: An Intellectual History from Sartre to Gorz*, Boston, Massachusetts: South End Press.

Hochedez, Daniel and Maurice, Cécile (1997) 'Règles et réalités européennes', *Pouvoirs*, 82: 77–90.

Hull, G. (ed.) (1982) *All the Women are White, all the Blacks are Men, but Some of Us are Brave*, Old Westbury, New York: Feminist Press.

Hunt, Lynn (1996) *The French Revolution and Human Rights: A Brief Documentary History*, Boston and New York: Bedford Books of St. Martin's Press.

ICFTU 'Mise en application du programme d'action pour l'intégration des femmes dans les organisations syndicales', http://www.icftu.org/equality/fcampaign0803. html, accessed 12 July 1999.

INSEE (1973) *Données sociales*, Paris: INSEE, 101.

INSEE (1995) *Les Femmes*, Paris: INSEE.

Institut français d'opinion publique (IFOP) 'La participation des femmes françaises à la vie politique. Résultats d'une enquête par sondage effectuée en juin 1953', in Duverger (1955a): 165–206.

Interparliamentary Union (IPU) (1997) *Hommes et femmes en politique: la démocratie inachevée, Rapports et Documents*, Genève: IPU.

Interparliamentary Union Parline database http://www.ipu.org/parline-e/parline. htm, accessed 10 November 1998.

Irigaray, Luce (1994) 'L'identité féminine: biologie ou conditionnement social?', in Halimi, Gisèle (ed.) (1994): 101–8.

Jauffret, Jacqueline and Joanny, Sophie (1995), 'Etre des porte-parole des luttes', *Cahiers du féminisme*, 73: 4–9.

Jenson, Jane (1982) 'The new politics: women and the parties of the left in Italy and in France', *Europa*, 5, part 1: 7–33.

Jenson, Jane (1987) 'Changing discourses, changing agendas: political rights and reproductive policies in France', in Katzenstein Fainsod, Mary and McClurg Mueller, Carol (eds), *The Women's Movements of the United States and Western Europe*, Philadelphia: Temple University Press: 64–88.

Jenson, Jane (1990) 'Representations of difference: the varieties of French feminism', *New Left Review*, 180: 127–60.

Jenson, Jane (1996) 'Representations of difference: the varieties of French feminism', in Threlfall (ed.) (1996): 73–114.

Jenson, Jane and Sineau, Mariette (1994) 'The same or different: an unending dilemma for French women', in Nelson and Chowdhury (eds) (1994): 244–60.

Jenson, Jane and Sineau, Mariette (1995) *Mitterrand et les Françaises: un rendez-vous manqué*, Paris: Presses de Sciences Po.

Jospin, Lionel (1999a) 'Intervention en clôture de la Conférence européenne "Femmes et hommes au pouvoir"', 17 April, http://www.premierministre.gouv.fr/PM/ D170499.HTM, accessed 9 November 1999.

Jospin, Lionel (1999b) 'Allocution devant le Parlement réuni en Congrès pour l'adoption du project de loi constitutionnelle relatif à l'égalité entre les femmes et les hommes', 28 June, http://www.premier-ministre.gouv.fr/PM/D280699A.HTM, accessed 9 November 1999.

Junter-Loiseau, Annie (1998) 'La démocratie locale à l'épreuve des femmes: le cas des femmes élues à Rennes', in Martin (ed.) (1998): 97–109.

Kandel, Liliane (1980) 'Post-scriptum: "une presse anti-féministe" aujourd'hui: "des femmes en mouvement"', *Questions féministes*, 7: 37–44.

Kandel, Liliane (1991) 'Du politique au personnel: le prix d'une illusion', in *Groupe d'études féministes de l'université Paris VII (GEF)* (1991): 21–34.

Kanter, Rosabeth (1977) *Men and Women of the Corporation*, New York: Basic Books.

Kergoat, Danièle (ed.) (1992) *Les infirmières et leur coordination 1988–9*, Paris: Lamarre.

Kergoat, Danièle (1993) 'Réflexions sur les conditions de l'exercice du pouvoir par des femmes dans la conduite des luttes, le cas de la coordination infirmière', in Riot-Sarcey (ed.) (1993): 124–39.

Knapp, Andrew (1999) 'What's left of the French right?: the RPR and the UDF from conquest to humiliation', *West European Politics*, 22, 3, July: 109–38.

Knibiehler, Yvonne (1996) 'Démocratie, désir des femmes', in Viennot (ed.) (1996d): 19–24.

Krakovitch, Odile (1996a) Contribution to seminar 'Actualité de la parité', *Projets féministes*, 4/5, février.

Krakovitch, Odile (1996b) 'Les femmes dans l'administration', *Après-demain*, 380–1: 16–19.

Kriegel, Blandine (1996) 'Parité et principe d'égalité', in Conseil d'Etat (1996): 375–84.

Lagroye, Jacques (1989) 'Vote et configurations des marchés politiques', in Gaxie, Daniel (ed.) *Explication du vote: un bilan des études électorales en France*, Paris: FNSP: 325–34.

Lalu, Vincent and Clément, Fabrice (1977) 'Les femmes face à la politique: celles qui luttent et celles qui ont peur', *Le Matin*, 8 December (FNSP Press Cuttings Service, Dossier FR108).

Lancelot, Alain (1968) *L'abstentionnisme électoral en France*, Paris: Armand Colin.

Laot, Jeannette (1976) 'Lutte de classe et libération des femmes', *Droit Social*, 1: 6–13.

Laot, Jeannette (1978) 'L'exposé introductif', in CFDT *Conférence travail des femmes et action syndicale* (Rapports et interventions): 1–20.

Laot, Jeannette (1981) *Stratégie pour les femmes*, Paris: Editions Stock.

Laroche, Françoise (1997) 'Maréchale, nous voilà!: Le cercle national femmes d'Europe', in Lesselier and Venner (eds) (1997): 153–64.

Latour, Patricia, Houssin, Monique and Tovar, Madia (1995) *Femmes et citoyennes: du droit de vote à l'exercice du pouvoir*, Paris: Les éditions de l'Atelier.

Le Borgne, Catherine (1980) 'La lutte des femmes de Plogoff contre le nucléaire', *Généraliste*, 9 avril: 1–2.

Le Bras-Chopard, Armelle and Mossuz-Lavau, Janine (eds) (1997) *Les Femmes et la politique*, Paris: L'Harmattan.

Le Doeuff, Michèle (1989) *L'étude et le rouet*, Paris: Seuil.

Le Doeuff, Michèle (1995) 'Problèmes d'investiture (de la parité, etc.)', *Nouvelles questions féministes*, 16, 2: 5–80.

Le Monde (1995) 'Conférence mondiale sur les femmes – Pékin 1995' (supplément) 31 août.

Le Quentrec, Yannick (1998) 'Les obstacles aux pratiques syndicales des femmes', in Martin (ed.) (1998): 141–9.

Le Trombinoscope: l'information professionnelle du monde politique (1999) Volume 1, Nanterre: Publications Professionnelles Parlementaires.

Leijenaar, Monique (1996) *Comment créer un équilibre entre les femmes et les hommes dans la prise de décision politique: guide pour la mise en œuvre de politiques visant à accroître la participation des femmes à la prise de décision politique*, Commission européenne, Direction générale 'Emploi, relations industrielles et affaires sociales', Unité V/D.5.

Les Verts (1994) *Le livre des Verts: dictionnaire de l'écologie politique*, Paris: Editions Dufélin.

Leschi, Didier (1996) 'Les coordinations, filles des années 1968', *Clio, histoire, femmes et sociétés*, 3: 163–81.

Lesselier, Claudie (1991) 'Les regroupements de lesbiennes dans le mouvement féministe parisien (1970–82)', in *Groupe d'études féministes de l'université Paris VII (GEF)* (1991): 87–104.

Lesselier, Claudie (1997) 'De la Vierge Marie à Jeanne d'Arc: l'extrême droite frontiste et catholique et les femmes (1984–90)', in Lesselier and Venner (eds) (1997): 41–70.

Lesselier, Claudie (1998) 'Contribution to Table Ronde', *ANEF*: 49–50.

Lesselier, Claudie (1999) 'Le Front national contre le droit des femmes, contre les libertés de toutes et tous', Ras-l'front website, www.Globenet.org/RLF/publications/publi-pref/chap10.html, 12 October, accessed 20 October.

Lesselier, Claudie and Venner, Fiammetta (eds) (1997) *L'extrême droite et les femmes*, Villeurbanne: Editions Golias.

Letablier, Marie-Thérèse (1995) 'Women's labour force participation in France: the paradoxes of the 1990s', *Journal of Area Studies*, 6: 108–16.

Lévy, Martine (1992) 'France: vers un équilibre dynamique avec les hommes', *Femmes d'Europe*, 70: 33–9.

Leyrit, Claude (1997) *Les partis politiques*, Paris: Le Monde-Editions.

Ligue communiste révolutionnaire website (1999) http://www.lcr-rouge.org/questce.html, accessed 12 October.

Lipietz, Alain (1994) 'Parité au masculin', *Nouvelles questions féministes*, 15, 4: 45–64.

Lipietz, Alain (1996) 'Ce n'est pas plus grave parce que ce sont des femmes: l'expérience de la parité chez les Verts', *Après-demain*, 380–1, janvier–février: 26–9.

Lister, Ruth (1990) 'Women, economic dependency and citizenship', *Journal of Social Policy*, 19, 4: 445–67.

Lister, Ruth (1997a) *Citizenship: Feminist Perspectives*, Basingstoke and London: Macmillan.

Lister, Ruth (1997b) 'Citizenship: towards a feminist citizenship', *Feminist Review*, 57, autumn: 28–48.

Logeart, Agathe (1997) 'La guerre des roses', *Le Monde*, 9/10 mars: 11.

Loiseau, Dominique (1996) 'Associations féminines et syndicalisme en Loire-Atlantique, des années 1930 aux années 1980', *Clio, histoire, femmes et sociétés*, 3: 141–61.

Loiseau, Dominique (1999) 'Du côté des syndicats', in Bard, Christine (ed.) (1999) *Un siècle d'antiféminisme*, Paris: Fayard: 355–66.

Loschak, Danièle (1983) 'Les hommes politiques, les "sages" (?) . . . et les femmes (à propos de la décision du Conseil constitutionnel du 18 novembre 1982)', *Droit social*, 2, février: 131–7.

Loschak, Danièle (1996) 'Les enjeux juridiques de la parité', contribution to seminar 'Actualité de la parité', *Projets féministes*, 4/5, février.

Louis, Marie-Victoire (1994) 'A propos des violences masculines sur les femmes: ébauche d'une analyse féministe du nouveau code pénal français', *Projets féministes*, 3, octobre: 40–69.

Louis, Marie-Victoire (1996) Contribution to seminar 'Actualité de la parité', *Projets féministes*, 4/5, février.

Louis, Marie-Victoire (1997) 'Des femmes ministres ne font pas un ministère des femmes', *Libération*, 23 juillet: 4.

Lovenduski, Joni (1986) *Women and European Politics: Contemporary Feminism and Public Policy*, Brighton: Harvester Wheatsheaf.

Lovenduski, Joni (1994) 'The rules of the political game: feminism and politics in Great Britain', in Nelson and Chowdhury (eds) (1994): 298–310.

Lovenduski, Joni and Hills, Jill (1981) *The Politics of the Second Electorate*, London: Routledge and Kegan Paul.

Lovenduski, Joni and Norris, Pippa (1993) *Gender and Party Politics*, London, Thousand Oaks, and New Delhi: Sage.

Lovenduski, Joni and Norris, Pippa (eds) (1996) *Women in Politics*, Oxford and New York: Oxford University Press.

Lucie, Renée (1993) 'Législatives 93: plus ça change, plus c'est pareil', *Parité-infos*, mars: 1–4.

Lucie, Renée (1996) 'Elections de 1998: candidats ou candidates?: Le temps des grands manoeuvres', *Parité-infos*, 16, décembre: 1–2.

Lyman, Stanford (ed.) (1995) *Social Movements: Critiques, Concepts, Case-Studies*, Basingstoke and London: Macmillan.

Machin, Howard (1994) 'Introduction', in Hall, Hayward and Machin (eds) 1994: 1–12.

Mangin, Catherine and Martichoux, Elisabeth (1991) *Ces femmes qui nous gouvernent*, Paris: Albin Michel.

Marchais, Georges (1977) Discours: 'Femmes pour changer votre vie', Paris: PCF.

Marshall, T.H. (1950) *Citizenship and Social Class*, Cambridge: Cambridge University Press.

Martin, Jacqueline (ed.) (1998) *La parité: enjeux et mise en œuvre*, Toulouse: Presses universitaires du Mirail.

Martucelli, Danilo (1997) 'Les Contradictions politiques du multiculturalisme', in Wieviorka (ed.) (1997): 61–82.

Maruani, Margaret (1979) *Les syndicats à l'épreuve du féminisme*, Paris: Editions Syros.

Mayer, Nonna and Perrineau, Pascal (1992) *Les comportements politiques*, Paris: Armand Colin.

Mazur, Amy (1995) 'Strong State and symbolic reform: the Ministère des droits de la femme in France', in Stetson and Mazur (eds) (1995): 76–94.

Mazur, Amy (1996a) *Gender Bias and the State: Symbolic Reform at Work in the Fifth Republic*, Pittsburgh: University of Pittsburgh Press.

Mazur, Amy (1996b) 'The interplay: the formation of sexual harassment legislation in France and EU policy initiatives', in Elman (ed.) (1996): 35–50.

Michel, Andrée (1959) *Familles, industrialisation, logement*, Paris: CNRS.

Michel, Andrée (1965) 'Les Françaises et la politique', *Les temps modernes*, 230, juillet: 61–91.

Michel, Andrée and Texier, Geneviève (1964) *La condition de la Française d'aujourd'hui*, Volume 2, Geneva: Editions Gonthier.

Millard, Eric (1998) 'Les voies juridiques de la parité: débats', in Martin (ed.) (1998): 265–73.

Millard, Eric and Ortiz, Laure (1998) 'Parité et représentations politiques', in Martin (ed.) (1998): 189–203.

Moi, Toril (1987) *French feminist thought: a reader*, Oxford: Blackwell.

Montreynaud, Florence (1996) Contribution to seminar 'Actualité de la parité', *Projets féministes*, 4/5, février.

Moreau, Gisèle (1983) 'Mort, le féminisme?', *Le Monde*, 20 décembre.

Moreau, Gisèle (1988) 'Mouvement social femmes et rassemblement', *L'Humanité*, 20 octobre: 6.

Morichaud, Nicole (1999) (secrétaire nationale du Mouvement des citoyens), Personal correspondence, 22 October.

Morris, Peter (1994) *French Politics Today*, Manchester and New York: Manchester University Press.

Mossuz-Lavau, Janine (1986) 'Abortion politics in France under the governments of the right and the left (1973–1984)', in Lovenduski, Joni and Outshoorn, Joyce (eds) *The New Politics of Abortion*, Thousand Oaks, California: Sage: 86–104.

Mossuz-Lavau, Janine (1991) *Les lois de l'amour: les politiques de la sexualité en France 1950–90*, Paris: Editions Payot.

Mossuz-Lavau, Janine (1994) 'Les électrices françaises de 1945 à 1993', *Vingtième siècle*, 42, avril-juin: 67–75.

Mossuz-Lavau, Janine (1995) 'Les conceptions politiques des hommes et des femmes ou le four cassé de la RMIste', in Riot-Sarcey (ed.) (1995): 259–79.

Mossuz-Lavau, Janine (1996) Contribution to seminar 'Actualité de la parité', *Projets féministes*, 4/5, février: 58–64.

Mossuz-Lavau, Janine (1997a) 'La percée des femmes aux élections législatives de 1997', *Revue française de science politique*, 47, 3–4, juin–août: 454–61.

Mossuz-Lavau, Janine (1997b) 'L'évolution du vote des femmes', *Pouvoirs*, 82: 35–44.

Mossuz-Lavau, Janine (1997c) 'Les Françaises et la politique: de la citoyenneté à la parité', *Regards sur l'actualité*, décembre: 3–14.

Mossuz-Lavau, Janine (1997d) 'Les Françaises et le Front national', in Lesselier and Venner (eds) (1997): 165–7.

Mossuz-Lavau, Janine (1997e) 'Les femmes et le vote: La France au regard de l'Europe', in Le Bras-Chopard and Mossuz-Lavau (eds) (1997): 81–94.

Mossuz-Lavau, Janine (1998a) 'La parité politique femmes/hommes: actualisation d'un droit demeuré formel', *Politis*, 11 juin: 22–3.

Mossuz-Lavau, Janine (1998b) 'Les femmes font de la résistance', *Le Monde diplomatique*, mai 1998.

Mossuz-Lavau, Janine (1998c) *Femmes/hommes pour la parité*, Paris: Presses de sciences po.

Mossuz-Lavau, Janine (1999) 'Les antiparitaires se trompent', *Le Monde*, 25 February: 17.

Mossuz-Lavau, Janine and Kervasdoué, Anne (1997) *Les femmes ne sont pas des hommes comme les autres*, Paris: Odile Jacob.

Mossuz-Lavau, Janine and Sineau, Mariette (1979) '20% d'élues?', *Le Monde*, 7 avril: 2.

Mossuz-Lavau, Janine and Sineau, Mariette (1981) 'France', in Lovenduski, Joni and Hills, Jill (eds) *The Politics of the Second Electorate: Women and Public Participation*, London: Routledge and Kegan Paul, 112–33.

Mossuz-Lavau, Janine and Sineau, Mariette (1983) *Enquête sur les femmes et la politique en France*, Paris: PUF.

Mouffe, Chantal (1992) 'Feminism, citizenship and radical democratic politics', in Butler, Judith and Scott, Joan W. (eds) *Feminists Theorise the Political*, London: Routledge: 369–84.

Nash, Kate (1998) 'Beyond liberalism?: Feminist theories of democracy', in Waylen and Randall (eds) (1998): 45–57.

Nelson, Barbara J. and Chowdhury, Jayma (eds) (1994) *Women and Politics Worldwide*, New Haven and London: Yale University Press.

Neveu, Erik (1996) *Sociologie des mouvements sociaux*, Paris: La Découverte.

Nolet, François (1980) 'Les partis et les femmes', *Que faire aujourd'hui?*, 8, octobre: 17–21.

Norris, Pippa (1987) *Politics and Sexual Equality: The Comparative Position of Women in Western Democracies*, Brighton: Wheatsheaf.

Norris, Pippa (1993) 'Conclusions: comparing legislative recruitment', in Lovenduski and Norris (eds) (1993): 308–30.

Norris, Pippa (1994) 'Political participation', in Githens, Norris and Lovenduski (eds) (1994): 25–6.

Norris, Pippa (1996) 'Women politicians: transforming Westminster?', in Lovenduski and Norris (eds) (1996): 91–104.

Nouvelles questions féministes (1981) Editorial: 'Féminisme: quelles politiques', 2, octobre: 3–8.

Ollier, Maryse (1978) 'Le mouvement des femmes et les partis bourgeois', *Quotidien du peuple*, 9 mars, FNSP press cuttings file FR108.

Parti communiste français (1966) *Pour le bonheur et l'avenir de nos enfants: recueil de propositions et réalisations du PCF en faveur de la femme, de la famille et de l'enfant*, Paris: PPI.

Parti socialiste (1972) *Changer la vie: programme de gouvernement du Parti Socialiste*, Paris: Parti socialiste.

Parti socialiste (1979) *Féminisme, Socialisme, Autogestion: les grands thèmes du manifeste du PS sur les droits des femmes*, Paris: Parti socialiste.

Pateman, Carole (1970) *Participation and Democratic Theory*, Cambridge: Cambridge University Press.

Pateman, Carole (1988) *The Sexual Contract*, Cambridge: Polity Press.

Pateman, Carole (1989) *The Disorder of Women: Democracy, Feminism and Political Theory*, Cambridge: Polity Press.

Perkins, Anne (1999), 'So far, so what?', *The Guardian* (G2 section), 29 April: 6.

Perrigo, Sarah (1996) 'Women and change in the Labour Party 1979–95', in Lovenduski and Norris (eds) (1996): 118–31.

Perrineau, Pascal (1995) 'Vers une recomposition du politique?', in *L'Etat de la France 1995–6*, Paris: La Découverte: 474–7.

Perrineau, Pascal (1997) 'D'une participation politique dirigée par les élites à une participation les défiant', in *L'Etat de la France 1997–8*, Paris: La Découverte: 18–21.

Perrot, Michelle (1994) 'La démocratie sans les femmes', in Halimi (ed.) (1994a): 33–40.

Perrot, Michelle (1996) 'Nicole Notat' (Témoignages), *Clio*, 3: 205–17.

Perrot, Michelle (1997) 'Les femmes et la citoyenneté en France: histoire d'une exclusion', in Le Bras-Chopard and Mossuz-Lavau (eds) (1997): 23–39.

Perrot, Michelle (1999) 'Oui, tenter cette expérience nouvelle', *Le Monde*, 25 février.

Perry, Sheila and Cross, Máire (eds) (1997) *Voices of France: Social, Political and Cultural Identity*, London and Washington: Pinter.

Pfister, Thierry (1978) 'Des femmes cherchent à s'affirmer en tant que telles au sein des formations de gauche', *Le Monde*, 11–12 juin.

Philippe, Annie and Hubscher, Daniel (1991) *Enquête à l'intérieur du parti socialiste*, Paris: Albin Michel.

Phillips, Anne (1993) *Democracy and Difference*, Cambridge: Polity.

Picq, Françoise (1991) 'Un féminisme hexagonal', *Raison présente*, 100: 69–77.

Picq, Françoise (1993) *Les années mouvement*, Paris: Seuil.

Picq, Françoise (1996) 'Les enjeux juridiques de la parité', contribution to seminar 'Actualité de la parité', *Projets féministes*, 4/5, février.

Pineau, Marie-Rose (1969) '1968 a-t-il changé les femmes?', *L'Humanité*, 22 March (FNSP Press Cuttings Service Dossier FR108).

Pinéro, Maïté (1981) 'L'UFF officiellement reconnue', *L'Humanité*, 16 September.

Pisier, Evelyne (1996) 'Des impasses de la parité', in Conseil d'Etat (1996): 385–93.

Pisier, Evelyne (1999) 'Contre l'enfermement des sexes', *Le Monde*, 11 février: 12.

Pisier, Evelyne and Varikas, Eleni (1997) 'Femmes, République et démocratie: l'autre dans la paire?', *Pouvoirs*, 82: 127–43.

Platone, François (1991) *Les électorats sous la Ve République: données d'enquêtes*, Paris: CEVIPOF, FNSP (Presses de la Fondation nationale des sciences politiques).

Portelli, Hugues (1993) 'Le parti socialiste', in Chagnollaud (ed.) (1993): 272–91.

Prendiville, Brendan (1993) *L'écologie: la politique autrement?*, Paris: Harmattan.

Pringle, Rosemary and Watson, Sophie (1990) 'Fathers, brothers, mates: the fraternal state in Australia', in Watson (ed.) (1990): 229–43.

Pronier, Raymond and Vincent Jacques le Seigneur (1992) *Génération verte: les écologistes en politique*, Paris: Presses de la Renaissance.

Proud, Judith (1995) 'Ecology parties in France', in Addinall, N.A., *French Political Parties: A Documentary Guide*, Cardiff: University of Wales Press: 131–52.

Questions féministes (1977) 'Variations sur des thèmes communs', 1: 3–19.

Randall, Vicky (1987) *Women and Politics*, second edition, London: Macmillan.

Randall, Vicky (1998) 'Gender and power', in Waylen and Randall (eds) (1998): 185–205.

Raulin, Nathalie (1999) 'Femmes d'exception à la haute fonction publique', *Libération*, 17 February, FNSP press cuttings file FR108.

Reader, Keith with Wadia Khursheed (1993) *The May 1968 Events in France: Reproductions and Interpretations*, Basingstoke and London: Macmillan.

Rees, Teresa (1998) *Mainstreaming Equality in the European Union*, London and New York: Routledge.

Rémond, René (1993) *La politique n'est plus ce qu'elle était*, Paris: Calmann-Lévy.

Remy, Monique (1990) *De l'utopie à l'intégration: histoire des mouvements de femmes*, Paris: L'Harmattan.

Renard, Marie-Thérèse (1965) *La participation des femmes à la vie civique*, Paris: Les Editions ouvrières.

Reynolds, Siân (1988) 'Whatever happened to the French Ministry of Women's Rights?', *Modern and Contemporary France*, 33, April: 4–9.

Reynolds, Siân (1994) 'Le sacre de la citoyenne?: Réflexions sur le retard français', Conference paper 'Féminismes et cultures politiques nationales', Lyon, 30 November–2 December.

Reynolds, Siân (1996) *France Between the Wars: Gender and Politics*, London and New York: Routledge.

Rieu, Annie (1998) 'Femmes élues en milieu rural: quels modes de gouvernance', in Martin (ed.) (1998): 85–95.

Ringard, Nadja (1977) 'Les éditions "des femmes" poursuivent en diffamation quatre femmes', *Libération*, 1 juin, FNSP press cuttings file FR108.

Riot-Sarcey, Michèle (ed.) (1993) *Femmes pouvoirs*, Paris: Editions Kimé.

Riot-Sarcey, Michèle (ed.) (1995) *Démocratie et représentation*, Paris: Kimé.

Rivais, Rafaële (1999) 'Opposer une politique volontariste à la logique des "Réseaux masculines"', *Le Monde*, 18 février, http://www.lemonde.fr/actu/societe/parite/articles/180299/reseau.htm, accessed 28 February 1999.

Rogerat, Chantal (ed.) (1978) *Les questions qui font bouger* (6ᵉ conférence CGT 'Femmes salariées aujourd'hui'), Paris: Antoinette.

Rogerat, Chantal (1987) 'Pratiques féministes et pratiques syndicales', *Cahiers du féminisme*, 41/42: 6–8.

Rogerat, Chantal (1996) 'Les femmes et l'organisation syndicale: entre le "général" et le "spécifique"', *Cahiers du GEDISST*, 15: 109–26.

Rosehill, Catherine (1988) 'Les syndicats à l'épreuve des coordinations', *Cahiers du féminisme*, 47: 27–30.

Rotjman, Suzy (1996) 'Après la manif du 25 . . .', *Cahiers du féminisme*, 75/76: 40–1.

Roudinesco, Elisabeth (1999) 'Une parité régressive', *Le Monde*, 11 février: 12.

Roudy, Yvette (1978) 'La stratégie du ghetto', *Le Matin*, 8 juin.

Roudy, Yvette (1985) *A cause d'elles*, Paris: Albin.

Roudy, Yvette (1995) *Mais de quoi ont-ils peur?* Paris: Albin Michel.

Rouge (1977) 'La coordination des groupes femmes d'entreprise parisiens. Les commissions femmes syndicales et le mouvement autonome', *Rouge* 14 juin (FNSP Press Cutting Service, Dossier FR108).

Rouleau, François (1999) (Lutte ouvrière: lo-uci@worldnet.fr) Personal correspondence, 3 November.

Rozès, Stéphane (1997) 'L'opinion entre perte de confiance et "esprit de révolte"', in *L'Etat de la France* (1997–8), Paris: la Découverte: 506–8.

Rule, Wilma (1987) 'Electoral systems, contextual factors and women's opportunity for election to parliament in twenty-three democracies', *Western Political Quarterly*, 40: 477–86.

Sanzone, Donna (1984) 'Women in positions of political leadership in Britain, France and West Germany', in Siltanen, J. and Stanworth, M. (eds) *Women and the Public Sphere*, London: Hutchinson: 160–75.

Sartin, Pierrette (1967) 'Les femmes et la politique active', *La Croix*, 14 février.

Savigneau, Josyane (1978) 'Intégrer le féminisme dans le socialisme', *Le Monde*, 17 janvier.

Savigneau, Josyane (1980) 'La journée internationale des femmes', *Le Monde*, 11 mars: 1.

Schain, Martin A. (1999) 'The National Front and the French party system', *French Politics and Society*, 17, 1, winter: 1–16.

Schneider, Robert (2000) 'Madame Europe', *Le Nouvel Observateur*, 1834: 53.

Scott, Alan (1990) *Ideology and the New Social Movements*, London: Unwin Hyman.

Scott, Joan W. (1996a) 'Egalité ou différence: le piège d'un choix impossible', *Parité-infos*, supplément au numéro 14, juin: 1–4.

Scott, Joan Wallach (1996b) *Only Paradoxes to Offer: French Feminists and the Rights of Man*, Cambridge, Massachusetts and London: Harvard University Press.

Servan-Schreiber, Claude (1996) Contribution to seminar 'Actualité de la Parité', *Projets féministes*, 4/5, février.

Simon, Catherine (ed.) (1981) *Syndicalisme au féminin*, (Questions Clefs, 1), Paris: EDI.

Sineau, Mariette (1988) *Des femmes en politique*, Paris: Economica.

Sineau, Mariette (1991) 'Autour d'une dette non reconnue: l'apport du MLF sur la scène politique', in *Groupe d'études féministes de l'université Paris VII (GEF)* (1991): 187–206.

Sineau, Mariette (1992) 'Droit et démocratie', in Duby, Georges and Perrot, Michelle, *L'histoire des femmes 5*, Paris: Plon: 471–97.

Sineau, Mariette (1994a) 'L'évolution dialectique des lois et des mentalités', in Halimi (ed.) (1994a): 183–95.

Sineau, Mariette (1994b) 'Femmes en chiffres', in Halimi (ed.) (1994a): 272–83.

Sineau, Mariette (1995a) 'Parité et principe d'égalité: le débat français', in Ephesia (ed.) (1995): 518–23.

Sineau, Mariette (1995b) Interview in *Parité-infos*, 12, décembre: 2–3.

Sineau, Mariette (1997a) 'Les femmes politiques sous la Ve République', *Pouvoirs*, 82: 45–57.

Sineau, Mariette (1997b) 'La parité à la française: un contre-modèle de l'égalité républicaine?', in Le Bras-Chopard and Mossuz-Lavau (eds) (1997): 119–42.

Sineau, Mariette (1997/8) 'Femmes en politique', *Alternatives non-violentes*, 105, hiver: 3–10.

Sineau, Mariette (1998a) 'La féminisation du pouvoir vue par les Français-es et par les hommes politiques', in Martin (ed.) (1998): 61–81.

Sineau, Mariette (1998b) 'Le scrutin uninominal majoritaire freine la progression de la mixité chez les élus', *Le Monde*, 31 octobre: 13.

Slama, Béatrice (1991) 'Quand la parole, l'écriture, étaient l'affaire de toutes . . .', in *Groupe d'études féministes de l'université Paris VII (GEF)* (1991): 105–22.

Sledziewski, Elisabeth G. (1993) 'Rapport sur les idéaux et les droits des femmes', paper given at conference on 'la démocratie paritaire, 40 années d'activités du Conseil de l'Europe', 6–7 novembre 1989, published in Réseau Femmes 'Ruptures', *Bulletin d'information, de liaisons et d'échanges*, 90, mars: 23–33.

Sledziewski, G. (1998) 'Vers la parité entre hommes et femmes', *Réforme*, 2776, 25 juin–1 juillet.

Spencer, Samia I. (1997) 'Secretariat, Ministry, or Service? Searching for a government structure to serve French women (1974–1995)', *Contemporary French Civilization*, 21, 1, winter/spring: 64–85.

Stegassy, Ruth (1978) 'Un désir d'ouverture', *Libération*, 17 février, FNSP press cuttings file FR108.

Stetson, Dorothy M. (1987) *Women's Rights in France*, Connecticut: Greenwood Press.

Stetson, Dorothy M. and Mazur, Amy (eds) (1995) *Comparative State Feminisms*, Thousand Oaks, London, New Delhi: Sage.

Stevens, Anne (1992) *The Government and Politics of France*, Basingstoke and London: Macmillan.

Storti, Martine (1978a) 'La moitié des électeurs sont des électrices', *Libération*, 14 janvier, FNSP press cuttings file FR108.

Storti, Martine (1978b) 'Toutes derrière et Chirac devant', *Libération*, 30 janvier.

Stuart, Robert (1997) 'Gendered labour in the ideological discourse of French marxism: the Parti Ouvrier Français, 1882–1905', *Gender and History*, 9, 1: 107–29.

Subileau, Françoise and Toinet, Marie-France (1993) *Les chemins de l'abstention: une comparaison franco-américaine*, Paris: la Découverte.

Subileau, Françoise, Ysmal, Colette and Rey, Henri (1999) 'Les adhérents socialistes en 1998', CEVIPOF, http:///www.msh-paris.fr/centre/cevipof/publications/ps.html, accessed 19 October 1999.

Surduts, Maya (1983) Interview, *Rouge*, 11–17 novembre.

Tarrow, Sidney (1998) *Power in Movement: Social Movements and Contentious Politics*, Cambridge: Cambridge University Press.

Terrail, Jean-Pierre (1995) 'L'essor contemporain de la scolarisation des filles et son interprétation', in Ephesia (ed.) (1995): 586–90.

Terré, François (1998) 'Egalité ou parité?', *Le Figaro*, 15 décembre.

Thalmann, Rita (1998) 'Le racisme est-il soluble dans l'oppression de genre?', in ANEF (1998): 15–20.

Thévenin, Nicole-Edith (1984) 'Identité, Politique, Théorie: un vent venu de l'Ouest', in *Femmes, féminisme et recherches*, AFFER, Toulouse: 152–61.

Thomas, Sue (1994) *How Women Legislate*, New York and Oxford: Oxford University Press.

Threlfall, Monica (ed.) (1996) *Mapping the Women's Movement*, London, New York: Verso in association with New Left Review.

Touraine, Alain (1994) *Qu'est-ce que la démocratie?*, Paris: Fayard.

Touraine, Alain (1995) 'Beyond social movements?', in Lyman, Stanford, *Social Movements: Critiques, Concepts, Case Studies*, Basingstoke and London: Macmillan: 371–93.

Tozzi, Michel (1982) *Syndicalisme et nouveaux mouvements sociaux*, Paris: Editions Ouvrières.

Trat, Josette (1993/4) 'Parité: de nombreuses ambiguïtés', *Cahiers du féminisme*, 67/8, hiver/printemps: 12–13.

Trat, Josette (1996) Contribution to seminar 'Actualité de la parité', *Projets féministes*, 4/5, février.

Trat, Josette (1997) 'Retour sur l'automne chaud de 1995', in Heinen and Trat (eds) (1997): 39–59.

Trat, Josette and Vigan, Marie-Annick (1993/4) 'Entretien avec Françoise Gaspard et Joëlle Wiels', in *Cahiers du féminisme*, 67/8, hiver/printemps: 9–12.

Trotignan, Yves (1985) *La France au XXe siècle – tome 1: jusqu'en 1968*, Paris: Dunod.

UR–CFDT Haut-Normandie (1978), 'Action et syndicalisation des femmes', in CFDT *Conférence travail des femmes et action syndicale* (rapports et interventions): 1–10.

Varikas, Eleni (1995a) 'Genre et démocratie historique ou le paradoxe de l'égalité par le privilège', in Riot Sarcey (ed.) (1995): 145–62.

Varikas, Eleni (1995b) 'Une représentation en tant que femme?: Réflexions critiques sur la demande de la parité des sexes', in *Nouvelles questions féministes*, 16, 2: 81–127.

Varikas, Eleni (1996) '"Le personnel est politique": avatars d'une promesse subversive', *Tumultes*, 8: 135–60.

Vedel, Georges (1998) 'La parité mérite mieux qu'un marivaudage législatif!', *Le Monde*, 8 décembre: 16.

Venner, Fiammetta (1995) *L'opposition à l'avortement. Du lobby au commando*, Paris: Berg International.

Venner, Fiammetta (1997) '"Une autre manière d'être féministe?": Le militantisme féminin d'extrême droite', in Lesselier and Venner (eds) (1997): 33–51.

Verba, Sidney (1990) 'Women in American politics', in Tilly, Louise A. and Gurin, Patricia (eds) *Women, Politics and Change*, New York: Russell Sage Foundation: 555–72.

Vidal, Pierre-Marie (ed.) (1998) *Le Mini-Guide: La France des régions*, Paris: Profession Politique.

Viennot, Eliane (1984) 'Des stratégies et des femmes', *Nouvelles questions féministes*, 6/7: 155–72.

Viennot, Eliane (1993) 'Colloque Choisir à l'Unesco: pour une participation accrue des femmes à la vie publique', in *Parité-infos*, 2, juin: 5.

Viennot, Eliane (1994) 'Parité: les féministes entre défis politiques et révolution culturelle', *Nouvelles questions féministes*, 15, 4: 65–89.

Viennot, Eliane (1996a) 'L'exception française: une très vieille histoire', *Après-demain*, 380–381: 5–9.

Viennot, Eliane (1996b) Contribution to seminar 'Actualité de la parité', *Projets féministes*, 4/5, février.

Viennot, Eliane (1996c) 'Parité: une larme de fond', *Parité-infos*, 16, décembre: 3.

Viennot, Eliane (ed.) (1996d) *'La démocratie à la française' ou les femmes indésirables*, Paris: L'Université de Paris 7.

Vilaine, Anne-Marie de (1978) 'Lorsque les femmes s'expriment dans la politique', *Libération*, 16 March.

Vilaine, Anne-Marie de and Clédat, Françoise (1981–2) 'Les femmes et l'écologie', *Dialogue des femmes*, Paris, Tome 2: 6–16.

Vincent, Rose (1977) 'Les femmes dans la politique?: Bien sûr tout le monde est pour, mais . . .', *J'informe*, 3 December.

Vogel, Jean (1994) 'La citoyenneté revisitée', in Vogel-Polsky, Eliane, *Les femmes et la citoyenneté européenne*, Commission européenne, V/D/5 Egalité des chances entre les femmes et les hommes, V/2337/94–FR, 1–46.

Vogel, Ursula (1991) 'Is citizenship gender-specific?', in Vogel, Ursula and Moran, Michael (eds) (1991) *The Frontiers of Citizenship*, Basingstoke and London: Macmillan: 58–85.

Wadia, Khursheed (1993) 'Women and the events of May '68', in Reader, Keith with Wadia, Khursheed (1993) *The May 1968 Events in France: Reproductions and Interpretations*, Basingstoke and London: Macmillan: 148–66.

Walby, Sylvia (1997) *Gender Transformations*, London and New York: Routledge.

Walner, Myosotis (1995) 'L'étoile de SUD', *Cahiers du féminisme*, 73: 17–19.

Watson, Sophie (ed.) (1990) *Playing the State*, London and New York: Verso.

Waylen, Georgina (1998) 'Gender, feminism and the State', in Waylen and Randall (eds) (1998): 1–17.

Waylen, Georgina and Randall, Vicky (eds) (1998) *Gender, Politics and the State*, London and New York: Routledge.

Wieviorka, Michel (ed.) (1997) *Une société fragmentée?: Le multiculturalisme en débat*, Paris: La Découverte.

Women of Europe (1979) 'Women and men of Europe in 1978: summary of the results of a survey on socio-political attitudes in the countries of the EC', Supplement 3, Brussels: Commission of the European Communities, June.

Women of Europe (1984) 'Women and men of Europe in 1983', Supplement 16, Brussels: Commission of the European Communities, October.

Women of Europe (1985) 'Elections to the European Parliament. Women and voting: an analysis by Faits et Opinions (Paris) coordinator of "Eurobarometer" surveys', Supplement 21, Brussels: Commission of the European Communities, July.

Women of Europe (1987) 'Women and men of Europe in 1983', Supplement 26, Brussels: Commission of the European Communities, December.

Wright, Vincent (1989) *The Government and Politics of France*, London: Unwin Hyman.

Ysmal, Colette (1990) *Le comportement électoral des Français*, Paris: La Découverte.

Ysmal, Colette (1995a) 'Le vote des femmes depuis 1945', *Revue des Deux Mondes*, avril: 21–7.

Ysmal, Colette (1995b) 'Les principaux partis', in *L'Etat de la France 1995–6*, Paris: La Découverte, 479–84.

Yuval-Davis, Nira (1997) *Gender and Nation*, London, Thousand Oaks, New Delhi: Sage.

Zancarini-Fournel, Michelle (1996) 'Marie-Noëlle Thibault' (Témoignages), *Clio*, 3: 218–22.

Zancarini-Fournel, Michelle (1998) 'Le Parcours ascensionnel de Nicole Notat: un exemple de mise en œuvre de la parité?', in Martin (ed.) (1998): 127–39.

Zylberberg-Hocquard, Marie-Hélène (1978) *Féminisme et syndicalisme en France*, Paris: Editions Anthropos.

Zylberberg-Hocquard, Marie-Hélène (1981) *Femmes et féminisme dans le mouvement ouvrièr*, Paris: Editions Ouvrières.

Index